Francis Francis

By lake and river

An angler's rambles in the North of England and Scotland

Francis Francis

By lake and river
An angler's rambles in the North of England and Scotland

ISBN/EAN: 9783337233297

Printed in Europe, USA, Canada, Australia, Japan

Cover: Foto ©Andreas Hilbeck / pixelio.de

More available books at **www.hansebooks.com**

BY LAKE AND RIVER:

AN

ANGLER'S RAMBLES

IN THE

NORTH OF ENGLAND AND SCOTLAND.

BY FRANCIS FRANCIS.

Author of "A Book on Angling," &c., &c.

LONDON:
"THE FIELD" OFFICE, 346, STRAND.
1874.

LONDON:

PRINTED BY HORACE COX, 346, STRAND, W.C.

PREFACE.

THE object of the following pages is to tell the tourist and angler where he may obtain fishing amongst the glens and valleys of the border counties and Caledonia, and what the fishing is like. To tell this as pleasantly as possible has been, of course, also an object, and I have ventured here and there to lighten the matter and to carry it out of the hard region of mere dry detail, in order that those who run may not only read, but be interested also, if possible.

FRANCIS FRANCIS.

THE FIRS, TWICKENHAM.

CONTENTS.

FIRST RAMBLE.

CHAPTER I.

CHAPTER II.

CHAPTER III.

CHAPTER IV.

CHAPTER V.

CHAPTER VI.

CHAPTER VII.

CHAPTER VIII.

CHAPTER IX.

CHAPTER X.

CHAPTER XI.

CHAPTER XII.

CHAPTER XIII.

SECOND RAMBLE.

CHAPTER XIV.

CHAPTER XV.

CHAPTER XVI.

CHAPTER XVII.

CHAPTER XVIII.

CHAPTER XIX.

CHAPTER XX.

CHAPTER XXI.

CHAPTER XXII.

CHAPTER XXIII.

CHAPTER XXIV.

CHAPTER XXV.

THIRD RAMBLE.

CHAPTER XXVI.

CHAPTER XXVII.

CHAPTER XXVIII.

CHAPTER XXIX.

CHAPTER XXX.

CHAPTER XXXI.

CHAPTER XXXII.

CHAPTER XXXIII.

FOURTH RAMBLE.

CHAPTER XXXIV.

CHAPTER XXXV.

BY LAKE AND RIVER.

FIRST RAMBLE.

CHAPTER I.

THE START—MORPETH—THE WANSBECK—MITFORD—ROTHBURY—THE COQUET—MOUNTAIN BURN FISHING.

I THINK Albert Smith, in by far his best work, Mr. Ledbury's grand tour, makes the following expressive observation :—"When the clocks had done striking the hour, which in Paris usually occupies about twenty minutes," &c., &c. This remark occurred to me at York, where I broke the journey North by stopping the night, for the clocks there appear not to be actuated by any particular guiding principle, being much addicted to the aberrations of those of Paris. Morpeth was the place to which I had resolved to steer, and, having slept at York, to Morpeth I went. Morpeth is a dull little town, with a gaol big enough to accommodate all the inhabitants, which may account for the dullness.

It was market-day when we reached Morpeth, but the market was evidently by no means a brisk one, and there was but a small irruption of farmers. The only striking object was a ragged and beggarly British Fakeer, who strove to excite sympathy and to promote the circulation of coppers by howling an astonishing refrain, composed of "Oh, Hallelujah! oh, Hallelujah! oh, Hallelujah! oh, Lord!" prolonging the last word to a kind of Little-Bethel-bellow that would have made him choir-master of the Rev. Stiggins's congregation without competition. The variety of keys and tones in which he managed to give the above words was very striking, while he had a species of *tremolo* movement for the aforesaid bellow at times, specially applicable to benevolent old ladies.

Catching a sight of the Wansbeck as I entered the town over the bridge, I saw that it was dead low, and yet dirty, which did not speak much for the chances of fishing. There had been a heavy thunderstorm a day or two before, which had just sufficed to send all the ditch-slushings and road-washings into the river, but had increased the supply of water infinitesimally. I determined, however, to do my possible to fish it, and selecting a very comfortable inn (Braithwaite's), took up my quarters there.

I applied to one or two gentlemen whom I knew to be sportsmen, or rather fishermen, who dwelt there, but beyond advising me by all means to move on, they appeared to be unable to render me any assistance, so I trusted to my own resources. There are five or six miles of open or non-preserved water about Morpeth; and no doubt, after rain, sport may be obtained. From what I saw of the river, I should say there is not much good fishing below Morpeth, though there is a sprinkling of good fish. The water, however, is very pretty, and but for the constant penning back by the mills, when the bed of the stream is left in many parts almost dry, it is capable of holding plenty of good trout. It would make a nice little breeding-stream, too, for salmon; but there are insurmountable weirs, and, save in very heavy floods in the winter, few fish ever do get up.

Above Morpeth the river belongs to some three or four principal proprietors, and here the river is very pretty indeed, in alternate stream and pool, and is generally well stocked with bright and lively trout of excellent quality, and running about three or four to the pound, and in some of the waters it is not difficult to fill a good creel. The chief desideratum is a little rain, without which sport is indifferent. At this period of the year, too (Midsummer), water is especially desirable, because, the sheep-washing being but lately concluded, the pools and streams are loaded to such an extent with the sickening and poisonous refuse that the fish are extremely averse to food. I stayed but three days at Morpeth, on two of which I fished. I might have stayed longer; but it was the fashionable time of year, and Morpeth, which is much resorted to by visitors, owing to its healthiness, and the beauty and variety of the walks about it, was rather full, and lodgings were not to be had.

The first day I fished below the town, in the open water. The walk was delightful, the river running through a ravine graced with hanging woods and rocks, interspersed with ferns and wild flowers in great profusion and variety. But the water and the weather were as bad as bad could be. Added to this, although the stream is well adapted to fly fishing, nothing is done here but bait-fishing, and constant minnow and worm much damages fly-fishing. That I did nothing did not at all surprise me, particularly as on my return I found the mill below the town had penned back the water, and there was no stream, and only water in the small holes and pools. I had written to one or two of the proprietors above the town, but none of them were at home, so some days would elapse before I got an answer. Fortunately, however, the steward of Admiral Mitford, of Mitford Castle, happened to come into the town, and he very kindly gave me permission to fish. Just, as I was starting the post came in, so that I did not get away until rather late. However, at length I ascended my vehicle, and I drove to Mitford, a distance of some two or three miles. It is a lovely spot, the scenery being similar to that below the town—hanging woods and deep ravines, with the crystal river now a mere thread at the bottom, winding a tortuous course between the steep wooded banks. The ruins of the old castle, which in the days of bows and arrows must have been a place of strength, frowning down upon the children whose great-great-great-grandfathers have played beneath its walls even as perchance their grandchildren may do, while not far from it stands the last ruined arch of Newminster Abbey, carefully railed in—and, oh! how carefully preserved! Archæologists, rejoice ye that such a delightful antiquarian feeling should exists in this out-of-the-way spot. No ruthless hand is suffered to be lifted against those sacred stones; and cursed and anathematised indeed would he be by his fellows who should dare to remove one block of it. For know, ye lovers of the things of eld, that while one portion of the abbey stands (and this is the only portion that does stand), the parish is held ever *tithe free*. Here is a motive, then, for respect to the remains of the past. Can stronger motive or more effective be, think ye? Alack and alas, were it not for this, I am forced to confess and believe that long ago the dust of its prelates might have "stopped a bunghole," and its mullions and architraves have graced a multitude of pig-troughs. While putting my rod together, the keeper made his appearance, and offered to show me the water.

He told me, and told me truly, that the water was so low and clear, the day so breezeless, that I should do nothing with the fly; and, to be ready for all hazards, he put a bag of worms in his pocket. I don't like large stream worm-fishing, although to use a worm properly in very low and clear water requires a good deal of skill. About a mile of the water above the house is preserved strictly for friends, and to this I cast a longing glance as I noted the many trout that dimpled the surface of the little pools as we walked along. It is evidently a trout paradise, and not often invaded by the angler. The upper part however, to which we wended our way, enjoys no such immunity, but shows a very decided difference. As we walked on, a good deal of game made itself evident. I almost stumbled over one hen pheasant with a nide of eight, all of whom could fly well. This has been an excellent breeding season for all kinds of game —indeed the keepers hereabouts say they never remember a better. I commenced fishing with the fly, but there was not a breath of wind to aid me. The fish were jumping out of the water; a score or more of them came at the fly sometimes, making an apparently fine rise at it, but they did not shut their mouths on it; sometimes following it for yards without attempting to seize it. The fly fisherman who is up to his work knows well enough what this means; particularly when, with a scorching sun and no wind, a heavy bank of oppressive cloud conceals the distant heavens to windward. Nevertheless, I worked on for some two or three hours, refusing the keeper's offer of a worm; but, at length finding that there was really nothing to be done, I took to the worm. It was of very little more use than the fly, for I only took three or four small fish with it; and even the keeper, who tried his hand for a pool or two and made nothing of it, was fain to confess that "he didn't thenk I should make up just a dish of fish thot day." I got tired of it at length, and, after trying the stream up for a mile or two of very awkward scrambling among the thick underwood along the banks, with now and then a slip and a stumble off the slippery stones into the stream, I gave it up, and returned homewards lightly loaded. With three or four inches of water in the stream, all this would have been very different, and twilight would probably have found me with a heavy creel still hard at work. I saw enough of the stream to convince me that it is at times well worth fishing, and that a very nice dish may easily be picked out of it. The fish, though small, are very bright, well made and flavoured, and extremely game and lively. There are several small feeders of the Wansbeck, which give good fishing at times, and where there is no difficulty in getting permission. Indeed the angler, if the weather and water suits, may do well at Morpeth for a day or two, though he will have perhaps often to drive to his ground some six or seven miles. On the succeeding day I bade adieu to Morpeth, and packing my belongings in the trap, was conveyed to Rothbury, fifteen miles off, to fish the Coquet. On the journey I passed over the Coquet at Wheldon-bridge, an excellent station for the angler, where there is a comfortable angling inn. The Coquet is a much more considerable stream than the Wansbeck, and quite capable in parts of affording salmon-fishing. It was very low when I reached Rothbury, but, as luck would have it, as I got there it began to rain, and continued at intervals heavily even into the next day, so that on the Sunday it was running well, and of that fine porter colour which anglers love to see in salmon rivers. While it was raining an old woman passed. "A saft day, sir," said the old dame on passing. "Delightful weather," answered I, beaming and getting wet through with the most cheerful complacency. "Ehow!" quoth she, looking at me as if I were last from Hanwell, "Ehow, sirs," slowly shaking her head, "F'hats to become of tha ha (hay) crap if 'tbides?" "F'hats to become of the fusshin if it disn't?" I asked in turn, with all the best of the argument, having the rain to back me. The query routed her. "Fussh'n! Fussh'n! Lord help us!" May difference of opinion never alter friendship.

Rothbury, at first sight, is a straggling, uninteresting-looking village, but it grows upon one—for, in whatever direction we look, the views are fine; and, however we may approach Rothbury, it looks picturesque and pretty. Situated in an indentation amongst the rocky Simonside hills, prettily embowered in trees, with the sparkling Coquet wimpling round it, with the fresh clear air of mountains abounding in wild thyme and fragrant shrubs sweeping down its street, it is indeed a healthy and desirable little spot, as the troops of well-dressed, cherry-cheeked, laughing children that meet one at every step abundantly testify. Rothbury is a great resort at times, for the smoke-dried denizens of Newcastle and Gateshead; for, added to its other attractions, there is a stretch of some fourteen miles of excellent trout-water of the Coquet here, which is open to all. It is as pretty and varied a water as heart of trout fisher could desire. It is tolerably well stocked with fish, which run from three or four to the pound to a pound weight. Trout have been caught up to 6lb., and there are a few caught yearly of 3lb. and 4lb.; half-pounders, and even three-quarters, being no rarities. The trout are very strong, and, for their size, show great play; while, such is the nature of the pools and streams, that very few of them, and those mostly of little account to the angler, can be netted;

the streams being so sharp and the bottom so rough, and the holts and roots so cavernous, that the river may be said to preserve itself. Here and there there will, of course, be a pool which a few large boulders or a stout stake or two would improve; but, generally speaking, not a great deal can be done with the net, and hence the greater part of the river is always well-stocked; and how delightful it is to feel, while pulling the trout out of the streams, that there is no leave to ask, and no keeper to fee! No wonder that Rothbury is popular. For the information of anglers and families, there is a comfortable little angling inn—The Three Moons—with a snug parlour and good attendance,* and there are plenty of clean, comfortable lodgings, with a coach from and to Morpeth daily.

Walking down the village, I could not but be struck by the march of civilisation. I was looking for *the* baker's, and found it difficult to find—there appeared to be but one, and that of a very retiring, unobtrusive nature; but of drapers and milliners, a round half-dozen at least. There, I believe you, we had the fashions i' faith. There were your crinolines, any quantity of them, like enormous parti-coloured parrot cages, in rows. There were your fardingales, and lappets, and tuckers, truly; and I could not help comparing the cases, and thinking, with Prince Hal, over Falstaff's tavern scores: "What, all these *sacques* to one poor pennyworth of bread? Oh monstrous!"

The rain, which I mentioned in my last, brought a foot of water into the river, which was much needed, as it was very foul from the sheep washing, so that the fish were quite sick and shy. The spate did not, however, half suffice to clean the river, though it certainly did some good; but from the rise taking place on a Sunday we were unable to take advantage of it. The trout-fisher of experience knows well that the time to make a good bag is when a flood is beginning to come down, and the water is rising. That is the time when the fish, on the look out

* This has since been rebuilt, and is now a comfortable and spacious hotel.

for the insects and other food brought down by the rising waters, feed most ravenously. The day after the fish are usually so gorged that they will hardly move at all; and this I found to be the case when, on the succeeding day, I went forth armed with my spinning-rod and a favourite old Allies' minnow. I chose to fish up, and at the first three streams I fished, to my surprise, I got a trout from each. I then met a brother angler, who told me the fish were taking badly. I certainly had not had cause to think so, and was prophesying a heavy bag. I, however, soon found that he was correct enough, for I went a long way without getting another fish or a run. Not knowing the water, I had chosen about the worst that I could have selected, having started about a mile above the town, just below the little village of Thropton, above which the water becomes very indifferent for a space. I worked on perseveringly, however, but only got five or six more trout, and those I fished hard for. This was a lamentable failing from what I expected. At length it came on to rain, and that so heavily, that I thought it worth turning homewards—and I got home at length, after a tiring walk in the rain, wet through to the skin. Northumberland is a fine county for rain when it is a wet season, which is pretty often. Mackintoshes partake of the nature of a delusion, and there is no means of dodging the drops.

On my return, I found Mr. Mavin, a fisherman, and a real one too, who had been sent to me by an acquaintance to show me the water; he advised me to go down below the town in the evening and try the fly, as the river would then be clear enough for it. I took his advice, and had an hour's pretty sport in a very nice piece of water, taking more and better fish than I had caught all the morning—thanks to a fly which I mounted, and which turned out a regular killer. This fly was one made by Martin of Brecon. It is a general killer, and, as I believe, one of Martin's own invention—buff crewel body, honeydun hackle, and light-coloured hen pheasant wing—and had I chanced to mount it earlier, I should have doubled my take.

The next day with Mr. Mavin to *cicisbeo* me, I went down the water about three miles, and fished up; we got away too late, however, and, although I began well, the fish soon went off. I thought myself a pretty good performer for trout with the single-handed rod, but I soon found that my attendant was a better one. He was wading, and I was fishing from the bank, and, of course, he had all the advantage of knowing the stream, and fishing with the most killing flies, &c. But he was picking up fish after they had done rising at me, and on looking at his flies for the cause, I found he was fishing with fine single hair, and with a light long double-handed rod, which he worked to perfection. I was no longer surprised, as I, trusting to the water being peat coloured, had been fishing with really coarse gut, with an old chub line in fact. The day was very bright at times, so that our take was very moderate, and the trout were of indifferent size; I scoring somewhere about a dozen in the day, and my attendant about a score, and better fish.

The water we fished was really beautiful—alternate pool and stream, with large rocks and stones. Here a gravelly, there a sandy, and again a rocky bottom, with overhanging trees casting the shade which trouts love, and under which they lie watching for the insects which ever and anon come sailing along, or drop from the leaves above. It is awkward casting unless you wade, and nasty wading when you do, as a ducking is by no means a rarity, the stones being slippery and shifty. Moreover, there are quicksands about. The unwary and unwitting angler may place his foot upon an apparently solidly-planted stone, when suddenly down goes the stone through the thin crust, like a plummet in a well, and the angler is lucky if he escapes with a ducking. I have always had a horror of quicksands and those sort of things since I spent half an hour above my middle in a Cornish shaky bog while I was snipe-shooting, when a boy. I was chasing a wounded duck, and plumped into a boghole up to my middle in my blind eagerness. I shall never forget that half hour. I had read that dreadful scene in "The Cruise of the Midge," where the niggers are swallowed up in the quagmire during the boat attack on the mangrove swamp, and I was fully penetrated with the horror of the situation. It was a bitter cold, snowy day, but the perspiration streamed down my face; when, at length, by laying my gun across and resting upon it, I managed, by clutching some reeds and twigs within reach, little by little, and with the utmost caution, to pull myself out of my uncomfortable position. Yah! shaky bogs, mangrove swamps, and quicksands avaunt! I'm a decent chiel, wi' a dread o' throupin. I'm free to confess that, had all the Undines invited me to "come unto these yellow sands, and there take hands"—in spite of golden locks, undulating forms, unearthly eyes, silvery moonlight, heavenly voices—in spite of any amount of mandolins twanged with the most inconceivable and bewitching sweetness, of lavish offers of nectarean draughts of nothing from pasteboard goblets—I should have declined the honour, and remembered Mrs. Caudle. There are good trouts in the pool where these sands be—but they would need to be very good ones indeed to tempt me to wade for them.

The next day I thought I would fish up a little beck, the Rye, which runs into the Coquet at Thropton. It is a kind of fishing I am rather fond of, rambling along up amongst the hills from wee poolie to wee poolie, with mimic cascades and streams such as you might almost make with a good-sized ewer; keeping carefully out of sight, and casting the worm neatly into these spots, and pulling out the spotted yellow jackets from every likely hole, and that to an extent astonishing to the uninitiated; wandering on, never tied to one place for more than a few minutes, calling on nature without notice, and finding her most charming when not adorned or interfered with by art. Now a sand-piper or water-ousel goes twittering away, or a waterhen scuttles into its favourite lair; while the pee-wit, or the golden plover, or, mayhap, the curlew, with their wild and musical, but melancholy notes, add to the sense of delightful loneliness which pervades this mountain beck-fishing. It is the *dolce far niente* of trout-fishing, for there is no bother about flies and tackle: a yard of gut—you can't lose it—and a couple of hooks is all your stock. There runs a little darkling stream under that hole in the overhanging bank or rock. You know that if you cast your worm neatly and properly into that stream, and guide the line clear of those stones (just where the lady-fern and Blechnum grow so luxuriantly almost in the stream), that you will catch a trout of half a pound *or less* to a dead certainty. You are as sure that he's there waiting for you as I am that that is Rothbury Church and yonder is Crag End. You needn't consider whether you shall try him with brandling, red-worm, black head, blue head, or marsh-worm—he will take any or all of them. Suppose you make a bungling cast—no matter, cast again; the only cast which is useless is that which does not permit him to see the worm, or which does permit him to see you. Barring these two contingencies, you may cast for a week; and the odds are a hundred to one that he takes your worm as soon as he sees it. And then the walking—save the brisk walk home with the heavy creel at night—what is it but a delightful lazy saunter from brae to brae, and from cast to cast? Then, too, you lunch, on a hard egg and a biscuit, as only a fisherman can, and after that lie down on your back in the heather, fern, or wild thyme, or all together, looking up at the ever-shifting canopy above; and you smoke your tobacco as though it were worth a guinea an ounce, while the laverock sings to you—"Lirra la, lirra la, la, la, he hu, he hu," higher and higher, till you lose him in the clouds. Hark now, the pretty little furze-chuck joins chorus with the yellow-hammer, who is whistling beseechingly for "bread and no cheese;" and goodman grasshopper, not to be outdone, stands on his stilts and swells his treble pipe, till you wonder he does not crack it in that "E alt" of his. The monotonous note of the corncrake, too, comes drowsily up from the lowlands, and the bees hum a midday lullaby; the brooklet murmurs softly peace and forgetfulness; the very "louping o' the trouts" in the little ruby-coloured pool below the Linn yonder makes itself heard through all, connecting itself in a wavering, indistinct, and dreamy manner somehow with something you have in hand—you are fast forgetting what. Degenerate angler! to be indulging in such a recreant forty winks as this. But here comes Queen Mab, in likeness of a midge, and, after buzzing in your ear, she bites your nose, d'ye see; while gossip Puck, in the fashion and habit of a cleg fly, carefully selects his ground, and, standing upon his head and forelegs, with hinder ones wide-a-tilt, so as to get a good, deep bloodthirsty grip of you, levies a contribution dire upon your under eyelid. Ha! has the Percy, or the Douglas, or Jockie of the Cleugh, or some other hero, with whom you are somehow engaged in an unaccountable struggle, dire and deadly, upon the fatal field of Something-or-other-burn, suddenly and unexpectedly driven his dirk through your left eye right into the very brain, and so dispelled the airy conflict? What a portentous collapse!—from Douglas to a gnat! And so you up and at it again. Yes! it certainly is the *dolce far niente* of trout-fishing; and, though I don't mind a hard day's work when there is anything to work for, I'm fond of the *dolce* too when there is nothing.

I fished up this little brooklet for some miles, trying here the worm and there the fly, but somehow "the throots were no in the humour—they wouldna' buckle to at a'." I could not make it out. It is a sort of sport I am a bit of a dab at. I was told there were plenty of fish, and there was no apparent reason for their not coming to the scratch. I had fished up to within a mile or two of the head, when I met a bricklaying being, a low beast, a pestilent democrat evidently, who had fished every hole just half an hour before me—a hulking brute. I should like to have told him what I thought of him, but he didn't look good to quarrel with; some of these cads can wrestle, you know, and pitch one over their shoulders, and I had no taste for any such aeronautic expedition. Of course, he had "five dizen of verra nice throots." I had a bare dozen. There's too much equality and all that sort of thing hereabouts for me, you know, out and away. Confound the fellow! how he must have enjoyed the day! and I hope his family enjoyed the fish. And after all, you know, it was all fair sport—he hadn't a pair of pole nets over his shoulder. He was very civil, and so we took a drop out of my flask just for good luck; and I hope he may always get as good sport when he goes out for a holiday, only, confound him, I hope he will start half an hour after instead of half an hour before me.

CHAPTER II.

PEPPERHAFF—SPINNING—BRINKBURN—CRAG END—THE LOWER COQUET—WEIRS, &c.

THE next day it blew such a gale of wind down the Valley of Coquet that I could not keep my minnow in the water, and so was constrained to relinquish the attempt. Towards evening some rain came down, and the water was coloured, and the next morning promised well for fishing. As it was towards the end of the week, however, having to wait for the post, it was late before I got away, and consequently when we reached our destination, which was a place called Pepperhaff, it was full late. Pepperhaff is an appanage of the Duke of Northumberland. There are some iron-stone or mining works there. The two or three huts that comprised the village—if it could be so called—reminded one more of Irish cabins than anything usually met with in England; one most wretched pig-stye of a place answered in every particular to the description of ould Barney's cabin in "The Fine Ould Irish Jontleman:"

I'll sing ye a song, and a fine ould song, made by a Paddy's pate.
Of a fine ould Irish jontleman, who lived on his estate;
His cabin it was kivered o'er wid a tatch and all complate
Wid a great, big, tundrin, tarein hole in the roof of the edifish, which was originally conthrived by the architect who made the plan of the same, to allow the smoke so gracefully to retrate,
Like a fine ould Irish jontleman, one of the oulden time.

The walls so old were hung around wid the divil a thing for show,
Save lashins of oak shillelahs, which had knocked down many a foe,
And there ould Barney sat and smoked in brogues and trunkless hose,
And quaff'd his naggin of potheen to warm his fine ould nose,
Like a rare ould Irish jontleman, one of the oulden time.

Certainly ould Barney was not visible within the doors of any of the Pepperhaffian domiciles, but his absence evidently created a void, and the pig, the crather, only seemed half happy without him. But, alas! Pepperhaff is not in Tipperary nor Donègal, though it ought to be. It is only fair to the late Duke to say that the ruinous state of the property was not at all owing to any neglect upon his part, as I believe he expressed a strong wish to have it put into a habitable condition, but the tenant was evidently of a mind with the old Scotch woman, who was ready to sacrifice her life rather than allow the hand of the spoiler to be laid upon her cherished "midden." The Duke was an excellent landlord, beloved by his people; indeed there was throughout his wide domain but one feeling towards the Duke of Northumberland on the part of his tenants, and that was of almost filial reverence. I never heard a man so universally well spoken of; and the Duchess was not a whit behind him in this respect, but worthily shared his duties and his honours.

We had to get some fresh minnows before fishing, and Mr. Mavin had brought a little net for the purpose; we soon caught enough to set me going (I had hitherto used the artificial minnow), and I waded into a likely-looking stream, popped on a minnow, using the tackle which is chiefly in vogue in this part of the country, and which consists of only two hooks—a large, longish-shanked one, and a smaller one a little above the large one, say half or two-thirds of an inch, for the lip. You bait as with Colonel Hawker's tackle, running the large hook down through the bait and out a little above the tail, crooking the bait so that it spins well. I explain this for the benefit of the uninitiated. The tackle is very simple; and if the fish are feeding well you don't miss many of them. If, however, they are coming shyly, I must confess that you do not kill one in three. When this is the case a single thread of gut, with a pair of hooks to stick about midway in the bait, is useful; some people to this add a triangle, which projects beyond the bait and spins around it so as to take the fish when they come short, but this is just Colonel Hawker's tackle, with a lip-hook added.

The first stream I went into I pulled out three nice fish—half-pounders, one of them a trifle over, and hooked another good fish of about ¾lb., which I got in to the side, but which retired at the sight of the landing-net. The fish then went off, and I only took another for some distance up. At length I came to a very pretty turn in the stream, where the water ran darkling away under the deep boughs, with a large rock at the head of the pool or stream, and behind which good fish might be expected to lie. "Plop" went the minnow as far under the boughs into the black water as was practicable; and, tug, swish, went the line for a couple of yards, almost cutting into my fingers with the dash of a Socdolager as he took the minnow and banged round behind the rock. "Now for twenty minutes' sharp work," thought I, "for it is either a salmon or a large bull-trout;" but my expectation was not fulfilled, the hook coming away free the next moment, to my great annoyance. The small slip-hook alone had taken hold, and the head of the minnow only was smashed. What the fish was I know not; but he was "a wheen muckle yan." Mavin said there were very large trout in this pool. It might have been a trout, but I incline to a sea fish of some kind. I caught another fish or two, and they went off as the day got warmer and brighter, refusing both minnow and fly. Near this pool where I lost the fish we secured a large stock of minnows. At one push of the little net, we got the bag nearly full, which would hold above a solid quart. These were taken home carefully and salted; and I can testify that they answer fully as well as a bait as when they are fresh; indeed, I am by no means sure that the trout do not highly approve of the flavour of them, as, after tearing and missing one, they will often come at another one most ferociously. Many anglers are often shrewdly put to it concerning the conveyance of minnows, &c., and therefore there is no harm in my mentioning the above facts, though they are no novelty to the generality of trout fishers. The minnows may be kept for weeks, until they resemble a bundle of dried caplins. Still, even then, unless a fresh stock can be had, they should not be thrown away, for as soon as the minnow becomes thoroughly wet, it fills out and looks almost as well as ever. The only drawback to salted minnows is, that they are soft, and do not stand long, a few sharp throws or a run soon destroying them. But there are times when no others can be obtained; and a dozen or so of salted minnows take up but little room in the angler's equipment.

In the evening I got a few nice fish. Morning and evening are the best times in the summer for a well-fished river like Coquet. From about three till seven the fish go off, and little or nothing can be done.

As we were walking out we met the coach, and the driver, the son of our host at Morpeth, had procured me a ticket for a day on the Brinkburn waters. The waters of Brinkburn Priory being considered about the best part of the Coquet fishing, we determined to fish it next day, but we found that both the conveyances were engaged—an important matter, look you, where there are but two in the place. It mattered little, however, as the day turned out badly and there was a good deal of rain.

Brinkburn Priory was founded in the reign of Henry I., by William de Bertram, Baron of Mitford, who endowed it and established the Black Canons there, dedicating it to St. Paul. It is most charmingly situated, deeply embowered in tall trees and hidden by overhanging banks, so that at a short distance it is invisible. Its invisibility had once, but for its owners, stood it in good stead. A Scotch army had ravaged the neighbouring country for miles and was returning to The Border, having passed close to the Priory without seeing it. So delighted were the monks at their escape, that, fancying the Scotch were out of hearing, they set the bells ringing for joy; but they rang so lustily that the sound attracted the notice of the retreating force, which thereupon turned about again and rectified the oversight by sacking the Priory. This was making them pay for ringing the bell with a vengeance. Can our lodging-house and swell hotel-keepers have learnt their lesson from the Scotch army at Brinkburn?

The Priory, though not extensive, is a fine old building, the architecture being Saxon and Norman. The proportions in the interior are very fine and harmonious. It has been restored, and that with a judgment and taste that do great credit to the owner; it belongs to the Cadogan family. To look at the roof I did a bit of climbing in a small well-tower, up about a hundred stone steps in the narrowest quarters I ever set foot in—a kind of chimney shaft with steps in the inside; I could compare it to nothing (having due regard to the relative proportions) but a cockroach going up the inside of a corkscrew a yard long. As I went up I continually looked through narrow slits to get a view of the country. That view was trees, at distances varying from fifteen to fifty yards, while, from the topmost one, the look-out was improved by the ruins of a jackdaw's nest or two. Having arrived at the top I looked down from the rafters of the priory, which threw their huge arms—or legs rather—downwards, and at that great height felt, as I saw how small the people looked below, like an unfledged sparrow on one of the girders of the Crystal Palace. I had a fine opportunity of practising a bit of Blondin, as there was a plank across to the belfry; but I had looked down, which Blondin, I am told, never does; besides, I hadn't a proper pole, and the only one I had stood a chance of being fractured against the slates if I tried it; so I carefully desisted, and came down the corkscrew again, cockroach fashion, and only breathed freely when I stepped off the bottom rung.

The modern dwelling-house stands close to the Priory, and is, of course, rather overborne by it—still the look-out, though confined, is very pretty; and the river, which forms a deep dark pool here, sweeps round the walls and gives it quite a fortress-like appearance. This deep pool, which is of considerable length, is called the "Wheel"—I hope I have spelt it right—and it harbours a number of large fish. The keeper told me that up to the last spate there had been about half a dozen old salmon in it, but the spate had carried them down. A July kelt may be no novelty, but as these old villains are great devourers of their own grand-children, I like to remove them out of harm's way, and always, if possible, serve them with a distress warrant if they do not vacate at the proper time.

The water at Brinkburn is beautiful water, with excellent streams, and is very well stocked with fine trout. But our day's fishing was unfortunately a decided failure (for Brinkburn). It was a regular July day—a blazing sun without a breath of wind or a cloud in the sky all day. I got quite tired of it at last, and gave up fishing as a bad job, and sat me down in the shade and hummed,

> Under the greenwood tree
> Who loves to lie with me,
> And tune his merry note
> Unto the sweet bird's throat,
> Come hither, come hither.

In faith he might come to a worse place. I got but nine fish, one of about three-quarters of a pound, and two or three half-pounders. A rather curious thing happened to me while spinning the minnow down a fine rough stream with a good length of line out. I had a heavy run apparently, and after a little "pully-hauly" I induced the rash stranger to show himself, and found my captive was a large eel, to my very great disgust. The state of my nice neat minnow tackle the angler may imagine —twisted and yarned in a filthy tangle, all frayed and daubed, tied in a score of slime-hidden knots; I cut off the hooks savagely, and having unfortunately plenty of time, I sat down and tied them afresh. But I had my revenge upon the caitiff, for I ate him; and, as he agreed with me, it was probably the only point we were unanimous upon, A 12lb. or 14lb. creel of trout is but an ordinary day at Brinkburn, and I could not but look with an envious eye over the walls of the priory into that deep pool, at the fine trout I saw "putting up their nebs," in various inaccessible places; and meditatively I thought how the good Prior of Brinkburn mayhap had, in years gone by, longed and mused to the same effect.

On Sunday afternoon, I took a walk to the top of Crag-end, one of the rough, rocky hills which hang over Rothbury—just one of those hills that artists love to paint, and giving that picturesque outline and blending of the neutral tints of the cold grey stones and the dark green and purple of the heather, and lighter yellowish green of the bracken, which one stands before, smothered in crinoline albeit, and admires so in a well-executed picture at the exhibition. For "Bracken green and cold grey stone" make capital subjects for pictures as well as poetry. Here, however, the objectionable goddess Crinolina had no power to interfere with the view, and I enjoyed it thoroughly. After a stiff scramble, during which I noticed a great quantity of the whortleberry amongst the undergrowth, we surmounted the hill, and found planted there one of the stations left by the Sappers and Miners during their survey; and from this as a resting-place I looked away over a wide brown stretch of moor, with hills and dales, and in the far-off distance the round humps of Cheviot rose like the huge paps of mother Earth herself. The intense stillness of the evening, the wide spread of patchy brown and apparently lifeless moor, gave an inexpressibly wild and primitive air to the place. Not even a sheep-bell tinkled, and I felt as if by ascending this hill I had cut myself off from civilisation for evermore. I could hardly realise that the other side of the hill presented such a different aspect. There is good shooting upon all these hills; that heather holds grouse, and these whortleberries are affected greatly by blackgame. They are not always so still and solitary, though, as to day, and

Crag-end shall see another sight,
When the twelfth comes, and sportsman wight,
Commanding fires of death, shall light
The darkness of its scenery.

Three or four years ago I surveyed the lower part of the Coquet from Wheldon Bridge to Warkworth to inspect the weirs and take plans of the salmon ladders which, as in the case of those of the Alne, are fully depicted and described in my work on salmon ladders. The river here consists for the most part of long deep strong reaches caused by the great weirs with fine deep weir-pools, full of broken water and big eddies. The trout in this part of the river are very fine, frequently being taken of 2lb., 3lb., and 4lb. weight, or even larger. Such salmon as frequent the river of course affect these places, and are now and then taken there, even with the rod. Bull trout are very plentiful in this part of the river, and they often run up to salmon size. At the lowest weir (Warkworth) is a salmon-trap—a species of elongated and enlarged cruive, from which the water can be shut by means of hatches, and the fish which enter it are left floundering on the dry bottom. Acklington, which is the second weir on the river, is a huge perpendicular stone structure 11ft. high, and the decay of the salmon-fishery in Coquet dates from the construction of this weir, which was impassable to salmon. Between this and Wheldon Bridge (where there is another weir) are two more dams, at Morwick and Felton. These weirs have all passes attached to them. The difficulty, however, is, as they are rather out of the way, to get the salmon to use them. Warkworth, with its ancient hermitage and lovely river scenery, is a favourite spot for tourists, who throng it in fine weather.

CHAPTER III.

GOOD FARMING—ALWINTON—SUDDEN SPATE—BURN FISHING—THE THRUM AT ROTHBURY.

I HAD been greatly struck by the admirable farming I everywhere noted in my journeys through Northumberland—it looked so neat and so very effective. The crops show a first-rate head, and the plant of turnips particularly was very fine, and I hardly saw an instance where they had missed. The fields generally were very clean too; women being very extensively employed in farm work. The tourist will often see a band of from twenty to fifty stalwart beings in petticoats—and who might be mothers to a race of Bersakers, such amazons do they become—hoeing and weeding away as though it were women's mission to exterminate weeds. There is something that reminds one of the Red Indian or the South Sea savage about this. Still they keep up the connection with civilisation, and once a week try to femininise themselves by putting on their crinolines—this operation, by the way, usually being performed in a convenient saw-pit or stone-quarry by the roadside, the monstrous structure being carried so far for convenience, as the Irish women carry their shoes—and, thus bedizened and translated, they display their "hoofs of dreadful note," and their other masculine proportions in "the toon" on the "mairket da." Farmers must have their work done, however, and generally, I should say, there are no better farmers in England than these Northumberland men. But the rentals they many of them pay would astonish a southern farmer; 5000*l.*, 6000*l.*, and 7000*l.* a year being not very unusual, and I heard of grass land letting at 6*l.* an acre.

Plenty smiles everywhere. The hills abound with sheep, while the valleys teem with magnificent herds of cattle. The sums of money realised here for wool are very considerable. But when the vast extent of sheepgrazing ground comprehended by the green-topped Cheviots and the many lesser ranges of hills is considered, this is not a very surprising fact.

But fishing is more in my line than farming, and I will leave my "muttons" for (to me) the more congenial subject. I had wished to see some of the fishing higher up the river, and now had an opportunity of joining two gentlemen who were going up to Alwinton to stay for a day or two for the fishing there. They had a seat in their conveyance at my disposal, and I gladly accepted it. Alwinton is about twelve miles up stream, and there are some nice burns which run in near it, and can be fished from it, the principal of which is the Alwine, though I believe there is a better one some two miles above. The morning found us ready. There had been a smart rain on the hills during the night, but the river had not spated as yet, and was low and clear. However, as it was still raining, and looked heavy on the hills when we started, we hoped the river might rise a little—enough to give us sport—and we drove off in high spirits. There was nothing worth note in the drive. We passed through the picturesque little village of Harbottle, with its ruined castle; and some two or three miles on we descended a sharp bank, forded the river, which still showed no signs of improving, though the rain had been heavy during our drive, and pulled up at the little inn, which is no bad refuge for an angler, who might make out well here for a week.

On seeking the river side we found there was too much colour for fly-fishing, so we betook us to the worm, and commenced wading up from stream to stream, casting into every likely pool and run, hooking and catching or losing trout. They are great worm-fishers in this part of the country, and the style in which some of them will operate rivals in skill the deftest fly-fishing. The day *promised* to be a good one, but promise is not fulfilment, and I soon had an opportunity of seeing the Coquet spate, which it did with a suddenness only seen in these mountain streams. One or two of the little runnels had been coming down the bank sides smartly, and I was rather apprehensive that we might, from the character of the river and the high land on all sides, get a rise in the water beyond our desires; and my apprehensions were soon justified. I was passing round a bush from one cast to another. I was not half a minute in my transit. While fishing the last stream the river brattled pleasantly and quietly in its accustomed manner upon its way—I could have forded it anywhere; but when I reached the next stream it was a roaring, raging, yellow torrent, that would have swept a man away. It came down almost in a bore. The river was suddenly bank full, and one of my companions, who was standing on a stone fishing quietly and unobservantly, found it, without warning, come down over his boots, so that he was glad to hop on shore as speedily as possible. It was at once evident that all fishing in Coquet was at end, and we must betake us to the burns, which might not be so unmanageable, and might be fished with worm well enough.

And a nice scramble we had all over those hills in search of the burn some two miles above us. Wading-boots and a mackintosh are not great aids to hill scrambling, very far from it; indeed I scarcely know anything so troublesome, useless, uncomfortable, and in the way—

Waterproofs sore, long time I bore, and waders were in vain;
Grown tired at last, I braved the blast, and much preferred the rain.

I think it was the late Lord Derby, who much preferred the gout to Gilbey. Sitting by one's study fire, with *materials* handy, and no dread of a fiery toe, one can only say that there is no accounting for taste; but to return to our hill side. It is a grand and picturesque thing to *look* at, to stalk up the Alps in big boots and a long coat fluttering in the wind, on the outside of a big grey horse, and to shout "Forward, my brave fellows!" any number of centuries or sentries, as the case may be, looking down on you, but it is quite another thing to scale Cheviotside, steep as a church roof, and slippery with rain, embarrassed in buckets and a horrid waterproof that flops about all wet and dabby, scarcely able to gasp out "Come along, old fellow!—what a beast of a hill this is! worse than the last, but not a patch on the one on ahead." One may say, "Look on this picture, and on this"—I believe Napoleon had rather a jolly time of it than otherwise, besides it is one thing to say "*va-t-on,*" another to say "*allons.*" What was worse, too, when we reach the burn, it ran in on the other side of the river. I tried the ford, to see if I could cross; but having had one or two narrow escapes in wading in spated rivers, I saw at once that the attempt was dangerous. I didn't want to form a subject for one of those agreeable newspaper paragraphs one drops on now and then, headed "Lamentable Occurrence," or "Shocking Accident;" so I yielded willingly to the whispers of discretion, and sat down on the bank, and looked at it instead, while we betook us to our sandwiches for consolation. But what was to be done? There was the burn—looking in fairish order, too; but as we could not get to it, and it could not well come single-handed to us, we turned at length upon our tracks, and bore away back for Alwinton, determined to try what might be done on the Alwine.

We found the Alwine in full spate, but quite fishable; and we were advised to try the minnow. We had a good stock, and at once commenced; and had the trout been large enough to take it fairly, no doubt I should have made heavy slaughter among them, as I had frequently five or six runs in a stream without hooking a fish—my tackle being somewhat large. After working up for a mile or so, and missing some scores of runs, I changed to worm; and now I had an opportunity of seeing what it was that had been running at me—six and even seven to the pound would be a large average for them. I got about four dozen of the little wretches, with half a dozen of perhaps four or five to the pound; and, having returned to Alwinton, I refreshed with some excellent Bass, and came away home. I regret I had not a better chance of trying the Coquet here, as I hear the river is very good for some miles up.

This was the last fishing I did upon the Coquet, for, anxious to get on, I left for Alnwick, *en route* for Wooler, the next morning. Generally, I believe, the upper part of the river is the best part. There are some fair fishing stations from Wheldon-bridge, which is close below the Brinkburn water, and by Felton; but I did not go to them, as I hear they are a good deal whipped. Indeed, this, I fear, is too much the case for really good sport late in the year wherever the river can be at all easily commanded from; and the local anglers on the river have long been noted for their skill in the use of their weapons.

The following description of the skill of the old anglers at the various villages on the Coquet is from Thomas Doubleday's "Old Angler's Triumph" in "The Newcastle Fisher's Garlands," and was published in 1830. It is very terse and forcible:—

At Shilmore they're guid at the mennim (minnow),
At Felton they're guid at the flee,
Lang Rothbury's streams for the brandin,
But Weldon, old Weldon, for me.
The Sharperton codgers are cunnin',
At Thropton they're guid at a thraw,
But up wi' the bonnie red heckle,
The heckle that tackled them a'.

Coquetdale has been famous in literature, and there are many angling songs of some standing and merit anent it; and the anglers who now frequent it, if not as skilful in constructing lyrics, are quite as skilful and active in the pursuit of fish. And, though considering that so much of the river is entirely open, and fair sport may be obtained—in the early part of the year more particularly—yet the state of the river must be very different now from what it was in the days when 300 or 400 salmon, sea-trout, and grilse were sometimes taken at one haul of the net between Warkworth and the sea; nor can the trout-fishing in Coquet be said to be equal to what it used to be, if we may believe the following lamentation of an old angler, which is given by Stephen Oliver the younger in his "Northumberland Rambles":—"Talk o' fishin'," says he, "there's no sic fishin' in Coquet now as when I was a lad. It was nowse then but to fling in and pull them out by *tweeses* and threeses, if ye had sae mony heuks on; but now a body may keep threshin' at the water a' day atween Halystane and Weldon, and hardly catch three dizen, and many a time not that. Aboot fifty years syne, I mind o' seein' trouts that thick i' the Thrum, below Rothbury, that if ye had stucken the end o' your gad (fishing-rod) into the water amang them *it would amaist hae studden upreet.*" I think I may say that this is about the best yarn of the abundance of fish I ever came across.

This same Thrum is a very curious spot. The stream has here worn for itself a narrow channel in the solid rock, and the water pours through it in places with a resistless sweep. In one spot the whole of the river pours through a narrow confined abyss scarce two feet in width. In other parts it widens to three or four yards, and the stream appears to have eddied out for itself in the solid stone a succession of chambers, looking like large pots or cauldrons, where the waters whirl incessantly, smoothing the stone almost to a polished marble surface. The length of the Thrum is about from 100 to 200 yards, and the name is said to be derived from the thread-like appearance taken by the river here—a thrum being the Northumbrian for an end of thread. This part of the river, where it is more open, is still a great resort for fine trout. It is one of the prettiest bits of scenery on the Coquet. Here there is a most picturesque mill, old-fashioned wheel, and all complete; a pretty little foaming weir; high rocky banks, o'erhung with spreading trees, and one of the finest pools upon this part of the river, where salmon are sometimes killed, and which is seldom without a sea-fish or two of some kind. The sky-line behind is broken up and closed in by high rocky hills, similar to Crag-End. I fear the little skill as an artist I once possessed has deserted me, or I might have been tempted to spoil some drawing-paper and good colour by transferring the mill on the Thrum to my collection of "reminiscences," with the necessary and graphic addendum, "This is a mill;" otherwise I really wouldn't promise but that, after a lapse of years, even I myself might not mistake it for some fabled or pre-Adamite monster, or some other unknown matter. It is a curious thing, but I never had a great taste for drawing anything but skeletons as a boy, and those I *was* great at. I came across an old Lempriere but a few weeks since that was full of them—a regular bone-house. There was a favourite one I have actually dreamt of and shuddered at, he was so more than real; I used to call him Τεττιξ (the nickname of our head-master, who was very like a grasshopper in his movements). He was a marvellous skeleton, that; he smoked a pipe and breathed flames, and had forty-six ribs, in defiance of the rules of anatomy. But to get back to the Coquet.

The angler who wishes to make a good creel in the Coquet, particularly late in the season, will find it no easy matter with the fly. The fish are very well educated, and "know a hawk from a hernshaw," and he will have to fish against professional fisherman, who can fish as lightly as he can, and know every trout in the river by name almost. There are several good fishermen, but Mavin is the best of them by far. He attends gentlemen, and knows all the best flies, places, pools, and dodges. If he has a fault, it is that he is a little too fond of fishing himself. His pet flies, with which he certainly takes a great many fish all through the summer, are, to make a bull, spiders, made with grouse and partridge hackle, yellow and lemon bodies respectively. He dresses a very neat fly, so that the angler can rely upon getting all that he needs in this line at Rothbury. If he wants his flies dressed upon *fine* gut, however, he had better send his own, as there is none to be got there.

There is a good deal of fair shooting on the hills about

Rothbury, a good range of grouse and blackgame ground, and this merges again into low-country game, which is also plentiful enough. Rents of shootings, too, are not expensive, from some few I heard of; but the shootings are yearly coming more into request. In conclusion, as concerns Rothbury, it is not at all a bad place for the angler to make head-quarters for a month, as he can get up or down the river easily; but I should recommend him to go early in May or April for the best of the fishing. It is a very pretty river to fish, is fairly stocked with trout, and no leave required save on one or two limited extents; it has plenty of good tributary burns, and there is a very comfortable angler's inn, while, as I have before hinted, Paterfamilias will find plenty of good lodgings, averaging at the rate of 10*s.* a room per week. That is about the tariff, and that is the rather peculiar way of paying. Living is reasonable, and there are famous healthy hills for the cherubs to skimble-skamble over, with no soldiers and very few policemen for the nurses; very nice and varied walks, not more than the average amount of toffy-shops in country places, no toy-shops, and only two doctors; a capital chemist's, a library, and any amount of millinery establishments for missus and the young ladies; no show places, and, consequently, no excursionists; a church handy, an energetic parson, and the river contiguous. George Robins could not say more for it, and I expect to be immortalised in Rothbury, and to have a monument erected to my—not memory, no, say "honour;" and if ever the principles of universal suffrage should be extended to representation, and if ever Rothbury should become a place of sufficient note to return a member to Parliament, I shall expect to have the representation of the constituency of Rothbury forced upon me. What a day would that be! In my mind's eye I see the two chaises put into frantic requisition; while the angler who wants one to go a-fishing will be scouted as an unsympathetic, unpatriotic, and hoggish individual. The four publics will keep open house out of pure philanthropy; committees will sit all day long in each of them at their own expense; every lodging-house will be specially retained without pay, disclaiming all views of petty lucre, and only desirous to emulate which shall construct and get rid of the greatest amount of red, white, and blue favours, all in the best Coventry sarsanet, in a given time. A gross of green parasols, as per Eatanswill, will be recklessly distributed by the attorney (if there is one, which I don't think there is—another virtue for Rothbury) as the proceeds of pure conscience-money in respect of overcharged and untaxed costs in some other election. The member in prospective, however, it must be clearly understood, don't bind himself to kiss or even hug all the children; though if some of the young ladies he saw there—ahem, ahem. The church tower will be hung with three dozen pocket-handkerchiefs, one dozen from each of the drapers, as a graceful and appropriate contribution, printed in the fashion of Union Jacks and British standards, if the said parson of the parish and the beadle thereof likewise don't render themselves obnoxious to these patriotic ebullitions; the very ballot boxes will be constructed out of the timbers taken from the wreck of the British Constitution, and out of compliment to the ladies, Home Rule and the grey mare will be proclaimed in Rothbury, and all sorts of attractions be put forward to signalize the occasion.

Before abandoning the Coquet, I may say that efforts have been made to reduce the bull trouts and to introduce the salmon; and, though most of the weirs have had passes constructed in them and a large number of salmon fry have been turned out, I fear the bull trout have got too far ahead ever to give the salmon a really fair chance; and, though the Coquet was in days gone by a fair salmon river, yet the tremendous obstructions caused by the formidable weirs constructed on it, and the alteration of the bed of the river by reason of destructive floods, has much modified its capabilities for producing salmon.

As I had to catch the coach from Alnwick, which leaves at half-past eight in the morning, and as it is a good twelve miles of steep hill and dale, we had to make an early start of it; and the grey of the morning had hardly cleared off the mountain-tops when I turned out, and, after a scrambling attempt at breakfast, mounted the shandrydan of a four-wheeler, and commenced the arduous ascent. A straight line across wide, dreary moors, with nothing but a shepherd and his dog visible in the distance. Snow-posts every hundred yards—significant fact of the delights of this country in the winter time! The wind a warning to razor-grinders. What a nice place to lose oneself in in a snow-drift! Now we mount another awful steep pitch; as I reach the top my nose, well-tutored for many long years to the peculiar savour, sniffed The Briny. Yes; there is no mistake about it. Father Ocean is somewhere to the fore, and half a mile on we catch sight of him, looking as oily as a Jew quack-doctor, and as mild as though his brow were never wrinkled and storms never affected him. All hail! old boy. You and I have had many a pleasant foregathering, and, I must confess me, surely many an unpleasant one too, for

When wind and weather come together,
Upon my soul there'll be stormy weather.

which has not unfrequently been the case during our acquaintanceship; and on such occasions sometimes, though not always, I experience throes, as if, like Mark Twain, I was striving "to bring up my immortal soul." If there is any very particular phase in any particular disease, worse than a bad attack of sea sickness, I am happy to say I have not yet experienced it; it would be superfluous perhaps, to say I hope I never, never, no never may. But we top another hill, and there lies Alnwick below us, with that magnificent structure, Alnwick Castle, in the midst of it.

CHAPTER IV.

OTTERBURN—A WATERLOO RELIC—ALNWICK—THE LAIDLEY WORM—WOOLER—A WRASTLING—A LOOK AT THE GLEN—EWART BRIDGE—WHITLING.

NORTHUMBERLAND is certainly one of the most interesting, if not *the* most, interesting county in England. The Englishman goes all over the world to see scenery—ruins, palaces, and battle-fields, and what not; but, when he has them altogether within a summer week's ramble close at home, he hardly seems to care about them; and many are the men who have looked down on the plains of the Pyramids, and pilgrimaged to Waterloo, who have never looked on Flodden nor cared for Otterburn. And yet their nerves have thrilled, their cheeks glowed, and their eyes brightened, as they read how

> Groom fought like noble, squire like knight,
> As fearlessly and well;

and, further, how

> The Dowglas lost hys lyffe,
> And the Perssye was lede awaye,

while they have but a dim and confused appreciation of the Pyramids, and were bored to death as they bought sham relics at Waterloo. Talking of Waterloo reminds me of a good relic story. A relative of mine was looking over the plains of Waterloo a short time since. The guide, a shrewdish *garçon*, was explaining the position of the French, English, and Prussians. "Here, Monsieur will observe, the French charged; and here, Monsieur, the English formed square. Yonder, Monsieur, is the farmhouse that was taken and retaken; and yonder, again, among the trees is where the great struggle, &c., &c., was," and so forth;

"and formerly, Monsieur, these trees showed traces of the battle, and were filled with bullets. Ah, sacrée! what do I see?—a bullet! No—yes! it is—it must be a bullet—a r-rélique of the gr-r-rande bataille." Frantic excitement—great digging with a huge clasp knife—much perspiration and exasperation, and at length out rolled a respectable bullet, which had been in the tree evidently but little time. "Monsieur will purchase a rélique of the grande bataille? Five francs will be but a bagatelle for the priceless relic." "Humph!" quoth my relative, a man not apt to be enthusiastic in such matters; "the tree, my friend, is a young one, you will perceive, certainly not twenty years old. The battle, my friend, as you are aware, was fought above forty years ago. Thank you, I will not purchase that priceless relic. Put it in the gun again, and fire into a larger and an older tree next time." The hint may not be lost, even as regards battle-fields nearer home.

But, while satisfied to be too often cheated upon foreign soil, Englishmen somehow are tolerably astute when they turn their eyes nearer home, and they throw away very little enthusiasm or money either on their own matters of this kind. There is scarcely an uninteresting mile in the northern part of Northumberland. All along the Border is "haunted holy ground." Druidical remains are numerous; every favourable hill has been crowned with the camps of Saxon or Roman; every favourable site has been a battle-field. Here are ruined priories, ruined castles, and tumble-down hermitages galore, as well as others of the same stamp, in good preservation, in all directions. Poetry and song and doughty deeds have ennobled and hallowed hill and valley, rock and plain. It is not possible for me to do more than barely hint at a tithe of these matters. It would take months, perhaps years, to go through Northumberland properly, and to see and find out all that there is to be seen. The artist will find delightful and picturesque scenery; the archæologist will be in a perfect *embarras de richesses*; the fisherman will find streams containing multitudes of trout, running in all directions; and the tourist will find all these things, and plenty of legends besides. One thing he will not find at all general, however, and that is good cooking; cookery is not an art the aboriginal Northumbrian excels in. Everything is pitched into the oven on the one hand, and the frying-pan on the other. As for boiling or roasting, they do not seem aware of it in a general way, and the meat too often comes to table dried up or greasy. I attribute much of this to the practice of the women to such a very large extent working in the fields, instead of their more legitimate sphere. This is a drawback, but not one the ordinary tourist-fisherman—who desires little beyond something to eat and drink, and somewhere to sleep, scenery, and mental fodder—will care to quarrel with perhaps. Well, he will find plenty of mental fodder about Alnwick, one of the most celebrated towns near the Border. How many times the castle has been besieged I will not undertake to say. Malcolm, King of Scotland, lost his life before it in 1093, and William the Lion, King of Scotland, was taken before it in 1174, as a stone near the town informs us. The stronghold of the Percies, it cannot but have a charm for the admirer of chivalry and poetic feeling. I am not writing a history of the town, and must, as I have said, touch these matters very briefly. There are, however, many objects of great interest about the town. Chief of all, of course, is the Castle, the seat of the Duke of Northumberland, which is a most striking edifice. It has been well and carefully renewed and restored within the last century, preserving its old outward form without alteration. The towers and pinnacles strike the visitor very much, being topped, though scarcely *ornamented,* with all sorts of strange figures of life-size, which appear to be doing a variety of incomprehensible, incongruous, and uncouth things; and I cannot but think the general aspect of the castle would be improved hugely by these figures, now so out of place, being consigned to some more congenial location. As they stand now, they give one at the first glance the idea that the towers are vast chimneys, and are given to smoking, and that these queer figures are the results of the taste of some ambitious fumifiers, as I believe the gentlemen who cure smoky chimneys call themselves. There are, besides, sundry old and curious arches and gateways to the town (one of which is said to have looked down upon eight centuries), and some beautiful churches. The visitor will often be attracted by a strange figure, which he will suppose to be St. George and the Dragon, and which is rather prevalent about Alnwick. This is a memento of the legend of the "Laidley Worm,"* a fabulous monster which was said formerly to have laid waste the country about Spindleston Heugh—a rocky hill between Alnwick and Bamburgh. This Laidley Worm was the daughter of the King of Bamburgh, transformed thus by her step-mother, who was a witch, and envious, according to the usual wont of witches. Her brother, who rejoiced in the striking cognomen of "the Childy Wynd," which, as there appears to be a good deal of transformation in the yarn, may suggestively enough be taken for a facetious transformation of "the Windy Childe"—this brother, I repeat, in revenge, in the end transformed his stepmother herself into a toad, she having failed to sink his ships as they were returning (which, by the way, had silken sails and rowan-tree masts—rowan-tree being unto witches what holy-water is to their papa). Not knowing that the serpent was his sister in disguise, the Childe went to attack the monster that threatened "to ruin the north countrie." Arriving at the cave, he drew his sword and gave the serpent to understand, in what could hardly be considered a serpentine manner or language, that he—that, in fact, if she hit him he'd hit her again. Whereupon the serpent or dragon requested him "to kiss her three times"—rather a staggering request to a young gentleman prepared for battle, especially when the ballad gives the following tempting description of the charms to which he was invited:

For seven miles east, for seven miles west,
And seven miles north and south,
No blade of grass or corn could grow,
So venomous was her mouth.

* "Loathly worm"—serpent or dragon.

Now, for a lady, or a serpent, or whatever she claimed to be, with such very striking peculiarities, to make such a remarkable request, and that without holding out any inducement whatever. might rather perhaps be considered as "coming it a little too strong." Amazing as the proposition was, our windy friend appears to have been nowise surprised at it, but fell to embracing the serpent as though it was the most natural thing in the world, the ordinary thing to do, and no more than serpentine etiquette on the occasion. The wind-up of the ballad is, of course, perfectly satisfactory to all parties:

> He sheathed his sword and bent his bow,
> He gave her kisses three;
> She crept into her cave a worm,
> But stept out a fair lady.

Whether the windy child was astonished even at this what Mr. Swiveller would have called "staggerer number three," the chronicler does not relate.

But the people in these northern parts appear to have been, if I may be permitted the phrase, rather "troubled with worms," for there is yet another legend anent "the Lambton worm." The origin of this one—take warning, oh! ye metropolitan anglers, who rusticate on the Sabbath at Twickenham and Richmond—appears to have been fishing on a Sunday. The heir of Lambton caught a fish on a Sunday, and threw it into a well. In utter defiance of all the rules of natural history, save perhaps such as may be gleaned from "The Vestiges of Creation," this fish persisted in growing into a worm or serpent. The fish might of course have been an eel; the eel have somehow been a conger, and the conger is a sort of first cousin to the sea serpent, if not the actual Simon Pure in many accredited instances, and thus the beast may be explained—but then the size is such a choker. This snake, "without a word of lie sir," grew to be 900 yards, or rather more than half a mile long. It is unnecessary to relate the whole of the legend after this sample of it; but as the serpent, when he was cut through, had a faculty very unusual in creation, to say the least of it, viz., that of growing together again immediately, it became very difficult to reduce his dimensions. Albeit the ambitious naturalist who went out to make a specimen of him attired himself in the costume of a lunatic knife-grinder, or got himself vandyked and embroidered all over with razor blades, and gammoning the snake to fight out the battle in the river, he soon got the best of it, for as soon as ever a chunk of the sarpent was whittled off, the current carried it away before it could reunite, and by this process the whole 900 yards piece speedily became "a remnant on a reduced scale," and was undeniably sold "a great sacrifice."

But I am devoting too much time to Alnwick, which, as I shall return to it, I will say no more of at present. The Wooler coach leaves at 8.45 in the morning, and by it I started. The drive to Wooler is very pleasant, the road passing over small rivers and burns full of trout, and by gentlemen's seats agreeably situated, we at length cross Wooler Water, and roll into Wooler. The coach is crowded to-day, Wooler games being on, and some of the best wrestlers on the border are expected. There was Jamieson, of Penrith, the champion of Cumberland, a perfect Hercules, a fellow "whose hug would make a bar grin, I guess." There was Scott, of Carlisle, a middle-sized, bull-headed-looking fellow, good-tempered, but determined; T. Davidson, of Castle-side, a smaller man in appearance than Scott, but active and rather less fleshy, with an angular, hard-looking phiz, that showed endurance; and last, but not least, there was Jamie Davidson, of Ilderton Moor, a mighty favourite with the Woolerites, a long, lithe, wiry herd, as hard as nails, with sinews like cords; always laughing and smiling, his hard mug beamed with grim good temper. The herds are swarming in from the hills, most gentlemanly and civilised-looking creatures in appearance, each with his pork-pie hat and inseparable "maud." For this sport is in great estimation with them, they being mostly good at a "wrostle." The women swarm, too, very solid, very parti-coloured, rainbow petticoats and stockings, and such "understandings!" with regular gorilla crinolines—oval, square, flat, triangular, any shape, in fact, but round. "An Englishman's house is his castle," says the law; but why—oh, why—should fashion make an Englishwoman's dress her cage? Anything so hideous and savage as these deformed structures, with which these good-natured, cherry-cheeked country lasses were then in the habit of disfiguring their comfortable proportions, it would be difficult to conceive. Hear the judgment of Paris, oh! ye Northumbrian damsels:

Lesbia hath a robe of gold,
  But all so tight the nymph hath laced it,
Not a charm of beauty's mould
  Presumes to stay where nature placed it.
Oh, my Norah's dress for me,
  That floats as wild as mountain breezes,
Leaving every beauty free
  To rise and swell as nature pleases.

"And so say all of us," "which nobody can deny." Bravo, Mr. Moore, *à bas la crinoline!*

Under the tutelage of my friend Mr. J. Thompson, to whom I owe many kind offices and much smoothing of the way for me, I went down to see the games. Putting the heavy shot was just over, and leaping with the pole had commenced. There were several competitors for the prize, but one after another fell off as the bar got towards the nine feet mark, until at length the trial lay between Jamieson, the wrestler, and an Irishman, one Larry something—nine feet three inches. It seems a great height to go over, but with a short run, the pole well grasped, and with only one false jump, the two men managed to heave themselves over, and drop the pole on the other side without touching the bar, amidst loud shouts "nine feet five." There are several attempts at this, but at last both men heave themselves over. It seems and looks incredible—nine feet seven inches. Larry tries and Jamieson tries; but it ends in Larry not doing it and in Jamieson coming down sair, so as to severely strain one of the sinews in the ball of the great toe, having previously had a similar accident. And no wonder; a ten or eleven-feet fall for a man of fourteen or fifteen stone or thereabouts is an awkward matter; and if he does it often, something must, as Robson used to say, "bust." The prize is therefore divided, and the wrestling begins, "Coomberla-and fashion," for eleven stone men. The names of R. Taylor and Adam Ross are called, and the men, stripped to their drawers, socks, and jerseys, step into the ring. Mighty neatly got up, too, and a good deal of taste and fancy is displayed in the wrestling toggery, for there is a prize for the man who is most *comme il faut* in this respect. Now they approach, stretch out their arms, neck is laid to neck, and shoulder to shoulder, and they stretch their long arms down, feeling along the backs of their antagonists for a favourable chance of getting a grip; and they are mighty cautious in getting it, because a bad or a good grip at once decides the throw; so that they do not take hold until sure of a favourable one, for when once the grip is taken, if either party releases his grasp, he loses the fall. Fifteen minutes is the outside time allowed for getting gripped or "fast," as it is termed Gradually the men feel their way. Now one catches, but the other doesn't follow suit, and so there is some more feeling and dodging. Now they are fast—a short fit of convulsive tugging and straining, in which all the skill and the strength is put forth, and down goes Ross to mother earth. Another couple take their place, and struggle after struggle takes place, considerable skill being shown; Scott of Carlisle and Davidson of Castleside being left in in the end to contest the prize. This they did in very fine style, Davidson gaining the best of three falls.

Then came the all weights' wrestling, when much disappointment was felt at Jamieson not being in a condition to try for the prize. His foot was so painful he could hardly stand on it. Every one was anxious to see him come against the wiry herd of Ilderton Moor—speculation and expectation had long been rife as to the result. It was not to be, however, and Jamie Davidson carried off the prize with tolerable ease, having grassed his opponents in fine style, swinging most of them off their legs as if they had been schoolboys. Then came a curious sport called "hitch and kick." A bladder was suspended to a high cross-bar, and the competitors had to run, spring up, and kick it. It was hung, to commence with, about seven feet or eight feet high, and gradually worked up to nine feet five inches, at which height a lithe young fellow (John Bell) managed to kick it, while the only remaining opponent failed. Then came jumping, &c., &c.; and, barring the break down of the grand stand, which took place at an early period of the festivities, all passed off well and satisfactorily. These games are an excellent institution. In the north almost every town and village of note has them at different times. It is quite unnecessary to point out the benefit derived from their encouragement, as it must be self-evident.

The next day, taking our rods, Mr. T. and myself sailed forth to the water belonging to Sir H. St. Paul, on the Ewart, which is the lower part of Glen. We put up trout flies, but it was blowing heavily, and ere we had got over a pool or two it came on a perfect hurricane again. It was almost impossible with my single-handed light rod to keep the flies on the water at all, so I gave it up and looked on at my companion, who having a double-handed rod, of course could fish heavier, and managed to make out somehow. We had tried a cast or two for whitling, which I believe is a term applied indiscriminately to the common white or salmon trout, and what may be called the grilse bull-trout. How this may be I cannot positively determine, but I am sure that under the name of whitling I have captured very different fish.

The wind came down more gustily and heavily than ever when we reached a fine round pool, called the Ewart-bridge pool. Here we made a pause, and determined to do our best, as it was full of these white and bull trout. The bull-trout run heavy, though they don't take the fly as well as the white trout. Presently one or two of these whitling begin capering about, and in a trice whitling flies were up. Mr. Thompson covered a nice rising fish, which, after two or three boils, came at him with a spring and he held him. The little fellow behaved marvellously like a small salmon, running, plunging, and leaping, after the fashion of white trout generally, but he was soon brought to book, and I landed him, a nice little fish of 2lb., rather lanky, but in good order. A few minutes after this, the wind being a little more favourable for me on the other side of the pool, I hooked one of the lively fellows, which gave me good sport on my light tackle; I soon landed him; he was near upon 1½lb. After this we rose several fish, but they got very shy after a lengthened residence in fresh water, accompanied with plenty of whipping. Presently I covered a good fish I saw rising at the tail of the pool; up he came with a dash, I struck rather sharply, and off went the fish with my fly and half my casting line. I had put a whitling fly on a very fine gut trout-cast, and paid for the temerity. Accordingly I sat me down disconsolate, and rigged out another cast, using stouter gut and two flies; but whether it was the stouter gut, or that the fish had had enough of it, or what, I cannot say, but I got only one more rise, and that a very shy one: so we went home and had our white trout for dinner, and very good they were—making our arrangements for the morrow meanwhile.

CHAPTER V.

WOOLER—WOOLER WATER—THE GLEN—OLD POLL OF BENDOR—THE BOWMONT AND COLLEGE BURN—A WHITE DEVIL IN THE COO-HAUGH—HEATHPOOL LINNS—BY YEAVERING BELL—THE GLEN AT COUPLAND—A MUCKLE WHISKY FLASK.

WOOLER is called the metropolis of the Cheviots, but for a metropolis it is not an extensive one. As a village it is neither picturesque nor pretty, but the neighbourhood is delightful. Here we are close at the feet of the Cheviots, which are remarkable hills, presenting, for the most part, no great difference in shape, being huge green rounded mounds of vast capacity, some of them nearly 3000 feet in height, but all of a similar character—green to the very top, here and there well clothed in heather patches along the sides, while the lower slopes are thickly clad in large masses of fern. These hills are of course grazed by thousands of sheep, and the mutton is scarcely inferior in fineness of flavour to the far-famed Southdown. On the tops of many of the hills adjacent to Wooler are found vestiges of camps of various dates of antiquity, Druidical remains, and other objects of interest; while the valleys have (more or less) stories and legends of battles, folk-lore, and other matters, attached to them. There are near Wooler, in all directions, numerous burns which, after a flush of rain, afford good trout-fishing; and as it often rains among these hills, and the burns that feed the larger rivers run in all directions, east, west, north, and south, it seldom happens but one or the other catches the rain; and when the rains are unusually heavy, however thick some of the streams may be, there will nearly always be found others which are fishable. Two things the angler here should always provide himself with, viz., a bag of well-scoured worms (these should be the smallest lobworms, which I always find the most suitable), and a couple of dozen or so of minnows, as fresh as they can be obtained, as the fresher they are the tougher they are. The fishing here is of so changeable a character, and after a shower of rain the streams come down so suddenly, that the angler can never calculate how he may have to make out his day's sport. He may go out with the notion that the stream he is going to fish is in capital order for fly-fishing, and he may find it almost too thick for worm or minnow. He may go out provided to fish with minnow—the stream may be roaring red, and before evening may be down again almost low for fly. Such is the change which excessive drainage has produced in our northern rivers. Every drop of rain is in the rivers almost as soon as it falls. They are bank-full and perhaps half over the fields for a few hours, and the next day one would hardly believe there had been any run of water into them for a month. Thus the angler must be well and thoroughly armed at all points to avail himself of his chance in these sudden changes, or he may have a long and tedious scramble over hills and bogs for nothing, for the lack of a small bag of worms or a bag of minnows which will not take up six square inches of space, and weigh next to nothing.

In the evening, after dinner (to which we came back after our rather blusterous day's fishing), I started out, determined to try the worm down Wooler-water to the Till. It is a pretty little stream, taking its rise near Hedgehope-hill among the Cheviots, and contains a good store of lively little trout, but it wants rain to fish well. Whether the water was over thick, or whether some tar-water which got into the stream had sickened the fish or no, I know not, but I only got two or three fish—one of about a pound, which, curiously enough, sprang ashore on to a bank of gravel the moment the hook struck him, thus saving me any further trouble about him. I tried one or two pools on the Till for whitling, but only rose one, for the Till was getting thick too.

The Glen is one of the best, if not the best, of the trout-waters in Northumberland, and the next day (having a permission from the Earl of Durham) we determined to fish it. Mr. Thompson and myself, thinking it would be in fine order, made a start for it; but, just as we started, it began to rain again, and before we got to the turnpike it was coming down heavily. We took refuge in the public house at Bendor, and listened for an hour or more to the groans of Old Poll, an old lady of nearly a century's experience of the vanities of this wicked world, and who has a most painful knack of doing little else but groan, and that in a most startling and cold-blooded key. For an hour the rain and Old Poll, with our fly-books, divided our attention; and still it rained on. We decided to face it at length, and we sallied out. The wind was driving over heavily from the dark field of Flodden, and the rain at present showed no signs of abating. As the day was so bad, and was, moreover, half-gone, we determined not to waste a day of our order on Lord Durham's water, but to go on to the upper Glen, where a namesake of Mr. T.'s had some water, and to look at the lower part of the Bowmont and College Burn. The College Burn and the Bowmont are the two streams which, united, form the Glen. They were all more or less coloured, College being especially red; and we had about half a mile of the head of the Glen to fish. I commenced on some sharp, rapid water, where I began to pick up the fish fairly, though they were small. We worked on, but the fishing fell off as we got higher up, and still the rain peppered us. Presently we reached the point of separation, and determined to fish up the Bowmont, as affording most chance of sport. A singular difference is observable in the character of these two streams. College is a rattling, good-sized mountain burn, dashing along over the stones, from pool to pool and from stream to stream; it was now the colour of London stout. The Bowmont, on the other hand, is here like a south country coarse-fish river, and looks more like a pike than a trout stream, resembling the Loddon or Windrush, deep and quiet, with a stream at the turns here and there. It was less red and more muddy than College: a coloured water or smart breeze is, therefore, wanting on the Bowmont to do much good. The fish in the two streams are as different as the streams themselves: in College they are most abundant, and it is nothing unusual to have three on your line at once; and they make but few sham rises, usually getting fast when they come at the fly. They are very small, however, and one of half a pound is not common. I have heard of twenty-four dozen of these fish being taken between ten and four o'clock. The Bowmont fish are nice chubby fellows, often running up to three-quarters of a pound; and on a fair day the angler may pick out half a dozen or a dozen half-pounders, with one or two of a larger sample. They often rise without taking, too—the fish, from the nature of the stream, being far better fed than in the College, and consequently more dainty.

I did not get on so well at first on the Bowmont as my friend. Out of compliment to me, or from some whim, he put up one of my flies, and, rather to his astonishment, it began taking fish fast. Finding this, I, after a time, was induced to try it too, and I put up a smallish Francis, when I found its qualities quite as much appreciated by the northern trout as by those in the south; and it did so well all that day and the next on Glen, that I seldom afterwards fished without it, and I can fairly say that I believe that it took a full half of all the fish I caught, and certainly most of the best ones. The difficulty which even I experience with regard to this fly is to get it properly tied. Either the hackles are of a bad colour, the fly is over-hackled and like a bottle-brush, or the body is as huge and fat as a moth's. The fact is, like all flies, it should be varied slightly in size and delicacy to suit the water. If the angler expects to go upon fine low waters, and to fish with a fly as big as the top of his thumb, and to catch fish, he deserves to fail, and should not blame the fly (which may suit other waters well enough) if he does. I have seen flies which have been shown to me as specimens of the Francis, which it was a disgrace to the tyer to send out.

But to return to our sport. We fished up the Bowmont for some distance, when, suddenly turning around I saw my companion divested entirely of his clothes, and standing stark naked, like Adonis, on the river brim, in the drizzling rain. At first I naturally concluded that he was suddenly overcome with some species of mania, and had become a piscatorial Nebuchadnezzar; but I was soon reassured. He had been catching fish rather fast, and, the wind being high, and the stream rather bushy and foul on the far side, he had had the bad luck to get hung up two or three times, and on each occasion lost fine new casting-lines, flies and all. The last occasion had taken his only remaining cast, so he suddenly resolved to re-collect his lost lines, and, with the decision and promptness which characterises him, at once slipped off his toggery and went in, as there was no other means of getting across. Now a bath in July is nothing very out of the way; but such a July as this has been here!—a shaving wind and sleeting rain!—"a raw and gusty day, the troubled Bowmont chafing with its shores," it required a little strong persuasion to face it. Mr. T. was some years since master of an excellent pack of otter hounds, which he hunted himself over all the numerous streams in this neighbourhood most assiduously and successfully; and therefore a jump into a pool was to him a mere matter of course. So, in he went, and, like Cæsar and Cassius, he "did buffet it with lusty sinews," and the first line was gathered. The others were some distance off, about a quarter of a mile down stream; and, dripping like a Naiad, or rather a Triton, he reappeared *in puris naturalibus* on the river-bank. Off he started down the bank over the grass land, to the utter amazement and horror of the cows, which grazed thickly thereanent. They had never seen such a thing before. What was this pale ghost that came skimming along the river-side over the greensward towards them? Nearer comes the spectre, and nearer yet! They cannot stand it—a mighty terror seizes them. Bogey or Jumbo is before them! Like the negroes, they evidently believe their devil is white, and the word was clearly passed that there was a white devil in the coo-haugh. *Vade retro, Sathanas!* and every cow turns tail, and, with heads down and tails up, they scour the far pastures in an awful state of mind. I believe my friend must have ruined all the milk for that day. But the other lines are collected, and T., all the fresher for his bath, is soon dressed and at it again. The fish rose but middlingly; altogether we managed to bag some four or five dozen, though I doubt if there was a fish of half a pound among them.

Having fished up the Bowmont for some distance, and seeing several fishermen making to the river, we resolved to leave it and take a look at the College, where there was some pretty scenery to see; so off we started. The water being too thick certainly for fly-fishing, we did not waste much time in casting, but scrambled along a gorge between the lofty hills on either hand; until the ground taking a sudden rise, the stream came out from a throat below, under the shade of hazels and ferns, black as ink, and inclosed, like the Thrum at Rothbury, between narrow walls of rock, save that these walls were in places some forty or fifty feet deep; a succession of falls or linns dashing along one over the other in the deep dark gulf below, from which the spray rose thickly; many sorts of ferns and foliage of various kinds hanging lovingly over the spot, which is called Heathpool Linns. Burns has aptly described it, or a spot evidently very like it, in the Birks o' Aberfeldy:

Bonnie lassie, will ye go to the Birks o' Aberfeldy?
The braes ascend like lofty wa's,
The foaming stream deep roaring fa's,
O'erhung wi' fragrant spreading shaws,
The Birks o' Aberfeldy.

Bonnie lassie, will ye go to the Birks o' Aberfeldy?
The hoary cliffs are crowned wi' flowers,
While o'er the linns the burnie pours,
That rising weets wi' misty showers
The Birks o' Aberfeldy.

It was, in truth, a charming spot in the very heart of the grand old Cheviots. It is easily got at, too, being close to a farmhouse, so that it is a great resort for pic-nics; and the only thing that spoilt the romance of the place (and it did spoil it) was the *débris* of a huge salad that had but lately been made there, for some scores of lettuce-leaves and sundry bits of old newspaper decorated and desecrated the spot.

We then turned us homewards, having a long walk of some eight or nine miles before us over the shoulder of Yeavering Bell, a curious hill of considerable height and singular shape, with some peculiar remains, in the shape of a wide stone circle, Druidical or otherwise, on the lofty summit. Tolerably wet through, we got home at last, tired and washed out. The next day we made a start for the water on the Glen at Coupland. The Coupland Water, then held by the Earl of Durham, is a very pretty water. It is well stocked with whitling, too, and the trout often run of a fair size, from half a pound to a pound, or a pound and a half even. Sometimes, of course, they are caught larger, but it is not usual. The river has some capital holes for the whitling all the way from Ewart-bridge up to the Cauld at Coupland. They are occasionally taken above this, even up the Bowmont, as they can get up above the Cauld by the mill-stream or in heavy floods. In a good wind, or early and late in the day, they may be caught; but they took badly the year I was there. Our sport at starting was indifferent, as the day was heavy and dull. We worked on for a few fish up to a fine deep pool, called The Foxholes; here we rose a whitling or two, but the wind was not enough on the pool to induce them to take. Indeed the pool is so overgrown and shaded that but few winds do touch it. Just above the pool is a nice rough stream, and out of this Mr. T. managed to coax a niceish whitling. Just then heavy thunder amongst the hills commenced, accounting for the sluggishness of the fish, and in about half an hour it obliged us to leave off fishing and take refuge in the keeper's cottage: the rain was very heavy. In the evening —(after looking over the kennel, and praising the condition of the pointers, which looked creditably fit for work)—the weather having cleared, we recommenced fishing. In the rough stream above The Foxholes I picked up some good fish, and tried hard for a huge fellow of 8lb. or 9lb., a bull trout, I think, which I saw feeding; but I had had a rise at the fly near about the same spot previously and missed it, and I fancied, as this fish persistently refused it, that I had risen and missed him. I got three nice trout of about a pound each, and a whitling; and besides these we had taken only about three dozen, of which perhaps a dozen were from a quarter to half a pound. The stream is here swarming with white trout or whitling fry, which are exceedingly troublesome to those who don't bag them, which is rather too much the practice on these northern streams, neither size nor sort being any safeguard from the creel, and smelts or trout of eight or ten to the pound are reckoned as "all fish that come to net." I could not make up my mind to kill the whitling fry, and so was much bothered frequently to get them off, or be rid of them; for they would keep rising, and, in spite of my not striking, often hooked themselves, and took up valuable time.

The heavy rain had so swamped the high grass, rushes, nettles, &c., which grow thickly here on the river bank, that we were well soaked again, at least up to the middle, before we reached the turnpike road once more, and it was late before, tired and wet, we reached home. On reaching home, I found, on looking at my landing handle, that the boy who carried it had managed to lose the brass screw at the butt end, and the two spare tops which the handle contained. I was much vexed at this, as, if the tops were lost, one of my best and most useful rods was placed *hors de combat.* Fortunately, however, the miller's man picked up both the tops and the brass butt screw, which is rather a large one of some inch and a half in diameter. There is a good joke in connection with this which, although a little at my own expense, I cannot refrain from relating. The miller's man brought back the tops to my friend T.; I was away at the time. He handed them over, saying, "Hey, sir! but a'm no surprised at the jontleman losing the taps, or onything else, for d'ye ken joost forbye them a' picked up the screw-tap o' a muckle whusky flask; an na doot but the jontleman 'll have been awfu' fou!" and he produced the large brass screw of the landing-handle, which would have argued a muckle flask indeed had it pertained to one, being, although of the same shape, about four times the usual size of the screw-taps to the whisky-flasks.

CHAPTER VI.

EWART BRIDGE—WHITLING—FLODDEN FIELD—THE TILL AT ETAL—MID-DAY MUSINGS—DANGEROUS WADING.

I HAD my journal to write up, and was rather tired with long walks, hard flogging, and repeated wettings, and resolved to have a day in for rest, but towards evening it looked tempting, and, taking our rods, Mr. Thompson and myself sallied forth to try the river by the Ewart bridge. Arrived at the river side, T. found that he had left one of the joints of his rod at home, and, substituted one of another rod, which did not fit; of course, this put out his chance of fishing. So I went to work *solus*. At the first pool I tried I rose a couple of whitling, and lost my fly in one of them. The trout, however, did not rise well, and beyond a bare half-dozen, I did little till I came to the Ewart bridge pool; here I got a fine whitling of about 2lb, almost fresh run, as I should judge. He had had a terrible mauling in the nets, having escaped with a severe scraping.

I rose another fish or two, and touched one, but got no more whitling, although I caught a very nice trout of about $1\frac{1}{4}$lb., a well-fed, handsome fish; and, as it was getting towards dark, we turned us homewards.

The next day, thinking that the Till would be in good order, we went down to it, resolving to fish it down to the mouth of the Glen; on arriving at it, however, we found it rather thick for the fly, and set to work with the minnow. I rose several whitling to the minnow, but could not get hold of them. I picked up a nice trout or two, but the day got windy and more windy, and the river came down thicker and thicker, until the trout went off altogether. We got about eight or ten fish only—true, they were all good fish, one which Mr. Thompson took being 1½lb. The Till here is a dull, sluggish river in places, but there are nice streams in it. It winds about in the most abrupt turns, and when there is a breeze on it, or a little water in it, it gives fine trout, though rather reluctantly. It would suit admirably for the introduction of grayling, which would be a great acquisition to it. The river flows over rich meadow land, and the banks abound in food, and this accounts for the fine size and condition of the trout, and also for their disinclination to take the hook. The Till trout are certainly (with the exception of the Tweed, of course) the finest fish in this part of the country, being fat, brilliant, well-fed fellows, running from ½lb. to 2lb., from ½lb. to ¾lb. being about the average when the fish are taking. They are very shy, and want much coaxing, however, in a general way.

We determined to take the next day on the Coupland water, as the stream was getting low, so, instead of fishing the lower water (being anxious to try our hands at the whitling), we drove at once to the pools below Coupland. Tackle was soon together, and I had hardly made three casts on the pool below the bridge when I had hold of a nice whitling, which danced about merrily for half a minute, when he danced himself off. A little disgusted at the opening of the day, I fished on, determined not to let the next one off so easily, if I was so far favoured; and in half a dozen throws I held another, which gave some good sport on my light rod before he was basketed. I rose one or two in the next pool, but the wind did not strike well, and they would not buckle to. On the succeeding pool, however, I got another. I had got hold of a few good trout, too, and the day did not promise badly; but the wind was a cross-wind, and, though tolerably heavy, it only struck here and there. Towards the afternoon and evening it blew a gale of wind again, but the trout rose well, and I managed in the evening to fill my basket with very nice trout. Indeed, this was the best day's sport I had had, since I should think my basket held some 20lb. of fish. Many of them, too, were very sizable trout. My companion thinking that the trout would not rise in such a heavy wind, went down to the Foxholes pool, to try for whitling, three of which he got hold of, but, for the want of a landing-net, he only bagged one of them. Tolerably satisfied with the day's sport, we shouldered our loads, lighted our pipes, and tramped homewards—*not* wet through, for a wonder.

I had written to Lady Fitzclarence for permission to fish the Till at Etal, and having received permission for a couple of days, which were named on my card, I took a gig and drove over. The drive is a pleasant one, passing by Coupland and under the hill of Flodden.

The Field of Flodden, fatal Flodden! is now cut up into a good many fields. Hedges and ditches have broken its expanse, and even Lord Marmion would have found a series of double posts-and-rails a series of obstacles to the perfect manœuvring of the *equites* not easily to be got over. The first flight in Leicestershire, in pink and velvet, might make a successful charge upon Flodden now, but Chester and Stanley, Lennox and Argyll, with iron pots on their heads, and twelve or thirteen stone of iron on their backs, would inevitably charge into the first bullfinch, with a yawner as a take-off, and stick there.

Flodden is situated on a short ridge of low hills, from one side of which—Flodden edge—the ground falls more gradually than from the other, and here is where the brunt of the battle was fought. Yonder, by that quarry, is the spot where King James made his last stand, and fell pierced with wounds, two of which at least were mortal, There, too, the little burn that "Clare" sought to obtain water from, but which ran with the blood of the combatants—the people here say—for four days after. The blood of trout is the only sanguined fluid that ever stains it now. See, there are a troup of mowers and merry haymakers hard at work in one of the fields, thoughtless how a grimmer mower and a feller haymaker has toiled upon that sod they now so lightly trip over; and yet the plough has often turned up one of the ripened stalks cut down and made by him, in the shape of skull or thighbone. The story of Flodden is briefly told. It was in the fair summer time of year in which I am writing, somewhat better than three centuries and a half ago, that King James crossed the border, with a large, well-officered and well-found army. Henry the Eighth was in France, and the command of the English forces fell upon the Earl of Surrey and Lord Dacre. Sitting on a green hill just above Wooler, a few years since, I traced the line of the English march, and the positions occupied by each army. On the far left, upon those three heights, encamped in a very strong position, lay the the Scotch army. To the right, on Wooler Haugh, lay the English army. Finding that King James would not leave his strong position, Surrey faced northwards, as if marching for Berwick, crossed the Till by yonder picturesque old bridge, and, keeping behind that high ground by Doddington, marched on as if for Scotland, until he reached Barmoor; encamped there the night, and then changing his route, instead of going to Berwick, went to the north-west by Duddoe to Twizel-bridge, so as to throw himself between the Scots and their country. He then crossed the Till again at Twizel-bridge, unopposed by James, crossed Pallinsburn, and met and fought the Scotch at Flodden-edge. The result of the combat is well known. The loss of the Scotch was frightful, and hardly a family in Scotland of any consequence but had to mourn a relative. Words cannot describe the closing of the scene better than Scott has :—

Then did their loss his foeman know;
Their king, their lords, their mightiest low,
They melted from the field as snow,
When streams are swoln and south winds blow,
Dissolves in silent dew.
Tweed's echoes heard the ceaseless plash,
   While many a broken band,
Disordered, through her currents dash,
   To gain the Scottish land;

To town and tower, to down and dale,
To tell red Flodden's dismal tale,
And raise the universal wail.
Tradition, legend, tune, and song,
Shall many an age that wail prolong :
Still from the sire the son shall hear
Of the stern strife and carnage drear
  Of Flodden's fatal field,
Where shivered was fair Scotland's spear,
  And broken was her shield!

But we pass another turnpike and pay another ninepence, turn to look at the cauld at Ford, which sadly needs to be done away with or greatly mitigated, and Etal comes in sight: it is but a collection of neat little cottages, with one small roadside public-house; with Etal House, the seat of Lady Fitzclarence, overlooking the village, and the remains of a fine old ruin, which I had not time to inspect, at the other end of the village. The hostess of the public either could not or would not take me in, seeming, in answer to our queries, as if she did not want the trouble; so there was nothing for it but to try a village on the other side of the river, and here I had no better success. On we went again, about half a mile further; and we found accommodation at last at the Bell, at Cookham, a small roadside inn, where the host was a relic, I suppose, of the celebrated English *bill*men who fought at Flodden, as *he* knew how to *charge* and how to manipulate a bill, though they certainly did their best to make the wandering angler comfortable. (N.B.—If the angler fills his flask with whatever he is in the habit of drinking, before he takes refuge in these parts, he may perchance find it very useful.)

I soon found my way to the river through the meadows, and walked down about half a mile of still, deep water, which is undeniable pike water. Soon I reached Etal, and here the principal pool between the two mills was reserved for her Ladyship's friends. Below the Barley Mill is some fine-looking water—alternate streams and deep pools. I commenced fishing it down, having on a light trout-cast, with a good whitling fly at the end. I had but fished half-way down the pool, when a great boil came up in the middle of the dead water. "A salmon or a large bull-trout, by all that's lucky!" thought I, and in my excitement I forgot the light trout-cast, and stuck it into him. The gut was as fine as hair, and he carried it all away. It was peculiarly exasperating, being the first and only rise of any kind I had had. Down I sat, in no very contented frame of mind, and put up another cast; but, hoping soon to make up for the accident, and auguring well from this rise, I went to work again reassured, and counting on fair sport. But "man never *is*, but always *to be* blest," and I reckoned without my host, for, although I fished on till dark, I did not rise another respectable fish, and I only got two or three small trout altogether. One pool—a somewhat shallow one, about a half mile or better below the mill—was alive with whitling, which was sheering about all over it, but would not look at a fly. I tried this pool again and again, but it was quite useless. Although the river was coloured slightly, it was low, and the water was full of filthy green slime. I could hardly make a cast without getting my hooks smothered in it, and it was precisely in these slimy spots that the best fish appeared to take delight in lying, for when I came by any of these spots, half a dozen or a dozen good trout would rush away into the stream, returning again as soon as I was well away. After trying till evening in vain, I turned homewards.

I made an early start of it after breakfast the next morning, determined to give the water a good trial. The day was not so favourable as could have been wished, being heavy and dull, with now and then bright sun and not much wind; and what little there was of it in a bad airt. I met the keeper, who was fishing when I got to the river, but who had done nothing, and did nothing while I was with him. He was a very good fisherman, throwing his fly like a master, and, of course, knowing the river and the flies that suited it well. It struck me, however, that his rod could very well have been dispensed with, as I had the day, and he knew it. From his want of success, I did not anticipate any great amount of sport myself; but I walked on below him, and tried my hand. For some time not a single fin of any kind could I raise. There was something more than usual in the weather to keep them down so; Till trout are at all times kittle fellows to get hold of, but to-day they seemed nailed to the bottom. But what I lost in the fishing was made up by the beauty of the scenery. The Till here runs in a sort of deep ravine, beautifully wooded with magnificent ash trees, interspersed with oak, larch, and other firs.

I sit at midday under a bank, overhung with shady hazels and waving ferns of various kinds, the river flowing quietly by at my feet. Under the deep shade of an overhanging branch upon the further side rises a cautious old trout, the only one rising in the pool. See how quietly the old gentleman comes up, sucking down an unlucky caterpillar or blundering beetle that has lost his foothold on the twig above. How like an usurer in his den the old scoundrel waits and watches his victims as they drop into the down stream of discount, until, hopeless and helpless, they descend into that Avernus, that limbo of a maw of his. "Throw a fly to him," say you? Throw your hat to him—throw your basket or your boots to him! Throw a lame duck to Levi, Levi, and Levi, of Westburnia, Spring-gardens, Mincing-lane, Cursitor-street, and Heaven (or the other place, more probably) knows where else. No, no! In the first place, my good friend, he is unapproachable. You can't get your fly to him, throw how you will. The eddy outside the bough will sweep it away long before he can see it. Let him alone—let him run his course—let him fatten; the inevitable law will hook him some day, never fear. Perhaps the next flood or the one after, when he is improving the occasion, and making a grand *coup*, some minnow or worm, fatter and more tempting than usual, may lead him to his fate; but to-day is not *the* day, so be content. And look at that water-rat, sitting on a stump trimming his whiskers, like a buck as he is. His little black eye glistening towards you, you think he doesn't see you; but make a feint to get up, and —"flop;" you see he is off, and that line of bubbles down stream marks his progress to some favourite lair. Yonder deep, still pool is a favourite haunt for huge pike, they say, and you can easily credit it. Twenty-pounders might lie *perdu* and unsuspected in it. It is a good haunt, too, for the robber otter—now, with his cousin, sly Reynard, the only robbers on the border whom the wardens of the Marches marshal their forces against. "Tak two coos, Tammy; tak two coos,"* goes the wood-pigeon in all directions, far and near, for it abounds here; and the soft dulcet note gives an air of repose and calm to the spot which renders it difficult to leave. But the luncheon of hard-boiled eggs is finished, and, after a sup of the flask, I am up and at work again. Before leaving this point of luncheon, I want to give a hint to brother sportsmen. Hard-boiled eggs are capital things for lunch, but there is one thing that is better, and that is a cold mutton chop. Have some cooked for breakfast, and put up a couple for lunch. Cut meat gets dry and tasteless, and sandwiches become like unto a sheet of pickled blotting-paper bound in boards; but a cold, uncut, succulent mutton chop is not to be improved on in the way of luncheon. To those who doubt it, I say—try it.

The day improved a little, a fresh wind got up, and I began picking up some nice chubby little trout. On my way down I had tried the pool for the whitling again, but with just as much

* This curious and capital interpretation or rendering of the wood-pigeon's note is thus accounted for in these parts. One Tammy Something-or-the-other went out one night to drive (steal) a cow. He had succeeded in his errand, and was making off with his booty, when passing under a tree, a wood-pigeon began his note, which, to the excited ear of the Borderer, said as plainly as bird could say it, "Tak *two* coos, Tammy; tak *two* coos." Roman augur could hardly have had more faith in birds than Tammy. "Hey, noo, and what's that?" said Tammy. "Tak two coos, Tammy; tak two coos." "A dunna but what a-weel," said Tam; "as weel be hangit for twa as ane;" and he went back for another, got caught thereby and was hangit, and laid the blame on the pigeon. The geese saved Rome, and the pigeon hanged Tammy.

success as on the preceding evening. They flew about all over the pool the moment a fly was shown them. One or two other pools lower down the river, of a similar kind, I tried with like success. The whitling declined the honour of my acquaintance totally. There was not wind enough, and the water was in very bad order.

One point I cannot forbear noticing, and that is with regard to the wading in Till, and my advice to all anglers is always when wading it look to your footing. There is a good deal of truth in the ghastly old rhyme which has so often been quoted:

> Says Tweed to Till,
> What gars ye rin sa still?
> Says Till to Tweed,
> Tho' ye rin we speed.
> An I rin slaw,
> Where ye droon ae mon
> I droon twa;

and to the appreciative eye Till has a most deucedly felo-de-se-ish look about it. There are constantly shifting beds caused by heavy and sudden spates and a loose soil, deep holes, and bends with hollow banks set with jagged stakes that look like monstrous teeth fanged like the mouth of the Jabberwock, and nasty currents, and swirly holes to drive you into them. I was wading along fishing a pool little better than half knee-deep where I was wading. I had walked down it about fifty or sixty yards, when, suddenly looking down, there at my feet was a black profound deep, where a sudden ledge of rock like a watery crevasse sunk down before me in a horribly abrupt and unexpected way, not eighteen inches from my feet. It was the merest chance that I looked down, because I was fishing the bushes on the opposite bank, where there was a suspicious dimple or two now and then. Another step and I should have found myself floundering about amongst the pikes and Lurlines of the Till, in twenty feet of water, and if I had not been able to swim, or even being able to with heavy wading boots and a lot of baskets and impediments hung all round me, I might not have been able to get out so easily. I need not say that I backed out of the position with the most judicious caution, and as I went along the bank a disagreeable refrain rang in my ears:

> Good luck to your fishing! Whom watch ye to night?
> * * * * *
> For a blue swollen corpse is a dainty meal,
> And I'll have my share with the pike and eel.

I felt like Father Philip after his escape from the kelpy, and sat down, smoked another pipe, and picked out a fresh fly. But it was all no use, the weather was dead against me, and after all I got about a dozen trout, when the evening became sultry, and heavy peals of thunder behind me came rolling up; anon, a loud crashing in the opposite direction, away towards Flodden and Yeavering Bell, announced that the storm was all round. The heavens grew darker and darker, and I had some two or three miles to walk to the inn; I was in hopes of being able to get there before the rain came on, but did not succeed, for before I was half-way it came down like a water-spout, and long before I reached it I was soaked to the skin once more. On the way home, walking along the side of the river, I saw a flash of lightning descend into the field on the other bank of the stream, about fifteen or twenty yards from me; I saw the place where it entered the earth—a slight cloud of blueish smoke, about as much as one puffs from a pipe, slowly ascended from the spot. It was perfectly calm and still at the time. The storm being some miles from me, no thunder accompanied the flash. Of course the storm (which soon passed off, though the rain held on all night) accounted for the disinclination of the fish to move: though the water was in very bad order, and would not have fished well had the weather been ever so favourable. The Till here is a fine large river, in alternate stream and pool; some of it forms very nice trout water, but much of it is mere dead, dull pike water, and I am rather inclined to think that the pike and otters don't allow the water to become overstocked. At times, I believe very good sport is had, but it did not fall to my lot.

A friend who was passing from Coldstream to Wooler gave me a lift so far in his vehicle, and at Wooler I got the coach back to Alnwick.

CHAPTER VII.

Alnemouth — Natural Upholstery — Hulne Abbey — The Alne—Midges—Weirs, &c.

It was the seaside season. Alnemouth, as a watering-place is, of all the places I ever saw, the best contrived one for the full and thorough enjoyment of the delights of laziness. "The delights of laziness?" methinks I hear a reader exclaim. Ay, my very dear sir! I repeat the phrase: The delights of laziness! Alnemouth is a village, on the sea-shore, with some bettermost houses on the outskirts which the gentry resort to; it is some three or four miles from Alnwick, whence a railway runs to within a mile of it. The beach at Alnemouth is a long flat waste of delightfully uninteresting sands. Above the beach, and amalgamating with it as it were, is a plateau of sand-hummocks covered with long thick, wire-grass. Bounding this inland, again, is a sloping cliff or high bank, covered with fern, with terraced walks along it and seats. There was no yachting, no fishing, only the herring fleet at anchor a long way off; no old men with spy-glasses to bore you to look at things; no pebbles to excite you into action, such as making good shots at the water with them. The sparsest amount of crinoline; very few of poor Leech's boots and petticoats, while nursery-maids and their charges were as scarce as plums in a school "stick-jaw." Only one bathing machine was visible—and here I make a point at fair game. Why a man should undergo that unpleasant process of encrusting his frame with unwholesome salts, I cannot conceive. Is it pleasure to step upon hard, angular or rounded pebbles of aggravating and laming tendencies, in the cold wind or blistering sun? Is it pleasant to have your eyes, nose, and ears filled—nay, saturated, with the bitterest, most acrid, and filthy to the taste of all nature's compounds? and is that compound improved by swallowing half-a-pint of it at a time through the medium of those passages? As for its being invigorating, I am not much of a chemist, but I should like to know how pickling a man can invigorate him, or make him better or stronger. If he wants to wash, let him wash in clean fresh water; already his body is naturally encrusted with filth, and upon what principle of invigoration or health does he encrust it still further? I always feel horribly languid and tired after sea-bathing; but some people bear an extra greatcoat better than others, I suppose.

But to return to Alnemouth. There was a very moderate amount of bathing—at least there was none on the day when I was there; and in fact there really was, as far as I could make out, nothing to do or see, and nothing whatever to distract one. So the devotee to laziness has but to smoke his pipe all day in the open air, and, in the most comfortable attitude he can assume, to enjoy himself. Does he incline to the perfectly prone position?—there is a stretch of sand that an army might lie down upon. Is he particular in the choice of a couch?—let him come with me up amongst the hummocks where the rank grass and ferns are, and there I will be his *cicisbeo*, his ready attendant, and will give him the choice of a hundred thousand couches, of all possible shapes and dimensions, and no two alike. There they are, nature's couches; this is her show-room, and nature is a more cunning upholsterer than Gillow himself, mark you. My visitor likes a couch, mayhap, with a rounded dip in the middle, a soft cushion of grass about the small of the back, a broad flat of sand for the shoulders, and a slightly elevated tump for the head, with fern on it to nestle in—he shall be suited. Then there must be a sand lump to raise the knee over, with perhaps a bunch of grass atop, so that the legs may dangle loosely and lightly and springily on the other side. Well, there it is. "Out of the wind, sir?" Yes, sir; on that side; there, if you please. Not a wind that can blow that you cannot get shelter from here, sir. Observe, hummocks on all sides; and, unless the wind blows straight down from heaven (which it does not do here, sir, whatever it may do in foreign parts), you are safe from it. Does my visitor tire of his couch?—does he desire one a little more extended?—a little flatter or higher, perhaps, with a better or a different view of the sea? He has not even to get up and look for it. Let him simply exert himself so far as to turn over. This does not sound easy; but I assure him that practice makes perfect, and when he has once really made up his mind to it, I do further assure him that the effort required is a very slight one, indeed not nearly so great as that of getting up. Is he stout, and to an extent protuberant? it is unimportant—he will find the soft sand and the hollows between the grass tumps very accommodating. Does his new couch not quite suit him? While his hand is in, he has but to turn over again—"'tis as easy as *lying*." If he is very difficult to please, then I repudiate him altogether, as not in a fit frame of mind to enjoy properly the delights of laziness. See him on his couch. If that be well chosen, every limb is free and resting, and he has no difficulty in getting at the materials for filling and lighting his pipe. How slowly and methodically—nay, how perfectly—that pipe is filled. There are no plugs or lumps in that tobacco, but when the pipe is lighted it smokes like a chibouk. The rings of smoke curl upwards, expanding as they go, until, reaching above the level of the sand hill, the light breeze catches them, and they become blue air. It does not rouse or excite the nerves at all to watch them. There is no variety to speak of; one is so much like another that even the organs of comparison are not called into play. The soft summer wind just gently soughs through the long yielding grass overhead. The glorious sunshine wavers on the grey sands in a misty, undefined manner, somewhat after the fashion of the water-mark on the back of an old, brown bank-note. The wavelets follow one another with a tiny wash upon the sands, barely to be distinguished in the hot hum of mid-day. You feel the ocean rather than hear it. "The sea," too, "is as calm as an infant's sleep." So much for the pleasures of Alnemouth.

I had procured from Mr. Holland, the Constable of Alnwick Castle, from whom I received many acts of politeness, leave to fish the Alne in Hulne Park, and on the day after my visit to Alnemouth availed myself of his permission. The day was tolerably favourable, and I made a start to the water above Hulne Abbey; but I got away rather late, so that I did not reach the river before mid-day. The walk to Hulne Abbey through the park is really a beautiful one; I have never seen one to equal it—a pretty river, a sward like velvet, a perfect arboretum of foliage, with plenty of interesting remains in the way of ruins, combined to render it agreeable. The park is very well kept and laid out, and the views are charming. I did not visit Hulne Abbey on this occasion, though I did so subsequently. Hulne Abbey, now a picturesque ruin, where you can be accommodated with tea and cakes at 1*s.* per head, was the first Carmelite monastery founded in England. It was founded by Ralph Fresborne in 1240, he having brought the monks from Palestine and settled them in a wilderness which at that time bore some fancied resemblance to Mount Carmel. Fresborne became the first abbot of the order. There are two magnificent pieces of tapestry in one of the chambers, which are in better preservation than any I have ever seen elsewhere. The abbey is now so hidden by the surrounding trees that it is not seen until the visitor comes close upon it. Just below it runs the Alne—a pretty little river, though somewhat dull and dead in parts, so that it always requires a wind to do much good in it. The fish in this part of the river do not run very large. Some years since a coal mine broke out into a small tributary brook which runs into the Alne at the head of the Duke's property, and the water killed the whole of the fish in this part of the river. The fish do not run above four or five to the pound, a half-pounder being rather unusual, I should think, where I fished (above Hulne Abbey). I might perhaps have hooked one in some five or six dozen fish. Higher up, however, above the brook referred to, the fish run of a much better size—$\frac{3}{4}$lb. and 1lb. being not uncommon.

I commenced upon a deepish little pool above the bridge, on which there was a good breeze, and immediately began to catch fish; and I did not quit the pool until a dozen and a half of nice little trout lay in the bottom of my creel. They nearly all took the red spinner, but they rose very shyly, often coming up two and three times before they seized the fly. From the sport I had in this pool I augured a big day; but somehow one is always wrong in one's auguries about fishing. As I went up, I found the river give fish much less readily. One or two streams and pools I fished for nothing, and they looked favourable ones too. However, I kept on working away—now catching fish, now missing or losing them; but never wanting the landing-net I was sorry to find, although I certainly lost some of the best ones in weighing them out as I did. I kept on getting a fish or two every here and there, and as I got towards the head of the park I found my creel growing heavyish; and having reached the little brook which carried the efflux of the coal mine above spoken of to the river, and which was thick and of an unwholesome-looking colour even then, I turned on my tracks, crossed the river, and fished back again to the bridge from the other bank of the river. The wind went down rather, and I did not get many fish on my way back. Moreover, the midges now became not only troublesome, but something infernal; and, in spite of my smoking furiously to drive them away, they visited my eyes, nose, ears, and forehead in a fashion that left large bumps upon them for a day or two. I slapped and I rubbed, I smoked and blessed the varmint, all ineffectually—fishing away meanwhile for few fish, with savage energy. I visited the Alne here subsequently, when these venomous little monsters were to the full as busy and vicious. I attribute much of it to the fallen timber, a good deal of which is scattered about in the shape of rotten branches and dead wood, reduced almost to tinder, which, I fancy, forms a favourable nest for them.

On looking over my creel I found I had between four and five dozen of nice little trout in it, nearly all of a size, and if there were very few large trout, there were not many very wee ones. I lost the evening fishing, moreover, as I had nearly two miles to walk to reach the gate by nine o'clock (the park gates closing at that hour), or I might no doubt have done better.

A few sea-fish get up the Alne at times, I believe, and there are below Hulne Abbey some long deep pools capable of holding them, I should say. But the Duke has such a succession of ornamental weirs, utterly impassable save in the very heaviest floods, that the fish have no chance. Indeed the Duke's fishings generally in this part of the world appear, by all accounts, to be managed neither wisely nor well; and he would greatly benefit both himself and his neighbours if he let the fish have a somewhat freer run.* There is a bit or two of open water on the lower Alne between Alnwick and the sea, and which gives some fine trout at times, but it is of course a good deal fished. The water is much more open, too, below Alnwick, and there are several mills in the tails and heads of which good fish are often met with. It will never be made into a salmon river, though white trout would do well enough in place of the bull trout.

A song on the Coquet has been sent to me. It is from the "Fisher's Garland." As it is well worth insertion, I append it, though it is rather out of place.

TUNE.—*The Miller o' Dron.*

Auld nature now revived seems,
  Cauld winter's blasts are fled,
And freely flow the sunny streams
  O'er Coquet's pebbly bed.

* All this has since been carried out, as most of the weirs on the Alne have had passes made over them, as may be seen in my work on "Salmon Ladders," published at the *Field* office, in which plans and sections of all the Alne passes are fully shown.

The mellow thrush frae Dewshill Wood
  Proclaims the dawn of day,
And to the Coquet's crystal flood
  The fisher wends his way.

CHORUS.

Then luck be to the angler lads,
  Luck to the rod and line,
Wi' morn's first beams we'll wade the streams,
  The night we'll wet wi' wine.

Nae mair we'll fish the coaly Tyne,
  Nae mair the oozy Team,
Nae mair we'll try the sedgy Pont,
  Or Derwent's woody stream.
But we'll awa' to Coquet side,
  For Coquet bangs them a',
Whose winding streams so sweetly glide,
  By Brinkburn's bonny Ha'.
Then luck, &c.

And we'll prepare our limber gads,
  Lang lines, and braw brass wheels,
We'll wile the trouties frae their hauds,
  And soon fill a' our creels;
We'll catch them here, we'll catch them there
  Wi' mennim, bait, and flee,
We'll thousands kill wi' hook and hair
  'Tween Thirlmoor and the sea.
Then luck, &c.

At Weldon Brig there's wale o' wine,
  If ye hae coin i' pocket;
If ye can throw a heckle fine,
  There's wale o' trouts i' Coquet.
And we will quaff the bluid-red wine,
  Till Weldon's wa's shall reel,
We'll drink success to hook and line,
  And all wha bear the creel.
Then luck, &c.

If ony Dolt our song that hears,
  Abuse the rod and fly,
May he to pay him for his jeers
  Have other fish to fry.

If ony Witling dare to lash
  The lads wha make the cast,
May he, to pay him for his clash,
  Dance in a line at last.
                Then luck, &c.

And O! in all their angling bouts,
  On Coquet, Tyne, or Reed,
Whether for maidens or for trouts,
  May anglers still succeed.
By Pont or Coquet, Tyne or Team,
  In sunshine or in rain,
May fisher ne'er put foot in stream,
  Or hand in purse, in vain.
                Then luck, &c.

The sun is on the mountain side,
  The daisy on the sod,
The river sparkles in his pride—
  Then fishers take the rod,
Since summer streams begin to dart,
  To streamy Weldon Post;
And he shall have the lightest heart
  Whose creel shall weigh the most.
                Then luck, &c.

—Rd. Rd.

CHAPTER VIII.

The Upper Till—Bewick Bridge—Chillingham Castle—Lord Tankerville—A Novelty—Rabbit Fishing—Ecce Iterum Vipera—The Chillingham Wild Cattle—The Lower Alne—The Kettles—The Pin Well—The Hedley Kow.

Some days before I had written to the Earl of Tankerville to ask permission to fish in his water on the Till, and on my return from fishing I found a very kind note from him, not only granting any permission I wanted, but inviting me to spend a few days with him at Chillingham, and to fish the water from there; and having accepted the invitation, I started the next morning by the coach for Chillingham. Chillingham is situated about two miles off the road between Alnwick and Wooler; and as the river, which is the upper part of the Till, runs under the road at Bewick-bridge, some five or six miles from Wooler, I determined, so as not to lose a day, to get off the coach, and fish from the bridge to the castle. The stream was rather low and the water bright, while the sun came out every now and then in a way that made success very doubtful; occasionally there came a cloud and a little wind, which I took advantage of, and I managed by about five o'clock to get a nice dish of fish; but they were hard to get, and required very careful fishing, as for four fish that rose at the fly scarcely one took hold. I worked on, however, until I got within about a mile of the castle, when, not knowing the dinner hour, I left off. The stream is pretty, though not large. There are excellent trout in it; I hooked two, which I lost, as they took hold badly, both of which were above a pound. There are a great many eels in the Chillingham water: looking over the bridge the next day, I saw five or six of some half or three-quarters of a pound each, and I should think a few eel baskets would pay well; but, as far as I could learn, eels are not much sought after or regarded by any one in the north—indeed, the country people will rarely eat them.

Leaving the river, I walked through an avenue of noble trees to the castle—a fine old building of Elizabethan architecture, with a spacious courtyard, through which you enter. It is situated upon the slope of an eminence, surrounded by magnificent trees, and backed by woods, through which the deer and the wild cattle, for which Chillingham is celebrated, roam unmolested. These woods afford in the winter the best cock shooting in the county. Lord Tankerville told me that above thirty brace were killed in one of them in one day in the previous season. The estate is generally well supplied with game of all kinds, and I saw numbers of hand-reared pheasants running about the park near the entrance. Far up above the slope, and bounding the park in that direction, is a craggy hill, which can be seen from all parts of the country, and on the top of which is a round double entrenchment, called Ross Castle, which is said to be of Celtic origin, as the name would indicate, the word "ross" signifying a promontory. Chillingham Castle from this aspect appears a long central building, with loftier wings at each end; these are thickly covered with ivy, which rounds them off, and gives antiquity in its most graceful form to the appearance of the castle.

I was very courteously and kindly received, and spent some days at Chillingham very pleasantly. Lord Tankerville is very fond of all field sports, and is one of the best shots in the county, and an enthusiastic deer-stalker to boot, as the numerous heads and trophies of his skill, which grace the great dining-hall (an apartment capable of dining some 300 or 400 people), indicate.

The next day, I went down to the river, Lord Tankerville walking with me. The day was very bright and the river low, and there was at first but little wind, so that I did not expect in a stream so sulky as Till usually is, to do much.* As I got on, however, the wind mended, and I got a very nice basket of fish indeed. There were between three and four dozen, and several fish of half and three-quarters of a pound; and, as on the day previous, I lost some very fine fish, owing to their taking badly, from the lowness of the water. Had the wind favoured me, instead of having to cast right in the teeth of it, I am convinced that, in spite of the low water and the bright sun, I should have had a big day; and, of course, as on the previous day, there was no evening fishing, the dinner hour not admitting of it, or the take, no doubt, would have been much larger. The Till trout are very game fellows, coloured gold and silver, bedropped with crimson; they are handsome fish, generally. There are few whitling and not many pike in this part of the water.

I saw, while walking up the bank of the river, a very curious thing. I would ask my angling friends if they ever angled for rabbits? if they ever caught a rabbit, for instance, when fly-fishing? I cannot account for the circumstance I am about to relate, but leave it to speak for itself.

As I was fishing up stream, several yards above me I saw something swaying about under water, which looked like a drowned cat, hanging apparently by the neck. On coming up to it, however, I discovered that it was a full-grown rabbit. I thought at first that it had been snared, had broken the hold, and somehow rolled into the water and got hung to a branch. I called Lord Tankerville's attention to it, when he got a long stick, and between us we "howked" the beast out, and I found that it had literally been caught by an artificial fly, it having

* It is generally considered that whatever one does on the Till here is equal, as a matter of skill and credit, to killing double as much on Glen or Breamish, so much easier are fish to kill on those rivers; and yet Breamish and Till are the same river, and separated from one another by a bridge only. Below Bewick-bridge the stream is Till, above it, Breamish; and the fish, also, within a very short distance, are said to differ in their habits and peculiarities.

been hooked in the shoulder by a fly which was the stretcher on a fly-cast, the bob fly being entangled round the branch of a tree that grew out under the water. The straining of the skin out from the hook showed that the rabbit had used some severe exertions to get free, though fruitlessly. We got both the flies off. They were in good order. The rabbit had apparently been in the water some two or perhaps three days; how it got hooked and in that position I cannot say. There are very few rabbits indeed about that part; and had anyone fishing there got his cast hung in this branch, he could easily have got hold of the branch and disengaged it. The cast, too, was quite a stranger; the flies not being at all such as are generally used on the river there, being of much larger size, and more like lake-trout flies. The river is closely preserved and watched, and is never fished save by his lordship and his visitors or friends. I have thought it over a good deal, but confess myself unable to solve this rabbit-angling satisfactorily. We confiscated the flies, but left the rabbit to the gleds.

The river here, though it holds very good fish, yet runs down so fine that at times fishing is hopeless, and whitling do not stay much in it. It struck me that if at the end of some of the pools where they are favourable to it, slight weirs of rough brush and stakes could be constructed, or big stones were laid across, so as to keep up an extra depth of some five or six inches, the river might be greatly improved. The floods in the winter are heavy, and of course would, without some little circumspection and management, wash away any obstruction which was too much opposed to them. Still the experiment might be tried with a few stakes and wattles, at a very trifling cost indeed.

In the course of the afternoon Lord Tankerville left me to go snake-hunting, and when he came home he brought with him a large black adder which he had destroyed, of above two feet in length. It was, in truth, a venomous-looking beast. There is a curious circumstance connected with it: Some time since, our friend Mr. Buckland, stopping at Chillingham, *en passant*, to have a look at the cattle, was during his walk in the park conducted over a sunny knoll, which attracted his attention somewhat. "What a delightful place—Don't you find lots of snakes here?" he asked with that enthusiasm for natural history, and particularly snakes, which even the "linked sweetness long drawn out" of the great viper question has been quite unable to dispel, or even to check in the slightest degree—though I confess I have wished more than once, that like the celebrated Indian acrobats Muley, Hassan, and Aali, who threw flip-jacks and swallowed each other, the last man throwing a flip-jack and swallowing himself, that the vipers, after swallowing each other, could and would leave a residuary legatee viper to all the rest, who might be induced to complete the feat, and so make an end of it—"Don't you find lots of snakes here?" asked our friend. His lordship opined that there might be snakes there, he couldn't undertake to say, but he would notice the spot more closely at the right season. A day or two previously he had happened, while crossing the knoll, to remember the circumstance, and looking about he chanced upon the newly-cast exuviæ of a large viper. Thinking that the owner could not be far off, he determined on the first sunny day, when the snake was likely to show out, to go forth and do battle with "the Laidley Worm" and the day in question being favourable, he went to the spot, found the adder and killed it, thus verifying Mr. Buckland's expectations and experience.

On the day after the fishing I went out with Lord Tankerville to have a peep at the park and a look at the wild cattle. The wild cattle are the *spécialité* of Chillingham. Much has been written and said of the Chillingham wild cattle, and there is no doubt that they are the last remnant of the large herds of cattle that once roamed free and unrestrained through the southern wilds and forests of Caledonia; as the country became enclosed and tilled, they gradually disappeared, a few at last only remaining in one or two places where they had been confined, amongst which was Chillingham, and this herd of about 100 head are now the only pure-blooded representatives of the original wild cattle. As regards their wildness, they are as wild as ever they were, and will not allow any one to approach them. If a man appears in sight near them, the herd immediately take to violent flight, and for this reason it is a great favour for strangers to be permitted to see them. Some of the cows often have calves by their sides, and when they are frightened they rush off in a stampede to their holdfast, a place called Robin Hood's bog, where they are never followed or molested. In going under the trees it often happens that the whole herd, in their mad race, will attempt to pass between a couple of large trees, much too close together for them to pass; a jam then takes place, in which the calves are inevitably crushed to death; and as they are very easily stampeded, the scent of a man being at times enough to cause it without their catching sight of him, or the dash of a deer by them (and the deer, when startled by man, have often a most annoying habit of rushing right through the herd of cattle), the keepers are obliged to be very cautious how they allow any one to approach them. They are beautiful creatures: pure white, with black muzzles, hoofs, and tips to the horns, and red ears. They are the most thorough-bred looking beasts I ever saw. The bulls are especially splendid brutes. We got within about eighty or ninety yards of them, but they would not allow us to come nearer, and it required careful stalking through a thick plantation and taking the wind to achieve even that. They did not run, but kept walking slowly and feeding away from us as if they suspected we were there rather than knew it. One of the old cows who had a calf by her side (there were three or four more who had calves also) was very suspicious, and stood for some time gazing fixedly towards us, and trying to get our wind. At length, partially reassured, she walked slowly after the herd with her young one. Once I made sure there would have been a bolt, for a hind which we had not seen was roused by us and ran towards the cattle, passing obliquely by them. Although it did not stampede them, it evidently rendered them more uneasy, and as they were gradually approaching a narrow part of their territory, from which there was no escape save by flight, we left them and walked back to the castle. The bulls often kill each other in their combats. An instance had occurred but a short time before. Two young bulls, uniting their forces, managed to thrash the old leader of the herd. For three days the old gentleman sulked by himself in a retired spot, goring everything he could in his blind rage, and gradually lashing himself up into increased fury. At the end of that time, one of the young bulls chanced to see him, and thinking that what he had done with the assistance of another, he was now man enough, or bull enough, to do by himself, he gave challenge to the veteran. A battle royal ensued, in which the old bull recovered his position and asserted his prowess by killing the young one. I saw the head—a remarkably perfect one. His lordship has made a collection of heads, in obedience to a suggestion made by the late Sir E. Landseer during his last visit. On the succeeding day I had to leave, having promised to shoot with a friend on the 12th, which was close at hand; and, having greatly enjoyed my visit, I left for Alnwick. By the way, I should say that as his lordship throws the greater part of his fishing on the Till entirely open to the public, only reserving for himself and his friends a small part near the castle itself, wandering anglers have no right to expect that that shall be thrown open to them also.

On the succeeding day I fished the lower part of the Alne below Hulne Abbey. The water was lower than usual, the sun bright, and there was no wind; and the fish, which appeared in this part of the water to be unusually well educated, were very shy, and would not come to the point at all. I chose to fish this lower part because, on the previous occasion, when walking home in the evening (there being a good rise on) I saw some rather fine fish putting up in the deep still dubs in that part. What was the cause of it, however, I know not, but there was no rise on this evening, the fish going off altogether at an early hour. Perhaps the unusual lowness of the water was the cause; howbeit they would not rise, and a bare half dozen was all my spoil. The river contained fine pools and occasionally some good streams, but the pools wanted wind, of course. It was a good deal fished, however.

Monday was the eventful 12th of August; so on the next day (Sunday), having an invite to shoot with Mr. Thompson on the 12th, I betook myself to Wooler again. Before dinner we walked up to a place called the Kettles, a curious glen among the mountains at the back of Wooler, the scene of a battle in lang-lang syne. There are traces of an encampment still to be seen. There is a big stone, too, called the King's Chair, and here once upon a time a certain king—but who he was, or when it was, or where he lived, the deponent sayeth not—did sit and did watch his army fight another army in the valley below, but whose army the other army was, or why they fought, or who got the best of it, your deponent won't undertake to say. There, too, is a large stone, much worn on all sides, like a huge grindstone, for hereon the soldiers of either side came to sharpen their swords when they were blunted and notched with hacking and hewing—at least so somebody says, but deponent voucheth not for the truth of the same, further than that there are well-worn stones on the spot indicated. On our return we stopped in an adjacent glen, at the Fairy's Well, commonly called the Pin Well, a small rough basin rudely fashioned from some half-dozen large granite stones, which contains bright clear water. The bottom is almost covered with crooked pins, in every state of preservation, from the new bright one of yesterday to the old rusted worn one of him or her now sleeping peacefully in the auld kirk-yard not far awa, and whose sons and daughters, or even grandchildren may be, have dropped in those later ones in their turn, to propitiate the good fairy of the spot: the belief, or kindly superstition of the place, being that if you utter a wish and drop into the well a crooked pin as an offering, the wish, by the aid of the fairy, will come to pass; and many a maid forlorn, and many a stout herd pining with hopeless love, have thrown a pin to the fairy and breathed the dearest wish of their hearts over that simple basin of crystal water in the dim twilight—half doubting, half hoping, the fulfilment of their wishes, in fear and trembling as the mist of the hills wreathed itself into fantastic and shadowy forms, and every stone, turf, or twig, assumed a fairy figure or shape to their superstitious and excited imaginations. The practice is kept up, though the superstition, however, like all others, is dying out before the march of civilisation. Alas for the country that has no superstitions! And what superstition could stand before the apparition of a pork-pie hat or the march of crinoline? Imagine the gentle and civilised Damon viewing that awful slice of a blackened chimney-pot on the top of his head, as he gazes at his own features in the sparkling glass of nature at his feet; or fancy Phyllis, with her three-cornered crinoline, tripping up to the Kettles in a gale of wind, to ask the fairy's kind interference between her and Damon-of-the-pork-pie, without being blown away by the indignant fairy. One almost regrets the days of wolf-skins and pigments!

One of the latest superstitions which held place in the Northumbrian bosom was that anent the Hedley Kow. The Hedley Kow was a sort of northern Puck or Robin Goodfellow—a most mischievous sprite, who constantly assumed all sorts of strange forms to delude, terrify, or punish travellers or farmers who might have stayed ow're late at the market or have indulged somewhat too freely in the "juice o' the bairly," as I am forced to confess they are somewhat prone to even now, for many of them yearly succumb and sink under the attacks of "the old complaint"—the execrable and poisonous stuff often vended at many of the houses of so-called entertainment under the name of "whisky" having much to answer for in this respect.* These wayfarers, in their

* It is a thousand pities that an Adulteration Act cannot be put in force here, and the scoundrels who manufacture and sell this vile poison (for it is nothing else) are not trounced, as they deserve. More than half the mischief that flows from the free indulgence in whisky, as it is called, is caused by its being so made or adulterated as to be not whisky, but downright poison, which is sold freely at most of the small public-houses.

acquired gift of double-sight, being too often prone to see more than is dreamt of in the philosophy of their less-gifted or more temperate, or, perhaps, stronger-headed neighbours, A rather absurd story is told by Oliver, in his "Rambles on the Border," of an adventure somewhat of this sort :—A decent farmer riding homewards one night, approached a part of the road famed as the scene of many an antic of the Hedley Kow; he saw before him another passenger on horseback, and, wishing for company, pushed on to overtake the stranger. No sooner did he quicken his pace than the stranger, alarmed, did the same. The hinder man shouted "Stop!" The one in front grew more frightened at the noise, and then commenced a race paralleled only by that of Tam o' Shanter, or Ichabod the pedagogue in the "Legend of Sleepy-hollow." Whip and spur was the order of the night, until the man in front, terrified out of his wits at being, as he supposed, pursued by a yelling, howling demon, which manifestly gained on him, pulled up, beaten and breathless, determining to attempt what exorcism could do, as running away failed. Turning around, in breathless and broken accents he adjured the astonished spirit, in the sacred names of the Holy Trinity, to say what he was,—when the supposed phantom, scarcely less alarmed than his neighbour at what had taken place, broke out with, "Whoy I's Jemmy Brown o' the High Field—wha's thou?"

CHAPTER IX.

THE 12TH OF AUGUST—A RAINY SHOOT—THE TOPS OF THE CHEVIOTS—WOOLER WATER—A NEW WAY OF POACHING—A WINDY SHOOTING—THE BREAMISH—BROOM PARK.

I DON'T suppose there is any day in the year looked forward to with so much interest and anticipation as the 12th of August. The great saturnalia of St. Grouse has numerous attendants and fervent acolytes. I won't say how I looked forward to it; I won't pretend that I was less of a boy, as it were, looking to the holidays, than my neighbours. The morrow must come in its time, so we drank success to it, and went to bed—and dreamt, of course, that grouse were like blackberries, and as easy to come at. Alas! for the waking reality.

It blew the day before, it blew all night, and I began to doubt for the day's sport; one thing was tolerably certain, that the grouse would not lie well after such high winds, and it only wanted a little rain to complete the destruction of our sport. It is unnecessary to say that we had it—but of that anon. Mr. T.'s shooting lay rather wide, and in smallish lots, so we had often a distance to walk from one part to another of it. The best part of his grouse ground lay eight miles off, near Heathpool Lynns, but there was a little bit of heath about half-way over the moors, where there was usually a brood or so, and where we expected to get a shot or two. We could have driven to within a mile or so of the further ground, but not wishing to miss the chance of a shot, we walked it, and it was a long grind of eight miles, over those moors, and it took just the sharp edge off one's walking by the time we really commenced shooting. The day opened fine, but very windy. We reached the half-way bit. The heather was rather thin, and had been heavily burnt, and in such weather it was, of course, very bad lying. My friend got two shots, but they were very long ones, and did not help us to fill the bag, and so we trudged onwards; and now it began to drizzle. Everybody (that is everybody who cares to read this) knows that sort of drizzle called a Scotch mist, and the insidious way in which it commences, sneaking into all the cracks, creaks, crevices, and button-holes, and laying a thorough foundation of damp, so that when the rain *does* come you are all over like blotting-paper, and a short sharp shower wets you through all over. So it began with us. At length we reached the moor. It was not of large extent, comprising a hill, part of another, and the moss between. As a foretaste of what we were to expect, we no sooner let the dogs loose, and took up the first brae, than away went four broods, one after the other, right off our ground, as wild and almost as strong as if it had been the 12th of November, instead of the 12th of August. They went to some friends on our right who were shooting, and no doubt had some fun with them, as we heard them rather busy in the quarter they had gone to, an hour or two after, while unfortunately the gentlemen on the moor to our left were not shooting; so that we got nothing driven to us for what we drove off.

The rain steadily increased, but we kept on bravely. Broods, pairs, threes, and fours, went away at 150 yards rises, and shooting appeared utterly hopeless, the moor lying very exposed, and badly off for shelter in the quarter the wind was.

Thompson and self looked at each other.

"What's to be done?" quoth I.

"Liquor," quoth my friend, with that presence of mind which helps him along where others would despair.

To this I readily acquiesced, as it was getting moist, and was "no that warm." And as the sun was over the foreyard, we piped to grog. The *dew* appeared, and disappeared as a natural sequence, and we once more braced our energies to the task.

Presently one of the dogs pulled up and looked round at me, as much as to say, "Here he is at last, governor;" and if ever a dog winked at me perceptibly that dog did. He was a well-worn veteran, in his last season; a good old dog, very grey and very knowing. Up got an old cock grouse, in a prodigious flurry, but my old double spoke out, and did for him as Dick Turpin did for the Bishop's coachman—see "Pickwick"—"purvailed on him to stop." Another got up to Mr. T., who also dropped his bird. We tried round the hill, and only found a cheeper or two; so we went to lunch, under the very partial shelter of a stell, which is merely a few rough stones heaped up into a rude wall, where the sheep are herded in bad weather. While at lunch the weather held up for a few minutes, the clouds lifted suddenly from the mountain peaks, and we caught a glimpse of truly a lovely scene and a fair country. One occasionally sees the efforts of the richest pictorial imagination depicted upon drop-scenes and in general scenes in our best theatres. The effect is very fine, the scenes are very beautiful; but I have once or twice in my life had momentary glimpses of scenes which exceeded anything that painter could devise or machinery effect. I saw a glimpse once on Killarney—a peculiar sun-glint through rain upon the lower lake, which I have never seen approached. I once went into a small beech covert of mine, when shooting in Buckinghamshire; there had been snow and frost in the night, and every tiny twig and leaf and spray was lined and fretted with frozen snow. Suddenly the sun broke through the trees, and such a striking and resplendent vista I never saw—no scene-painting could convey it. Here, again, among green mountain-tops innumerable, was Nature in truth unapproachable. Those wonderful Cheviots—they are so like in shape, and yet so various! The pitch of the hills down into the valleys is often so steep that it is barely possible to walk along it. The round curving humps at the top being completed, down they go with a precipitous sweep, sometimes into pretty cup-shaped smiling valleys, green, and apparently smooth as a billiard-cloth, with little burns whimpling and winding along the midst of them like silver threads; sometimes they go down almost sheer, forming a deep, dark precipice, into a shaded, gloomy, mist-ridden gorge, such as Sinbad and his friends might have picked the diamonds out of by means of lumps of eagles' meat. You could almost fancy that herd above the precipice Sinbad himself. There the hills were all around us, some clad in a rich patchwork of green with purple heather, others decked in light yellowish-green wavy fern, half way up the sides; others again dressed in small oak, or with scattered juniper and yew darkly dotting their base; while, out beyond them all, we had a glimpse of the vale of Tweed—a very land of Goshen and promise, it looked so fair. There was the merse of Berwick extended before us like a map; far away the eye rested on Dunse Law; and near to us, the beautiful Eildon Hills, which Scott loved so well to roam over, dwarfed into insignificance by the gigantic mounds of Cheviot, had yet an abrupt and ragged beauty of their own, which shrunk not from comparison with their huge brethren. Yonder, too, is Yetholm, the gipsy territory; that spur of a hill is a corner of Yetholm Common. But lo! the Prompter rings his bell, and the heavy drop-curtain of mist descends again upon a scene which will ever dwell in my memory.

Down comes the rain again, but, invigorated by lunch, we are up and at it again, and, by dint of hard walking and good shooting, we managed to screw the bag up to $7\frac{1}{2}$ brace and a plover. We killed a bird badly diseased, too, which I sent up to the *Field* for examination. The day was terribly against us. It rained from lunch out without intermission. Only one brood did we get near enough to shoot at, and at that my first barrel missed fire altogether, and my second hung fire owing to the wet. Mr. T. was wide of them, and had a very long pop to no use. All our birds were singles, or scattered birds, My gun missed fire several times, too, or I should have scored at least another brace or two of grouse, and a couple of plovers.

If the walk out was undesirable, what was the walk home? I had not a dry thread on. Twelve hours pitiless pelting on those unscrupulous Cheviots had reduced me to a walking sponge: the rain ran in and out, how, when, and where it listed. My boots, of course, were mere water-buckets; my powder was paste; my tobacco undeniably damp, not to say wet; while matches could not be coaxed to go off anyhow, but smoked and stank away with a dull, phosphoric smell and glare in the dying twilight without ignition. And still the rain came down, swish, swoop, over the dreary moors for eight blessed miles. How it did come down, oh dear! searching out every joint in one's harness, creeping insidiously in at the back of one's neck, and as Miss Miggs said, "running aperiently down one's very back." Eddying into the gulfs and bays of one's costume, so to speak, with a shiver and a shudder, and then out again, down one's trousers and into one's boots—clothes were mere cullenders, and hats were streamers. And then the walking, sliding, slipping, bumping, bogging, with arms reversed. Our little party manfully faced it, and struggled homewards. We got home at last. A warm tub, dry clothes, and a good dinner soon put us all on our legs again, and we fought our battles o'er again, and thrice we slew the slain. I always think the chat over the weed, after a hard day's shooting, is as enjoyable a thing as a sportsman meets with. The "I say, T., do you recollect that shot you made over the knoll at the back of the dell? By Jove! old fellow, that was a clipper." "Yes, and that wasn't half a bad one *you* made out of those glitters, when that old cock was stealing away up the hill;" "and how well Rake found that single bird," &c.

On the 13th I took it easy, being a little stiff after my long tramp; in the afternoon, however, we drove some two or three miles up Wooler water, calling on Mr. Hughes, who owns a portion of one bank, to ask permission. Wooler water is a pretty burn, rising at the foot of Hedgehope, one of the highest of the Cheviots, being second only to Cheviot itself, which is 2658 feet in height. The trout in Wooler water are not large, though at times plentiful, but it gets a good deal fished; when there is a little water in it, a fair basket may be made. The greater part of it is open, and it is wormed *ad nauseam*. There are a few whitling in it, and the bull-trout run up it later in the season. The scenery through which this pretty little stream runs is most charming; and the angler who is a lover of nature will hardly regret a wander up either of the valleys through which the two burns run which unite to form Wooler water a few miles above Wooler, even if his creel be a light one at the day's end. We went a little above the junction. As we reached the stream I saw two anglers, one upon each side, literally *worming* their way downwards; and above them we found two more, so that the water had been uncommonly well worked by the time we reached it. Under these circumstances it was not to be wondered at that our sport was small—in fact, we did almost nothing; a bare dozen of small black trout being all that we could compass. Owing to the above inauspicious circumstances, even though there was plenty of water in the brook, and it was well coloured, the trout would not feed; for when they did come at either fly or worm, they took very badly. I worked it down for about a mile and a half, but gave in at last and went home. It is worth a trial, however, if the angler have a spare day, and the water be in order.

The herds have a curious way of poaching here, as well as in the College and other small burns about the neighbourhood. They go with a heavy mallet, and having driven the trout under the large stones they strike the stone a smart blow. The jar somehow stuns the trout, and they are easily picked up. This is said to be a very destructive method of poaching, but I have, never seen it in operation.

On the 14th we made another trip to the moor, but the day, which was threatening and windy at the commencement, turned out even worse than the 12th. The wind was tremendous, and the rain showers cut into us as if they would drive through us. The grouse were wilder than on the 12th if possible, and such an effect had the weather had upon them that I saw a large number already packed, although I believe they had never been shot at. Up to lunch time we did nothing. The grouse got up and went away at distances which for the time of year were incredible. After lunch we sallied out from our "bield," determined to try our best. We had been sitting under the lee of a small hill, but when we rounded it and met the full force of the blast it was tremendous. We could hardly make way against it; our coat-tails were whirled wildly around our heads, and one hand was employed in keeping our hats on. The rain came like bullets, and battered us about at its pleasure. The very dogs flatly refused to face it, but lay down for shelter in the long heather, looking piteously at us, as much as to say "Really, now! this is too bad. You never can be such fools, you two fellows, as to go out into this." We coaxed them up, however, and on we went. Just then an old cock grouse got up wild, a long shot from me, and, catching the wind, he was going away with it like lightning. "Nothing venture, nothing have," thought I. So, although I did not imagine for a moment that it was in powder and lead to stop such a skyrocket, I put up the gun, and, holding a good yard and a half before him, I let him have it. He came in for the full charge, and spun over, coming down with the wind as dead as a stone. I paced the distance, and it was a good eighty-four yards. Allowing twenty yards for the drift of the wind, which it was fully, it was "a lang shot," and I was very proud of it. It was a good omen, too, for we managed to pick up three brace more in our last round, Thomson coming in for the lion's share, and shooting remarkably well.

The homeward journey was perhaps a trifle worse than that on the 12th, though I managed to keep my tobacco and matches dry, and there was consolation in that. Had the weather been reasonably favourable, we should no doubt have had two very nice days' grouse-shooting; and it was the more unfortunate, as the 13th, on which we decided not to go up to the moor, was a fine, warm, sunny day, well adapted for the purpose; and I hear that the grouse behaved very respectably upon the other grounds near us.

Mr. Burrel, of Broom Park, had given me permission to fish that part of the Alne which runs through his property, and, thinking that it would be in fine order, I started the next morning with Mr. Thompson's brother, who was kind enough to accompany me, and to drive me over to fish it. It was a longish drive, some thirteen miles to Broom Park, and I had better have taken it from Alnwick, from which it is less than half that distance. About half-way we passed Percy's Leap. Walled-in, within a small enclosure, and shaded by small trees, are two large stones, which are said to mark the distance which Sir Ralph Percy leaped on receiving his death-wound at the Battle of Hedgeley Moor, in 1463. The incident is touching. Fighting as a partisan of Henry VI. against Edward IV., he received his death, and, while dying, he exclaimed, in evidence of his fidelity: "I have saved the bird in my breast." I had the curiosity to climb over the enclosure, and pace the distance from stone to stone—it was eight yards and a half. A mile or two further on we passed over the Breamish. It was in full spate, and of a fine porter-colour. The Breamish is a capital stream, and gets a good deal fished, as there is a good bit of it open to the public, or was up to very lately. The Breamish, as I have already said, is another name for the Upper Till. The Breamish trout partake somewhat of the fine quality of the Till fish, but from the different character of the water they are better risers, particularly in the spring, when it is advisable if possible to give the more open parts of the stream alook up, as it is a good deal fished, being rather get-at-able, particularly by anglers who come on the coach from Alnwick. This, however, is chiefly for the brown trout fishing. In the autumn the sea fish get up, and then the wandering angler may chance to make prize of a much nobler quarry. Mr.

Moffat, who knew the Breamish well, recommends as flies the red and black hackles, the smoky dun ditto, dun fox, black gnat, little dark dun, blue dun, tawny fly, ash fox, ashy dun, crane flies, great light dun, little ditto, hare ear and woodcock, case winged orange fly, cream camel, small black fly, barm fly, red and black ants, fern fly, &c., and I may add that the collection will kill fish in every stream on the border, bar none, when fish are taking. Breamish is also a capital worm stream when coloured, and minnow, too, often takes very large fish in it. But to return to the Alne. Soon after we passed over a very thick and muddy little brook, which was running down (which proved to be the upper part of the Alne), and pulled up at the inn at Alne-bridge.

Here we made inquiries as to the way to the park, &c., intending to find out the keeper's lodge, but somehow we missed the turning, and walked a long way round the outside of the park without coming to the entrance. Not wishing to lose more time, as the day was getting on, we made inquiries of a man at work with respect to the river, &c. He pointed out all that we required, and we made our way to the stream. It was very thick and muddy, and fly-fishing was clearly out of the question. As the river appeared rather small upwards, we took downwards. I intended to try the minnow, but, after getting a fish or two out of the nice little sharp stream we first hit upon, we found the river for a long way down was nothing but one long dull dub, with very little stream. No doubt the water contained very fine trout, and, with a good wind upon it, and a clearer water, I can easily conceive that it would give good sport to the fly; but it was of course quite unfit either for minnow or worm, so we viewed it rather blankly, for it looked as if a day's sport was very problematical. We went on, however, until we came to a mill. Below the mill was a nice little stream or two, though small; but when we came to them we found a man fishing with worm, who of course had skimmed the cream off the water, if one may be allowed to use the expression. We got a fish or two from the streams notwithstanding; but a little below we found the river resume its dubby character—so, hardly knowing what to do, or how to make the day out, we slowly turned upwards again. The water, I thought, was a shade clearer, and I saw a fish or two rise, so I determined, although it was still very thick, to try a fly. It did not do, however. While we were trying it the keeper came to us, and advised us to try the water above the bridge, where we should find some nice streams, suitable to either minnow or worm, and we at once made for them. Here we found the river, though a mere burnie, a very pretty one, and a continuation of wee sharp streams and holes; and had we chanced to come upon this part of the water in the morning, we could easily have filled our creel. But it was getting towards evening, and after fishing it up for some little distance, and picking up a few nice trout, we had to give in, as it came on dusk, and we had a long drive home before us.

CHAPTER X.

COUPLAND CASTLE—THE EARL OF DURHAM—THE CAULD POOL—THE TWENTIETH—EMANCIPATION OF THE BLACKS—THE BOWMONT AND THE GIPSIES.

THE day after I received the invitation to Chillingham, there came another invitation from the Earl of Durham to stay at Coupland Castle, for the purpose of fishing the Glen. As the Glen is the best trout-stream in these parts, and I was desirous to give the whitling pools close to Coupland Castle another and an early and late trial, I gladly accepted his lordship's invitation, although, as I have related, I had already fished the water. I shall not, therefore, dwell much upon it now. The sport I had during the two days I fished it was of the same character as I had previously enjoyed, save that the whitling would not take. The first day the river looked all that could be desired; it was just clearing off, and of a fine light porter-colour, but the fish did not rise well, being gorged with the food that had come down with the rain of the previous days. The whitling, too, were evidently restless, and desirous of moving on in the fine running water; but the cauld under Coupland barred them. But for this cauld the upper parts of College and Bowmont would be stocked with whitling, to the great delectation of the herds and the Yetholm gipsies, who are supposed to be the great poachers of all the streams and fields in these parts; a good many fish do get up by the mill stream. The cauld pool above the dyke, and just below Coupland Castle, is the finest pool by far on the river, being broad and deep enough in parts to hold salmon, and of considerable length and capacity; about a mile and a half above it is another cauld, but less difficult to surmount than the Coupland one. Were this one raised, and a pass placed in the Coupland cauld, the whitling would get an extra mile and a half of very fine water, full of good pools and streams suited to them, with much good breeding ground, and Lord Durham's fishing would be greatly improved. There is one point, however, that would require consideration, viz., at present the pools below the Coupland cauld, which are swarming with whitling, are close under the noses of his lordship's keepers, the kennels being not 200 yards from them. Were this abundance transferred to the pools below the cauld, a mile and a half up, it might prove a serious temptation to the Yetholm folk. I have touched upon this subject, and given reasons *pro* and *con.*, because a passage has been, I believe, talked of once or twice. Coupland Castle is beautifully situated, standing on the top of a high-wooded bank, at the foot of which runs the Glen. The house itself, which is a delightful country seat, contains all the means and appliances for comfort without being unwieldy or oppressive. It is surrounded by trim gardens and well-kept lawns, from which the flower-beds, well stocked with all the good old-fashioned, sweet-smelling flowers, greet the senses with a smiling and cheerful good-morrow as the visitor steps, refreshed, from his bath out into the early sunshine of the fair summer morning. The preserves around the house give good shooting at lowland game of all kinds, while within a mile or two his lordship has a capital tract of grouse-shooting, on which I heard of one gentleman, who was staying at Coupland Castle, bagging his twenty-five brace in the day, bad as the season and weather had been.

The second day of my stay was windy and rough, but the wind did not strike well on the pools below the cauld; so, after trying them for a short time, without much sport, I went up to the cauld pool, on which there was a nice breeze. I should say, that whenever leave is given to fish to strangers, the cauld pool is always excluded, as it adjoins the gardens, which are immediately over it; and as the house is very close to it, it would be trenching rather too much upon the privacy of the family. But there is plenty of excellent water below, and therefore the deprivation to the angler is slight; and the cauld pool being rather dull and still, does not always fish well, as it is a good deal sheltered, and not every wind strikes it; moreover, there is not much of it which everybody could fish, even if they had leave, as it is much overgrown with large trees, which stretch their arms over the bank very awkwardly in places. Two things served me in fishing this pool—one was much practice in fishing very wooded places, and the other the power to throw a long line when it is required. Some years since I fished a good deal in Buckinghamshire, in a small but excellent trout-stream there; a portion of this stream, where many very excellent fish are, is quite overgrown with trees. The practice I got there stood me in good stead here. Before coming to the trees, there was an open space for some twenty or thirty yards, which was quite open and treeless. Here I found the fish very shy at taking within ordinary distance, though they were rising freely enough. I tried them, and passed on to the trees; where the fish, being less fished over, rose more boldly, and I got several nice fish—one or two of above a pound, and several from a half to three-quarters. They took a cow-dung fly, dressed by Wright of Sprouston, very well indeed, nay almost exclusively. Coming back, after I had fished the pool over, to the open part, where the fish were still rising, I fished it again, and the difference in the behaviour of the fish was most marked. It then occurred to me to try a few longish throws beyond the ordinary fishing distance to which the general run of anglers pitch their fly, and, oddly enough, I found the fish beyond that distance take remarkably well; a fish at ten or eleven yards would leave off rising when the fly came over him, but one at thirteen or fourteen and over took the fly freely. Evidently the reason here also was because they seldom had a fly put over them. I feel convinced that a middling caster would hardly have taken a dozen fish in the cauld, and those of no great size; whereas I managed to get between four and five dozen of very good ones, nearly as many having been taken by a relative of his lordship's a few days previously I understood. The Glen runs away very quickly, for although it had been in full spate the day before, it was now down to its natural size again. There was, of course, no evening fishing, as dinner occupied the usual evening fishing time, so that my take, all things considered, was a good one. The next day I left Coupland; Lord Durham was very kind, wishing me to prolong my stay, and to pay them another visit in the event of my coming again to the Glen. Indeed, Coupland Castle, so charming both for the beauty of its situation, the pleasant sport afforded in its precincts, and the thoughtful urbanity of its noble owners, will long retain a green spot in my memory.

The 20th came full upon my departure from Coupland. I had promised my friend, Thompson, to shoot blackgame at Heathpool Lynns with him, and we made our way to the farmhouse in good time. I have described the scenery here before, so need to dwell no more upon it. Leaving the higher hills and heather to the grouse, we took to the waving bracken and boggy valleys, which blackgame love. We walked for some time before we got a point at black, though we got a number of points at partridge, which, much to the surprise and aggravation of our dogs, skimmed away unharmed by us, having eleven more days' lease of life. It was very amusing to watch the puzzled expression of Rake, the younger dog, who could not make this out at all; once or twice he looked round, when he was on partridge, to see if we were within distance, and then stiffened himself up an extra screw, as though to say, "I won't do anything wrong; here I am, and here I'll stay, and if you don't kill 'em, mind, I'm not to blame, don't blow me up. I wash my paws of it." As for the old dog, Old Dick, he knew all about it after the first point or two. At length Rake stood in the corner of some tall fern near a rushy bottom. "Black" was the simultaneous whisper, and up got a young cock hardly arrived at his full plumage. He flew past me along the bottom, and the shot was so easy that I missed it with the first barrel, and T. immediately wiped my eye. Of course we were all upon the expectation of seeing the rest of the brood, but, though we hunted and tramped over the ground all around, we found no more. It was evidently a stray one. Lower down in the bottom the dogs began to draw upon partridge, and after drawing about fifty or sixty yards up got a fine covey of partridges. We were now about to take lunch, and had carried the basket down to a spring, when, as I was crossing the ground a second time, a blackcock got up and I dropped it. I loaded immediately, and T. joined me, when, on searching about, seven or eight birds of a brood got up. We each killed our first birds, and both shot at the same bird for a second which was, of course, considerably chawed up in consequence. Three other birds got up directly afterwards, one of which T. killed; the whole brood of about a dozen had been lying exactly on the spot whence we flushed the partridges. Having marked in several of the birds, we were about to follow them, when the farmer, who had been ill and in bed, came down to take us to some other ground, over which he could take friends; and this having the reputation of being very excellent ground, and as we could find the rest of the brood we were leaving any other day but could not shoot the other ground, we rather foolishly left our marked birds and went on to Trow Burn. It was very pretty shooting, but awfully stiff walking. We were shooting in tangled fern, often up to our necks, with now and then a boggy undergrowth, and the huge flowering rush by way of a change. The sides of the hills were abominably steep and high, and up and down, from the very top of the hills down to the rushy bottom of the valleys, were we constantly obliged to clamber and scramble backwards and forwards. It was heavy work with the sort of jungle we had to force our way through. Of course it was impossible with two dogs to beat the hundreds of acres of this stuff that lay before us, so we skimmed through it as well as we could, though we might have left scores of birds, or even broods, untouched and unfound; yet nearly all the birds killed were old ones. We saw, too, a great number of old grey hens, but they none of them, save one, appeared to have broods. The late and hard frosts had evidently cut them fearfully. After a long round, we made the bag up to seven and a half brace, and got back to the farmer's. Had a tithe of the old hens we saw reared broods we might very easily have trebled our bag; as it was, we only found two broods all day, and in one of them the birds were too small to shoot at. We plodded homewards over Yeavering Bell—a long tramp, *but, not being wet through*, I thought little of it.

I had an invitation to Carham Vicarage, the residence of Mr. Thompson's father, in order thence to study the beauties of Tweed. The best way to get there appeared to be to fish up the Bowmont, and as Mr. H. Thompson, who had been staying at Wooler, was driving over to Carham, he offered to take my luggage over with him on the 21st, to meet me the following day at Mindrum, about six miles up the Bowmont, and to pilot me thence to Carham, some five miles further. I was glad to accept his offer. We drove with him some distance past the turnpike on the evening of the 21st, leaving him to continue his journey to Carham, while we had a farewell hour or two upon the Lower Glen water, between the bridge and Sir H. St. Paul's, a part of the water I had not yet seen. It is a very fine piece of water. Indeed, to my mind it is better than the upper water at Coupland. It is not so often fished either, and it contains very fine trout. We got an excellent basket of trout, some three dozen, and the best for size which I saw at all, several of the trout being ¾lb. and 1lb. and over, and few under ½lb. T. also got a whitling, but I could not delude any of these wary fellows even though we worked on to Ewart-bridge pool, and found them rising when almost dark.

This was my last trial of Glen, and I left its banks with regret. It was fished once a week in the season by an excellent club. The Glen is the property of M. Culley, Esq., from whom

Lord Durham then leased it. Mr. Culley is a most ardent angler, and is a member and patron of this club, and some excellent fishermen there are in it. The best basket made in the year I was there was some 33lb. or 34lb.; Mr. Thompson, also a member of the club, coming in second with about 28lb. or 29lb. Considering the size of the fish in these rivers, these are great baskets to make. Thirty-four fish of 1lb. each is no bad day; and even sixty-eight of ½lb. one could manage to put up with, and the season was not a first-rate one. I once killed 43 brace and 45 brace on two successive days on the Lathkill, but then the fish run of a better size there than in the rivers further north; but I was heartily sick of my load by the time I got home each night.

To the above I must now add that Mr. Culley has now resumed his right over Coupland Castle and the Coupland water of the Glen, Lord Durham's lease being ended. He is a first-rate performer with the rod. What leave may be obtained in the Glen now, I cannot say, but if the river is to keep up its character at least it would be sparing; but before leaving the Wooler country, I may say that there is still a good deal of water open even to the wandering angler on the Till, Bowmont, Breamish, College, and Wooler water, besides smaller burns, good when there is water in them, but useless at other times. Indeed there is no part of England where there is such a quantity of open water as all along this border country, few of the tributaries of the Tweed being entirely closed to the angler, and many of them entirely open; but anglers multiply every year, and the open waters get more fished, and more poached too, unfortunately, and though a good catch may be made now and again, the habitual large takes of former years are not to be looked for.

The next day I drove up to Canne Mill, on the Bowmont, and I commenced operations a little above it. It began to rain and blow, the wind, with its usual perversity, insisting for the most part in blowing steadily and heavily down-stream. Fortunately where the river wound about much I now and then managed to fish up, and I took some fairish fish. They were rabid at the red spinner and the cow-dung, a few taking my blue dun; and at one time I thought I should have filled my creel, but towards the afternoon the wind was so troublesome that I could not cast properly. With a nice up-stream wind one might, I think, have filled two creels. I got a good basket of fish, however—about seven dozen. Possibly I might have caught more had I dwelt longer over good spots; but I had about five miles of water to fish up to reach Mindrum, and not knowing the country, I was afraid of being late, so I got on rapidly.

It is said that the Yetholm folk poach the Bowmont heavily, as it runs so near them. It may be so; but there certainly are a great number of fish in it, notwithstanding. In one or two places where there was a bit of a fall and rapid, the fish were rising incessantly, keeping the little pools in a constant commotion, like a pot boiling. The Yetholm gipsies are of course the scape-goats for every deed of plunder or rascality committed far or near. I fear that, as poachers, they deserve some of the animadversion cast on them. But a certain personage (decidedly the first gentleman in Europe) is never so black as he is painted. The gipsies still occupy Yetholm as of yore, and are mighty touchy upon all matters affecting their privileges, and the great families of Blythe, Douglas, Faa, and Young still flourish. Old Blythe, their king, was lately dead when I was there, and the territory of clothes-pegs and toasting-forks lamented his loss. Wet through, but walking and fishing my way upwards, I worked steadily on for Mindrum. Arriving there in the fall of the afternoon, I found my friend, Mr. H. Thompson, waiting for me, and we took our way over the hill for the Vale of Tweed and Carham, which we reached long after dark.

Before leaving Bowmont, I would give the angler a word of advice. If there is not a good rough wind, or if the water be not coloured with rain, do not go to Bowmont. It is all very much like the lower part, and though there are a good many streams every here and there, the greater part is dub—unmistakeable dub. In these, if there be wind or they be slightly coloured, you will kill fish, and plenty of them. If it be calm and clear, you kill a few fish in the streams perhaps, but the dubs are of course unapproachable save in the evening. If the weather be favourable, though there is no scenery to recommend it, the angler will certainly do well to pay Bowmont a visit, as he will easily fill his creel, and may often get hold of whitling. No leave whatever is required until he almost reaches Mindrum, where a small portion of it is preserved.

CHAPTER XI.

A BACK DAY ON TILL FROM WHEATWOOD TO DODDINGTON—THE PIKE OF THE TILL—BOB THE POACHER—THE VOICES OF EVENING—CARHAM—THE TWEED—CARHAM WHEEL—JAMIE WRIGHT, OF SPROUSTON—THE TROUTIN' DAY—A DAY'S TROUTING ON TWEED.

ON looking over my notes I find one day's fishing omitted. As it describes a part of Till not touched on yet, I must crave permission of my readers to go back to it. The 19th was a very windy and squally day. I thought the Till would be slightly coloured, but not enough to prevent worm-fishing. Minnows I could not get, or I think I could have done well. Accordingly, I sallied out to Wheatwood-bridge, about a mile and a half from Wooler, to fish down to Doddington-bridge. I tried above Wheatwood at first, with the fly; but the wind was too furious and the water too thick. I then went below the bridge, and the water tempted me to try a worm, and in the very first stream I got a nice trout of nearly a pound. This induced me to keep on, although I saw the footsteps of an angler in the sand, who had evidently fished every bit of the water before me; I had met him upon the bridge; and he was giving it up as a bad job. I, however, having nothing else to do, determined (for the sake of seeing this part of the river) to persevere. The water was nicely coloured, and had it not been for the fierce gusts of wind, which precluded my holding the rod for two seconds in any desired position, no doubt I should have made up a splendid dish of fish, for I got scores of bites; but it was utterly impossible to command the rod—it was whisked here, there, anywhere, by the wind. I could not tell when I had a bite, and the hooking of the fish was a pure matter of chance. As to casting the bait to a nicety under bushes or banks, or between weeds, it was not to be done; and so I went on from dub to dub, and stream to stream, renewing my worm every ten minutes or quarter of an hour, after a visitation from a good trout, for there were none but good ones on the feed to-day, and occasionally, when the banks were high and sheltered, perhaps catching a fish. For some distance the river is a nice alternation of stream and pool. The pools are deep and rather dead, but they hold good fish, and some of them have capital pike. The Till pike—which more resemble a Trent pike than any I have seen elsewhere in shape and make—are well fed and shy fellows; they do not run large so far up the river, one of 6lb. or 7lb. being uncommon. They are very fine eating, however, as I can testify from having dined off a 4-pounder at Mr. Thompson's, which was stuffed and baked in a savoury gravy, and was marvellous daynteous meat. Let not the ardent pike-fisher of the metropolis fancy that a visit to Till would repay him—I do not think it would. Till pike feed on trout, the fry of the *Salmonidæ*, and the choicest of large minnows, and are very capricious; a few are caught now and then by the rod and line, but the greater number of those that are caught in this neighbourhood are nightlined, there being sundry poaching brothers of the angle in these parts who turn a shameful penny in this way. There is one lanky Scotchman, in particular, a long fathom of drunken humanity, who haunts the river side with a rod. Ye piscatorial deities, such a rod! It would give Farlow a fit of the strongest convulsions if such a thing were displayed before him as an instrument for the capture of fish—verily, indeed, "a thing of shreds and patches." Here shines forth an old umbrella-stick, there the remains of a broken whip-stock; anon a green hedge-twig vamped on to an old parasol-rib furnishes a top with curious properties, while the butt bears a suspicious resemblance to a superannuated wooden leg. It looks more like a geometrical instrument constructed for the purpose of teaching the young idea the variety of angles which can be formed by two right lines. Bob is as angular as his rod, and Bob and his rod always put me in mind of the first proposition of the 1st Book of Euclid, and the sight of them usually set me demonstrating the problem, for poor Bob never could "describe an equilateral triangle upon a given finite straight line" after a successful day's fishing, though he might often be seen trying involuntarily to make the circles concerned in the same, and holding forth in the market-place in an erratic discourse, interpersed with bewailing howls of psalmody, which usually merged into a determined three-day's drunk, terminating in a lock-up, and perhaps a visit to Newcastle—not always at his own expense or with his own consent. The rod, however, of course was a mere blind, seldom used save when in company, for he always betook himself solitarily to lonely and unfrequented parts of the river, and his basket (a mysterious-looking affair) generally contained a dozen or so of rude night-lines, if report does not shamefully ill-use the estimable Robert; like other great men, Bob *may* suffer from calumny, though I doubt it. But, to continue my own fishing.

Although I got a good many bites, I did not get one fish for every half dozen; still I picked up fish, and good ones. At length the river became one long consistent dub, dead and apparently streamless for about a mile. This, of course, it was useless to attempt; so I got down below it, and commenced where Wooler water enters, but Wooler water was thick, and made Till a deeper colour than it was above. The river here too, is a little more exposed, so that the wind was even worse; but there are some very nice streams, and now and then I did get a fish. I had passed Doddington-bridge, and was working down, when evening came on, so I turned about and fished up again. The wind fell as the evening closed over me, and then the fish left off feeding; so I tackled up, and strolled slowly up the river bank, enjoying the quiet evening walk after the blusterous and unquiet day. And now nature began another phase of her existence, and the voices of the evening made themselves manifest. The voices of the evening! Who hears them like the angler, as he returns by the river-side meditatively conning over the incidents of his day's sport?

Hark to them! "Key-wit," complains the lapwing, "key-wit, key-wit," as, disturbed from his lair, he hovers about—now far off in the next field, and now menacing you overhead. Anon the water hen, with sharp shrill note, suddenly surprised, flaps over the pool heavily to the sheltering bushes on the far side. Hark, too, how the subsiding wind rises and falls alternately—now hushing the willows and reeds like a nursing mother, now wailing and sobbing like a tired child amongst the hollow banks and sedges, then away over the wide meadows to seek its home amongst the giant hills that frown upon us in the twilight distance. Halloa! "Quack, quack, queek, queek," and a brood of flappers beat the water in wild and scrambling alarm, while the old parent duck, with her warning quack, sweeps by you in hasty flight. "Scape, scape," an errant heather bleater, a wanderer from the hills, springs aloft as you pass a rushy muddy pool: he is heard, but you see him not, unless by chance he flits before the moon, which is rising and making the river gleam like a bran new service of plate, and tipping every bough and leaf, rush and reed, with molten silver. Who is that grey and ghostly fisherman deserted by his fellows that stands so lone and still by the shallow pool yonder? Who? Trust me, friend angler, he is your rival, and can show you a trick of fishing you could hardly equal him in. Take him up for night poaching, an old scoundrel, if you can; but faith he is hard to catch. But now he hears or sees you, and so his broad pinions are spread wide too, and grandfather heron flops off with no sound but the heavy beating of his broad wings, and more speed than you give him credit for. Haply as you leave the river, in the alders, by the dyke side, you hear the soft sweet notes of the sedge-warbler, for he sings at night—as sweetly too, though not so powerfully, as Philomel herself. Phew! what a pother is here! ay, you have disturbed a large covey of partridges from their jugging place. They are strong on the wing too, and it wants nearly a fortnight of September yet: they will try your skill on the first, friend, and you will hardly get so close upon them in a week from that time. And so you walk on, sometimes musing, sometimes marvelling, as each new voice salutes you, that you never noticed "the voices of evening" before, though you may have heard them a hundred times; but it is your mood to hear, and note them too, to-night, and you do so wonderingly, as though they were all new things and this some other hemisphere, and so you tramp on homewards under the moonlight. Is your creel light, friend? What then! your heart is light too, and there be other things to admire in the world besides fishes, so take that by way of consolation.

My creel was not abundantly stocked, holding about a dozen and a half, but they were all fish of from ½lb. to ¾lb., with one or two of 1lb.; and yet if one did that within 100 miles of London and called it nine brace, you would regard it as highly satisfactory.

And now for the Tweed, the glorious Tweed, sung in song and praised in story by how many hundreds of abler pens than mine; pens that have earned immortal fame for their wielders in all parts of the world where literature is prized. The Tweed is a magnificent salmon river, of unbounded capabilities of production. Rising on the confines of Peebleshire, for more than for a hundred miles the Tweed hurries onward to the sea, presenting throughout its course one long and uninterrupted home and nursery for the salmon. But even the facilities offered by the Tweed itself are as nothing compared with those afforded by the hundreds of miles covered by its multitudes of tributaries, many of which are large and important rivers, all of them presenting, as breeding places for the young fish, resources so boundless that it would be impossible to estimate what might be the amount of salmon it could produce if it only had fair play. It is, however, much too closely netted at the mouth, and should have a shifting weekly close time, while the pollutions in many of its tributaries are something awful, and if not checked ere long threaten to extinguish the fishery altogether.

Apart from its capabilities as a salmon river, the Tweed and its tributaries present unlimited sport for the trout-fisher. The Tweed trout especially are magnificent fellows, equal in point of size, flavour, and gameness to almost any produced by the far-famed rivers of the south. The average run of Tweed trout, on a fair fishing day will run from three to the pound to 1½lb.—say from ½lb. to 1¼lb.; but trout of 2lb., 3lb., and even 4lb. are not uncommon, while occasionally they are taken of larger size. The fly-fisher from the south will often be puzzled when he comes to Tweed what fly to select for his cast; for it produces and sends down so great a variety of flies, that, although the fish may be rising in hundreds, it is often very difficult to tell what fly they are rising at; added to this, the myriads of small and delicate flies, scarce larger than midges, which often throng its waters to the great delectation of the trout, preclude all hope of accurate imitation. This fact has caused the use of a number of general flies, known usually by the names of the inventors, and, to save the trouble of selecting and searching for the right fly, Tweed fishers are too apt to pin their faith to these flies in all instances. Now there are times when these flies kill well enough, as there are times in other rivers when almost any moving thing in the shape of a fly, not absolutely unreasonable in size, make, and colour, will be taken by the fish; and there are of course other times when a little discrimination would perhaps serve to stock the creel fairly which otherwise goes home somewhat light; and sure I am that there are many well-known flies admitting of accurate imitation which might be used at almost all seasons on the Tweed with advantage, and which would serve better than a blind reliance upon general flies, though, as I have said, there are often times when the general fly will be found advantageous.

I got to the Tweed rather late in the season for trout

fishing, and my hopes and chances of sport were not considerable, as the trout were fast losing condition, and changed their colour ominously within a short period of their capture.

I had written to ask permission to fish of the Earl of Home (to whom the greater part of the Carham water belongs) some time previously; but at that time he had a large party staying with him for the sole purpose of salmon fishing, so that he was unable then to give me permission to fish for salmon, nor would there have been any boat for me if he had; indeed, his boats were all daily double-manned with fishermen, which is very unusual—a rod to a boat being quite enough, either for sport or comfort. He, however, gave me unlimited leave to trout fish; and, after the departure of his party for the grouse-shooting, he very kindly gave me all the leave which I required, and, as the sequel will show, I had at least one good day's sport upon his water. Carham Water is about the best salmon water on the Tweed—the casts from Birgham dub down to Ladykirk comprising magnificent rapids, deep swirling pools and eddies, rough broken water and still dubs, available in every state of the weather and water, and seldom or ever without fish. For hours, when the wind has been low, and the sun too bright for trouting, have I sat upon the bank above Carham Wheel—a deep, tumultuous, swirling pool, where the largest salmon lie in security—or gazing at the splendid rattling stream at the "Kirk End," watching the silvery salmon springing aloft every now and then, of all sizes, from 20lb. to 5lb., and thinking futilely, as some overgrown monster flashed into the sunlight, and fell back into his native element with a huge splash, "Ah, my boy! If I only had a good salmon-hook stuck in the gristle of your nose, I'd give you something to jump for;" and yet there are not a tithe of the salmon in these waters that there used to be but a few years ago. What a stretch of river it might be, and how thronged with fish, under other circumstances!

Carham Vicarage is very pleasantly situated on the banks of

the river, and the kindness and hospitality I received during my stay there added one more grateful memory to the many already stored up in my mind of "the kindly North."

There had been a considerable flood in the river some days previously, and trees were floating down the river wholesale. The river rose eight or nine feet, and kept in fine running order for several days; and, had there been any quantity of fish left at Berwick, the river would have been well stocked from end to end. This flood had, however, been going down when the rain of the day before came on, and apprehensions were expressed when I reached Carham that "she would be down in the morning," the meaning whereof was not that "she," the Tweed (all rivers are "she's" here, as in Wales), would be lower, but would come down from the hills again higher and thicker; and I was told if she could be seen from the windows, she would be too high for fishing. It is needless to say that in the morning I looked out anxiously, and, sure enough, there, at the bottom of the glebe, was a thread of silver discernible high up the banks; and fishing, as I saw when I went to the river after breakfast, was hopeless, for, from the rain of the day before, it had popped up some four or five feet again, and was as thick as need be. As it was possible that it might be in order for the minnow by the evening, I wasted no time, but walked up the river-bank to Sprouston, to see the water, in company with Mr. H. Thompson. We also wanted some flies of Wright, who abides there. Wright is one of the neatest and best tyers on Tweedside; but he needs no notice from me, his name being known far and wide. He was at home, and at work; and we sat and chatted with him for an hour while he and his assistants plied the pliers and dubbing-hook on some salmon flies which he had an immediate order for; and very pretty and deadly-looking flies they were—*chef d'œuvres* of their kind. We got all the information, too, we could as to what was doing amongst the salmon in those parts; how one gentleman had killed half a dozen, and another three the day before; the flies they used, and so on. The morrow, it was prophesied, would be a grand trouting day. Leaving our order with him, we came away at length.

In the evening, though somewhat late for the take, we sallied forth and commenced just above the "Kirk End." I fished with the minnow, Mr. Thompson with the fly. We did not do much. I caught a couple of nice fish, when, casting over a shallow usually dry, but now covered by the flood, I got hung in a twig growing on it, and in my endeavours to clear my tackle I broke and lost three parts of the trace. I marked the spot exactly, and looked some days after, when the river was down, for the tackle, but could not find it, so suppose it was carried off by an eel, as they are very plentiful in the Tweed. As I was rigging out a new tackle, Mr. T. came down to me to tell me the fish were taking the fly freely, and I went up to the spot where he was fishing to try the fly; but by the time we had effected the change the trout went off, and I only caught one more, so that we got but six or seven; they were, however, very nice fish of from three-quarters to a pound each, some of the fish being bright or silvery, like a Thames trout in the height of condition. The season was evidently beginning to tell upon their rising. A week or a fortnight before this time they would have risen till ten o'clock, and perhaps later; now, however, they had commenced the early closing movement, and eight o'clock found them putting up the shutters and retiring to rest, and from this rule I did not find them depart subsequently.

The next morning, though rather bright, was a fine trouting morning apparently, as the river looked in splendid order. And here I give an appropriate Tweed trouting song, written (it is needless to say) by a local genius, and certainly far from being devoid of merit. There is a feeling and taste in the lines which will recommend them to every angler, while the quaintness of the old Border language and expressions will by no means detract from their value. I owe this song to the attention of a friend who was staying at Mr. Thompson's while I was there.

THE TROUTIN' DAY.

I'll mount the creel upon my back, and aff wi' merry glee,
And ha'e a gallant troutin' day, wi' minnits* an' wi' flee;
I ken ilk stream and wimplin' pool, ilk plantin', brae, and mead,
By Beaumont fair, by sleepy Till, or by majestic Tweed.

Your swivel mount, the minnie spin, the water's porter-brown,
And try the cast aboon the cauld, belaw sweet Coldstream town.
The wind is saft, the sky is grey, the colour o' the tide
Proclaims the spate frae Slitrig brae, or Yarrow's mountain-side.

The laverock's chirlin' in the sky, far—far aboon our ken,
The blackbird's notes are ringin' high, frae out The Quarry glen;
The brairdin'-beart† sae sweet to smell, a' wat wi' dewy spray,
Makes high our bounding spirits swell on sic a troutin' day.

The saft wind pirlin' through the trees, the gowans at my fit,
The big trouts boilin' at the flees, as owre the stream they flit;
The salmon wans upon the ford, just new run frae the sea,
The swallows swarmin' owre the tide, a' please the fisher's ee.

Fling owre to where the eddies boil, upon their rocky bed—
I hae him fast, the greedy-gowl, he stuck it like a ged.‡
The tackle's stout, the haud is fast, for landin' famous ground;
I've worked him down, he's out at last, his weight aboon a pound.

Another and another, still—they're rising by the score;
I dinna think I ever saw them tak sae weel afore.
But night is closing in at last, my pouchen heavy feel,
I scarce can get my lid made fast, wi' sic a stockit creel:

I'll hame on Sandy Foster ca'—o' fishers he's the sire—
And wi' the lave we's hae a blaw aroond his kitchen fire.
The warmin' cheerer circling bright—the weary turning gay—
A' listenin' to the hard-won fight—that crowns a troutin' day.

The fish upon the table spread, in ashets§ bright and clean,
The big anes a' laid uppermost, *for love o' being seen.*
The cantie laugh o' harmless glee, the royal lots o' fun,
Wi' auld Tam Smith, blithe Uncle John, or canny Willie Dunn.

Oh! Coldstream fair! there's ane, at least, that bears a love for thee,
A fervent, deep, and stirring throb, that time will never dree!
I'd sooner starve at Coldstream-cross, and bite a crust that's brown,
Than row in wealth and luxury in ony ither town!

---

* Minnows † Barley
‡ Pike § Plates

Fine as the day was, it belied its appearance, for the sport turned out to be very indifferent, and, instead of the heavy creel we anticipated, we got but little over a dozen fish, and none of any large size. I attribute it to the fish having gorged themselves in the flood of the day before, having also been well fed in the heavier flood which occurred previously.

Until noon scarcely a fish showed himself; then they began to rise fairly, but at what fly it was very difficult to determine, there were so many varieties on the water. The fly called by Yorkshire fishermen the little needle brown was very abundant, and, had I had any good imitation, it might have done; but the flies which they were really taking were very diminutive duns, pale blue and yellow, not larger than the smallest midges, but the most perfect and beautiful little insects conceivable. It would be utterly impossible for the rude hand of man to imitate them, so all that one could do was to keep whipping away with a good specimen or two of some of the larger flies which also abounded, and to hope the fish might sooner or later take to a change of diet. I kept up a red spinner of Ogden's, and the blue dun previously mentioned by me, with a local general fly, said to be a great killer at times. On this occasion, however, I did not get a fish upon it, nor, although I tried it subsequently, did the fish appear to fancy it at this time of year. I got seven or eight upon the two former flies by perseverance, Mr. T. doing about the same execution. It was very annoying to keep on throwing over rising fish, the only visible result being to stop their rising. In this part of the water stone causeways have been built out into the river, with the view of saving the banks, but I think they have not served the purpose they were designed for, as the river whirls round inside these dykes and dams, and makes large eddies which in floods rather damage the banks than save them. These eddies are fine places for the trout, however, and in the centre of them may be seen a large sheet of foam, whirling and twirling about without ceasing; into this all the flies which come down into the eddy are drawn, and this foam is a perfect larder for the trout, who follow it about in its gyrations, and rise within its precincts incessantly, the black water in the midst of the foam constantly marking and betraying their risings as they suck down the insect of their choice; and, having such a selection all ready to hand, they are the most perfect and determined gourmands in that choice. The object of the fisherman is simply to cast into this foam, wherever it may be, for where it is, there the fish are; and, if he has the right fly, he may pull the big trouts out at every cast, or two while the rise is on, for they have their distinct times for rising and for leaving it alone; and when the rise is not on it is next to useless to keep thrashing the water with a fly, though perhaps minnow, worm, or creeper, as the case may be, may then be advantageously employed.

Our creel, as I have said, was light when we were compelled to go in to dinner. After dinner, the evening was cold, and the fish did not come on at all, not being hungry, I suppose.

The next day was worse still, for the river had nearly cleared, and the day was bright, hot, and without a breath of wind all day. The trout certainly rose, as on the previous day, about noon, but they were shyer than before. We got some half dozen of fish, however, in the evening; but the early closing had spoilt the evening-fishing altogether, and we were obliged to abandon it at a comparatively early hour.

CHAPTER XII.

TWEED FISHERIES — MUCKLE SANDIE AND THE BAILIFFS — JUMPING A HORSE OUT OF A QUICKSAND—DAN THANKLESS —KELSO—MELROSE—ABBOTSFORD—A DAY AT THE SALMON.

THE Tweed, since its fisheries have risen in value so much, is very fairly preserved in these parts, and comparatively little poaching goes on. Now and then a well-mended kelt is condemned to die an unrighteous death by pot-hunting sportsmen who ought to know better. Formerly there was a good deal of wholesale poaching with nets, but I do not think there is much now; various kinds of set nets used to be very common, and the poachers, a cunning and daring race, were "aye hard to grapple." There is a good yarn told of one Muckle Sandie. Muckle Sandie was a huge and a most determined poacher; he had his net set for salmon on one occasion when two bailiffs chanced to come upon it; having procured a salmon, they stuck it in the net and laid down under the bank in hiding, determined to take Sandie *in flagrante.* But Sandie was no the chiel to be had that fashion, and the bailiffs waited in vain. The day passed, and not a soul but one solitary woman with a keel * on her head, to fetch water, came near the river. Still they determined not to give up, and stuck to it manfully all night. The next morning the bailiffs, tired out with their long watch, went disconsolately down to the river's brink determined to take the net as they couldn't catch the delinquent, when—"Hey! what! Gone? Never!" But it *was* gone—clean gone. But "How, when, where, who, or which way?"

* A sort of pail with a long handle.

"Gude day, sirs; an what ails ye? Hae ye tint onything?" asked a stalwart female with a keel on her head, who came down to the river for water at the moment.

"Tint onything!" roared the amazed bailiffs, "what's come o' the net?"

"Ehow! the net! Wast that'n ye was speering after? Am thenkin, then, ye joost had a lang leuk at naethin; for it was awa in the keel or the clock chappit twal yesterday. And Sandie bid me gie his respectfu' thanks for the muckle fine fusshe in't to ony ane that speered on it."

Under the pretence of fetching water the morning before, she had whipped the net out and into her keel, and bore it off under the very noses of the unsuspecting bailiffs, who not only lost Sandie's net, but their own fish, and got laughed at into the bargain.

The eels, too, were terrible poachers of the fish caught in set nets, for I have it from a friend that he has constantly known the whole of the insides of fish thus taken eaten completely out, nothing being left of them but the bare skin. If the eels could be taken, without in any way interfering with the salmon, they would form a most valuable item in the Tweed fisheries, while the salmon-fishing could not but be most extensively benefitted by their being thinned.

On Saturday evening I determined to betake myself to Kelso, *en route* for Melrose and Abbotsford; being so near the great sights of Tweed side, I could not forego them.

We started for Carham station. On the way to the station we passed through the turnpike-gate; by it runs a little rill—a mere insignificant ditch; nevertheless that ditch or rill separates England from Scotland, and we were now over the Border. The pike-house is said mostly to stand in England, but the hearth-stone is in Scotland. Here, then, was the identical line of the Border, on which so much has been written, and of which so much is even now styled "debateable ground." Here we could to a few inches decide which was England and which Scotland.

I have one amusing extract concerning the Border, and the line it takes, sent me by a friend, which I here append :—

The *Scottish Chronicle*, or an abridgment of the "Black Book of Paisley," says : "Scotland is divided from England by certain marches from the East Sea called the Scots Sea, to the West Sea called the Irish Sea, from the mouth of Tweed till it come betwixt Werke and Hadden (Wark and Haddon), where the march leaves the river ; thence it passeth south-west by secret ways known only to the inhabitants of that countrie, till you come to Redden Burne, and so up the said burne till you come to the height of the fells of Cheviotte ; from thence west by the tops of the fells to a march ditch, and from the march ditch to the river of Carshope, and down Carshope till it fall into Liddel, till Eske and Liddel meet, and passing along the north side of Eske it goeth endlong a ditch till it come to the river of Sarke, and down the river Sarke till it fall into Solway, where the waters of Annan and Nith, running severally into Solway, all meet in one channel in the Irish Sea, 'making plenty of fishes.' Here, by the flowing and ebbing of furious tides, made through many lands ends, and partly by the inundations of the said waters, there are very dangerous quicksands called Solway Sands, that no man can safely pass over them without danger except they have an accustomed guide, because of sinking holes, that are frequent in them. Being every tide overflowed with the sea, the travellers take their journey through them at a low or ebb water. If any man or horse fall in his fellow-travellers casting their cloaks or other cloths about the place where he sinks, by their running often about, the sand swells up to a height, and so vomits out that which is fallen into the sinking hole. Upon the banks of Solway in June and July the country people gather up the sand within the flood mark, bringing it to land and laying it in great heaps, thereafter they make the salt spring water, and cast it upon the sand with a certain deuice, causing the water to run through the sand into a hollow pit purposely made to receive it, which water being boiled in a little vessel of lead there is made thereof good white salt, after the temperance of the weather. This place is called 'Saltcoats.'"

I have heard of jumping out worms from their holes in this way, but jumping a horse out of a quicksand is quite a novelty.

Carham station, though an insignificant affair, stands on a somewhat famous site, for here stood the stronghold or tower of the last of the Border robbers—one Dan Thankless. Yonder, where that *débris* of coke, coals, ashes, rusty iron, and railway refuse, cumbers the soil, was the corner of his kail-yard ; and close by, in the ditch by the roadside, similarly bestrewn, under the knotted elder-bush, Dan Thankless's unsanctified bones lie buried; for be it known Dan fell not in raid or battle, nor was he hanged upon a gibbet after the fashion of his kind; neither was his head erected upon a spike, a terror to evil-doers, nor his body drawn and quartered by willing but rude and unskilled anatomists. No, Dan, to his immortal disgrace and the shame of his race, died peacefully in his bed, and consequently it may have been considered as well-nigh time that his profession became extinct. How would his forbears have raged with indignation could they have forseen that their kail-yard should become the site of a vile commercial transaction in the form of a railway-station, and even the very hearthstone but a convenient slab for the money-changers and ticket-sellers, where actual buying and selling would be carried on, and where one policeman, armed only with eighteen inches of painted ash-stick, would be sufficient to check anything like a reiving of pocket-hankerchiefs or a "driving" of portmanteaus. Oh, profanation! But let us hope of Dan, that, like the renowned Tom Bowling—

Though his body's under *ashes*, &c., &c.

We slept at Kelso, and got on to Melrose uncomfortably early the next morning. At Melrose, the first thing I noticed was that the names of Walter Scott and John Knox were not likely to be forgotten, for they graced two houses in the main square; but though the names at first a little staggered me, I soon saw that their representatives were but "mute, inglorious Miltons" after all, for the fictions of the one extended not beyond a belief that reels of cotton and silk contain the exact amount specified on them, while "the Reformation" of the other would possibly be never directed to anything but rolls—the one doing a smart stroke in haberdashery, the other being connected with the baking interest.

Of course, being Sunday, nothing could be seen in Scotland. The abbey was religiously locked up, so that the simple and apparently harmless privilege of strolling through the sacred precincts was denied to us. As possibly, however, such a privilege might, by ill-conducted people, be grossly abused, and the abbey turned into a bear-garden, no doubt the proprietors have reason for inclosing it, and placing it under lock and key. We strolled down to the river, however, and had a peep at that, for they could not very well lock that up, or no doubt they would. It is very pretty, but does not look like very favourable salmon water, though there are, I believe, some good casts in it, particularly above the cauld. Most of the water here belongs to Messrs. Broadwood, the great pianoforte makers. Later in the day we strolled up the nearest of the Eildon hills, at the base of which Melrose is prettily situated. These hills are not of great height or bulk, though they are in their way very picturesque; and the steepness of their sides, and sharpness of their outlines, make them not only very striking, but hard to scramble up. From the top of the nearest one we had hopes of a fine view, but the afternoon set in misty, and the view was much circumscribed and interrupted; we did now and then, however, get a charming peep of the valley of the Tweed, with Galashiels and the other small towns and villages which grace its banks.

In the evening I strolled out to the abbey, and as the moon was rising, I had an opportunity (above the closed gates) of seeing the beautiful view so well-known to the admirers of Scotch guide and hand-books. Through the tall window (the crowning beauty of the place) shone the rising moon, showing up the delicate and lovely tracery, and gilding the salient points, and no doubt flooding "the long-drawn aisles" with its silver light; but this, alas! I could not see, owing to those envious gates, though I would have given a handsome sum to have been permitted half an hour's stroll through them under such circumstances.

> If thou wouldst view fair Melrose aright,
> Go visit it by the pale moonlight.

says Sir Walter Scott—("but don't go on a Sunday evening," he might have added)—and hereupon he gives such a description of the beauties of the scene that it is difficult to believe that Sir

Walter never *did* visit the abbey by the pale moonlight. Nevertheless, it is asserted that he did not, and upon apparently good authority, and I am not aware that the assertion has ever been contradicted.

The next morning I visited Melrose. Now, I am not about to enter on a description of it. It would be treading ground which has been far too well and frequently trodden before, and the reader desirous of a more intimate and archæological acquaintance has only to take up the handbook most convenient to himself, to have a better description, and to know more about it than I can tell him. I will only briefly say that Melrose is almost the only fashionable ruin much bepraised and visited which has not disappointed me. To say that it is beautiful, that the architecture and effect is almost entrancing, is to repeat well-used and very well-deserved praises. Two things, however, jar upon the sensitive visitor (at least I consider myself a sensitive visitor, and they jarred upon me), viz., the situation, which is nowise favourable to its charms, and the repulsive neatness maintained in the interior, which gives it the air rather of a modern Roshervillian ruin, than of a really venerable pile. Carefully swept, and garnished with every little fragment and carving of gurgoyle, frieze, or mullion, built up apparently into hideous little gimcrack altars to bad taste and petty misadornment, one feels inclined to seize a large shovel and send each mass flying to their natural resting-places in forgotten and neglected corners—only there are no such things, for every corner is most particularly attended to, so much so that even the spiders must get disgusted with their quarters, and the bats dissatisfied with such unquiet lodgings. I could think of nothing but some amiable old annuitant surrounded by a score of sycophants and flatterers, who polish his boots and brush his hair, and keep him alive for what they can get out of him. I paused before the grave of the wizard Sir Michael Scott, and wished I could have invoked the aid of the grim old sorcerer to give the harpies (who spoilt my intellectual feast by befouling the viands with their abominable taste, and who worried me with stereotyped descriptions) a gliff that would make them shy of the abbey for ever and a day.

Abbotsford, which is a short half-hour's drive from Melrose, is a very nicely-kept, singular, and interesting curiosity-shop. The building itself is perfectly indescribable, and how such an apparent confusion of peaks, pillars, towers, and chimneys ever got thrown together is a mystery. Fortunately for me the view of it is very well known, so I am not called on to attempt description. The inside is as remarkable as the outside, for the collection of curious and rare things therein displayed is so very varied, and at the same time so interesting, that the effect produced by the contemplation of one singular object is immediately destroyed by the next, which is to the full as curious; and this goes on until the confusion of mind produced by the attempt to form a notion of the outside is thoroughly completed by the interior, and the visitor comes forth quite prostrate and bewildered with what he has seen, and half an hour's walk in the grounds, with a long gaze at the placid Tweed flowing here so peacefully along, is absolutely needed to arrange his ideas, and to get some distinct notion of what he has really seen. The collection is perfectly wonderful, but so rich and diverse that a mere walk through it cannot give any satisfactory reminiscence of it. Then the variety of ceilings and architectural adornment; the odds and ends of windows, carvings, medallions, and of heaven knows what besides, would almost lead the matter-of-fact stranger, who did not know where he was, to ask, "Wasn't the owner and projector of all this a little—just a little—cracked? and, if not, how on earth did he avoid becoming so?" The library seemed to me the only room in the house where there was simplicity and repose. There was Sir Walter's desk, and there his chair. "Don't sit in it, please." Everybody wishes to, and as thousands visit the house weekly, and sometimes excursions of hundreds at a time, if it were permitted, the chair would have to be renewed yearly. Is not this species of vulgarity a wonderful thing? is it not confined to and symptomatic of the true British snob? What satisfaction can a stupid heavy-sterned Briton derive from sitting in Sir Walter's chair, and wearing it out? Does he imagine that the divine afflatus can be communicated by the contact between his well-filled nether-broadcloth and the chair of the immortal dead? or that, like little boys, he will imbibe learning by application to the breech? But to the library: there was the gallery, with the little door out of Sir Walter's bedroom, through which he could descend to his desk at any hour of the day or night, without interruption — delightful privilege. Then, too, the books! thousands of rare and valuable tomes. My fingers itched, my eyes watered for them; I felt "Kleptomania" coming over me. Here was a wonderful old black letter volume, full of wonderful engravings of arms and armour, and worth its very weight in gold; would it be possible to drop it out of window and pick it up promiscuously when walking round the garden? But what if I were caught *in flagrante?* Would a wrong address help me? No. Would it be of any use for me to say I was eighteen when I was eight-and-thirty? I doubt it. Would the magistrates or counsel sympathise with my youth and beauty, or my lofty and distressed connections? I fear not; besides, the attendant never gave me a chance; so my mania was ungratified, and I was un-committed. I could willingly have spent a month or two in that one room. To the lovers of curious and rare things, Abbotsford is a mine of wealth worthy of a score of visits; but the taste shown in the whole thing is, I cannot help thinking, a little questionable. No doubt better judges of such things will look upon all this as only two or three removes from "flat blasphemy;" but what are people's impressions worth if they do not describe them truthfully? so I will take my chance, and abide by them.

On my return to Carham in the afternoon, having permission from Lord Home to fish the Carham waters I determined next day to make my first essay on Tweed with a salmon-rod, and, having procured half a dozen well-tied flies from Wright, I set all in order for the ensuing morn. Somehow the salmon—although there had been one or two fine, dark, windy days for them—had not been in a taking humour at all; one, or at the outside two, small grilse being, with a blank sometimes, the amount of sport obtained. Still, there were a good many fish showing themselves, and a change of wind or weather, or some alteration or modification in ozone or some of those inscrutable agents which may or may not have to do with the taking of fish, might ensue any day, and put them in a good humour; and, of course, I hoped it might come to my luck to be on the water on that day.

On the next morning I looked out anxiously at the weather: apparently it was all that the heart of a salmon-fisher could desire. Dark and windy, with a good water—not too low. In fact, to look at the day, one would have expected to get four or five fish at least, and perhaps half a score, or perhaps a big one or two. Breakfast ended, I walked up to "The Wheel" with my rod, and there was Willie Scott, his lordship's fisherman, waiting for me. A nice, douce civil lad is Willie, and a capital fisherman, too—one who takes it for granted that the gentleman who is going to fish with him has some knowledge of the use of a salmon-rod, and has some knowledge of hooking and playing a fish, and who does not conceive it necessary to shout a host of useless and exasperating directions into his ear when he is doing his best, and which only tend to make him nervous and irritable—a frame of mind not favourable to successful fishing, as is too often the wont with fishermen of greater self-pretensions to skill in their art. Now, I have sometimes met men who think that a salmon cannot be killed unless they vociferate and advise to "do this or do that;" and who will not let you fish in your own way, nor strike in your own way, nor do anything in the way you are accustomed to do it, and who, having succeeded in making you lose your fish, take on themselves to blame you for doing so. It is "Ah, sir; if ye'd only just done so and so." I once lost three fish in succession, I firmly believe, through trying to follow the advice of one of these wiseacres. At length I hooked a fourth, and he commenced anew, as if nothing had happened. I turned round, and pointing to a tree some twenty or thirty yards behind me, I said, "Have the kindness to walk to that tree, and when I want you I will call for you." I killed my fish, and also the next I hooked. A word of advice as to the presence of a sharp rock or some unseen danger is all that a moderately-skilful fisherman requires, and the more quietly this is given the better.

The rod was soon up, and the fly selected by Willie lapped on, the fly chosen being the one locally known as the "dun-wing." We rowed off, and I commenced on the head of Carham wheel, a magnificent cast, and fished it carefully down; every now and then a huge fish would heave himself aloft, or a lively grilse come dancing up, sometimes barely a yard or two from the hook, but none of them cared for a taste of the dun-wing; and having fished it down, we came back and fished it over again with a silver body—a very striking fly—but in vain; not a fish would move. Once more we shifted to a doctor. Every moment I expected to see a big boil, or to feel a pluck at the fly; but blessed are they who expect nothing, for they are never disappointed, and I was. I fished it on the top, I fished it deep, a foot under water; I fished it slow, I fished it quick; I played the fly roughly, I drew him steadily along on an even keel—but it was no go. It was, of course, unaccountable; but that is nothing, because it always is unaccountable. Clearly enough they wouldn't come, so we went on to the next cast. Fished Ship End, Long Ship—Flummery, I think it is called—and at last half-way down the Kirk End stream. "There he is!" said Willie Scott. I was looking at a couple of stones on the other side of the river, having marked a good fish opposite to them, and being desirous of putting the next cast over him. So I did not see the fish; but as I did not feel him either, I concluded that he rose falsely. I tried him again and again. I fished the stream out, tried other flies, but he would not come again, so I left him. On I fished, cast after cast, but did nothing. Then we lunched; and after lunch I went to it again, and at last, in a cast rejoicing, I think, in the euphonious title of "bluidy breeks," up came a small grilse of about 4lb. at the dun-wing, and after a nice little scamper here and there the net was slipped under him, and *we drank his health.* I had been afraid of a blank, but that was saved. I fished on until the evening came on, but did not extract another rise out of the sulky dogs. So ended my first day.

CHAPTER XIII.

Fishermen's Rights—The Floors Water—Mr. Fawcet and Salmon Fishing—Two Days at Kelso—A Good Day at Carham—Tweed Flies—The Salmon Fly—Bamborough Castle—The Three Idiots.

The Tweed fishermen are a very independent set of fellows, very civil, when not upset, with a certain pride in themselves and their calling, but quite sensible to the difference between good and scurvy treatment. Not a hundred years ago, a gentleman well known on Tweedside was fishing with one of them, whom, for the sake of individuality, we will call Davie. Soon after starting, the gentleman killed a ten-pounder, and, greatly pleased, took out his flask and drank "to the fusshe," and, without offering Davie a sup, returned it to his pocket, blew out the feathers of the fly, and went to work again. The stream was heavy, but Davie never shirked it, and ere long "his gentlemen" was in another. This was killed, too, and out came the flask again. The gentleman, much delighted, laughed, slapped his thighs, prophesied a big day, drank to the fusshe again, and put up his flask—all as a matter of course. But the deuce of a drop got Davie. Davie glowered on't. "He didna joost like the prospec—it was no the sort o' thing he was usen to at a'." However, he put off from shore into the stream once more, bent to his work with desperation and a dry throttle, and again the lucky fisherman was in his fish. A third time they got to shore, and a third time the fish was landed—a noble fifteen-pounder. Laughing, joking, chuckling, in the highest glee, the angler again brought out the flask, again drank to the fusshe, and again, without passing it on, returned the bottle to its abiding place. Davie rose from his seat. "I'm thinking we'll have an amazing day, Davie," said the gentleman. "A'm thenkin ye wull," said Davie, drily, as he stepped out of the boat and handled the chain. "Hallo; what are you about?" asked the fisherman in wonder, as Davie, having dragged the boat up, commenced locking the chain to the post. "Mon," said Davie, "Ef ye drink by yeresell, ye may fusshe by yeresell, and gang to—for me," and, putting the key in his pocket, he stalked off and left the astonished angler to his meditations.

They are extremely jealous of their reputation, too, as the following anecdote will show. A friend of mine was one day fishing with one Tammy, when he hooked a large fish, which showed them great play; at length, having nearly tired the fish, he brought it round, and once or twice Tammy failed to gaff it, not being able to put the hook into the part he wished. "Ah," said my friend, growing impatient for the fish's landing, "Ah! confound you, Tammy, you never could gaff a fish properly, for yere always looking for the tail, so as not to spoil the fish." Down went the gaff, and off came Tammie's coat, and in a monstrous rage he began squaring up at my friend after his fashion. "Ye tell me a canna gaff a fusshe!" said Tam. "Ye tell me a canna gaff a fusshe!! A'm roosed—a'm roosed to deeds o' bluid, ye ken, when ye tell me a canna gaff a fusshe! Tak aff yere coat, mon, for a'm roosed to deeds o' bluid. Ye touch my honour when ye say a canna gaff a fusshe! A'll ficht wi' my best friend gin he tells me a canna gaff a fusshe. Tak aff yere coat, mon, for a'm roosed to deeds o' bluid, ye ken—a'm roosed to deeds o' bluid! Tak aff yere coat, or a'll trample on ye." "I'll not take off my coat, Tammy," said my friend, quietly, "but by the lord! I'll give the coroner a job if ye can't swim, for I'll throw you overboard if you miss him again." Whether Tam thought my friend looked as if he, too, "was roosed to deeds o' bluid, ye ken," or that he had done sufficient to vindicate his wounded honour, or whether the fish at that moment presented so tempting a mark that Tammy could not resist the opportunity, or whether both circumstances combined to interrupt the course of his ire, I know not; but he retrieved his character, and wiped off the slur cast upon it by my friend, by at once gaffing the fish with a skill and dexterity which left nothing to be desired; and as he was a twenty-pounder, and my friend's whisky-flask was always as free as the air to a deserving boatman, no doubt,

> If any pain or care remained,
> They drown'd it in the bowl.

If the angler wishes for sport, he will certainly find it advantageous to treat his fisherman at least as well as he treats himself.

I had applied to the Duke of Roxburghe for leave to fish the Floors water, and had received a very courteous permission for two days' fishing, and determined on the day after my return to Carham to make a trial of it. It was, apparently, a good day for salmon-fishing; and having heard the water very highly spoken of, I anticipated a big day. I took the train to Kelso, and soon found the Duke's fisherman, Mr. Stevenson, who in due time piloted me through a portion of the park to the river just below Floors Castle, which is beautifully situated, and forms a lovely and imposing view from Kelso-bridge. We commenced operations on a reach of rather heavy, dull water, which stretches from the cauld up-stream for about a quarter of a mile. Here there are some good casts for heavy fish, which find good lying ground. We fished it carefully down to the cauld two or three times with a good choice of flies; but on this day, favourable as it looked, their mightinesses were not in the humour to put in an appearance, for I did not get a rise, and indeed I saw very few fish move. After lunch we fished on up the river for above half a mile, trying some fine likely streams, but it availed nothing. At the upper part of the water there is a short sharp current between two rocks; it is an awkward bit to cast properly over without wading, as the angler has to cast rather up-stream.

At the throat, however, I saw a grilse leap out of the water, so I resolved to try him, and at the second cast he came up—but only to look, for I neither fastened nor felt him. I tried him again, and again he came, but more faintly, and with a smaller boil than before. After giving him a rest I tried him again, but he would not look at it. I changed my fly, and at intervals I put several other flies over him, but it was of no avail, and I was obliged at last to leave him. I then fished the water down to the landing place, and tried the slack water again, but I got no other rise, and, being tired with a long day's flogging and so little encouragement, I gave in, and tackled up to a blank day. Just as I was putting up my rod, not ten yards from the landing-place, a huge twenty-pounder came up with a prdigious plunge, as though to say, "Here I am you see, but I wasn't to be gammoned by your bunches of feathers and tinsel." On this very spot, some three days before, Stevenson told me that a blind gentleman,* whom he was fishing with, hooked and killed a handsome fish of above 20lb. weight. As I was walking back to the inn to get some refreshment it came on to rain, and having let the last train to Carham depart, I had to walk home. The weather held up for a time, and thinking it was going to clear up, I left my rod and tackle to save carrying back for the next day, and I made a start; but I had scarcely got a mile from Kelso on the road for Sprouston ferry, when it came on again harder than ever, and I walked the whole distance—and a long and wearisome walk it was in the pelting rain—reaching home at length soaked to the skin.

The next day I made for Kelso, fearing that the river would come down, if not already risen, as it had rained nearly all night. When I reached the river, however, I found that it had not started as yet. It was a tremendously squally gusty day, blowing so at times that the boat could hardly make head against it. Stevenson did not like the look of it, and indeed there was every

---

* Professor Fawcett, late M.P. for Brighton.

prospect of a very rough day's work cut out for him; but it struck me that this was just the very weather to suit the dull water and the big fish, and I was in great hopes of hooking a big one if the water did not rise, as, when it does begin to start, it is useless to attempt salmon fishing on Tweed, and indeed on most other rivers. I had not taken three casts above the landing-place when I rose a fish at the silver body, but he did not take. I tried him again and again—changed flies, but it was useless, and I fished down to the cauld without another rise. On the very brink of the cauld there is a good cast, and at the second or third cast into the smooth, gliding water, a sudden boil and a sharp pluck at the silver-body announced that I was fast. I had been in hopes that it was a good fish, but five minutes' middling play brought a 6lb. grilse to the net, and I was soon thrashing away again, but I could not coax another to move. The washing of the waves against the banks began to thicken the dead water; so I thought, as the water was deep and there were large fish, that I would try something a trifle more showy, so I changed to a Ballina fly, and subsequently to a parson all toppings, and cock of the rock, a mighty showy fellow. but it was all unavailing. And now I fancied the river began to rise, and when we reached the landing-place doubt was changed to certainty; she had shot up three or four inches, but was very slightly discoloured. It was quite enough to destroy all chances of sport, however. Still, in hopes that by an outside chance something might be done, I worked on, being desirous to try the fish which I had risen twice on the previous day. When we reached the cast, however, the river had risen full six inches, and the nice fishing stream was lost in a rattling torrent. I saw a couple of fish disport themselves there, however, and as I could not now at all reach the spot, not having wading boots with me, I handed the rod to Stevenson (who had), and he tried it, but could not fish it properly, as the stream was too powerful. We left it at length without a rise, and we fished the river carefully down to the landing-place without even seeing another fish. From the way the day commenced, I was certainly in hopes of having a better bag to show; but the rising water no doubt put an end to sport.

There are some pretty streams in the water I fished, particularly opposite to and above Floors Castle, altogether there are twenty-two recognised casts on it, but of course they are not all in order at the same time. On the lowest of all, "Maxwheel," which seldom gets the wind on it properly, some years ago, the Duke of Roxburghe killed twenty-seven salmon and grilse in one day when the wind served.

The next day I took another turn at the Carham water. Another gentleman, who had permission, had sent word a day or two before to say he should be down, so that he had the choice of the best water. Willie Scott was engaged to attend him, and was waiting, expecting him down by the train.

I had to take Birgham Dub—a large wide stretch of rather still water—and I went with a capital boatman and experienced fisherman, whose name has escaped me, Mr. H. Thompson taking a trout-rod and occupying the bow of the boat, for the purpose of getting a dish of fish for breakfast. It was not a likely-looking day, being a trifle sunny, and with very little wind; and, the Dub requiring a good brisk wind, our chance of sport looked small. We fished it over, however, for an hour or two, and only saw one fish move. By this time the train had come in, and Willie Scott's gentleman had not put in an appearance; so we were at liberty, much to our satisfaction, to take the lower water; so we dropped down to the wheel, and fished it down two or three times. The day began to cloud over a little, and I was in great hopes of getting a rise out of the wheel; I was the more anxious, too, as the fish are usually heavy there, and I saw some big ones rolling up. I fished this magnificent cast very carefully, tried most of my best Tweed flies, and one or two taking-looking strangers, every minute expecting to see the big boil which heralds a quarter of an hour's active excitement. But it never came, and having given it a fair chance, we went to lunch. As this was the last day I could spare, I must say I did not feel delighted with the aspect of things—I hardly anticipated a blank on such fine water, but I did not quite like the look of it. However, never despair; and the result proved that there was corn in Egypt yet, and that a bad beginning has often a good ending.

No sooner was lunch over than we put off again, and with "silver-body" temptingly skimming the water, I fished down a short distance, till I came off "The Prison," or "Long Ship End," when a sharp pull and a bending rod told glad tidings. Oh! how musical is the sound of the reel! Talk of a solo on the sacbut or saxhorn, or the grinding of the most melodious hand-organ that ever drove Professor Babbage frantic, or gladdened the heart of an *ennuied* nursery-maid in charge of a covey of craving two-year-olds. Pshaw! "What fairy like music steals over"—not "the sea," but the river?—"voice of the mermaid," indeed! What's a mermaid to a multiplier? not that I ever use a multiplier, save for the sake of alliteration. Talk of the Sirens, forsooth! Had the wise Ulysses only been a salmon fisherman, the click of a reel would have fetched the wax out of his ears, and brought the artful old scoundrel to book in the twinkling of a bed-post. I landed at The Prison, and the fisherman landed the fish in The Prison—only just in time though, for he was getting too near the stakes to be pleasant, one of which, being loose, came up entangled in the net. The fish was a reddish one, of about 6lb. We put off again, and in half a dozen throws, almost on the same spot, another tug and another bend of the rod proclaimed another fish on. Again we landed, and after a little gentle persuasion I induced my friend to come within the sweep of the net. It was the fellow fish to the other; there was not a quarter of a pound between them. A little below this I struck something which at first I thought was a grilse. In playing it I thought it was a good trout, but on getting it in we found it was a fish called on Tweed the silver-white. It was about ¾lb., a very lively, handsome, brilliant little fish, and, as I proved next morning, delicious eating. As to the real name of the silver-white, I believe that it is neither more nor less than a young white or salmon trout, and that is the opinion of many other good judges; it differs widely from the orange fin or black tail, which is the young of the bull trout. Pleased with the prospect of sport, we got on, without losing time, to the Kirk-end. Half-way down I saw a large fish come up, and, as it looked a feeding rise, I marked the spot carefully. It was a few yards below two sunken stones, over which the water swirled and eddied temptingly. At length we got to the cast. I threw over it, and, thinking to coax him, let the fly sink deeply; just as the line was at its full extent, I felt something touch it as if it had brushed against one of the stones over which I was fishing; raising the point slightly to clear it, I felt the slightest possible tug—more like an obstruction than a tug. "There he is, sir!" sung out Willie, who had his eye on the rod-top; and "there he is," I felt; and I struck sharply, but I was too late, for the cunning rascal had cheated me. Fishing so deeply there was no rise to be seen; and he came so gingerly that I was deceived at the first pressure, and too late at the second. I felt like an abandoned criminal. "Hey, faith, that's a big yan! That's joost the way those big yans often rise. Hey, mon, what a pity ye didna yack it into him!" quoth the boatman. But it was of no use crying over spilt milk. I anathematised my want of judgment and decision, but that was useless now—of course he wouldn't and didn't come again. As I had marked the fish, and was fishing over the spot where he had risen, I have no doubt it was the fish I saw, which was a fish of from 15lb. to 20lb., as I judged.

In a stream called, I think, the Kitchen Craigs, I got another rise, but I made no mistake this time; indeed, the fish took care of that, and I stuck fast in a lively grilse, which jumped about like a pea on a hot shovel, leaping and running bravely. He soon came to net, however, a beautiful little fish of between 4lb. and 5lb. weight, just fresh from the sea, with the sea-lice on him thickly, and as bright as silver sheen. Things were certainly improving.

We now turned upwards again, as evening was coming on, and I took off my silver-body with which I had killed all my fish, and put up a white-wing. Fishing up I came again to the Kirk-end, and at the head of it I got hold of an obstinate sullen fish of nearly 8lb. He was not very handsome, being rather red, nor did he show much sport, but he was not landed until it got almost too late to try for another. I had had a very fair day since lunch-time, having, including the silver-white, "killed five sea-fish out of six rises," as Willie said—which is not bad work; and I make no doubt but the sixth would have shared the fate of the others if I had but been aware of him. So tackling up, I bade adieu to Tweed—indeed, this was the last time I used a rod in the North.

The Tweed flies I used were the dun-wing, the drake-wing, and the white tip. These flies are well-known, and have been described over and over again. The fly I killed best with was the silver-body—a grey, ghostly, very shrimpy-looking fellow; the body all silver foil, the tail golden pheasant topping, with a small sprig of jungle cock; two or three turns of silver twist with yellow tag above it, and one turn of black herl over the butt of the tail; silver twist, with light grey hackle, with black centre and points; grey drake feather hackled at shoulder, with a mixed wing composed of strands of bustard, gold pheasant tail and tippet, puce macaw, brown drake, green parrot, red under-feather of gold pheasant's tail (two or three sprigs of each of the above), with a good bunch of grey drake, gallina, and wood duck, and a single topping over all with blue macaw veins, make a very nondescript cold grey wing, if properly mixed. I have been particular in describing this fly, as I found it a killer. The white tip is a well-known Tweed fly, with a dark body, and a pure white wing. It shows well at night, and should always be the *dernier ressort.*

With regard to trout-flies for the north, the southern angler should not listen to any nonsense that half-bred fishermen talk about Cockney tackle and London flies, and who advise him to leave his London-made flies at home, and trust to the village tinker and all that sort of fustian. You can get the best materials in the world in London, if you only know how to select them. I found my southern flies kill well enough. So the southern angler should by no means leave his book at home, for the flies of the south are the flies of the north: the duns and spinners of the south are the duns and spinners of the north. But, if the young angler mistrusts his judgment, and fears or does not know what to select, he had better drop a line to Wright of Sprouston, or Forrest of Kelso.

Before leaving the subject of flies, I give a song, written I believe, by a well-known fisher on Tweedside, and sung also by him at various festivities. I have to thank the same friend for it who got me "The Troutin' Day":

THE SALMON FLY.

Come, see me dress the salmon-fly,
  With feathers bright and gay,
Of ev'ry hue and brilliant dye
  That tempts the scaly prey;
With azure pinions of the jay,
  The tail of buzzard brown,
Mixed with the gorgeous colours frae
  The golden pheasant's crown.

In harle from off the peacock's tail
  I'll wrap the polished steel,
And modestly will blend the hale
  Wi' freckles frae the teal.
The flossy silk, sae saft to feel,
  A'doon the breast will hing,
While hackles, bright as cochineal,
  Will form the under wing.

With purple from the gay macaw
  The topmost wings are drest,
And tinsel bright in mony a raw
  Binds round the gaudy breast.

A plume from out his orange crest
  The cockatoo will lend,
Which droops behind in graceful rest,
  To cover barb and bend.

My fly is dress'd—I'll throw the lure
  To tempt the salmon bold;
A deadly barb, both sharp and sure,
  All swathed in shining gold.
The brightest rose bears 'neath its fold
  The prickly thorn conceal'd,
While sweets that mankind dearest hold
  Aft rankest bitters yield.

Vice aft appears in Pleasure's garb,
  Let giddy youth beware—
Beneath may lie the polished barb,
  'Mong feathers bright and fair;
Deep hidden 'neath sic tinsel glare
  The wiles of life may lie,
And brilliant follies gild a snare
  As deadly as my fly.

The day after leaving Carham I had to go to North Shoreham to make inquiry of the fishermen and others regarding the encroachments of the French. While visiting North Shoreham —as a change from its herring barrels, offal, rotten weed, and general amalgamated association of stinks—I ran over to Bamborough to have a look at that gem of the north, the castle. I nearly missed seeing Bamborough, but rejoice that I did not, as the loss would have been irreparable, for it would be difficult for imagination to conceive anything grander or more magnificent than the *coup d'œil* of Bamborough Castle. As you approach it from the village, there is a simple massiveness of outline and conception which fills the delighted eye, and harmonises wonderfully with the real massiveness of the work itself. Rising from a rock which springs up abruptly from the sea-shore, it seems to have grown from it, and to be a part of itself. One face domineers the ocean, while the other keeps watch and ward over the land, and calmly gazes upon the rocky hill of Spindleston

Heugh (whilom the dwelling of the Laidley worm), which stands over against it frowning and snarling with ragged tooth-like rocks, as though it was ready at any moment to spawn forth from its crevasses another monster to destroy Bamborough and persecute creation, if it could only withdraw itself from the lordly, lion-like regard of that sublime old castle. This is strong praise, but I can only say that if I knew stronger I would use it, for I never saw anything of its kind that surprised or pleased me so much as Bamborough. There, too, was no bad taste—no sweeping and garnishing—no snobbery—no petty Roshervillean adornment—and, better than all, no hungry, empty-headed, chattering attendant to distract your senses and spoil your views. All was simplicity and repose. There was vigorous old age, appropriately clad, not befrizzled and becurled like an antiquated beau or a metropolitan grotto. An artist could repose on the rank grass that decks the sandhills around Bamborough, and gaze at it for hours without feeling repletion. It can hardly be called a ruin, though it dates from the Conquest, and portions of it even show Roman origin. The solidity and strength of the original building may be conceived when I state that time and ruin have touched but little of it, for not only is the castle habitable, but it is a most comfortable residence, and all the outbuildings are in good order and repair. There were kings of Bamborough at one time, and truly it is a regal residence; as a fortress, in the days of bows and arrows, it must have been impregnable, and even now Sir William Armstrong would find it a very hard nut to crack, for there are whole flights of steps in the solid stonework of the outer walls, which I should think in some places are forty or fifty feet thick. Beyond the castle are the Farn Isles, the scene of Grace Darling's exploit. Poor Grace! she was one of "those whom the gods love." The Farn islands from Bamborough, sleeping peacefully in the calm still sea, are inexpressibly beautiful and smiling; but when swept by the furious north-east wind—the roaring of the stormy surge, and the battling of the fierce currents that run between them, they must be a sublime and splendid spectacle. These islands abound in wild birds, which visitors formerly amused themselves by destroying, wasting powder and shot to show the little skill they possessed, as three-fourths of the birds were useless when killed. Various conveniences are kept ready in the castle for the relief of wrecks, which oft bestrew the fatal islands and the dangerous Budle sands. There are some noble charities also wound up in the existence of Bamborough, so that it is not only beautiful and grand, but confers very practical and solid benefits.

Two days after I was, thanks to a friend of Mr. Thompson's, shooting a moor but three or four miles inland from Bamborough, which, with the Farn Isles, lay, as it were, almost at our feet. It was a magnificent day, and we drove to the moor from Wooler. Half way we passed the village of Chatton. There is a whimsical anecdote anent Chatton which I give. Some years since a traveller, a stranger to the place, was wending his way towards Belford *viâ* Chatton, and, not knowing the road, he was afraid of missing his way. He accosted a man whom he met on the road, with "Can you tell me if I am on the right road to Belford?" Instead of answering the question, the stranger caught hold of his coat, and with a stupid smile said, "Hey, mon! what braw buttons ye gat! Faith, but their bonny anes." Seeing that the poor fellow was an idiot, the traveller released his coat, and got on out of the way as quickly as he could. About half a mile on, he met another stranger hastening along in a hurry. To him he repeated his question as to the road to Belford, whereupon the stranger, without answering it or noting it, said, "Hey, Jenny MacLauchlan's gan to kill a soo (sow), and a'm to have the blether (bladder). Hoo!" and with a shout, a skip, and a caper that fairly discomposed the traveller, the fellow bounded on his journey. "Good gracious, another idiot! The Lord be thanked," muttered the traveller, "they were neither of them mischievous, and I am well out of it," and he continued his journey with increased apprehension as to the road. About a mile onward he met a third stranger. "Sir, can you tell me the road to Belford?" he asked. "Mon," said the third stranger, "if ye gang to Sandy Scott's, dinna ye ate hairy crowdie;* it's a bad thing for a sair belly." And with this solemn adjuration and a great shake of the head, the third idiot continued his journey. "The Lord help us!" said the alarmed traveller to himself, "has the county lunatic asylum been broken open, and all the inmates turned loose? or is this the normal condition of this particular part of the country?" Ruminating on these questions, he reached Chatton at length, and then the thing was explained. There were three brothers named Mackenzie, all daft, but harmless, and all herds, and he had chanced to meet them one after the other.

The moor was a nice level one, very easy to walk, and contained mixed shooting, but the grouse were wonderfully wild for the time of year. It was only by walking round or over the tops of knolls, and by such means, that we could possibly get a shot at them. On the open they were up and away at two and three hundred yards, and sometimes at double that distance. We managed to bag a couple of brace, but we had relied rather on the black game, for which the moor was very favourable, from the little streams that intersected and the quantity of covert along their banks; but they were very scarce, and we only found one old hen and a brace of fine young cocks, which I bagged with a right and left (they were very easy shots), and a few wary old cocks, that were wilder even than the grouse. We found several snipe, but, as we were shooting with very large shot, to accommodate the wildness of the grouse, they mostly managed to slink off between the crevices, only one falling to friend T. The bag was a mixed one, consisting of two brace of grouse, one of black cock, one brace of partridges, one snipe, a couple of hares, and a rabbit.

The next day we went partridge-shooting at Wooler, on a small farm shot over by T. We did not start till mid-day, and, as the

* Crowdie is a species of porridge.

turnips were thick and high, we lost a good deal of time, hunting for cripples; but we managed to bag fifteen brace and a couple of hares—almost all of them being done to death in one field, and that not a large one. The corn was not all down, there being a patch or two about, and we did not go into it, or we might easily have increased our score. The next morning we went to another little farm, a plot of two small turnip-fields, and three or four stubbles, appertaining to the parsonage. There were a couple of coveys in it, and we knocked them about a little, getting four brace and a half out of them, when it came on a pelting rain, and we left them, and went home to lunch. After lunch we went to the other farm again which we had shot over the day before. The rain had washed out all scent; the dogs could do nothing, and most of the birds were scattered, from our having killed their parents I suppose the day before, and they would not stir until you almost trod on them, and hardly then. It was not at all favourable, and we got only the same number as we had bagged in the morning.

On the ensuing day I paid my last visit to the grand old Cheviots, for we shot Heathpool Lynns again. We had very bad luck with the black game. As we were beating along the bottom, where we had found them on the previous occasion, our attendant, who was stationed on the side of the hill to look out, walked into the very midst of seven of them. They went away like skyrockets off the moor. We then tried a place called the Black Bog, and instead of approaching it along the bottom, as we ought to have done, we very foolishly came in at the top, and a fine brood of eight or nine got up wild, only one passing me within shot. He fell to my first barrel, among the rushes in the bottom; my second being directed at a bird that was evidently hit by my companion, but got off.

After this we only found a few old cocks, which were unapproachable, and one young cock, which got under my feet and flew towards T., so that I could not shoot, and T. being, I suppose, equally in difficulty, somehow managed to let him off.

We killed eight brace and a half of partridges, one blackcock, three hares, and two couple of rabbits; and, leaving the game at the farmer's, to be sent home next day, we trotted home gaily, over the shoulder of old Yeavering Bell, to whose bold crest, gleaming in the silver moonlight, I paid a last and lingering adieu.

The wandering angler may do far, far worse, than spend a summer among the Cheviots.

Before leaving the Tweed, it may be well to say a few words about the trouting upon the Tweed and its tributaries, on which an angler might spend many summers with advantage. Much of the Tweed, particularly of the upper section, is open to anglers; and, indeed, little difficulty is thrown in the way of trout fishers until they reach Galashiels. From there to Kelso the proprietors more or less object to strangers, though there are portions of the river still open; but there is quite enough of Tweed and its tributaries still open to render the angler quite independent of leave. From Kelso to Carham the river is open to trouting, as is most of the water from Wark downwards. All the lower portion is well marked, and the towns and villages on the bank have all excellent inns for the anglers' accommodation. On the upper part, supposing the angler starts from Innerleithen, or, say, Peebles, he will find a convenient inn at Broughton. The next is at the Crook, and some little distance above there is, or used to be, an inn called the Bield. These points of refuge will enable the angler to fish most of the upper waters of the Tweed and many excellent tributary burns. But—and this applies to many other inns in the wilder parts of Scotland in August—it is as well to find whether quarters can be had beforehand, as the inns are frequently full of grouse-shooters; and even before this anglers and artists often keep them full for weeks together. From this the angler can cross over to Tibbie Shiel's, fishing up Talla and down Meggat Water—a first-rate burn. Here he has St. Mary's Loch and the loch of the Lowes, both holding fine trout, and the latter pike and perch; and thence he can either work the surrounding district, or make down the Yarrow to the Gordon Arms, whence he has the choice of fishing down the Ythan, *viâ* Traquhair, to Innerleithen; or he can continue on down the Yarrow, *viâ* Yarrow, to Selkirk; or he can cross to the Ettrick at Tushielaw—an inn will be found half-way to Selkirk, at Ettrick-bridge; but portions of the Yarrow and Ettrick are preserved. Tib Shiel's needs no notice of mine; it has a world-wide reputation already. The tributaries of the Tweed often deserve the name of rivers; and these, again, are subdivided into fine streams, fed by innumerable burns, all of which more or less hold trout, a few only of which are really closed to the angler. On the south bank, we have first the Till, with its tributaries, the Glen, College, and Bowmont, many portions of which are open to anglers, though the Glen is the least so; but enough has been said of them. Then comes the Teviot, a considerable river, with its tributaries, the Kale, Oxnam, Jed, and Ale Water, the last being the largest. Some of these streams produce capital trout, but they are preserved in parts, and much polluted in parts. It would, of course, be well for the angler to find out which parts are preserved, and the limits, which can hardly be given here, as they may be altered yearly, as proprietors take up the whim of preserving. The lower part of Teviot is preserved by a club at Kelso, but I think tickets can be had. Starting from Kelso, the angler will find fairly convenient stations on most of these streams, and on some of them towns of some size, with railway accommodotion. The next stream of note is the Ettrick, which is joined a little above Selkirk by the Yarrow, which flows from St. Mary's Loch. Both of these streams are more or less preserved in the lower portions; they are excellent streams, and have already been referred to. Then comes Manor Water, a few miles above Peebles, a fair stream, with abundance of small trout, and some good ones in the lower reaches, and in Glenwrath burn. Several fair-sized burns then come in, and next Talla Water, a fairish trouting stream. Crossing over to the north side, we come on Biggar Water, which is not so good as it used to be, and where the trout are scarce, and the Lyne, which is worth notice, being one of the finest fishing streams that flow into Tweed, and with excellent burns; and Eddlestone, which runs in at Peebles, and is not worth notice; and next the Liethen, which runs in at Innerleithen, where, as is the case with many other waters, there are plenty of trout, but small; and next the Gala, which debouches at Galashiels—there are plenty of good trout in it, but it is a good deal fished; and next the Leader, an excellent stream, most of which is preserved, three smallish bits only being open. Some distance below Kelso the Eden falls in, but it also is almost closed to the angler, as is the Leet, which comes in at Coldstream. The Whitadder is the last, and certainly the best of all the tributaries of Tweed; its largest feeder, the Blackadder, holds large trout, but is a good deal preserved, though there are parts of it open, but it is not nearly as nice a stream to fish as the Whitadder, and the Whitadder is not preserved to nearly the same extent as the Blackadder, though it has been so overfished and so unfairly fished that several proprietors are beginning to talk of closing their water to the public. In the season the Whitadder holds grilse, quantities of bull trout, and plenty of whitling. The upper waters and head tributaries abound with small trout; the stations, too, at Allanton, Dunse, Ellemford, and Longformacus are well placed and convenient. Anglers should be careful in fishing these waters not to give offence, if possible, to the proprietors, but to behave as sportsmen and gentlemen if they wish these privileges to be continued. For in many instances, where waters have been closed to the public, this has frequently been caused by the gross misconduct of wandering fishermen, who have no notion of how they ought to behave when walking over the property of others. Anglers should always strive to be unobjectionable and inoffensive, and, beyond all, should do their best to avoid trespassing where water is preserved. This is the last of the Tweed tributaries, most of which can be got at by rail from Berwick; while in Beloe of Coldstream, Wright of Sprouston, and Forrest of Kelso, the angler will find first-rate purveyors of angling requisites. From the head of the Tweed the head waters of the Clyde can be struck as they intermingle.

SECOND RAMBLE.

CHAPTER XIV.

THE START—A TEMPERANCE HOTEL—A TEMPERANCE DINNER—A PLEASANT EVENING—BAG-NETS ON DEE AND DON.

ONE of the most difficult things to accomplish is a good start. In racing, in rowing, in coursing, and in commencing a narrative, a good start is everything. The next best thing to making a good start is the making up for a bad one. Now, I made a bad one, but of that anon. Let us begin at the beginning. The first thing the angler considers, when he is about to start upon an excursion, is the momentous one of tackle. Quite wonderful is the lot of things, never wanted before, which all of a sudden he finds himself in need of. It is bad enough if he is only going to fish one river; but if he is going to fish from half a dozen to a dozen, it is then necessary that he should be armed at all points and provided against all necessities. I don't know how many visits I paid to Farlow's. I must have bored that most patient of tacklemakers to death: I must have sat upon him like an incubus: I must have been as bad as the "fiery brown" to poor Martin Kelly, who died of it. Many were the conclaves, and deep was the erudition called forth in those all-important consultations. I had intended to start on Thursday; but just before starting, a matter of business occurred to delay me. Two days were lost by it, and I was only able to get off on Saturday. I always prefer the night train, as one gets over in sleep a great deal of the long, wearisome twenty-hour journey to Aberdeen. Accordingly, on Saturday night, I got to the Great Northern, and then found that we could not book further than Edinburgh, in consequence of the objection to travelling on the Sabbath in Scotland.

I determined, however, to go to Edinburgh, as it wonld give my friend Chalkley—who accompanied me in search of the picturesque, he not being much of a fisherman—an opportunity of seeing that city; and it would give me an opportunity of calling upon my kind friend, the editor of *The Scotsman;* and thus our rather untoward start would be turned to a fair account. I will not describe our journey. We had the carriage to ourselves, and we rather enjoyed it. But at length we were shunted out at Edinburgh. I had never stopped there for a night, and could not call to mind the names of any of the best hotels, so I asked the guard, who had been very attentive, to tell me the name of the best.

"Well, sir, ye see there is the Waverley; that's a capital hotel; but then it is a temperance hotel, and perhaps that won't suit you."

I fear that I made some strong observations on temperance hotels in general, for he said quickly, "Ah! then, sir, you had better go to Quilp's, for that is a capital hotel." I am circumstantial in my account of how I got there, as I do not wish it to be believed that I went there knowingly.

We went to Quilp's: we breakfasted, and then walked round the town, and went up to Arthur's Seat, and the Castle—and saw the lions, in fact, returning a little before dinner-time. There was a table-d'hôte at five o'clock, as I had been told, and I determined to join it. It was a few minutes before dinner when Mr. R. called on me. He wanted me to dine with him, but I had already elected to dine at home.

"Well," he said, "You will come in afterwards, perhaps, and take your wine with me, as of course you will not get any here."

"Not get any!" quoth I. "Why not?"

"Why, I suppose you are aware that this is a temperance hotel?"

"A what!" I exclaimed, bouncing off my seat with amazement; while poor Chalkley, who is ordered by his physician to live generously and to take a fair allowance of wine and a moderate supply of spiritual comforts, fairly gasped at him in unspeakable horror—"A temperance hotel!" The words were spoken, and he was clearly serious.

"You don't mean it?" He nodded. It was the nod of doom to all who know what it is to be a stranger in the town of Conventicles, encompassed in the "sanctified bends of the bow" upon a Sunday. I looked at the dinner-table. Sure enough there was a huge water-bottle to every two men, and tumblers enough to swim in; but there was no wine glass to be seen. The spirit within me—which was principally bile, by the way, incidental upon railway refreshments—was grievously moved. I know I was wroth, I fear I was profane. But I soon cleared up, for there was a "sweet little cherub that sat up aloft," in the shape of a brandy-flask, in my bedroom, locked up in my portmanteau; and I said as much.

"Then, whatever you do, don't let the landlord know it, for he is a desperate fanatic in his profession, and I expect he will consider it incumbent on him to 'cast out the spirit,'" said my visitor, rising to take his leave.*

Shall I describe that dinner?—a dinner presided over by fanatically temperate commercials, a species of being which, judging by experience, is a shade or two more disagreeable than intemperate ones would be. Shall I tell how dreadfully they ate and drank, and how that water disappeared?

"Sammy," I whispered to poor Chalkley, who has a hydrophobia for water as a drink, and who laboured in serious silence over the unmoistened viands—"Sammy, there's a young man on the next form but two as has drunk nine tumblers and a half of water, and is a swellin wisibly afore my werry eyes."

"Don't!" said Chalkley; "dreadful, isn't it? I never

---

* R. himself got a clip from the temperance flail, for when the landlord heard from him how the mistake had arisen, he said, "Weell, weell, Meester R., it joost puzzled me sairely to ken hoo ony friend o' yours ever cam' this gate." He told us the story in the evening, even at the expense of a laugh at his own cost, but it was too good to be lost.

experienced anything like it. I'd give a sovereign for a glass of sherry!"

"No go, old fellow; try the water. Only think of the good you are doing to the microscopic world of science in preparing subjects of animalcular interest for future investigation!"

Shall I detail how they carved? and how one commercial, whose ideas of carving were of the most primitive kind, shaved a ham sideways, cutting off all the fat at the first slash, and leaving none for future consumers; and how he asked, "If any gent said 'am?" and how several gents did say "'am"—very few, in fact, saying anything else when they desired that viand. Shall I tell how a villanous old kelt, which blushed for its untimely appearance at table, being red where it should not be, and not where it should, was served up to us under the fiction of salmon; and how *they* ate it, and how I rejoiced at the way they would want brandy some hours after, and wouldn't get it; and how many other things filled up the sum of our great affliction? No; I forbear!

In time—for all things have an end, even the temperance dinner (which is, mind you, a pretty long operation, too, for temperance in drinking by no means includes temperance in eating)—came to an end, and we betook ourselves to the more congenial and hospitable home of our friend.

He had asked the late Mr. Stewart, the "practical angler," who was about the best trout-fisher in Scotland, and another friend or two occupied in the guild of letters, to meet us; and we had a delightful evening among practised conversationalists, in which wit without coarseness, and humour which would have been acceptable even to the most scrupulous, ruled the hour. Stories of the Wilsons, scraps from Tibbie Shiel's, anecdotes of leading professors and reverend divines—lights of science, and pillars of the Conventicle—followed each other in rapid succession. But time, the inexorable severer of the best of friends, put an end to our enjoyment. In Scotland hospitality is a much more active virtue than it is in England, and even the most serious business cannot prosper unless a libation be poured out on the shrine of Ben Nevis and Lochnagar; talking *is* dry work, no doubt of it, and I fear me that if we had pulled up at the door of our hotel, and told our host how much of contraband material we had about us, how subversive our contents were to the dearest and most cherished principles of the constitution of his uncongenial caravansery, he would never have allowed us to "run our cargoes," but we should certainly have had to pass the night on the door-step, in penance for our short, or rather long—comings. On the way home, Chalkley, moved by the spirit, insisted on singing, in a nasal and lugubrious key, something which commenced in this wise—

> Good people, who around do dwell,
> Abjure the temperance hotel;
> For if you don't you might as well
> At once be doomed to go ——.

"Ye munna mak that noise, mon," said the harsh voice of a guardian of the night, breaking off ruthlessly Chalkley's harmony.

"Whatsh that he shays?" he asked.

"Says you musn't make that row," I replied.

"Row," said the indignant improvisatore. "Row! whatsh he call a row? Wash only shinging a hymn. Wheresh harm in shinging a hymn on Shunday night?" and he wanted to argue the point, but I wouldn't stand that, as the Scotch bobby, as a rule, is not amenable to argument.

On Monday morning we made our flitting, and as the train stopped for half an hour at Perth, I walked across to Mr. Pople's, at the British Hotel, to ask what was doing. He told me that the river had not fished well yet, and little had been done; but it was getting into order, and they soon expected to be making good bags. On rolled the train through a rather interesting country, until at length we closed up with the Aberdeen coast. The coast looked smiling and pleasant, and glimpses of little coves and caves, with tiny strands, dotted with rocks, over which the green water played and circled like dimples on the cheek of beauty, greeted us as we rushed onwards. The morning was calm and lovely, and the fresh sea-breeze was exceedingly invigorating to asphyxiated Londoners. Here and there the white wing of a gull, or a sail far out in the horizon, lightened up the picture. But there was an alloy even in a scene so fair, and my wrath was greatly roused by the sight of the bag-nets which fringe the coast at every available point. At every jutting of the rocks, at the entrance and exit to every little bay, cove, or nook, there were one, two, and even three sometimes, of those infernal machines blocking up the fair way of the salmon, and plundering the rivers. Every time we could catch sight of the shore, there were bag-nets, bag-nets, bag-nets! I should think that in that fifteen or so of miles south of Dee mouth there must be—I would almost say—hundreds of them, to judge by what I saw. Now, bag-nets are expensive things to work, and it takes a good many fish to pay the wear and tear before any profit can be realised, and the quantity of fish they must rob the rivers of is enormous. Mr. Russell, in his admirable work on the salmon, states that the Dee and Don are injured by these nets to the loss of 18,000*l.* of yearly rental; and I have very little doubt but that he is right in that estimate.

Meantime, I hear that little is doing up the Dee; that the season is not so good as it was expected it would be. The fish have not got up yet. But how it was to be expected the fish could get up, or how long it would take them to run the gauntlet in and out of all the bag-nets between Stonehaven and Aberdeen—to say nothing of the tremendous draft nets, which require curtailing too, at Aberdeen—I am sure I don't know; and how it is that any fish get to the river at all until the extreme end of autumn is a wonder. For, to look at the ingenious way in which these nets intercept the salmon's course, one would be fairly amazed that any fish at all should escape them. One comfort is, that after having fished out the rivers, they will fish each other out. Meantime rod-fishing is worth 10*l*. a-week on the Dee, and people are glad to pay it, and think themselves well off if they get a fish a-day for it. Contrast the position of the rod-fisher and the bag-netter, and I think my readers will own that there is a very large screw very loose indeed somewhere.

CHAPTER XV.

THE DON—KINTORE—PISCICULTURE AT ABERDEEN—CRUIVES OF DON—THE DON AT INVERURY AND ALFORD—THE DEE FROM ABOYNE TO CAMBUS-A-MAY.

"THERE'S cauld kail in Aberdeen," I believe—though in what particular part of Aberdeen that undesirable vegetable preparation may flourish, I cannot say: certainly we did not discover it. Our kail was very superior in quality, well cooked, and abundant, for our host of the Royal did his best to make us comfortable, and to show us all that was to be seen. I looked up my old acquaintance Mr. Brown, the inventor of the phantom minnow, which is the very best artificial bait ever yet invented, who brought me a few specimens of his cunning handiwork in the fly way, as superior slaughterers on the Dee and Don, to test; and I decided to stay over the next day and go up the Don, on a part of which Mr. Brown has a ticket. Accordingly on the next morning we made a start up to Kintore. The Don is a very fine salmon river, and perhaps one of the best trout rivers also, in Scotland, the part up about Alford being particularly famous as a trout water. It is said to be a late salmon river, but I fancy the reason it is a late river is because the salmon cannot get up earlier, however good their intention, as the stream is blocked by all manner of mills and a set of cruives, of which I will speak presently. There are paper mills on the river, which are not very particular to a little refuse, I am told. When will the Legislature take the misdeeds of mills and factories in hand?

The Don runs through a fertile agricultural country, and this would, of course, account for its giving such good trout. The trout are plentiful, and run up to 4lb. weight, and sometimes even larger. A singular contrast is presented by the two rivers which empty themselves at Aberdeen; for while the Don is of such a character as I have described, the Dee runs through a sterile tract of wild moorland; so that there is an old rhyme which says—

> A rood o' Don's worth twa o' Dee,
> Unless it be for fish and tree:

the Dee being a superior salmon-stream to Don, and the upper portions clothed with valuable woods. But to return to the Don. A long stretch of the Don, between Aberdeen and Kintore, is very dead, dull water; and this, it is said, abounds with pike, though the pike do not grow of any large size; still they no doubt take sharp toll of the smolts. The water at and above Kintore is pretty salmon water—sharp streams and fine pools; and the river is easy to fish and wade. Just the reverse again with Dee, which is hard to fish, and awkward and even dangerous to wade. Rods were soon ready, and we went to work, I using one of Brown's dun turkey-winged flies; and Brown following me with the phantom; while Chalkley walked the bank and rejoiced in the picturesque. We fished, and we fished, but we saw nothing but a few dead kipper-kelts, which had died after spawning. And here is another contrast; while many of these dead kelts are seen on Don every season, very few are seen on Dee. I got a pull from a fish of about four pounds, under a large bush, but I scratched him smartly and he would not come again; and Brown got a haul at the minnow.

"Here's a good pool up here," said Brown; "we call it 'The Dark Nuik (nook);' and if there's none of those rifle-laddies there, pop-poppin' aboot, we may see a fusshe there—though he'll be a kelt, mayhap, for the chances are twenty to one in favour of a kelt."

I could not quite make out the rifle allusion till we came to the pool, when it was quite plain enough. They had stuck their target and butt up on the bank, about the centre of the cast; there being a straight range along the bank just there, and a high cliff to take stray balls on the other; and, consequently, when there is practice going on, it is not possible to fish the cast, which, considering it is the best cast on the water, is rather trying. However, there was no practice to-day, so to work we went; and as the cast was too long for the minnow, Brown put up a fly. I fished it down about two-thirds, but the wading became too deep for my "Fagg's;" so I gave it up to Brown, who had wading breeks, and who could therefore command the lower part. And here he got a pull, and after a fair amount of suspicious rolling and tumbling I tailed out about the best kelt I ever saw. He was wonderfully "weell mended;" and but for a little redness of the vent, and breadth of the fish at the anal fin, it could not have been told from a clean fish. It was thoroughly well-coloured and shaped; and there was no parasites in the gills, which were as bright and as red as need be. We did no more, and it came on a heavy snowstorm, so we tackled up, our only spoil being three trout, of which two came to the salmon-fly and one to the minnow. Two of them were in capital condition for the time of year, being half-pounders; the other, a pound fish, was rather dark on the belly. We ate the bright ones for breakfast, and very good they were.

The next morning Mr. Robertson took us to see an apparatus for incubating salmon ova, set up by Mr. Adams, the manager of the Don and other fisheries. Mr. Adams had erected his apparatus (which consisted of some thirteen or fourteen large slate troughs three parts filled with gravel, on the old plan) in a small office opening out of the ice-house; and the cistern, which supplied a never-failing flow of the Don water, owing to constant pressure being on, was actually in the ice-house, so that a low temperature could always be kept up. In these troughs he had some 40,000 ova, and outside he had two other troughs containing a further number just hatched out. These fish, when reared, are to aid in replenishing the Dee and Don. A spar out of one the cruives would answer the purpose far more effectually to my mind. However, Mr. Adams is sanguine in interesting many of the proprietors in the work of artificial hatching and rearing, and expects to get it done upon a much larger and more complete scale; and I trust his hopes may be realised, as it is a step in the right direction, and great praise is due to Mr. Adams for the trouble and pains he has taken in the matter. No one who has not had the charge of such an apparatus can appreciate the amount of trouble and anxiety consequent upon it. After showing us these matters, he took us to see a sight which I confess was rather less gratifying to me—viz., the cruives of the Don. I had wished to show my friend Chalkley a salmon freshly hauled out of the water; and as the only chance in the then state of the water was up at the cruives, we walked up. On the way we discoursed on the smallness of the usual size of the spring fish on the Dee and Don, and Mr. Adams told us that the average size was decreasing rapidly in the Don; that whereas, some years ago, the average for salmon was 13lb., last year it had sunk to 10lb.—a great falling off; and if I may judge of the fish I saw at the fish-house and at the cruives, this year it will be considerably lower, as I do not think one of the fish I saw, out of hard upon fifty, would have scaled 10lb.

At length we reached the cruives, which are pleasantly and romantically situated under hanging woods. The weir, to my astonishment, was without a queen's gap; and on my return home I turned out "Paterson" and looked to the Scotch Act, and, to my further surprise, there was no provision whatever about gaps. Regulations as to the *cruives* and their construction are left in the hands of the commissioners; but not a word about gaps. To return to the cruives on Don. There was more water than usual coming down, and the consequence was that the boxes were under water, and could not be got at. This, I think, is in consequence of the dyke being put up so high, in order to prevent enough water going over the waste part, which would perhaps let salmon up it, and it drowns the boxes. The dyke is also so long and straggling that whatever water does come over is too thin for salmon to get over; and when a flood comes on, the boxes cannot be opened, owing to what is called stress of weather, but which is in reality the bad construction of the waste dyke to the cruives. Of course it may be said that if the water comes over the cruives, the salmon could go over them too; but then it is a question whether the salmon would do so, but would not rather go into the boxes and remain there; and if these are set, and cannot be got at when a spate is on, the Sunday slap cannot be of much use. The best way would be not to allow the boxes to be railed in or covered at the top. Mr. Adams told me, however, that little was really done in the cruives, as the upper heritors had, sometime since, compelled them to set the spars of the hecks full three inches apart, which would let a fish of considerable size through; and that, if it were not for the net which is kept going below the boxes, the fishery would not pay them. This, of course, may be so; and many fish may, when they can avail themselves of it, go through. The cruives, however, certainly look rather severe, and the net keeps the ground pretty clean; and, although there are few clean fish up the river as yet, twenty were taken in the net at one haul that same morning—so it looks as if the Don would be an earlier river if it could. The great fear of most of the proprietors at the mouths of rivers is, that if they let many fish up they will never see them again. If they would only try to learn the problem of the Galway fishery, and if they would only argue, "If I let a salmon up, and that salmon deposits its eggs, a very large number of its progeny will come down, and I shall then probably reap ten or a dozen fish by deferring the capture of that one"—we should soon have a much better system prevailing in our rivers, and salmon would speedily be abundant. But the lesson seems hard to learn; the nimble ninepence being everywhere preferred, no matter at what cost and risk.

A short distance below the cruives is the Brig o' Balgownie, celebrated by Byron in "Don Juan." Attached to the bridge is a mysterious prophesy—to wit:—

Brig o' Balgownie black's your wa',
Wi' a wife's ae son and a mare's ae foal,
Down ye shall fa'.

Whether the wife has not produced the "ae son," or the particular "ae foal" has not come to light, or the two have not come into conjunction, the Brig stands yet, maugre the prophecy. Perhaps the wife's ae son is that celebrated New Zealander who is still in the womb of the future, and who, in the ripeness of prophetical fulfilment, shall contemplate the ruins of "mair brigs than ane." It is a single Pointed Gothic arch, with nothing very striking or formidable about it. I fear me that "the boy feelings of the youthful poet must have been somehow mixed up with the consciousness of an imperfect Gradus and a neglected Delectus, and, consequently, Balgownie's scenery, &c., &c., was just a transcendental way of "creeping like snail unwillingly to school."

There is a club on the Don, but, of course, it is a local one, and not easy to get into; but capital fishing can be had at one or two stations by staying at the inns. The nearest to Aberdeen, perhaps, is the Minton Arms, at Inverury, kept by Mr. Jno. Annand, where both salmon and trout can be taken. At the Forbes' Arms Hotel, kept by Mr. John Law, at the Bridge of Alford, about twenty-eight miles from Aberdeen, there is also good fishing for trout and a few salmon; while at the Haughton Arms Hotel, at Alford, kept by Mr. Reid, there is five miles of very fair trout fishing and a few salmon in April and May. Mr. Browne has very kindly furnished me with this information as to the Don, and also with a hint or two for the Ythan and Deveron.

On our return from the cruives, we bade adieu to our attentive host of the Royal, and, wending our way to the station, we were soon panting and puffing away up to Dee-side, on, I suppose, the slowest railway in the world, for Ballater. When we reached Aboyne, where the rail terminated, or, rather, I should say, died a sort of natural death, we found that the coach did not meet that train, but met the morning one ; so we were obliged to stay the night at Aboyne.

The Aboyne water is the very cream of the Dee, as, although it is a long way up, salmon usually run through the lower waters (the pools not being holding pools), and make straight for Aboyne. A part of this is rented by Mr. Cook, of the Huntley Arms,* and it is very fine water, and usually shows capital sport, so that the three tickets for it are generally all taken before the season. The ordinary take of a *good* rod is about forty fish to the month. The year before I was there, an unusually good year, one rod took eighty-four fish in the month. The fish are the property of the sportsman—so that, if this gentleman had been commercially-minded, it was not a bad thing. The spring fish in the Dee certainly run small, for, though ten or twelve-pounders, or even fourteen or fifteen, are not altogether strangers, the great run of the fish are about from five to nine or ten pounds. Much larger fish, however, do run late in the season, as 20lb. kelts are not uncommon. The Dee depends rather for its water upon the snows which remain in the mountains. A warm sun, a south-west wind, or a little warm rain for a few hours, will usually produce a spate ; and the prospects of the spring fishing may usually be gauged by the snow on the hills in March and April. April is the best month for Dee, if the water be right.

On arriving at Aboyne, I found, as I expected, all the rods occupied ; so my chance was out there. One gentleman offered me the opportunity of fishing with him the next day, when we could take pool and pool about—an offer so liberal and kind that I was glad to avail myself of that chance of seeing the water. Accordingly, next morning we drove a few miles up in the coach, which is, as Paddy would say, "an omnibus, bedad ;" and which was but thinly tenanted now ; although in the tourist season, as my acquaintance remarked, "you could'nt hang a snipe on it." Our plan was to send our traps on to Ballater by coach, and fish up

* Now Mr. Johnstone.

the water to Cambus-a-May, which was then the extent of the Aboyne water; thence I could walk the remaining four miles to Ballater. As we were starting, the news was brought in that a head of some fifty fresh fish were then going up under Aboyne-bridge, which was right joyful and acceptable news, as sport had not been first-rate hitherto, although I saw, when I arrived, a couple of fish which one gentleman had taken that day: they ran about 4lb. and 6lb. or 7lb. each. Soon the coach stopped, and set us down; and we made our way to the river-side, where the gillie was waiting us. Rods were to, and I commenced—with very little anticipation of doing anything, however, as the day was excessively bright and still, and the water low and exceedingly bright. Indeed, the Dee is almost always bright, and seldom discolours much, being, from its rocky bed, one of the clearest and brightest rivers in the country. I was surprised when, looking down upon a fine salmon-pool, called "the Red Brae" (which, by the way, is the name of some pool on most Scotch rivers), from a considerable height, to observe how distinctly I could see all the pebbles at the bottom, when the sun was shining. They say you can see every pebble in twenty feet of water. So you could in the Thames, at one time; but now, alas! you cannot see every dead dog at the bottom, even in twenty inches of water.

I worked on, however, from pool to pool, my companion taking a turn here and there, but we neither rose nor saw a fish; and when we got within about a mile of Cambus we parted—he fishing down towards Aboyne, and I taking the water up towards Cambus. He did his best to describe the casts I had to fish; but, not having a gillie with me, I soon found that my labours might be in vain, and that I might be thrashing nice-looking water, but not salmon-casts. Chalkley had been chirruping like a bird: the moors and hills delighted him exceedingly—he was saturated with the picturesque. His foot, like Mr. Briggs's, was clearly on his native heath, and his name *pro tem.* was unquestionably and unmistakeably Macgregor—particularly as he had bought a Scotch cap, which became him so much that persons paid him the compliment of mistaking him for a native. He now wandered off up-stream, promising to meet me above, and, being somewhat tired, I sat down, and indulged in a smoke and a reverie.

The silver Dee rolled at my feet, swirling and gurgling along from stream to pool, and brattling over shallows pleasantly enough. But the rifts and splinters of trees, the huge displaced stones, the remains of rails and fences carried away, and all the *débris* of the last winter's floods collected high and far up the banks; the torn and barked trees, and bushes everywhere rasped by masses of floating ice, showed what Dee could do when she came rushing from her mountain fastnesses in all the resistless force of the winter's spate. The mountain peaks, near and far, were clad with snow, and looked like silver-haired sons of old Terra watching over the body of their father. The brown heather glowed in the afternoon sun. The silver birches, feathering away up the mountain-side, the lovely and graceful maidens of the forest, with their hair unbound and shorn of their summer tresses, were relieved by the dark green firs in the background; while above them gigantic crags, split by the weather into many a rift and scaur, seemed nearly threatening to topple over into the river below. The cock grouse was crowing his challenge far and near; the little ouzel popping and dipping along from stone to stone, while a solitary sea-pyat, or oyster-catcher, flapped lazily up-stream, uttering from time to time its shrill melancholy pipe. It was a lovely scene! What a land this must have been in the fine old reiving, ranting days of the clan feuds! How I could fancy the secret march of the hostile clan stealing along through yon dark woods and overhanging rocks. And then the sudden attack on yonder village or the adjacent fortress. The sacking of the same, The Milonic feat of the "lifting" of the cattle. The triumphant march of the victors "bock again;" their pibrochs sounding louder and louder, and clearer and clearer, as they approach down the glen there—

commencing with an indistinct whine, and ending in a full-blown and overpowering bray of victory, until they burst into sight amid the glancing of steel, the tossing of bonnets, and waving of tartans. "By Jove! sir," as Chalkley would have remarked, "it was enough to make a fellow almost pleased to have his property reived and his throat cut in such a decidedly romantic and picturesque kind of manner, you know." Of course there is no accounting for taste, and pre-Raffaellism is a wonderful invention. But to my narrative

---

CHAPTER XVI.

BALLATER—CHALKLEY'S VAGARIES—ABERGELDIE—BALMORAL—PRINCE ALBERT AS A SPORTSMAN—NUMBER OF DEER—OTTERS ON DEE—PERILS OF A DEE SALMON.

NOT knowing the salmon casts, I sauntered on up the bank slowly, until I came to the little public-house at Cambus, expecting to find Chalkley there before me. But the picturesque apparently had gotten fast hold upon him, and he was not there. I sat me down upon a stone, and waited for more than an hour; but he did not come. Having about four or five miles to walk, on an unknown road, I thought it advisable, as it was getting towards dusk, to step on, imagining he must have gone on before, and I made my way on towards Ballater. Cambus-a-May, which consists of a public-house and a boat, is in the region of some mountains which are locally called the Cairngorm mountains, and fine specimens of cairngorms are often found thereabout. By the river-side about there seems to be a capital place for blackgame. I saw, at least fifty grey hens, all in one flock apparently, perched up in the tops of the birch-trees, feeding on the young buds, or some other comestible they found to their taste. I had also, while coming along the bank, disturbed several pairs of grouse, which were healthy and strong, and, if the early summer be propitious, will no doubt throw forward broods. Anon, I arrived at Ballater. Here I met my friend, Mr. S., just coming in from fishing; he had done nothing, but two of the other gentlemen had each a fish. Sport with him had been but middling; he had three fish on one day, but had had two or three blanks. The water was not quite right, being rather low, and there was not as many fish up as there had been the previous season.

But where was Chalkley? The Invercauld Arms had not received him under its fostering roof. I could see a mile or more up the road, and could not make him out. Evening was coming on, and I began to grow uneasy. He was not in the habit of moss-tramping. He was not accustomed to moors. He might lose his way, and wander about, goodness knows where. He might tumble into a bog-hole, and never tumble out again. He might fall over some crag or precipice—there were plenty about the Cairngorm hills—and never be found save by the eagles. And I thought of dismal tales of dark mysterious lochs, in silent misty glens, where mortal living foot had never trod; of savage crevasses; of being frozen to death in the snow, and then found, months after, like the traveller in the Canadian snow-storm—

> With his hat on his head, and the reins in his hand;
> The dog lay crouched at his master's feet—

frozen stiff in the foundered sleigh, while the beautiful "Morgan Brown" steed had floundered its last into the snowdrift. I commend those charming lines to such of my readers as have not read them. I know nothing in poetry so truthful and forcible as that picture. It occurred to me just then, and I fancied Chalkley with his hat on his head—he always liked to have his hat on his head—and with his empty flask, instead of the reins, in his hand; and—but, by Jove! he hadn't any flask. I remembered he would not take one. No whisky, and out on the mountains all night; for, as he had not come in yet, he *must* have lost his way! Things were getting serious—very much so. I got in a funk. I ordered a gig to go out somewhere, anywhere, in search of him; when, just as excitement was at its highest pitch, and everybody was very uneasy about him, in walked the delinquent, as smiling and satisfied as possible. Of course he would do so; I might have known it. That is just the way he always does. He thought I should have done something extraordinary, of course—walked back a few miles to Aboyne, I believe. However, we were all right now; and, as dinner was ready, we all went to it. Mr. P., his son Capt. P., my friend S., Chalkley, and I—we made a pleasant party. There was one other angler, a Mr. A., who had a rod on the water, but he did not join us. We five took all our meals together, and made a delightful evening when the dinner was disposed of, and the pipes and cigars put in requisition. Then came the history of the deeds of the day, in flowing chat—broken only, perhaps, by an occasional snore from the sleepy party in the easy chair. It was matter of common interest "how this one rose that fish three times at the point of the brae," and how "the other got the fish at the head of the moor-pool just before dark;" and after trying this or that, he succumbed to the charms of the "yellow eagle;" and so on. But the gossip of anglers is endless; it is a sport that can be talked and written about for ever.

There were no rods to be had on the river, all being taken up. So the next day I walked with Mr. S. down the north bank. Soon after we started it began to rain, and it rained off and on the whole day. The burns began to swell; indeed S. had to carry me across one, as I had no waders on—a proceeding which aroused Chalkley's bile. He was wet through, and accused me of detaining his macintosh in my carpet-bag for some occult mysterious purpose, and therefore he offered S. half-a-crown if he would drop me in mid-stream—a proceeding rendered very probable by the fits of laughter which seized upon S. at the serious manner in which Chalkley propounded his highly-advantageous bargain. We got safely over, though in a very tottering condition.

In one fine pool below a high bluff cliff, a good fish came up, and was hooked. After some play, just as his nose was brought to the gravel, off he went. Much vexed at his bad success, for this was the fourth fish running he had lost, Mr. S. went to work again, and, after fishing another pool, he thought to look at his fly, which was found utterly smashed—an accident one is particularly liable to on Dee-side, from the precipitous rocks at one's back. "Pity I didn't look at that before," quoth S., "might have saved my fish." On went another fly, and on went S. Two pools lower, in a fine run, up came a fish in mid-stream. He was a little red from long residence in the river, but was a good clean fish notwithstanding. After a turn or two, he went off too. We fished a few more pools; and as the water was now rising rapidly from thawing snow, we went home. The fish had possibly been disturbed by the rise a little, as both Mr. A. and the Captain had hooked and lost fish as well as Mr. S.

The next day the water was up a foot, and Mr. S. had the upper water, which runs up almost to Balmoral, but for a part of the way only on one side, the other belonging to the Prince of Wales and the Queen. On the way up we passed Abergeldie, a quaint, old-fashioned place, with all sorts of queer turrets and peaks, and a sort of Flemish mediæval look about it. It is not a large house. It is rented by the Prince of Wales for the shooting. They have a strong rope made taut across the river there, on which works a cradle, and by this means persons can cross the river or obtain anything from the opposite shore—which is a great convenience, as the high road runs hard by, and there is not a bridge either up or down for nearly four miles. Abergeldie has an interest of its own attached to it. It is beautifully placed, and groups of fine birch trees grace the banks of the river near it. It gave the origin to the song, the "Birks o'Abergeldie," and most appropriately too; but Burns, I think, very unjustly and unfairly robbed it of its fame by turning the old burthen of the song into "The Birks o' *Aberfeldy*." It was a place of strength in olden days, when reiving was in fashion. Balmoral we only got a peep of from the road, and it did not look so palatial a place as I expected.

The upper Ballater water is, to my fancy, prettier water than the lower; of course, being further up-stream, the fish do not run up there quite so soon; but to counterbalance this, it is not nearly so often fished, being rarely so more than once a day, and not often that, as the practice is to go up to the top and fish home to Ballater; whereas the lower waters are fished from both sides, and both out and home. Mr. S. got hold of a nice little fish just above Abergeldie, and the gillie was getting the gaff ready when, as the fish's nose touched the shore, he managed to make off, which was exceedingly provoking, as it made the seventh fish Mr. S. had lost after hooking. He had lately invested in a new and rather heavy greenheart rod, the top of which was unusually large and stiff, in order to pick the line off the water quickly, so as to facilitate long casting. New fish are usually rather tender in the mouth, and it may be that the stiff top did not give to every plunge so readily as it should, and thus the hold speedily cut out. I cannot account for his ill fortune in any other way. We fished very hard, pool and pool about; but we did not even see another fish, and eventually we scrambled into the cart, and so home to dinner; the captain having one fish and Mr. A. another, some others having been hooked and lost.

The next day we went down the south bank, fishing pool and pool about, but we did nothing. The captain, however, had a fish, and we ate most of him for dinner, and finished him off for breakfast. Mr. S. had unexpected business which called him away, and offered me the use of his ticket; but as I could not stay long, I used it for one day only before I left. The next day I had leave on the Balmoral water; but having letters to write and answer, did not get away so early as I could have wished. We drove to Balmoral, however, and I found one of the keepers awaiting me; a very nice, intelligent fellow he was, thoroughly versed in his business.

Balmoral is beautifully situated, and a more charming summer residence it would be difficult to conceive. Embosomed in woods, whence its more prominent towers and turrets peep forth most attractively, it is almost surrounded by high hills and lofty mountains, portions of which give admirable grousing, while other parts comprise the deer forest, which alone extends over some 40,000 acres. The grounds about the castle are not very extensive, and have not been spoiled by any attempt to make them appear what they are not. The moor and the forest have been partially cleared, and pleasant winding walks have been cut amongst the rocks, trees, and heather; but these distinguishing features of the Highland landscape flourish luxuriantly in all their native grace and beauty. Here and there a group of hardy shrubs may have been added to diversify the shades of green; but no violent changes have been attempted. The castle itself is much larger than would appear from the road, and is capable of entertaining a pretty large company. It is impossible to give any idea of it, as it is exceedingly and charmingly irregular in construction, being a collection of small turrets—some of them in the Flemish style, others in various styles; yet the eye dwells upon the mass of clean cut stone with pleasure. The outbuildings are disposed conveniently about the grounds—the stables here, the poultry-house there, the dairy elsewhere—peeping out from the trees, which also surround them on the hill-sides, more like Swiss chalets than outbuildings. The rapid Dee runs through the grounds, forming many a pleasant stream and pool.

I should very much have liked to have a look at the inside of the castle, of course; but Her Majesty has a very natural objection to having her private residences made show-houses of —and this one is especially sacred to her, for here her late husband spent many of the happiest hours of his life. It is delightful to hear the way in which he is spoken of by all here who came in contact with him. Elsewhere he could be misrepresented and slandered; here, at least, he was only known as a kind landlord and an honourable and worthy gentleman, who administered to the large estates under his control with a wisdom and liberality that endeared him to all around him. To point how misrepresentation was put in force in one instance, in trying to fix a want of true sportsmanlike feeling upon him, I cannot avoid referring to the old story of his firing into a herd of deer at random ("into the brown of them," as it is called), as a raw shot sometimes in moments of excitement fires into the brown of a covey of partridges without selecting any one in particular, and wounding many but killing none—a most unsportsmanlike proceeding. Now I took particular care to inquire about this matter, and to find out what sort of a shot Prince Albert was at deer. The keeper who was with me said that he was by far the best shot at deer with a rifle he had ever seen in his life. The Prince of Wales, he said, was a good shot, but he was not nearly so good as his father. Indeed no one he had ever seen could hold a candle to him. He had seen him kill deer dashing between the trees at speed, over and over again; and one day (the occasion, possibly, when he fired into the brown of them) six or seven deer came past him in one of the corries. He had with him three double rifles, and fired as the deer passed the six barrels in succession. Five of the deer fell dead in their tracks, and the sixth ran about a mile before it fell. Each deer was slain handsomely and fairly with the single rifle bullet. There are not many men in England or elsewhere who can ditto this feat, and it is most improbable that any one capable of it would ever "fire into the brown" at any game. I made other inquiries as to this fact in other quarters, and the story was confirmed in every particular. Many of the hills round about are crowned with mementos of Prince Albert, raised spontaneously by the tenantry, whose grief at his loss might reasonably enough rest upon some solid foundation.

There are nearly one thousand head in the royal deer forest; I saw very many slots of the deer in the snow on the river-bank, where they had crossed to feed on the turnips when driven down from the mountains by the deep snows. Some of the slots were very large. The grouse-moors are abundantly stocked, and very extensive. On these moors the farmers are never allowed to burn the heather at all. They come to the keepers and say what they would like burnt, and the keepers burn it, taking care to burn it in patches; and, as most of the burning is conducted when the snow lies in patches over the moors, the burning never can go too far, or get beyond control, as it is speedily extinguished by the snow. To those who do not know of this system of burning, I strongly recommend it. I saw it in progress, and it answers capitally.

I tried the pools near the castle, but got no rise. At length I came to the iron bridge across the river, and just below it was a nice-looking cast. I had made a few throws, and was raising my line—which appeared to be sucked into the eddy behind a rock—when I found some resistance—I raised it higher, and I felt a tug. I tightened it, and found that a salmon had kindly hooked himself without my knowledge. I had seen no rise, and felt no pull. He showed himself once, and was a nice clean fish of about 10lb. or 11lb.; but he wabbled about so strangely that I could not make him out. Presently the hook came away, and on the point of it was a scale, so that he had been hooked foul, and must have rolled across the line as I raised it. I fished on some distance, but did nothing until I got near to Abergeldie, where, in a fine broad pool, I got a rise; but nothing more. I gave the fish five minutes, and then went at him again, letting the fly go much deeper in the water—a practice which I invariably adopt whenever a salmon rises and refuses. It will nearly always bring him to hook; and this time, sure enough, he took it fiercely enough. He gave a little nice play, and duly came to gaff—a good fish, nearly 6lb., though a little coloured from his residence in the fresh water. In a very fine stream, perhaps the best-looking in all the upper water, I got a rise and a pull from a fish, which, of course, had seen all he desired, and would not come again. Some distance further on, the keeper, who had the rod for a cast or two, rose another fish; but he declined also, and I suspect must have tasted the feathers. We saw no more, but got to our dog-cart, and so home, crossing a fine burn, the Muick, a tributary of the Dee, which flows from Loch Muick, a lake up amongst the mountains, amidst magnificent scenery. I had not time to hunt after the picturesque, but Chalkley, who pilgrimaged to it, described the falls and the rocks, &c., &c., as lovely. The lake and burn give capital trouting in the season. Close to the lake Prince Albert had a small hunting-lodge built, just large enough to accommodate him for the night, when he was up there shooting, to save the trouble of coming back to Balmoral. The Queen often rode up and joined him there.

Ballater is charmingly situated, and forms a sort of watering-place for the Aberdonians, who flock out there in the summer time, taking lodgings and enjoying the invigorating mountain air, and excursioning to Balmoral, Brae Mar, and even Blair Athol; while, for picnicking, Ben Muick, Loch Muick, Craigendarroch—a remarkable wooded crag, hard by—and many other spots, form most agreeable refuges, where quarters of lamb, lobsters, salads, champagne, Bass, and general flirtation, form an agreeable relaxation to the pleasure-seekers.

The day after I fished Balmoral, I had Mr. S.'s ticket for the south side of the lower water. The water is pretty, but I fear there was no great abundance of fish in it. We wanted warm winds, melted snow, and fresh spates to bring fresh fish up. Above the town, in the higher part of the lower water, there are some very fine pools, especially the moor pool, one of the best and nicest casts on the water. I did nothing, however, beyond raising one fish, which came very shyly in the dusk of the evening; he had been pricked, I fancied, and on inquiry I found the captain had been very attentive to him, and often raised him.

There are a great many otters on the Dee, and some very large ones are frequently seen. Portions of fish were constantly turning up along the banks of the river; and the evening before I left, just above the bridge, there was found on a little island, a huge baggit, nearly 20lb. in weight, and full of roe, with only the otter's bite taken out of the back. Supposing an otter to require a fish a day, he takes as much as one rod would from the river during the rod-fishing season; only the otter is fishing all the year round. and if there be very many otters, as there are said to be, the wonder is that any salmon are left in the river. I strongly recommend the most stringent measures being adopted to keep them down. If these be not adopted they must speedily make a considerable clearance in the fish. They cannot be hunted in so large a stream, but they may be trapped and shot.

Nothing surprised me more than the great scarcity of kelts in the river. I never at that time of year saw anything like so few. There appeared to be hardly any, and I fear that the previous year must have been a very short breeding. If it was not, where were the kelts? It was supposed that by taking the nets off a month or so before the end of the season, a sufficient supply of fish could be insured for breeding purposes, but I do not believe that any such untimeous provision would be found to serve in the long run. This trumpery concession on the part of the nets amounts to saying, for nine-tenths of the season hardly a fish shall get into the river, and then, when they are no longer of any use to us, being gravid and unsaleable, you anglers may do what you can with them. We could not well outrage propriety by fishing on a Sunday, so we throw that in as well. Now the Sunday slap was all very well when there were only one or two sweep nets at the river's mouth to contend with. The fish ran in past the nets easily, and stocked the river, but now they have fifteen or twenty miles of bag-nets to run past, and the Sunday slap just transfers the fish from No. 99 bag-net to No. 95, half a mile nearer the river mouth mayhap, but hundreds, nay, thousands of miles from the upper waters of the river, if the doctrine of probabilities as to their reaching it be entertained. Moreover, now, instead of a few sweep-nets at the river's mouth, nets of vast capacity, which take the entire river in, are shot one after the other, so that the escape of a salmon is almost miraculous. Again, every pool and stream for miles up here has its little coble and net. The fish never knows when his enemies have done with him; and then proprietors wonder that the fish don't rest in the lower pools. Rest in the lower pools! I only wonder they rest until they reached the mountain-tops, where the first burnies come from. I wonder they don't jump clean out of the river to escape it altogether. Only imagine a man condemned to pass through London knowing that for a considerable part of the way his life is in constant and imminent danger. In street after street enthusiastic Volunteers, with double-barrelled breech-loading Enfields—if there be such things—lurk in doorways and blind alleys to pot him, as though he were a rabid cur, as he goes by. If he steps aside into an area, it is a pitfall or horrible *oubliette.*. From every window here and there, stalwart matrons hurl accumulated paving stones and heavy articles of domestic usance upon his devoted head. Yawning chasms, of which he has no warning, are dug by viciously-minded contractors in gas or water, with prepense malice, that his bones may be broken and his mangled body captured in the open sewers below. While from every bye street mad cabman and infuriated bus-drivers dash at him, seeking to run him down as a common foe and a scourge to humanity. Now I ask any one, after having threaded all this sort of thing from Bow to Oxford-street, whether he would consider himself justified in stopping in his tremendous race for life until he had left even Uxbridge far behind, and found himself out upon the breezy heaths of Beaconsfield. I know I wouldn't; but then I wouldn't go into a river at all—I would do as the stake-netters aver the salmon do, spawn in the sea among the rocks and islands, that the salt water might kill all the eggs; or, if any progeny survived contrary to all probability, I would be of the veriest old Saturn Saturnine, and eat 'em.

CHAPTER XVII.

LOCH KINNORD—CRATHES CASTLE—THE BARON OF LEYS—THE FEUCH — MACBETH'S CAIRN — DEE FLIES — BALLATER AND ABOYNE FISHERIES—THE YTHAN, INVERNESS—MACBETH—VITRIFIED FORTS—THE NESS—MR. SNOWIE.

BEFORE bidding adieu to Ballater, I must take occasion to praise the capital accommodation to be found at the Invercauld Arms, and the unvarying assiduity and attention of Mr. Cook to his guests. Nothing could be more *comme il faut* for an angler's hotel. 3*l.* 3*s.* a week was the tariff of board and lodging for anglers; for this they had a room to themselves; and one great trouble was avoided, viz., from the time the angler entered the inn until he paid his bill he had not to put his hand into his pocket; everything was charged at a regular fixed rate in the bill, even to the gillie's hire, which was 2*s.* 6*d.* per day and his whisky, which was limited and charged at 1*s.* per day. His lunch was included in the 3*l.* 3*s.* So that there was no doubt as to what one should pay for this, that, or the other; attendance and all was included in the bill, and at a much lower figure than nine anglers in ten would probably give if it were left to their own judgment. As these small matters are often amongst the worries of an angling trip, I recommend the practice to all landlords of angling hotels, as it gives their guests complete satisfaction at no loss to themselves. The provender was good and liberal, and the angler could have anything he liked to devour at any time of the day; and he could calculate beforehand to a fraction what his expenses would be. In some seasons the fishing is very fair, though, of course not equal to that at Aboyne; but then it was just half the price. I heard from Mr. Cook after I left it improved very much, many good fish being been taken. In April, which is the best month for the Dee, it would be better still, as there was a great deal of snow on the hills, and the Dee depends for its spring freshes on the snow.

On our way back to Aboyne we passed a fine loch—Loch Kinnord. It is a beautiful sheet of water, some miles in extent, with fine wooded islands upon it, and is full of very large pike, which are not often fished for. Adventurous pike-fishers who are constantly making inquiries as to where they shall go, might well take a month here in October; and if they were to get a boat up by rail from Aberdeen, I am sure that their takes would be something new in pike-fishing, both in size and numbers. The two next days I went up to fish the water of Sir James Burnet, Bart., on which, through the intervention of a friend, I had procured permission. Finer pools and streams it would be impossible to imagine; they are all than can be desired; but the fish will not remain in them, having been so worried by the nets. They rest there after their first rush perhaps for half a dozen hours or so, and then go on; and when the great run of fish takes place, in early spring, in the grilse season, and, in the autumn, capital sport is often obtained; but at any other time the only chance, as I think, of sport is after a good spate or on a Monday, when a few stray fish may have made into the river. Tempted by the fine appearance of the pools, and by the fact that the first day was a very unfavourable one, bright-steel sky, and bitter east wind, although I had no sport, I tried it again, and caught one big beast of a kelt, about 14lb.

Crathes Castle, the seat of Sir James, is one of the finest and most interesting buildings on Dee-side. The older portion of the castle bears marks of great antiquity, and the old doorways, rusty portcullis, and barred windows evidence ruder times when more of "the right of the strong arm" was in vogue than those we live in. Other portions of the building are apparently Flemish, from the gables and peaks, and attached to these is a portion of even later date. It is beautifully situated on an eminence, amongst superb trees and fine old shrubs. I find in Black's Guide an account of a former ancestor yclept the Baron of Leys, and of him there is a humorous ballad writ. It appears that he had become entangled in some foreign *liaison*, and, being desirous of concealing his identity, with true Scotch caution, when asked his name by his ladylove gave her for answer a series of absurd names which could not be easily identified certainly. Thus answers the Baron of Leys to his love's importunity:

Some ca's me this, some ca's me that,
  Whatever may best befa' me,
But when I'm in Scotland's King's high court
  Clatter-the-Speans they ca' me.

To which his true love, who is evidently in a bad way, and to whom her rose, no matter by what name it is called, would appear to smell equally sweet, maketh answer:

Oh, wae's me now, O Clatter-the-Speans,
  And alas that ever I saw thee,
For I'm in love—sick, sick in love,
  And I kenna well fat to ca' thee.

Thereupon the Baron of Leys, who is evidently quite unworthy the *tendre* he had established, sayeth:

Some ca's me this, some ca's me that—
  I carena what they ca' me;
But when wi' the Earl o' Murray I ride
  It's Scour-the-Braes they ca' me.

And so on. I wonder what the ladies would ca' him?—an out-and-out loafer, I strongly suspect, for obtaining love upon false pretences. I should like to try him by a jury of matrons, all with marriageable daughters; a maiden of fifty, or the "mother of the modern Gracchi," for counsel against him, and a Mrs. Chief Baron for judge; and if they didn't "scour his braes" and "pipe-clay his weekly accounts" for him, I know nothing of the sex. "Clatter the speans," indeed! a pretty clattering of the speans there would be about his devoted ears. Evidently the baron had fears of a breach of promise before his eyes.

Opposite to Banchory, which is close to Crathes, the Feugh—one of the largest tributaries of the Dee—rolls in. It is a foaming, rocky stream; but many salmon and grilse at times run into it, and it sometimes gives capital sport. Not far from Banchory, upon a wild open heath near Lumphanan, is Macbeth's cairn. Here Macbeth is said to have been hunted down and finally slain; and near the cairn, remains of rude entrenchments are seen, and weapons of ancient warfare have often been turned up, giving evidence in favour of the assertions made by the older chroniclers. Some years ago, when visiting a moor near Lumphanan, I saw this cairn. The country around is very wild and desolate—indeed, the whole of Dee-side is replete with objects of more or less interest, and it forms a favourite summer-tour route for excursionists.

The flies used on the Dee are peculiar, being dressed upon very long shanked hooks made expressly for the purpose. Three or four of them are peculiar to the Dee, and I will endeavour to describe them. The first is called the Red Wing. The body is composed of one-third dirty orange-yellow towards the tail, and the rest of claret (inclining to purple) mohair; broad silver tinsel. Tail, a golden pheasant's saddle feather, and two or three turns of the tinsel as a tip. The hackle is a very large black heron-hackle, the fibres of which reach from the head of the fly to as much beyond the point as possible; the hackle should be wound up about two-thirds of the body; at the shoulder is lapped round a teal feather. The wings are two long strips of swallow-tailed gled set flat, so as to support the fly in the water, or the dun reddish feather sometimes found in the turkey's tail does almost as well. The sister fly to this is called the Tartan. The body is dressed with one-half dirty orange, and the upper half scarlet mohair; broad gold tinsel, two turns of it for the tip, and a red, gold-pheasant breast-feather for tail. Over this body is run a sandy red hackle, one side of the fibre being snipped off pretty closely; over this is run a large grey heron's hackle—I think they come from the rump; they are very long in the fibre—indeed, the difficulty with these Dee flies is to get feathers long enough in the fibre. The grey hackle is laid on over the red for two-thirds of the body; at the shoulder is a teal hackle, as in the other fly. The wings are two strips of silver-grey speckled turkey. It is a singular looking fly, giving one the idea of a huge spider. The White Eagle is even a greater monstrosity. The body resembles that of the Red Wing. The tail is a breast feather as in the Tartan. From head to tail is wound what is termed an eagle's hackle, but it is the fluffy part of a golden eagle's feather just over the leg. In fact, upon a cursory inspection, the fly looks like the stump of some feather. The shoulder is decorated with the invariable teal hackle, without which it seems no Dee fly would be perfect. The wings are slips of the silver-grey barred turkey, with black tips; and a very monstrous-looking production is the result. Nevertheless, it kills well towards evening; and if dressed small, and with less of the eagle on it, it will kill well by day. Another fly of the same cast is the Yellow Eagle, which is just the same fly, only the eagle feather is dyed of a bright lemon yellow. I have heard many theories as to what a salmon mistakes the usual run of flies for; but for what he can possibly mistake a "yaller aigle" (as it is called in those parts) passes my comprehension utterly. There is nothing like it that I ever saw, either in earth, air, or water. These flies are used large in spring and high water, and smaller as the water fines down. The other flies used, are patterns used also upon other rivers—golden and claret, or golden and copper bodies, with claret hackles, jay shoulders, and mixed wings do well enough; but the herons and eagles are the speciality. The same flies a size smaller do for the Don. The Ballater water is, I believe, still open to the public by ticket, taken from Mr. Cook, of the Invercauld Arms; and I hear that part of the Aboyne Water also, which has been closed to the public for some years, has this season been re-opened by Mr. Johnstone, of the Huntley Arms, Aboyne, who has fishing for three rods above and below Aboyne Bridge. As the Dee fishing is always in request, an early application for tickets is always necessary, and the lessee of the Fife Arms, at Braemar, has also a good stretch of the river for the use of his customers. Before working up to Inverness I may give a little information on the Ythan.

The Ythan, a river formerly famous for its pearls, runs into the sea, at Newburgh, a dozen or so of miles north of Aberdeen. It is a moderate salmon, a fair sea trout, and a capital brown trout river, and fishing may be obtained at Newburgh, to which a coach runs from Aberdeen. Here, by staying at the Udney Arms Hotel, kept by Mrs. Allan, the angler may get very fair sea-trout fishing; and somewhat higher up the river, at Ellon, by staying at the New Inn, Mr. Lamond's, a salmon or two may be got late in the season. From Aberdeen we journeyed to Inverness.

Inverness is called the capital of the Highlands; and from the beauty of its situation, the associations which belong to it, and the noble river which flows through it, it deserves the appellation. The first thing which strikes the tourist is the castle, a very handsome building of reddish stone, which stands on a high mound overlooking the river, and dominating the town. The present building is of modern date, and comprehends the gaol, the court-house, and the other county buildings; upon the same site, however, other castles have stood and perished. Formerly, in remote antiquity, a castle stood upon an eminence to the south-east of the town. Here it was said that Macbeth murdered Duncan: the best authorities, however, deny this. Macbeth, nevertheless, certainly had possession of this castle, which was destroyed by Malcolm Canmore, Duncan's son; and a castle was built upon the site of the present one, which was destroyed and rebuilt several times before the present one rose. The whole neighbourhood seems to recall Macbeth. While coming here in the train, which is only equalled in slowness by that of the Deeside railway, ten miles an hour being held to be fair travelling, Chalkley was infected seriously with Macbeth-ianism—if I may say so; he was perpetually looking out for wild heaths, and blasted trees, and ugly old women in dilapidated garments and clothes-props, and he quoted Shakespeare tremendously. One of the passengers ventured to remark that it was rather close with all the windows up, On ordinary occasions Chalkley would have said, "Really! Do you think so?" Now, I should have said the thermometer was somewhere about twenty-eight on this occasion. He fixed the old gentleman with his eye, and replied, "Sir, the air bites shrewdly; it is very keen; it is a nipping and an eager air"—which much perplexed the old gentleman, who got out carefully at the next station.

"How far is't hence to Forres?" he asked of a big guard with a huge red beard, in a deep, sepulchral voice, and with a theatrical wave of the hand.

"Joost saxteen mile, sir," answered the literal-minded official; adding, "and if ye want to gat oot ye'll mok haste, or she'll be ganging."

"Behemoth!" muttered Chalkley; and he retired within himself.

Inverness has rich and fertile land round it, and has a peculiarly mild climate; and is surrounded with lofty hills, so that it combines lowland and highland advantages. One of the pleasantest walks I ever saw is open to the public here. The Ness makes a series of large islands just above the town, which are accessible from either bank by light suspension-bridges. These islands, which are more than a mile long, are beautifully and thickly wooded, and a more charming retreat in the summer-time can hardly be conceived. Here a band plays on summer evenings, and the lads and lasses dance to the music under the greenwood shade; while the salmon and trout spring from the crystal Ness on either side to catch a glimpse or a hearing of what is going on, like so many dolphins looking after so many Arions. I noted this to Chalkley, who punned on it in a manner so vile, that I hardly dare to reproduce his perpetration.

"And very proper, too; there's good authority for it.

> Meantime some rude Arion's restless hand
> Wakes the brisk harmony that *salars* love—"

quoth he, and the villain took to flight; for he knew that the largest boulder I could lift would be hurled at him, even though, like Ajax, I should have to rend from its parent "no small part of a mountain."

Opposite to these islands are two very remarkable eminences, one of which is a little round steep hill, beautifully feathered with light wavy trees; this is called Tom-na-hurie, or the Hill of Fairies. It is now converted into a cemetery—rather an awkward place to get the bodies up to, I should think. Whether the fairies will still patronise it under these circumstances remains to be seen. The other (Craig Phadric) is a peculiar hill, crowned as my informant—Lord Saltoun—pointed out, by a vitrified fort. Now, I did not know what a vitrified fort might be, but I did not like to show my ignorance by asking. My archæological education, I suppose, was left imperfect in this particular, and I determined to look it out in some of the authorities at my disposal when I got home, and I did so; but none of them gave me any inkling of the composition of vitrified forts. They were glib enough upon "those remarkable remnants of antiquity, vitrified forts and vitrified cairns," and so forth; but that was all —not a hint of their construction or origin. So I went to Chalkley, who looks as if he were chock-full of all that kind of information.

"Chalkley," I asked, in as careless a way as I could assume, "seen Craig Phadric?"

"Well—yes—only from a distance, though."

"Anything peculiar about it?"

"Oh, dear, yes—a most remarkable monument of antiquity —a most charming and delightful—old—a—a—place; one of the most perfect specimens of a vitrified fort, you know, in the kingdom."

"Dear me, you don't say so!"—"Just so—yes!"—"Vitrified fort!" said I reflectively, dwelling on the word. "By the way—what is a vitrified fort? I don't fancy I ever saw one."

"A vitrified fort! oh! ah! I suppose—that is—oh! it's a fort that has been vitrified I should say. Can't say I ever saw one exactly myself—that is to say, not closely, you know."

"Well, but, how the deuce—or what can the process consist in?"

"I'm sure I hardly know, unless it is done all over shiny outside, like the pumice-stone houses one sees at deserted watering-places, or the inside of the large red crockery pans one's always tumbling over in back-yards, and such places."

Still, we never came to any satisfactory conclusion, and, to this day, we are both in a state of debased ignorance on the subject.

The Ness is the queen of Scotch rivers. It is such a large and splendid stream, and the pools are so wide, that, when a heavy salmon is hooked in one of the larger pools, he gives magnificent play. I believe that a fish which inhabits wide open waters usually gives five times the sport you get out of one which inhabits a more confined locality. The one runs fast and free, knowing he has plenty of room do so; the other wobbles along dwarfed in his ideas of resistance by the poky hole he dwells in.

The first thing I did was to call on Mr. Snowie at the great repository of all sporting intelligence in this part of the country. Both Mr. Snowie and his son gave me every assistance in their power, and both interested themselves warmly in trying to procure for me all the sport they could. Mr. Snowie has been for so many years a respected and trusted providore of sport to so many patrons, that comment of mine on the useful post he occupies so well is needless. No sportsman ever thinks of passing through Inverness, if he has a few minutes to spare, without a run into Snowie's to hear what this one or that one is doing, and what his own prospects are; for Snowie generally knows quite as well as he does, and often much better.

My arrangements were not completed, and I had an hour or two to spare, so I walked up with Mr. Snowie, jun., to a fine long pool which he had leave to fish. The kelts were jumping about, and some fine sea trout popped up now and then; but, though he fished it over twice, he only got a couple of rises, and did nothing, and did nothing. The afternoon was very raw with a shaving east wind. It was a very bad taking day. The next day was what is called an open day on the "Four Cobles water." The Four Cobles water is the lowest water, and comprises several fine pools, which fish well at the proper season, about July and August, if the river is in condition. A part of the Four Cobles water belongs to the town, and the town have let it upon condition that one day in eight shall be open to the public to angle over the *whole* of the water, and about harvest the pools are lined with anglers; and it is not an uncommon thing for a good rod to pick up his two or three, or even more, fish a day—of course, the day is looked forward to with great eagerness. Being desirous of seeing the water, I walked up with Mr. Snowie, jun. There were not many anglers out, and the weather was just what it had been for a week previous—dark, with an uncanny east wind. So little or nothing was done. I saw one fellow with a small sea trout, and a brown trout of 1lb. and better. The latter was caught with worm, and was not in good condition. The Ness gives very fine trout-fishing at times, many of the fish running very large, some being taken up to 6lb. and 7lb. weight. Mr. Snowie fished down the same pool as he had the day before, and with like fortune. The water is fine water to look at, and when the river is in order, or about a foot or eighteen inches higher than it then was, it is good fishing water; but it was getting rather low now.

The warm westerly breezes and genial sun had melted a considerable quantity of the snow on the mountains, and many of the rivers were in full spate; and never was water more wanted or more grateful.

CHAPTER XVIII.

BAPTISM IN THE NESS—THE FORCE OF FASHION—A DAY ON THE NESS—CHALKLEY—THE BLACK STREAM—A FISH AT THE TWO STONES—ANOTHER AT THE BLACK STREAM—A 20-POUNDER LOST AT THE TWO STONES—KELTS! KELTS! KELTS!

THE first Sunday we arrived here the Baptists held high ceremonial. Two new sisters were to be received into the bosom of their communion, and a very ostentatious dipping of the damsels took place in the river Ness, in about the most conspicuous part of the town. They were led down almost waist-deep into the river by the officiating priest, who then, supporting them in his arms, gently laid them back into the water, taking care that they should be thoroughly immersed. It was a bitter cold day, with a N.E. wind, and a more pitiable spectacle than those females presented when they came out of the water would be difficult to imagine—drenched, dripping, and chilled to the skin, they marched off amidst the comments of an enormous crowd of spectators, who assembled to see the ceremony. One of the regenerated fair ones was a young and rather good-looking girl; the other was not remarkable for beauty, and came in for a trifling modicum of chaff.

I do not know whether regeneration or revivalism, which is getting popular in Scotland, is altering the fine old spirit of the Scotch damsels, as evidenced in many a good tale and sly joke of Burns, Allan Cunningham, and a host of others. I hope not, but civilisation is making tremendous advances. The newspapers are full of huge millinery advertisements, and the fashions get here as soon as they do in London, and are adopted more readily. And the ubiquitous piano, too—shade of Broadwood! what doleful snarlings from wire-haired instruments, in the extremity of torture, one does hear every now and then; and when one does hear such a piano so out of tune that the major keys all sound like minors, hammering away at one of those *very minor* Scotch tunes that seem to have neither ending nor beginning, but to go groaning away on the same interminable note, without change or cessation, then I say that that celebrated feat of music performed by Richard Swiveller, Esq., on the flute, to the deprecation of melancholy, would be the music of spheres, whatever that may be (and it is something very transcendently beautiful, I have no doubt) in comparison. "She," I overheard one strapping lassie say to another, contemptuously, "She can't play nane; I can play Bonnie Doune, and the something-or-other polka." I would rather have overheard anything smacking of the old tale, told by Allan Cunningham, of a damsel on Nith side, even though it evidenced somewhat more of freedom of manners than prevails now. In those parts a backward or slow lover was looked on with the greatest contempt; and during a wordy war between some young ladies one day, in which various young men's names were brought into discussion, some reference was made to the supposed sweetheart of one of the fair ones present. "Him," quoth the indignant maiden, "him! why I tried him wi' a lanely room and a lighted candle, and he had na even the sense to blaw it oot and steek (stop) the door."

But the change by no means affects the women alone, the men are quite as badly bitten by it. The kilt, of course, one rarely sees, and then on some shopkeeper from Glasgow or Edinburgh; but if the women have cast off their linsey woolsey, the men have kicked off hodden-grey with equal alacrity. They must all be gentlemen now. A sort of mania for dress seems to have seized on the Highland peasant, and he will go through any amount of privation to come out strong on a Sunday. You wonder who the distinguished-looking party before you is. It is the laird, or the laird's son at least; and yet, no, it can't be. You can hardly believe your eyes when they assure you that that howling swell is neither more nor less than your dilapidated gillie, Angus, who has carried your basket and cleek all the week at 3*s.* 6*d.* per diem. You would as soon think of asking him to shoulder your gaff in his present costume as you would of asking the minister to take a hand at "put" on the door step. The English labourer will spoil his outside for his in; the Highlander, on the other hand, mortifies his inside for his out. But I am wandering away into matters which are very foreign to fishing, and which, perhaps, the reader cares but little about.

Having written to ask permission of Lord Saltoun to fish his portion of the Ness, his lordship very kindly drove into town and took me out to his water without delay. On the way I could not but admire the lovely scenery which distinguishes this part of the banks of the river Ness. When the trees are in full leaf the variety of foliage that towers up and above the banks must be very beautiful, as here much of the bank on one side is in his lordship's private grounds, and huge Portugal laurels, rhododendrons, and other hardy shrubs, break and diversify the masses of birch, fir, and larch. On one of the banks for a considerable distance a great deal of destruction had been done last winter in a tremendous gale; large trees had been uprooted and cast aside as though they were mere saplings, and immense branches had been torn and twisted off the parent trees in places with as little apparent difficulty as a boy would tear off a twig. No one who has not witnessed it can have any conception of the tremendous force with which the wind seems to rush down the rifts and glens in an alpine country. In this instance, gathering force as it comes from the fastness of Mealfourvonie, a mountain near 3000 feet high, it strikes upon one of the lesser but more precipitous crags upon Loch Ness side. Thence it whirls across the loch with redoubled fury, and woe be to the boat that encounters its wrath; and when at length it is hurled upon the south side of the great glen of Scotland, Lord Saltoun's firs pay pretty dearly for the stramash it causes. Precisely the same thing had occurred at the Prince of Wales's place on Deeside—Abergeldie; it was quite extraordinary how easily the largest trees seem to have been rent away by the tornado.

As we drove along the banks, the number of huge kelts that we saw splashing and leaping about was surprising. Indeed, the river was full of them, though few clean fish were to be taken in the Ness as yet—July and August being the best months—the Ness not being a spring river for angling purposes, though very early, indeed, for the nets. The fact is, the fish are anxious to get up to the warm water of the lake, and so do not at that cold season dwell in the Ness, but run straight through to the lake, whence they manage to make their way still onwards up to the Garry and other rivers which form the head waters; and thus the Garry, which is a long way further up the country, is a good spring river, while the Ness, through which all the Garry fish have runs, holds but few clean fish; still it does hold some; and the probability of a clean fish just makes one obliged to play the kelts carefully until one is certain of their identity. I have heard people say that they can tell a kelt from his play at once. If they can, I can only say that they are cleverer than I am; for I have often mistaken the play of a kelt for that of a clean fish, and been agreeably surprised to find that that which I had set down a kelt turned out clean. I am sure that many clean fish are lost from the anglers losing all patience with the kelts. For although kelts often give capital sport, better than many a clean fish, yet the disgust one feels at seeing their long, lanky bodies and big heads, and their generally miserable appearance; the certainty that they are spoiling the pool, if there is a clean fish in it; and the anxiety one feels about one's fly, and the rage one gets in at finding the hackle and tinsel cut—so disgusts the angler that, as I have said, he is very apt to pull them out anyhow, so that he can get rid of the obstruction; and if, as frequently happens, he has hooked a clean fish, the mouth is fleshy and tender, and away he goes, when in all probability, the angler catches a farewell glimpse of him as he makes off, and it just dawns upon him that he has lost *the* clean fish of the day. Of course this only riles one all the more with the kelts; and to have to play a brute carefully, when you are morally sure he is a kelt, but have not had an opportunity of being ocularly so, is trying work.

Having arrived at the water, we found Johnnie Macdonald, the water-keeper, awaiting us, and Johnnie forthwith conducted us to the top pool, where I was to begin. Though much of the fishing could be done from the bank by wading, yet as there is a boat to each pool for those who don't like to wade, and as I had a bad cold, I eschewed the wading and took to the boat. The first pool is a very curious pool; it has altered a good deal, I am told, of late years. The river enters it in two converging streams, some distance apart, and the whole of the space between them is one black, dead, glassy back eddy, and if your line gets out of either of the streams (which are not very powerful), it is sucked into this back eddy and drowned. I never hooked a fish in this part of the pool, though curious to see what the effect would be. Of course, if the angler wants to fish this eddy, he ought to go down stream and throw up.

I fished the streams twice, with a different fly each time, and got but one nasty little kelt; and as the wind, which was still in the old quarter, E. to N., and was all wrong, blew the boat up against the stream, we could not fish it properly, and so left it. The next stream was a regular kelt stream, with very little chance of a clean fish in it, so, as it was pretty safe work, I handed the rod to Chalkley, whose ambition to catch a salmon—no matter whether clean or foul—was at the highest possible pitch. His dreams of fishing had never soared to such an eminence, but now that the consummation was within his reach there was no holding him. The spirit of the land was upon him (I don't mean whisky, of course, as it was only eleven in the morning). His eye blazed, his *porte* was—shall I say *sublime*, no—erect, as erect at least as the swaying and bumping of the boat would permit. He steadied himself, took the rod in his hand with a stern resolve, waved it gently as Zephyr backward, and more gently than Zephyr forward, and the fly just tumbled into the boat again somewhere about his legs. Again and again he essayed; I tried to teach him, but somehow, as the saying is, his fingers were all thumbs, and his hands all left ones. He would let out fifteen or twenty yards of line, and like Miss Tox, he would "make an effort." You would think from his corrugated brow and compressed lips he was going to cast 140 yards of line at least; then he would bow the rod gracefully down to the surface, and the fly would gently alight on the water, about two feet from the rod point. Nevertheless, so rabid were the kelts that they came at him regardless of the expense, and fairly ran off with the fly. "Never strike your salmon," says the good old school, and Chalkley never struck his, and thus achieved the acme of perfection. The kelts came and boldly tweaked him by the nose, as it were, and he held the rod out to them to do as they liked—and they did so. Taking the fly and leaving it just when they chose, at last one did manage to jam the point of the hook between his teeth somehow, so that he couldn't let go, and began to pull. Then Chalkley caught the infection, and pulled too. To see Chalkley wind that fish up, as though he had been playing the "Dead March in Saul" on a hand-organ which might have been expected to explode if it were ground too fast, was the finest thing I ever saw in fishing. I laughed to that degree that the very kelpies must have been amazed and confounded. With a gravity befitting such an important capture, Chalkley hauled in his first salmon, and I feel pretty sure that if the law—for which Chalkley has a wholesome reverence—had not objected, that illustrious fish would have figured in a glass case, like Mr. Briggs's. I think he caught another, and then, seeing that he was not really fishing the stream at all, and throwing away what chance there might be of a clean fish, I resumed the rod and hooked two or three kelts for him, handing him the rod to play them. We fished the stream down, and went to the next cast, called the Two Stone Pool, from its having two large stones at the end of it. It was a fine wide pool, and, though rather low, was still in fair order. As this was the best and most likely cast for a clean fish, I fished it over carefully twice, but, alas! nothing but kelts repaid my labour. Thence we went to a fine stream called the Black Stream, from the bed of the river being very dark coloured; it is the finest stream on the water. We missed on the way a very nice-looking pool called the Laggan, it being too low to give a chance of a clean fish. The Black Stream was no more propitious to us than the others, and we got nothing but kelts; one big beast, about 15lb., contrived to hook himself in the vent, and managed to haul out close upon 100 yards down the stream, when finding the rod would be strained if I pressed it further, I laid it down and took hold of the line, and by this means, with care, towed him all the way home again; and it was hard work, for the moment he got into the stream fairly, he put his broad fan-like tail broadside to it, and it was like pulling against against a wall. However, he came in at last, and I whipped off his adipose fin, as I did of all the kelts I caught, and returned him; and as it was getting dusk we tackled up and went home, having pulled out above a dozen kelts. Chalkley was rampant with delight: 'That was something like sport, you know; only it would certainly have been an improvement if they had all been clean fish" a sentiment, I need not say, I warmly concurred in.

The next day we were not with Johnnie till twelve, having letters to write, &c. The upper pool gave us a kelt, as usual, the stream only one; they were all still in it. The Two Stone Pool was not to-day inclined to yield kelts, and I fished it down to the upper stone, when I got a rise and a hold, and away went the fish down-stream rather briskly.

"Hallo! Johnnie, this looks more like business," said I.

"'Deed, sir, it's a deal more like the play of a clean fusshe than any I've seen the day."

Just then out he came nearly a yard high, bright and clean as a smelt.

"Faith, he's a nice fusshe; haud him carefully, sir. I'll land ye, and ye can play him better frae the bank."

Landed I was, and after a good deal of scouring the pool we got him into the net (an implement, by the way, which Johnnie abominates), a fine fresh-run fish, with the sea-louse on him, about 10lb. in weight. We duly christened him, and then went to work again. However, we did no more in the Two Stone, and so went on the Black Stream, not to lose time. I had not fished it down twenty yards when I got a very shy rise under water, and the next moment I was fast. He was a dull, sluggish animal—a kelt as I thought—and I was just handing the rod to Chalkley when I caught sight of his tail as he passed the boat. It looked very muscular and clean-cut. "Why, Johnnie, he's—eh!"

"Weel, I thenk he's joost a kelt; but play him carefu'; we'll soon see." Just then he put his back up.

Very brown back that for a kelt, Johnnie.

"Weel, it is, sir, indeed; and there's a scar on his side I misdoot. Haud him carefu', sir, haud him carefu'." The fish showed himself. "Faith, his clean enoo'; he's just a wee coloured with the river."

And up came the anchor, and we got on shore; and after a long bout of rather slow play we got him into the net, a very nice fish of about 11lb. or 12lb. He was slightly discoloured from having been some weeks in the river, and on his side were marks of seals' teeth where he had been sharply cut. This, perhaps, had made him slow in moving up. The very next throw I got a sea-trout of about 1lb., which I gave to Chalkley for his breakfast, but we did no more; indeed, I had reason to be rather proud of what I had done, as two clean fish are not got every day in the Ness in March.

The next day we went forth doubly armed, for Chalkley, having been told by Lord Saltoun to try his hand, determined to go on his own hook; and having borrowed my small rod and my Faggs, and invested in some flies, &c., he set forth upon his mission with a high and stern resolve. Chalkley's notion was clearly that wading-boots were an invention to get wet in, and the first thing he did was to walk deliberately into the water as far over the tops of the boots as he could conveniently go. I believe he would have walked on up to his middle, if the stream had not been rather sharp. Being now quite cool and comfortable, he hammered away with varied success. I believe he really did land two or three kelts all to himself. He was completely happy, except when he came to pull off my waders, when, sitting down rather abruptly and elevating his legs for some one to help pull his boots off, he shot some two bucketfuls of water which were in them back into his "rudder-case," as Jack-Tar would nautically term his nether integuments.

"Oh! oh! Oh, Lord! Now, that's too bad. I didn't mind as long as I kept that warm and dry. As for the feet, you know, I think that's rather jolly; my feet are as warm as a toast."

My friend has his peculiarities in this respect, *e.g.*, where others would be or are shivering with cold he finds it all quite warm and delightful; and when, on the other hand, some people complain of sultriness, he would opine that it was the sort of weather when you might put on a great coat and yet not find it too warm. However, the last blow was too much even for him. The centre of his gravity had been roughly invaded, and he had a serious objection to such an unwarrantable liberty. He had been wading persistently over the tops of his boots. They were, of course, full of water, and it took three strong men to pull them off. His stockings were wet through, so he had to walk home in his boots. Wading in the Ness is nasty work, as coming from such a large deep lake, although comparatively warm in winter, she is desperately cold in summer; and many a life-long rheumatism has she bestowed upon her more assiduous votaries.

My sport, besides a few kelts, on this day consisted in hooking a beautiful 20lb. clean fish in the Two Stone Pool. At the second or third cast on the pool a fish rose so shyly that I thought him worth more careful attention. The sun was bright, so I waited for a cloud; and when it came I came with it, and the fish came also, and away he went for a spin down stream, making a couple of most brilliant runs, and taking out some seventy yards of line, coming to the top with a plunge, but not jumping. I worked him up a little way, but down he went, further off than ever. Excitement was now getting up, as we were feeling pretty sure that he was clean and fresh-run. Carefully I worked him up, little by little, until I got him up level with the boat in the shallower stream on the inside, when I had a good sight of him, and he proved to be a very handsome clean fish of about 20lb. It was the only sight I did get of him, however, for, as if aware that he was in dangerous quarters, or, perhaps, catching sight of us—away he went spinning the line out like lightning, and taking fully eighty yards in his run, when just as I was going to land, so as to keep abreast of him, away came the hook, and I—I—collapsed. I ought to have landed sooner.

The next day we did naught but kelts. Chalkley waded again. This time I lent him my Woolgar's; and as I cautioned him seriously that if he got wet in them he should pay the penalty, he behaved himself with respectability and moderation, and hauled in, I think, only one kelt, but he got quite a dab at throwing, and did not smash more than two or three flies. This was Saturday, and I bade by friend Johnnie adieu, as I did not intend to try the water further.

A capital attendant is Johnnie Macdonald—cool, quiet, and unobtrusive. He seems to know where you ought to be and where you want to be, and there the boat will surely be. He never offers or obtrudes advice. There is no "Keep up the point of yer gad, sir," "Wind up the line, sir," and "Don't let him do this, that, or t'other, sir," "Ah! sir, if ye," &c., &c.,

&c., all of which is to me so exasperating that I feel tempted always to do the very opposite of the advice, out of pure aggravation. Johnnie sits down quietly, and says not a word unless spoken to. But if his advice is sought it is generally worth attention.

CHAPTER XIX.

DRUMMOSSIE MOOR—THE BATTLE OF CULLODEN—BEN WYVIS—THE RITES OF BAAL—DRUIDICAL CIRCLE—THE ROMAN WALLS ON THE NESS—A MONSTER KELT—THE SWITCHER—THE BEAULY—A DEATH AT THE CRUIVE POOL—EILAN AIGAS AND THE FALLS OF KILLMORACH.

Drummossie muir, Drummossie muir,
  A waefu' day it was to me,
For there I lost my father dear,
  My father dear and brethren three.

Their winding sheet, the bluidy clay,
  Their graves are growing green to me,
And by them lies the dearest lad
  That ever blest a woman's e'e.

Now wae to thee, thou cruel Duke,
  A bloody man I trow thou be,
For monie a heart thou hast made sair
  That ne'er did wrang to thine or thee.

THUS sung Burns of Drummossie Moor, upon which the battle of Culloden was fought, on the 16th of April, about 120 years ago. Drummossie moor is but some five or six miles from Inverness, and accordingly on Sunday afternoon Chalkley and I pilgrimaged to the spot. The ground rises steadily from Inverness up to the moor, which is a wild, open plain of table-land, a mile or so in width, and sloping down on all sides—on the right to the river Nairn, which runs through a deep, rocky, and woody defile, and to the Moray Firth on the left. How somewhat irregular troops as the Highland clans were, compared with their adversaries, could have been brought to fight a battle upon ground so entirely unfavourable to them, and where their enemy's strong points (his cavalry and artillery) could be employed with such fatal effect, when, by marching a few miles either way, they could have occupied a position which would entirely have neutralised these advantages, it seems difficult to understand. It needs no military *savant* to appreciate fully the utter folly of the choice. The object was to prevent the Duke of Cumberland from forcing his way to Inverness; but to fight a battle upon the worst possible terms, and with the almost certainty of losing it, was not the way to cover Inverness. It appears that there was much internal dissension and jealousy amongst the different clans and between the various leaders, and a want of sufficient firmness and capacity to control the whole. In fact, many of the clans appear to have behaved like sulky children. The Mac This's wouldn't fight because the Mac That's were upon their right, and the Mac Those marched off because the Mac T'others were on their left. Thus it has ever been with the clans. Everything was sacrificed to private jealousy and private vanity. Individually, the Highlander is the finest raw material in the world. In a rush or a determined charge to the death they are magnificent, as a thousand traits of battle can testify, from Culloden to Coomassie; but here there seemed to be a want of consistency and adherence which utterly destroyed them. Many other circumstances aided the defeat of Prince Charles; his troops had been harassed by a long, weary night-march and want of food. The Duke of Cumberland's army lay before Nairn, and a night surprise was attempted. The Highland troops marched from a little above Culloden House yonder, which lies embosomed in trees, so peaceful and smiling, that one would hardly think so bloody and tremendous a strife could ever have taken place so near it. One seems to expect that it should wear some distinguishing mark whereby everybody would at once recognise it as Culloden House, instead of a mere ordinary-looking country mansion. Thence, however, marched the army towards Nairn, until they reached a place called Knockanhuic.

There the intention of a night surprise (which would not have been a surprise at all, as spies were going and coming between the two armies all night long) was abandoned, and the troops marched back again to the rear of their starting point, a distance, by the map, of about 16 miles. (We could trace most of the line of march from the road, but young plantations begin to break up the face of the country somewhat.) Sixteen miles of needless moss-trooping by night, with loss of rest and want of food, with dissatisfaction, disaffection, private feud and jealousy, want of head or control, or definite purpose, are terrible draw-backs to success in a battle. The English army came up fresh and fit for the day's work. By those farmhouses now called Old Lenach the English right wing was stationed; right across the road on which we stood was the Highland position. The artillery mowed them down terribly, the dragoons cut them up terribly, and the battle soon became a disgraceful rout, the credit of which was only redeemed by that one terrible charge so characteristic of the Highlanders, when, throwing themselves upon their foe with all the rage and fury of despair, they clove their way through fire and steel, through rank after rank of the foe, nor ceased until the last arm among them was powerless, and the last claymore broken or beaten down. That heap of rounded mounds, not far from the roadside, attests the noble daring which strove to the death to retrieve the fortune of the day, and forms the last resting-place of those gallant Highlanders:—

> Few, few shall part where many meet—
> The snow shall be their winding-sheet;
> And every turf beneath their feet
> Shall be a soldier's sepulchre.

Conditions all strictly borne out in this instance, as the snow lay white and brilliant everywhere, and not a yard of where we stood but some poor fellow slept below us. To the right, about a mile off, still stands a huge solitary ash tree, whence the hope of the Stuarts bolted somewhat early in the battle. A mile and a half onward is a huge round boulder, of enormous dimensions, whence the cruel Duke surveyed the progress of his army. All his talents as a general, all his energy as a commander, are blurred and degraded by the cruelty he displayed towards his conquered foe. Would, for our own credit sake, we could doubt the truth of much that is told of the doings of the villainous soldiery, but it is all too well attested. Hosts of wounded men were shot in cold blood days after the battle. By yonder old tower, so quaint with its battlements and mouldering quakers,* a great number of officers were murdered—I can give it no other term. A large barn, in which many had taken refuge, was positively set fire to by his orders. A war of extermination, in which the Highlanders were treated like rats, and murdered wherever they were caught, without regard to age or sex, was commenced, and carried on with devilish ingenuity and perseverance. The savagery of Red Indians could not go further than the soldiery did. Well might the poet weep and lament, for such a page, let us hope, blurrs the history of but few nations. Not long since, by the quaint tower I have noted, stood one of the old guns left on the field of battle. It has been removed to Culloden House. On the field by the roadside where the fight was hottest, a sort of monumental cairn was commenced, but has been abandoned; and as the "hottest parts" of the battle-field are now planted thickly with rising plantations, in a few years much that is worth seeing will be obliterated. National feeling may have something to do with this, for such sores cannot be healed even in a century, and feeling is still rife, and the Duke still cursed in this neighbourhood. Chalkley and I sat down upon some of the stones about the cairn, and drank "honour and peace to the brave on either side," and smoked the reflective pipe; but as the afternoon was getting on, we abriged that ceremonial somewhat, and made our way on, as we had planned out a long ramble of some seventeen or eighteen miles. About a mile on was, according to the map, a capital

* Dummy wooden guns, now dropping to pieces in grim mockery.

bridle-road. I wonder what the notion of the framer of that map was of "a bad bridle-road." Snow was lying everywhere, and, of course, added to the difficulties of making out the track across the moor; and we stumbled along, sometimes on the moor and sometimes on the road, and sometimes in a diabolical rut, and so on; at length the capital bridle-road divided into two capital bridle-roads, and which excelled in point of capitalness it was very difficult to say. One seemed to lead towards Fort George, out towards the mouth of the firth; the other was more towards Inverness; so after debating which was the origin of the supposed capital road, we choose the latter, which soon (after for some time losing all its capital,) went into the Bankruptcy Court, and expired altogether; but we knew that if we kept straight on towards the shore of the firth, we must in time cross the lower road which runs along it. The afternoon had been a little cloudy, but now the sun shone out clearly, and a scene of remarkable beauty and splendour burst upon our view. Before us was the blue firth, with its range of dark hills, amongst which the Beauly Loch ran far up a broad and tranquil sheet of water; beyond this, and full thirty miles away (though it did not look ten), rose the gaunt mass of Ben Wyvis, one of the highest, if not *the* highest, of the Scotch mountains, very considerably over 4000 feet in height. From almost its base, lump after lump seemed to be borne up into the air as if the Titans had been lifting the earth on their backs, until one gigantic boll towered above them all, dwarfing the lesser range of hills (which showed all sorts of shapes and sizes), and everything else, in fact, into insignificance by his hugeness. Covered with snow, the gradations and indentations were singularly effective. Fleecy clouds would pass along, throwing alternate shade and light, and anon destroying the outline of the grand old mountain, and leaving it doubtful which was cloud and which snow-clad hill, when the sun would suddenly glance out, and there was the outline of the mountain-top gleaming in the midst of the blue air like burnished silver. I have seldom gazed upon a more gorgeous spectacle. Anon we scrambled, after a long round, down towards the road we were searching for; it had been our intention to examine some Druidical circles which abound upon a point of land that runs out into the firth, but we got too far down, and only came upon one which is close to the roadside; that, however, is very perfect. The altar-stone and its supports are in very fine preservation, and some two-thirds of the ring very well defined. The interior of the circle is hollowed out like a bowl, "and here," said Chalkley, with powerful unction and immense solemnity, and standing in a reflective attitude, before the altar-stone, "and here the rites of the sanguinary Baal were performed 2000 years ago. Here the maddening shriek of the miserable victim of the darkest and most hideous superstition that has ever disgraced and defiled this beautiful land, sir" (appealing to me as audience), "was heard, while men of apparently venerable aspect, with beards flowing down like the tails of the Angola sheep (which are carried upon little platforms, I believe, behind 'em), burnt their wretched votaries by hecatombs, packed like caller herrings in a fishwife's basket. They might wriggle, they might writhe, sir, they might poke their heads or their arms out between the bars, as I've seen 'em do in the *Penny Magazine*, sir, but they were within the toils, bound in withes, and their veins must burst and their sinews crack, and the very small amount of brains they did possess must frizzle in their brain-pans, sir; or here, perhaps, the arch-druid, arch-scoundrel, sir, arch-villain, sir, arch-arch-arch-blackguard, sir, mangled and gagged the throats of his unhappy disciples with gilded sickles all set with teeth like saws, in order to prolong the torture, of course. Don't tell me, I've seen pictures of 'em—lots of 'em—and know all about it. Relics of superstition and horror, I abandon ye, for Inverness is four miles off, and we shall be an hour late for dinner," and winding up his pathetic picture with this remarkable practical termination; away went Chalkley, five miles an hour, as if the arch-druid had kicked him.

Below the water belonging to Lord Saltoun on the Ness, and between that and the Four Cobles water, are some remarkably fine pools, called the Home Water. It was upon this water, on the pool called the Lower Home Pool, that Mr. Denison, the brother of the late Speaker, hooked that enormous salmon, that kept him at work all night, the paragraph about which went the round of all the papers, at the time of the occurrence. Mr. Denison hooked the fish about eight o'clock in the evening, and lost him about four in the morning, the fish keeping him going pretty nearly the whole of that time. He was seen many times close in to their feet, and was an enormous beast, but could not be gaffed, and was at last lost by the handle of the reel becoming entangled in Mr. Denison's watch-chain: eight hours hard at work and then to lose him after all, is very hard lines! In all probability the fish was 50 or 60lb., perhaps more. I had permission from the gentleman under whose charge the water is in the spring to fish this water, and having engaged the services of a rather well-known character, one Andy the Switcher, also known as the Northern Switcher, I made my way to the Upper Home Pool, and found the boat all ready and was soon at work. After a few casts I saw a large wave come after the fly, but nothing more. I waited again, and again a huge wave, with this time a slight break; a third time I waited for a cloud and fished deep, and he took, and I at once found I was in something considerable. I therefore landed, and commenced a series of operations somewhat similar, I conclude, to Mr. Denison's. Presently, I caught sight of the head and shoulders of a very large fish, far off, too far off to be certain what he was, but they looked so broad and thick that my pulse quickened with the hope that Fortune might cast in my way a big, clean one. I knew that 30lb. fish had been lately taken up the Garry? why might not this be one detained in the Ness? It was not violently likely, still there was an off chance which obliged me to play him a little carefully—not that I could have hauled a beast of the size I had on about as I pleased, if I had wished to ever so much. Nearly an hour and a half was consumed in steadily giving and taking line: now he would make a great charge out towards the other side of the stream, which was something like 100 yards wide where I was; every now and then whirling his huge body up to the surface with a heavy roll, and just breaking the surface, but not showing himself clearly: then he would work across again to my side, and come within fifteen to twenty yards of my feet, but we could not make sure of him; at last, in one of his rushes across and down stream, as he turned, he again showed his head and shoulders, and this time Andy saw him: "Weel, weel, weel," and he beamed all over, "he is an a-fu' big fusshe, to be sure, and I'm no certain that he isn't clean; he's verra thick and deep for a kelt; haud him carefu'." Another half hour went by, and our friend began to cave in a bit. At length he fell over on his side, almost within reach, and then, but not till then, we saw and were sure he was an enormous kelt. My net had been laughed at at Ballater as such an exaggerated, such a tremendously large affair. Large as it was, it wasn't half large enough to land this brute; and after several ineffectual efforts, Andy got his head into the net, and managed to scoop him on shore. It was a huge kelt, as I have said, very broad and deep in shape, and weighing, I should judge, about 35lbs. Andy said he was the largest kelt he had ever seen, and he was certainly a giant. He would have been hard upon 50lbs. if he had been clean. After shaving off an adipose fin bigger than the palm of my hand, we committed his carcase to the river, and, after a little panting and blowing, he made his way again out into the stream. I would very willingly have given a five-pound note to catch him when he came into the river again. Strange, what small appliances will bring down the strength of the largest fish. The fly I caught him on was a wee grilse fly, not much larger than a large sea-trout fly; and the gut was not very stout—single gut, and somewhat worn. After this feat of fishing, which took rather a large bite out of the day, I went on again, and fished the pool down. It was a long one; and by the time I had worked it out fully, it was too late to try another, and we went home, having taken several other kelts, but no clean fish.

The next day I had some letters to write, and I made Andy go on before me, and fetch the boat across to the other side of the river, walking up the Caledonian Canal path myself until I arrived at the Lower Home Pool—a magnificent stream, and the one in which Mr. Denison hooked his monster. Having mentioned the Caledonian Canal, I would wish to note here that by this very Home Pool are some apparently serious leaks in the lofty embankment of that canal, and if they are not properly attended to and stopped in time, some day some accident will happen here. In one part you can hear the water rushing like an underground torrent through the stones below the surface, where it has cleared away for itself a regular subterranean conduit; and not far from one of these places, perhaps 14 or 15 yards, is another of these underground streams roaring and rattling along like its fellow.

I caught a lot of kelts in the Lower Home Pool, one of them, up in the heavy water, of 20lb. weight; but he was a lively beast, and did not take so very long to haul out considering. Here I tried the talents of my friend Andy the Switcher. The bank behind is very lofty, and is, further, exceedingly stony and precipitous. By keeping the point of the rod well out and the fly up stream, I could manage to cast off fairly, but my Switcher showed me his quality by switching the pool all over, every throw being as straight and true as need be. To switch, you give a sort of half toss in, not enough to take the fly completely off the water, or over your head, but so that it shall first touch the surface of the water a little above and at your side. Then switching the rod downwards smartly towards where you want it to go, away it goes to its destination. It is easy enough to compass, if you are wading and have a yard or two of water behind you; but when you are well over a rocky shore, nothing is easier than to smash half-a-dozen flies running. I used to switch well formerly, but had abandoned the practice for many years, and now renewed the cast at the expense of several flies. The lower pool gave us, however, but a few kelts, although we saw one or two clean fish show in it; and we were so long over it that we could barely find time to try the upper pool, so we merely scraped over the tail of it and tackled up.

The next day we tried both pools, being incited thereto by the sight of the clean fish the day before, but nothing but kelts came of it, save a brown trout or so. The day after, being tired of the kelts, I thought I would try for a dish of brown trout, as I had seen a number of very fine ones rising on the further side of the stream on the previous day, there being a good deal of early blue dun on and some March brown. When I got to the water, however, it was cold, raw, and gusty, without a fish moving. I did put up the rod—tried a few casts for form's sake—and that is almost all I could say: I did nothing. All the next night there was a warm rain and west wind.

Having obtained permission to have a day on the Beauly, I started off by train the next morning, having appointed Mr. Geddes, the keeper, to meet me at the station. The Beauly is a very fine salmon river, belonging chiefly to Lord Lovat. The Master of Lovat often has splendid sport. In the Beauly, a few years since, I believe he took 156 fish in five days, or about thirty-one fish per day. The majority of the fish, however, were grilse; but such a feat of fishing has never before to my knowledge been chronicled in this country. The manner in which it came about was from the fish having run up to the two great cruive pools, where they were stopped from going further, the haicks being in, but the traps not set; consequently a large number of fish were collected in these two pools, and the Master being a very powerful man, and using an enormous flail in the shape of a twenty-five foot rod, no doubt made short work of them.

Mr. Geddes was waiting for me, and we walked a mile and a half up to the cruives. Where the stream divided, and forms a couple of splendid pools—the one upon the further side being the better of the two—I put up a remarkable fly called the snow fly, made on a very large round bend hook; the body being blue pig's wool, the hackle large black heron, and the wing a bunch of peacock's herls, with a shoulder of bright orange mohair; and as long as there is any snow water in the river, this fly is used, and has been for many years, The cruives were perfectly open and free to the run of the fish. Indeed, it is only when they are running *en masse* that they are put in work. I tried tbe near pool once with the snow fly, but did nothing—on the further side I changed it for a fly a size smaller, and I rose a nice fish well down the stream. I tried him again and again with all sorts of flies, but he would not have them. The day was woefully bright and hot—quite a summer's day, with hardly a breath of air or a cloud. The water too, was rising, from the west wind and warm weather, and all this was against fishing. I then tried the other pool all over with the snow fly, and after fishing down a very fine run, under a high cliff of rock on the further side, I was going to reel home, when at the very end of the edge up came a splendid fish, but he came all the wrong way, down and across stream. The eddy having taken and partially drowned my fly, I tried him again, but he would not have it. Nearer in, another fish rose, but he would not have it either; and further down again, I saw another nice fish that jumped clean out of water at it, and although from his eagerness I argued well for his taking, he refused. After a time I tried the first fish again, and this time he came up more like business; I felt him, but he got only a scratch, and, of course, was down for the day. After this we went to some very fine pools further down for a mile or so; but whether it was that from the very high wind I could not fish them properly, or that the bright sun and rising water prevented the fish from taking, I did no good, and after a couple of hours' unavailing flogging, I came back to the cruives again, which are the surest find on the whole river. The sun was now down a little, and the afternoon looked much more likely. The first pool I drew blank; the second I fished the stream over as before, and two-thirds down up he came, and I held him. He was a rather sluggish fish, making no great dashes, but he was very "hard in the head" and struggled long. I got him out at last, a firm fresh fish of 10lb. As I had to get to the last train, I feared to stay longer, and so tackled up and made off, finding, when I got there, that the station-master had made a mistake in the morning and put me an hour wrong as to the last train, which hour I had to spend unprofitably in a very dull station, instead of "profitably," as I think it would have been, by the river side. The Beauly is celebrated for much beautiful scenery; and the falls of Kilmorack, and the island, called Eilan Aigas, in which Col. Fraser resides, are beautiful parts, well worth looking at. The spot, too, where the boiling kettle was placed into which the salmon were supposed to tumble and boil themselves when jumping the fall, is also shown to the curious tourist. The Beauly is a capital grilse and autumn river, and has been to some extent relieved by the doing away of the many stake nets which formerly thronged the firth.

There are one or two rods to let on the river on application to Mr. Snowie, of Inverness, to whom all anglers who want information as to them must apply; and the proprietor of the Beauly Hotel has some nice casts which he lets to gentlemen staying at his hotel.

CHAPTER XX.

A LAST DAY ON THE NESS—THE RESULTS OF OVER CONFIDENCE—THE NAIRN—THE HILL OF CLAVA—THE PHŒNICIANS AND BALACLAVA—NESS FLIES—SIR ALEXANDER GORDON CUMMING—THE FINDHORN—ALTYE—THE DUNGEONS OF GORDON CASTLE—INCIDENT AT THE SOLDIER'S POOL—TROUT LOCHS—THE SLUIE POOL—NETS ON THE FINDHORN—FLIES FOR THE FINDHORN.

I HAD intended to visit the Thurso, and had hoped to get permission to try some of the Sutherland rivers, but I waited to hear good news from the former in vain. It had turned out so badly that it was useless for me to go to it. My hopes of the Sutherland rivers also fell through, for I failed to get permission on one or two; and though I got permission to fish one of them, the Helmsdale, subsequently, it came too late for me to avail myself of the offer, my engagements being quite made up, so that my waiting had not been of much avail, and I turned to another quarter.

A very fine spate had been on in the Ness, and I resolved to have a farewell day at the Home and Saltoun waters, thinking that the kelts must be cleared out, and fresh fish come in. The Home was an utter blank. The other I tried on so tremendously gusty a day that we could only fish a sheltered spot or two, and I landed nothing but kelts, which still pervaded the water. I lost a clean fish, however, from handling him roughly, and mistaking him for a kelt. I saw him at parting, and he was a little pink, but perfectly good. So much for being too knowing!

Skirting Culloden Moor towards the east runs the river Nairn.

This river lower down has some nice pools, and which, after a little run of water, are generally supplied with a few salmon and sea-trout; in fact, if it was looked after better, and had not been like all the smaller rivers here away, completely stripped by the nets, it would be a nice little river, and capable of yielding a very satisfactory revenue. In 1830, the year after the Morayshire floods, Col. Rose, of Holme, his fishing in the Findhorn being for a time rendered worthless, "went in for" the Nairn rod-fishing, and, by watching the net-fishers at the mouth, killed from sixty to seventy salmon! After a spate, sport can still be obtained. There was not much chance of salmon and sea-trout being so high up as Nairn-side so early in the season, and I went rather to look at the river, and because it was a picturesque bit of scenery, than for anything else; and having induced Mr. Snowie, jun., to *tutoyer* me over the water, we started to Nairn-side with our trout rods, thinking to find a little amusement with the fly. In due time we reached the river-side and found the Nairn in heavy spate, thick and turbid. As to fly-fishing, it was an absurdity; and indeed any fishing at all looked most hopeless, as she was too full even to make eddies for the worm. Still, it was quite evident that there was no chance at all but to poke into any little hole behind a stone or a turn in the bank with a worm; and I ferreted my fly-book over for a worm-hook, but could not find one, when my companion lent me a set of Stewart's tackle, and capital tackle it is, and catches three fish for one at the old single large-hook plan. The next job was to find a split shot or two for a sinker; but no split shot were to be had. I pulled over everything, and turned out every pocket, but no such thing was found. Nothing at all like it, not a bit of lead, absolutely nothing that would do. What was to be done? The tackle would not work at all in the heavy water without a sinker, and just as I began to despair, Snowie ingeniously came to the rescue; he kicked a hob-nail out of the sole of his boot, and I tied that on to the line with a fragment of silk, and it answered capitally. We turned up the stones along the river and gathered a few worms into a fuzee-box as we went along, and with these makeshifts I managed to delude a couple of dozen of wee trout, which ran about five or six to the pound. But the walk, or rather scramble, for it was all up and down work from Nairn-side to Daviot-bridge, was beautiful; the scenery well repaid one for the trouble—precipitous cliffs, crags, and scaurs banked up the river, so that we often had to make a bit of tall climbing to get from one bend of the river to another. These rocks, a month or so later, when the ferns which grow here profusely are out, must be lovely. Close to Daviot-bridge a good-sized burn falls into the Nairn, and as it was just then very full of water, it made quite a fine fall, pitching down, as well as I could make out, some forty or fifty feet. A little further down the Nairn is the hill of Clava, *unde derivatur* "Clava?" and query, what relation is it to "Balaklava?" Clava is well known as containing the finest Druidical remains in this part of the country, many very fine and perfect circles being found there. Now the Druidical worship was the worship of Baal, and it was brought to England, I believe, by the Phœnicians, and the Phœnicians hailed from a place tolerably adjacent to Balaklava. I have not a lexicon by me, and am anxious to find out the meaning of the word, as it seems to me that there must be some connection, which at this moment I am ignorant of. I have a dim notion that clava means "a sword," bala "a hill," or "a fort upon a hill," but I am by no means certain. I was informed by the proprietor of this portion of the Nairn, in a very indignant letter, subsequently, that I had been poaching his water without leave, as it was not open to the public. I could only plead ignorance and apologise. The way in which I had been led astray was clear, and certainly, whatever else I did, I did no harm to the water, for the wee black trouts I took were not worth the catching. Fishing may be had, however, at Nairn.

On the morning I went to the Nairn, Chalkley left me. I mourned his loss, for great was the deprivation. But his *lares* and *penates* could not get on without him, and so he retired full to the very bung with the pictureqne. He had gorged himself so much upon it that he looked and talked like an animated tour, a veritable splinter of the great Dr. Syntax, who was the first searcher after the picturesque on record ; and, allowing him to be this, I claim for Chalkley to be the second.

The flies used for the Ness are very small ones for so large a river, the greater portion I used being grilse-flies. Although the Ness is a large, wide river, the pools are not very deep, particularly when the river is at all low. The flies which I found most taking were pig's-wool bodies, the lower half yellow, the upper half a red brown, "fiery brown," I should call it, only there is much difference of opinion as to which is the real fiery brown colour. I believe the late Martin Kelly was the best authority known on this point, having had much experience in that particular colour; a grouse hackle at the shoulder and a wing of golden pheasant ruff and teal with one topping, a small topping for tail, and silver twist. The fly is varied by having a light blue upper half to the body, with hackle of the same over it, and grouse over that, the rest of the fly dressed as in the last. Another variation is to substitute green for blue, or even claret. The wing may also be varied with turkey or mallard, and a few sprigs of bustard or teal. "The doctor" also does well in the summer, and the "silver doctor" likewise. The Popham is also used at times with effect, but it is not a fly that I care much for, and is very troublesome to dress. There is another fly, brought out, I believe, by Snowie, called the Highlander; but of that anon. I did little with it on the Ness, but it proved a slaughterer elsewhere.

Before concluding my notice of the Ness I may say that I have heard from Mr. Snowie that the custom of fishing the Four Cobles water one day in eight on the part of the public still holds good, but besides this the water has been taken by the brothers Mackay, who rent the net fishings below, and who hold it for three days a week. They let the rod fishing by the season, *3l. 3s.*, or by the day, *7s. 6d.*, and as there are some very nice streams and grilse and sea trout take well in them, it is by no means dear fishing. The tickets issued have, all the Mackays' days printed on them, and also the other days which belong to Mr. Baillie.

About this time I received a very kind invite from the late Sir Alexander Gordon Cumming, to spend a few days at Altyre, and take stock of the Findhorn; and having finished up at Inverness, I went to Forres, and in good time found myself under the roof of my most hospitable entertainer. Altyre is certainly a most delightful country residence, embosomed in woods, surrounded by pleasant gardens and trim lawns decked with the most magnificent and gigantic Portugal laurels I ever saw, one of which measured one hundred yards in circumference but a year or two since; with avenues and winding walks amongst ornamental shrubs, and the rarest of coniferæ, which abound there. Well supplied in its immediate neighbourhood with all the resources needful for the enjoyment of a great variety of field sports, one need scarcely wish for anything beyond in a country residence. I shall always retain a lively recollection of the pleasant days I spent there in the companionship of a host who was an accomplished angler, and, like myself, enthusiastic in everything that related to his favourite pursuit.

On reaching the house the first thing I was introduced to in the porch was a collection of most awful looking implements, some of which appeared to bear a startling relationship to an iron apparatus termed "the scavenger's daughter," whose acquaintance I first made in the Tower of London. "Ah!" said Sir Alexander, "those are a few trifles from the dungeons of Gordonstoun, where we used formerly to keep *our* prisoners. Those," pointing to a huge rusty iron bar, with two tremendous shackles fixed on it, "are the leglets—we put their legs into them; and these," pointing to another delightful instrument of a similar kind, but smaller, "were the bracelets that decked their wrists; and this little trifle," taking up a huge affair like a slice of a tremendously ponderous gas pipe, "is the necklace they wore—not a comfortable thing to eat one's dinner in. That is the water dungeon-gate from Gordonstoun," pointing to a clumsy, heavy iron grating; "my ancestors kept them in dungeons sometimes where they were up to their knees in water." "Nice sort of people, your ancestors," thought I.

We then sent for Duncan, Sir Alexander's angling attendant, and discussed the state of the river and the chances of fishing on the morrow, which were said to be very small, as she was full and running from bank to brae; and, worse than all, she was not falling. On the next morning this report was further confirmed, so that fishing for that day on the river was out of the question. Accordingly we strolled down to the farm and looked at the live stock, Sir Alexander being a great rearer of fat cattle, and having obtained many awards and prizes at various cattle shows. Many of the beasts showed great promise, and one young leviathan bid fair to come out very well indeed at the next show. In the afternoon we decided to drive down to a small loch on the grounds called the Loch of Blairs, which had been artificially stocked with small burn trout some four or five years before, from the burn that flows through the property. These trout had thriven famously, having many of them increased to 1½lb., the majority of the fish being from ¾lb. to 1lb. We did not expect to take many, as it was thought to be much too early for the fish to rise. To our great surprise and gratification, however, they did rise, and very fairly; and we got about a dozen of fourteen or fifteen inches long each. Fine game fellows they were, making a capital fight of it, many of them getting off in their struggles. The fish were in fair condition, too, and ate very well at table. They took a March brown and a soldier palmer pretty freely, and I can fancy no pleasanter sport on a fine summer evening than to float about on this pretty little loch and to pick up a dozen or two of speckled beauties such as we obtained.

The next day the river was declared to be big, but fishable in places, and we sallied forth intent on slaughter, I taking a trout-rod, as there was a good chance for sea-trout.

The Findhorn has obtained a very unenviable notoriety, from the great size and the sudden impetuosity of its floods. Bridges are often carried away and much damage done by it. The floods often come on with most dangerous suddenness, rushing down the river like a bore, and overwhelming everything that may come in its course.

"Some years since," said Sir A., "I was fishing a pool yonder called the Soldier's Pool, from a soldier having been drowned in it. I had crossed a straggling branch of the river almost dry shod. While I was fishing I observed that the river was changing colour, and looking up I saw a huge red wave coming down beween the high rocks above, with a roar like distant thunder. I made a rush for the place I had walked over ten minutes earlier, not over my ankles, and before I got across it was above my waist, and I hardly stood on the shore when the whole river was one huge, rolling, seething flood. It was a close shave, for twenty seconds later nothing could have saved me. People and horses and carts caught in this way are constantly carried away—in fact, the Findhorn is about as dangerous a river as any in the kingdom. I need not say after this that when we fished the Soldier's Pool, I cast a curious glance up the river occasionally.

The tremendous floods in the Findhorn in 1829, known as the great Morayshire floods, are a matter of history, a large book having been written on them by Sir T. Dick Lauder; and the gallant rescue by some boatmen of a farmer and his family, who were surrounded on a small plateau by the roaring flood, is still told as one of the deeds of daring done during this dangerous period. The destruction done to property was enormous, this river as well as the Spey in places rising fifty feet above its usual high level; and it is perfectly astounding and inconceivable to see the places pointed out as the level of the flood at that date. So filled up were many of the best salmon-pools, and so torn about the bed of the river, and so charged with alluvial matter was the water for a long time after, that the salmon deserted it for years, and it was feared that they would not come back to it again. The estimated damage on the Altyre estates by this flood exceeded 8000*l.*

Some miles up the river is a celebrated pool called the Sluie Pool, the net-fishing of which belongs to the Earl of Moray; and in the annals of the house, there is a letter from the present Earl's ancestor to his Countess, who was in London, stating that during the night before they had made a tremendous haul of salmon, to the number of 1300, in the Sluie Pool. Long might the Sluie Pool be dragged now without producing 1300 salmon; indeed, I almost doubt if the entire river proper produces as much in the whole season. Hard by this pool, which is a very remarkable one, is a very striking natural phenomenon. Up to about this point the river runs through old red sandstone or freestone cliffs. At this point the freestone suddenly ceases, a large block of plum-pudding stone crops out, and then the primary granite commences as abruptly as the freestone terminates, and the river at once assumes a totally different aspect, running over a rock bed and through rocky channels; and great as is the contrast, it is difficult to say which forms the more lovely scenery, the fine bold striated cliffs and precipices of the freestone, or the more rugged and jagged rocks of granite. Both are remarkably fine throughout the greater part of its course: the Findhorn is pre-eminently beautiful, and the charming winding drives cut through the Altyre grounds, and wandering in and out of the woods along the banks of the river, are much sought by visitors and lovers of the picturesque in the summer.

The river was still very high for fishing, and the first pool was a blank. While fishing down the next, a fish rose in very slack water near the side. He was supposed to be a kelt, from the unusual place he came up in. He declined to come again, and we left him. At the top of the same pool I got hold of a very nice fresh-run sea-trout, 2½lb., and one or two other smaller ones, and some yellow trout. Sir Alexander fished three or four more pools up the river, but without getting a rise. At length we came back to the same pool again, and came over the fish which had risen previously; and, by dint of coaxing and changing of the fly, he came up and took boldly, and after a little sluggish play, he was landed, proving to be a beautiful clean fish of 10½lb., as fat as a little pig, and round as a top. I have seldom seen a handsomer fish, and certainly never ate a better one. We had a slice of him at dinner, and he was full of curd, and as crisp as though he had been crimped.

The next day was Sunday, and we took a long walk through the Altyre grounds and woods. The property extends for nearly seventeen miles in one direction. These woods were very widely planted and cultivated by the late baronet; and the care bestowed upon them has not been thrown away, as they are now producing a very handsome return. Planting is still carried on by his successor with great spirit. No less than two millions and a half of plants of fir, larch, spruce, &c., have been put in during the past year and a half.

During our walks we obtained magnificent views from various elevated parts of the grounds. From one place, called the Gallow's-hill, we could see portions of no less than eight different counties. This Gallow's-hill is rather a remarkable place. "We had formerly," said Sir Alexander, "the power of life and death; we summoned our own court, and tried our own prisoners; and if we found them guilty we just hanged them out of hand. We hung a fellow here during the last century, one Macgillicudy; he was tried for stealing wood to the value of fourpence, found guilty, and sentenced to be hanged. I may say it was not the only offence by many that he had been guilty of, but it was the last straw that broke the camel's back, and his neck into the bargain; and we caught him, convicted him, and hanged him on a gallows on this very spot, in the sight of the whole country side. By Jove! I wish we had the power now; I know three or four fellows I'd hang straight off," concluded Sir Alexander, with characteristic energy. During our walk we flushed a great many pair of woodcock, which breed largely thereabout; and, after glancing over a well appointed kennel, in which were a number of very promising young Gordon setters, we found that our rambles had given us a capital appetite for dinner.

On Monday the river was in very fair order, and though the day was rather bright, we expected to do great things. The lower pools were a blank, until we came to the Soldier's Pool. "Now here I will make you a bet I rise a fish," said my host; and, being incredulous, I made a bet (which I owe to this day, by the way, as it was in whisky), and so, at the word, up came the fish. He was, however, but lightly hooked, and after a flounder got off. It was but a little round hole; I did not at all expect there was another fish in it, but from under a rock on the far side another fish came at the fly, and missed it. He made another offer with a like result, and then refused all other temptations. Onwards we went, after some heavy scrambling, up about a mile or so to a pool, called the Ledenreich, and here, after fishing it blank, Sir A. was just winding home to walk out when a fish took him, and, after being set down for certain as a little kelt, he turned out a nice little clean fish of 6½lb.—the fish seldom running so small as this in the Findhorn; but, somehow, they seemed to run small in all the rivers that year, which I look upon as a sign of over-fishing and unnatural deterioration. In the next pool above we had another bet of more whisky (for which I am also a defaulter), and lo! as if the fish had been ordered, up jumped a 9lb. fish, and after some smart play and running down over the rapid into Ledenreich, I clipped him. We then went back to the Soldier, and found the fish we had risen at home. He came and took at once, but was so lightly fixed that he also got off, and we went home with two only; we had expected much better sport, but the draught nets were getting no fish below, in spite of the fine spate. All they caught was the body of a poor girl who had been accidentally drowned some miles up a day or two previously—caught in the spate, no doubt, when attempting to ford the stream. Sir Alexander wrote to me subsequently that from that time forward he took only five other fish; so that a fine April spate of nearly five weeks long, with four Sundays in, and fine running water, produced to the only rod upon a long reach of the very best water on the river just eight fish and no more, and the nets in the river, hardly any at all, the only fish obtained being those taken in the fixed nets at the mouth; and this in a river that formerly gave 1300 fish at a haul in one pool. The stake and bag-nets at the east of the river mouth, however, have been taking nearly everything that has appeared at the *embouchure.* Can stronger evidence be needed of the mischievous, destructive, and unfair nature of the present system of stake and bag nets? Not so many years ago the Findhorn would have been filled with fish by such a spate as I have noted; now they do not and cannot come in. The last Scotch law did not benefit the Findhorn one bit; the most destructive nets still remained close to and completely dominated the eastern mouth of the river. Rivers which run into the sea without any wide long estuary have not benefitted much by the interference with the stake nets. What is wanted is a new definition of the mouths of such rivers, which should be made to extend for three miles on either side of them at least (five would be better), within which stake nets should be abolished. The nets noted were set up but a few years ago, and in the first two or three years they returned tremendous profits to their proprietors, but it must have been at the expense of the stock of the river.

The next day I had to flit to the north, but as I did not go until two o'clock, we utilised the morning by driving up to a most picturesque and charming little loch, called the Loch of the Romach, which is inclosed amongst high overhanging hills and woods, and looks more like a wide river flowing through a wooded ravine than a loch. On the way up we could not but notice the immense damage done to the plantations by squirrels. These little pests eat the bark of the trees round about two-thirds up the tree; the wood dies, and then in the first gale of wind the top of the tree snaps off, and the tree is spoilt. There were literally hundreds of trees thus spoilt as we drove along, and the mischief done must be very serious. As soon as the boat was prepared we embarked, and drifted slowly down the loch, fishing towards the shore. There was rather a stiff breeze blowing, and it was very early in the year; nevertheless we managed to hook out about two dozen of very nice trout, some of them approaching a pound—the majority about half that weight. Later in the season the sport is very pretty in this little loch, and very abundant likewise; but fine tackle and small flies are needed. Sir Alexander and another rod killed one hundred trout in one day a few years back. I found the March brown, the soldier palmer, and the coch-y-bondu tolerably persuasive both on loch and stream at this season.

The flies used for the Findhorn are mostly silk bodies and of largish size—dark-blue, green, olive, and claret; large toppings for tails, and well-mixed wings, with whole teal or small bustard feathers in them, and two or three toppings or jungle-cock feathers, heavily tinselled, and hackled variously with jay or gallina at the shoulder.

CHAPTER XXI.

The Blackwater—The Alness—The Carron—Good Sport—The Oykel—The Cassley—The Shin—Andrew Young—"Ephemera"—The Fleet—The Brora—The Helmsdale—Conon Angling—Publics and Angling Hotels.

On arriving at Inverness 1 found an invitation awaiting me to fish the Blackwater, and a permission to me to fish the Conon, very kindly obtained for me by Lord Saltoun from Seaforth Mackenzie. The Blackwater is the largest of the tributaries to the Conon, and is a capital little river. The fishing part of the river is only about one and a half miles long, the fish being stopped from further ascent by a high fall, but the whole of this mile and a half is fishable; and as the river had the reputation of being full of fish, and they take well in the Blackwater, I was glad enough to get the invite, and hurried off the next morning to Alness, which was the trysting-place. Unfortunately time was so brief that I could neither write nor telegraph to make arrangements, and was obliged to chance catching my friend; and the chance, as chances will at times, turned against me.

It was a drizzling morning when I reached Alness—what the Scotch call in some parts a "saft," and in others "a fresh" day. It drizzled in that persevering manner which threatened to turn to something a trifle heavier before the day was out. My friend had missed the train that conveyed him towards his fishing by about half a minute, and had returned home, intending to go by the next; so I made sure I should catch him, and waited at the station. He did not come in, and the train went without him; so I walked up to his house and found that he had not long started to drive, *viâ* Dingwall. There was a train to Dingwall at one o'clock, and by that I thought I should perhaps catch him. I had an hour to wait, and spent it looking at the little river Alness, which runs through the village. The Alness is a very pretty river, a size or two larger and better than the Nairn. Some of the lower pools are really very fine pools; and formerly a good many salmon, and plenty of grilse, with abundance of very fine white trout, were taken in the river. But it has been fished out and poached to death. There is a quarrel between some of the smaller holders, while the principal proprietor unfortunately does not care about it; and thus a really excellent river, which might produce a very handsome revenue and capital sport, is utterly sacrificed. It seems really a thousand pities that rivers like this and the Nairn should be neglected. They may not be first-class rivers, nor even, perhaps, second-class; but I know, if I had the fishing of them, that with a little artificial propagation I would soon make them yield me a very handsome income. But a few years since a salmon or two, or two or three grilse, and a dozen of fine white trout of from one to five pounds weight, would not have been a very unusual day's sport in the Alness; now, I fear, it would be a very unusual one.

When I got to Dingwall, I found that my friend had driven up to the river, which was eight miles off. As it was raining very heavily, I thought he would hardly continue his sport, and that I should most likely meet him on his road back; and thinking also that I should have quite as good a chance of seeing the river on the morrow, I remained in mine inn, and thus lost my opportunity of seeing the Blackwater, and of having a good day's fishing. My friend returned at night with five fish, having hooked and lost five others. The river, he said, was full of fish; but (there always is a "but" when anything good is in the horizon) the lessee of the river himself had come up that very day to fish, and whilst he was there, of course we could not expect to get on so short an extent of water. I heard afterwards that he had very good sport, which is a decided departure from the bad sport which may almost be looked on as the rule in most of the Scotch rivers this season. My friend, however, to make up for the disappointment, very kindly offered to take me over to the Carron, on which he had permission for a couple of days; and, having made arrangements for next morning, we parted.

The train did not get to Alness until late; but we made a start at once for Ardgay, which was eighteen miles off, across the mountains. The day was lovely, and the drive delightful, as my companion knew all the moors, and all about them, and what sort of sport they afforded, and who rented them; and so the time passed pleasantly, until after rising steadily for a long way, we began to descend upon the fine bold scenery of the Dornoch firth. A short distance out of Alness we passed a very snug little wayside inn, called the Stittingham Inn. Hard by it is a pretty little loch, which gives good trouting, and the Alness, which also gives good trouting, is not far away; and there are some good burns in the neighbourhood. For retirement, cheapness, and fresh air, and a little light fishing, it is to be commended. The Dornoch firth is the outlet of several rivers: the waters of the Carron, the Shin and the Oykel discharge themselves into it; but it is very shallow, and the sands are bare at low tide; but when the tide is running out, and there are heavy spates in the rivers, it runs furiously; and should a stiff breeze blow from the east, it makes a very nasty sea.

In due time we reached Ardgay and put up. We had something to refresh the inner man, and then got our rods under weigh to fish a few of the lower pools, as, being late, we could not do much that afternoon. The first pool we tried is called the Gledfield pool, and fishes fairly when the river is high. I did not know what fly to put up, but our attendant (an old fellow who knew all the rivers within twenty miles of Alness) seemed to have a fancy for a "Highlander" of Snowie's; so I put it on, and after a few casts I rose and hooked a nice fish, which, after exploring the various recesses of the pool, came to net and scaled 8lb. My companion very kindly and liberally made me take the best water. As we were going up to the next pool we met a gentleman coming down, and my friend stopped to talk to him, while I fished the next pool, which I was hardly half over, when I rose a fish ; he did not come kindly, so I gave him five minutes, and then tried him again, and he came and fixed himself. He was rather a dull fish, but I got him in at length, and he weighed 9½lb. After this we tried two or three more pools—pool and pool about; but the evening got very still, and nothing more came of it. So we just skimmed over the Gledfield again on our way home, and got to our inn. I was up early the next morning and tied a couple of Highlanders before breakfast, and it was fortunate I did. The morning was cloudy, dull, and still, but there was a haze about which I did not like; and by the time we were at work the haze was away, and a regular August sun was beginning the day. I rose a fish in the first pool, hight the Raven ; but I knew that it was hopeless to expect any to take in such weather. It was very trying, for it was almost the only really good chance I had had of a capital day's sport, the river being in superb order and full of fish, and not another rod on it; while I could command every pool from the bank. But the sun broiled away, and fishing became a toil, a mechanical labour. I rose another fish in a pool called "The Oak Tree," but, of course, it was useless. Old Bob kept on trying to support our spirits by saying "Ye ken there's wather in her, an' that maks a' the difference." But it would not do—water or no water, they would not rise, still less take in such a blaze of light and glare. I fished on, merely hoping to move a fish or two, that I might know where they were, so as to cast them at once without loss of time in the evening.

My friend rose a fish in a pool called the Bulwark, and, as it was a rough stream, he had hopes; but, although the fish came again and again five or six times, he always came with his mouth shut, and having at length bullied him into the sulks, he was obliged to leave him. I went on to the falls, where is a splendid pool, which a farmer at work there told me was full of fresh fish, as he had seen them jumping all over it in the morning; but, rough and swirling as the water was, they would not rise now. I waited an hour for a cloud and got one at last, but it was of no avail; I just wasted my time, and all would not do. My friend got a couple of sea trout, and as he had an appointment at home in the evening, he left me about half-past six to finish the evening out alone. As he went, I hailed him with: "Now I will go and catch your fish in the Bulwark." I went down, just to try my friend at the Oak Tree, but he was "not at home, thank you." I then went to the pool next above: in three casts I rose a fish, gave him a rest, rose him, and hooked him; he took one turn and made his *congé*. I felt exceedingly riled, and hummed "Bad luck can't be prevented" in the most savage key. I fished the pool on down, and about two-thirds down I rose another fish; he touched the fly, so I did not expect to see him again, but casting in a little time after to the same spot, deep under water, either he or another fish took me and made a jiggering match of it just inside a ledge of rock; but I got the best of the match at last, and jiggered him out, and he weighed 8lb. I do not know any sensation so trying to the angler's nerves as a jiggering salmon. I always expect to lose a fish that takes to jiggering, though it is by no means a proof, as has often been stated, that such fish are lightly hooked, or even hooked in the lower jaw. I watched a fish which was jiggering, not long since, and he whirled and twirled himself round and round with extraordinary velocity, as if he wished to wind himself up the line, as I have seen a conger do sometimes; but when he came up he was very well hooked in the lower jaw, and I had to cut the hook away with a part of the flesh, before I could get it out. But to return to my fishing. I then went to the top of the pool, and began it over again; and just where I had lost my first fish I rose another, and hit him very hard; but casting in the place a minute or two after, another fish rose and took me. Either the little pool was full of fish, or they rose and rolled over the fly and were touched in the tail or body, and did not heed it; from their rising so much in the same spots I could not help fancying the latter was the case. The fish I had hooked was the brother of the other, but more lively; and he ran all over the pool and thoroughly disturbed it. I tried it again, but could not get another rise, so I went up to try my friend's fish at the Bulwark, while my gillie went into a house to borrow a cloth to roll and carry the fish in; and long before he came out again I was yelling, "wild as the scream of the curlew," for the net, for at the third cast our friend made a lovely rise in mid stream, but rabid for it this time, and we were soon dancing a two-handed reel with the marriage lines between us. In good time, however, my gillie came to the rescue, and we baled out the voracious stranger, the best fish of the lot, 9½lb.; a little lanky, however, and not quite so well made as the others.

What a strange feeling it is in human nature, particularly sportsman-human nature, that love of wiping a friend's eye. I admired that fish twice as much as either of the others, and thought with what exceeding charity I would write to my friend and tell him that I had done it, and how he would recollect that I had said that I would do it. Curious beings are sportsmen, particularly fishermen.

Each of the three fish had contrived to cut the tinsel of a fly, so that my Highlanders were sadly shorn of their attractiveness. I put on another fly, and went to another pool some 500 yards up and caught a sea-trout, and rose and touched another salmon; and, as the evening was now closing over us, we waded across the river to our dogcart, which stood waiting, pleased with the wind-up to what promised at one time to be a disastrous day. I have very little doubt, if the weather had been as favourable as the water was, that we should have bagged some ten or a dozen fish at least, if not more. Tickets may be had to fish one side of the Carron on application at the inn the Balnagown Arms. I think the charge is 7*s.* 6*d.* a day, and you give up the fish; but the angler must not calculate upon always getting sport. I was exceedingly fortunate in happening upon the river on the very day when she was in the best spate; but the river falls very rapidly, and if no rain came, and nothing happened to keep her up, she would be down again dead low in a couple of days. Of course, being small, and with a mountainous and rapid course, the water runs away at once; and the river, which will be in fine order in the morning, may be full low at night. If the angler chances to be on the spot or within easy reach, it is worth a visit; but I would scarcely recommend anyone to come from a long distance, as they might have to wait for weeks without a spate. From this I went back to Conon to fish the Conon, but before leaving Ardgay I may as well record what I know of the rivers on this coast of Sutherland, and in the neighbourhood, as all this country is now much more easily got at than formerly.

Most of the rivers from the Dornoch Firth northwards, within the county of Sutherland, belong to the Duke of Sutherland. The public have little or no chance of getting at them save by permission, they being either held by the Duke or in private hands. The duke's factor, Mr. Peacock, of Golspie, is very liberal in permissions. The Oykel, with its principal feeder, the Cassley, rises away by Assynt. It contains a long stretch of fishable water, extending from the falls above Oykel Bridge down to its junction with the Dornoch Firth; it is a capital grilse river, and often shows very fine sport. It belongs, as does the Carron, to Sir C. Ross, and can be fished for about five miles by staying at Oykel Inn, and paying 10*s.* 6*d.* per day. The fish have to be given up, but the sport is worth the money at times. For salmon fishing, spring is the best time, but the summer gives the best grilse fishing. I had leave on it, but I could not afford the time to go to it. The Cassley is a nice stream, and also shows fine sport at times, particularly if there is a flood to bring up the grilse. The river belongs to different proprietors, of whom Sir C. Ross is one: his water can be fished by ticket, by application to his agent, Mr. Forsyth, of Parkhill; and a portion of the Eanig may be fished by staying at the inn, and there are two or three decent pools in it—Rosehall is the best station for it. Next comes the Shin, once well-known to the lovers of the angle, when held by my old friend and gossip, poor Andrew Young, than whom an honester and more enthusiastic salmon fishery reformer never existed, and with whom and his friend "Ephemera," of *Bell's Life*, my earlier career in the course of salmon fishery reform was associated. The Shin used to be a magnificent salmon river, and should be so still. When Andrew Young had it the fishing ran to from 12*l.* to 13*l.* or even less than that per month for a rod. Goodness knows what it is now, four or five times as much, if it has followed the fashion, as doubtless it has; and what the sport was at times may be gathered from the fact that my poor old friend "Ephemera," or rather Fitzgibbon, as his name really was, killed fifty-two salmon and grilse in fifty-five hours of fishing, which should be good enough for anybody. What would Manchester and Liverpool pay for such sport now? The Shin is a largish river, and runs out of a very long loch, and, therefore, keeps in fishing order longer than most of the northern rivers, but still it will run low after long dry seasons, or when the waters are shrunk by frosts, and then the fishing will be indifferent for a season. On the Shin are two falls, the lower one is hardly worth the name, and is of no consequence, the upper, however, stops the fish until about May, when they really mean heading, and then, as the fall has been mitigated, they go above it. The angling there is only middling. Below the fall, however, there are twenty good salmon casts. Tickets by the month are let, and the prices vary with the month. Mr. Peacock, the duke's agent, who, as I have said, lives at Golspie, is the person to apply to for information. Snowie knows the best flies, and will supply them. The rail to Invershin makes approach to the last three rivers easy. The Fleet is a small salmon river not much worth notice, except for the fact that off the mouth of the river, or, perhaps, one should say in the estuary at some states of the tide, salmon may be taken in the salt water with the fly. Mr. Peacock occasionally grants permission for it. The Brora has never been open to the public, being held always by private individuals. It is a very nice river, and produces a good quantity of salmon, and is, moreover, a capital early river, fishing well in February, and holding plenty of clean fish much earlier even than this; the reason of which is simply that it runs through a large loch, and has therefore a comparatively high temperature. The same thing has been observed of many other rivers placed in a like position. On the Ness, for example, the fish must run very early to get through Loch Ness, and reach the Garry so soon; for the Garry is one of the earliest and best spring rivers in Scotland, and the same must be said of the fishing in Loch Tay. Loch Brora also gives excellent sport with salmon, grilse, and abundance of sea trout. Mr. Peacock is the person to supply any required information in respect to it. I think at present it is let by the month. The Helmsdale at one time used to be let out in rods, but it is I fear among the "has-beens," and is let, like the Brora, by the month. It is also, like the Brora, a very early spring river; it is a larger river than the Brora, and larger flies are required for it; the fish, too, as a rule, run larger. From February to May, if there be water, the Helmsdale, as a rule, fishes well. I also had permission on the Helmsdale, while at Inverness, but it was rather late for it, and the river was low and out of order, and time pressed, so I did not avail myself of it. There is a large loch at the head of the river, and many smaller ones as feeders, which contain very fine trout, and some charr. The Berriedale and Wick are the only two rivers remaining south of Thurso, and they are little worth notice. The railway now runs to Helmsdale, and next year opens to Thurso, which will be of great convenience for sportsmen. The scenery is varied and delightful, but to get back to Conon.

Conon is not a very picturesque village, and the Conon itself is a large, heavy river, somewhat like the Ness in character. It forms the head of the Cromarty Firth; it is the outlet of several smaller rivers—the Orrin, the Blackwater, and others, all good salmon-streams; while the main river drains the waters of several lochs far up towards its source, some of them, as Loch Fannick, being of large size.

Most of the salmon entering the Conon at this time of the year are running for the tributaries to which they belong; and being a good deal worried with nets, and the cruives with which the river is fished, they do not take well until they reach them. Thus you may see a dozen fish rising in one of the streams, and not be able to prevail upon one of them to look at a fly. Some of the streams are both long and heavy, and it is no joke on a warm day to wade in heavy waders and to work one of those streams steadily down from top to bottom with a 20-foot rod. Oh! my beloved brother of the rod, do you know the taste of beer—of bitter beer—cooled in the flowing river? Not you; I warrant, like "The Marchioness," hitherto you have only had "a sip" occasionally—and, as Mr. Swiveller judiciously remarks, "it can't be tasted in a sip." Take, then, your bottle of beer, sink it deep, deep in the shady water, where the cooling springs and freshes are. Then, the day being very hot and bright, and the sun blazing upon your devoted head, consider it a matter of duty to have to fish that long, wide stream (call it the Blackstone stream, if you will); and so, having indued yourself with high wading breeks, walk up to your middle and begin hammering away with your 20-foot flail Fish are rising, but not at you. No; they merely come up to see how the weather looks, and what o'clock it is. So fish away; there is not above a couple of hundred yards of it, and you don't want to throw more than about two or three-and-thirty yards at every cast. It is a mere trifle. An hour and a half or so, good hard hammering will bring you to the end of it, and then—let me ask you *avec impressement*—how about that beer? Is it cool? is it refreshing? does it gurgle, gurgle, and go down glug," as they say in Devonshire? Is it heavenly? is it Paradise, and all the Peris to boot? Ah! if you have never tasted beer under these, or similar circumstances, you have, believe me, never tasted it at all.

There is a very snug little angling public at Conon. Perfect happiness is not to be found anywhere on earth, perhaps; but the nearest approach to it is to be had in a really good angling public. I say "public" in order to mark the establishment I refer to. Had I said "inn," my meaning might have been misconstrued, and I might have been supposed to indicate something of the hotel breed, whereas nothing is further from my thoughts. The hotel does not do for fishermen. It is all too stately and too *imposing* in every way. There is your solemncholy waiter, with his white choke and his impressive civility, both of which you know you will have to pay for in the bill. Yes, there he is, with that everlasting dirty napkin shifting from one hand to the other, with his oppressive politeness. How can you venture to eat your dinner before that individual without ordering a pint of *that* sherry?—and, oh! that sherry. What is it? There was a wonderful beast shown to the London public many years ago under that title, "What is it?" No one could say, excepting that whatever it was it was very nasty. The sherry reminds me of that beast. You know how bilious it will make you, and you tremble while you consume it. You hate it worse than salts, for it will make you more uncomfortable, yet you feel constrained to order it; and should you venture to order tea instead of dinner, and something hot and comforting with it, you feel like a culprit; as if that white choked incubus were an innkeeping detective, finding you out in making away with a meal by compressing two uncomfortable meals into one comfortable one, and covertly disposing of that pint of sherry in a highly swindling sort of manner. If you order beer with your dinner, how like an ogre that waiter glares at your wine-glass—oh! that inevitable, overpowering, and all-pervading wine glass! Why will they put it on the table in that matter-of-course sort of way, which is so trying to weak-minded individuals like myself? What fits of indigestion that wine-glass has given me! Empty or full, the result is pretty nearly the same.

But my angling public—there, indeed, I am monarch of all I

survey. There is no awful waiter with weekly washing bills for his neckties. There is no need to ask where the smoking-room is. No. I interfere with no one else's comfort but my own when I pull up in front of the fire, put my feet on the hobs, and light my pipe, without "By your leave, or with your leave." There is the couch and the easy chair—not easy with the strained easiness of upholsterers, but with the easiness of long dwelling heads, shoulders, backs, &c. Somehow, all in dents and holes as they are, every dent and every hole fits something about you. Do I ring, I am instantly waited on by a neat handed Phyllis, whom I address as Mary or Susan, and we have quite a conversation as to what is required for my refection, or other comforts; whereas the waiter is not an individual with whom I consider it as pleasant to converse, I expect him to supply me with so many pints of conversation to order. And the hostess, who is always so glad to see you and so sorry to lose you, makes everything so pleasant, that you quite share in her views.

Some time since I was mightily taken with an anglers' inn, and I wrote some verses which I append, as they may answer the purpose of an angling song, with a good chorus, which is always desirable.

THE ANGLERS' INN.*

Of all the pleasant places
  That in my mind do dwell,
The anglers' inn, unto my taste,
  All others does excel;
For many a heart, o'erborne with care,
  Relief and comfort finds,
And in the jovial angler's inn,
  Throws sorrow to the winds.

Chorus—Then sing the angler's happy life,
    And sing the rod and line;
  And sing the gentle sou'-west wind,
    That wafts the tackle fine,

* If the angler likes this song well enough to wish to sing it, he may, in default of having any other tune for it, contrive to jingle it out to the air of "The Poacher."

And blows it to the fish's mouth.
I think you'll all agree,
There's no place like the anglers' inn,
For perfect jollity.

Then come, my friend, the spring's new breath
Invigorates the air;
Unto the well-known hostelry
Along with me repair,
Where the sheets do smell of lavender,
And it's welcome we shall be,
For the merry, buxom hostess has,
A smile for you and me.
Chorus—Then sing, &c.

A taking day has ended,
Our creels are crammed with fish;
With scale and fin of goodly size,
We've laden every dish;
And o'er a cheering pipe and glass
Our doughty deeds we tell.
On every happy day like this,
How memory loves to dwell!
Chorus—Then sing, &c.

Or in the dainty garden,
Where flowers of every dye
Surround the well-trimmed yew tree seat,
With the river rippling by.
We muse upon the sport we love,
As erst in days of yore
The elders of our craft have done,
Who've lived and gone before.
Chorus—Then sing, &c.

And when the hand that cast the fly
Can cast the fly no more,
And death shall land us fairly
Upon that unknown shore—
May we like yonder river glide,
So calm, so peacefully,
From time, that owes us no regret,
Into eternity!

Chorus—Still sing the angler's happy life,
Still sing the rod and line;
And sing the gentle sou'-west wind,
That wafts the tackle fine.

Though fortune cross and cares perplex,
While time be left to me,
If these be mine, fate cannot frown
On my felicity.

Such would be my praise of the angling inn; but if I dared to approach the description of the superior hotel, I hardly know how I should treat the subject. Let us see; it ought to be in measured cadence and metre—indifferent hexameters with a rhyme to them, for example—something, perhaps, in this way:—

THE ANGLER'S HOTEL.

Come to the Angler's Hotel, hard by some murmuring river—
Murmuring there you may dwell, troubled with qualms of the liver.
Neat are the wines, and the fly's neat as the charges imported
Into the bill, and the beds downy as landlord reported;
Golden the sherry with bile; port, you'll be certainly ill by;
Claret entitled La Rose—*Rose* by Bill Gladstone, or Gilby!—
Brandy *sub rosâ* B. B., by tricks that would puzzle the Magi,
Changeth to Hennessy's best, taken "sub tegmine fagi."
Blue are the sky and the hills, blue you will look in the morning;
Blue, very blue, are the pills needed for slighting the warning.
White are the napkins and plates, white is the "choke" of the waiter;
Black are the chops and the steaks, dainty, unwary Piscator,
Hint not that lean is the fare, landlord will else be observing,
"Gents as come constantly there never find fault with the serving."
Eat and be thankful, nor say words that may sound like a curse, or
Think of the bill yet to pay—things may grow worser and worser.
Shell out the "fives" and the "tens," knowing the hope to be vain O
There to establish the "mens sana in corpore sano."
Bleeding at every pore, quacks recommend still depletion;
Landlords shall make you deplore rabid and rapid secretion.
Having once settled the bill, deaf be to any detergents;
Hasten away, and you will surely remember the servants.

CHAPTER XXII.

The Conon—The Orrin—Reason for Superstition in the Highlander—Taffy and Sandy—Flies for Conon—The Spey—Aberlour—The Fiddich Burn.

During the first part of my visit to Scotland the weather had been cold and raw, with very searching and chilling easterly winds, which speedily made their mark upon me in the shape of a severe cold. But, cold or no cold, the work must be done, and, barking away like a faithful watch dog who expects thieves about, I threshed my way onwards in spite of cough, snow, or easterly winds. The weather, however, was not good for fishing, for, besides these cold winds, there was little or no water in the rivers. But all this was changed now; the wind was "westlin," and was melting the snow upon the Highlands galore. The sun shone out without a cloud, and the weather was one constant blaze during the whole time of my visit to Conon. It rained the night before I came away, and the day on which I was obliged to travel was a fine dark moist fishing day, as is somehow always the case.

The first day I searched out a Mr. Fergusson, a smith in Conon, who is a first-rate operator with the rod, and knows the river intimately. He came with me, and the first afternoon we fished up to the cruives, and for some distance above. But we did not go to the upper pools, being aware that there were two gentlemen already there who had been fishing them all day. The lower streams are fine streams enough, but evidently never *hold* fish. The fish rest in them as they are running up for a very short space, just as they do in the lower pools of the Dee;

but they are a good deal harried by the nets and worried by the cruives, and consequently they do not rest for any time until they get a mile or two at least above the cruives; and from the restless state they are in while in the lower waters, of course they rise badly and take worse. You may see lots of fish rising, and they may even come at your fly, but they are mighty shy takers. I did not have very much experience of them, but in what I had I found this character which I had already had of them pretty correct.

While we were fishing the first stream, which was a fine long heavy stream, some seventy yards long, the netsmen came up and shot round the eddies on the further side where most of the fish lay, and they got one fish of about 7lb. or 8lb. They had been doing well, however, all the week. Subsequently they fished a shallow side stream which leads away up to the further cruive in the dyke, which is of a very peculiar shape, and is very long and straggling, bending downstream like a tongue. This side stream, however, is a favourite one with the salmon for running up, and though they have to run up to it often quite bare backed, scuttling away over the stones and gravel for several yards, where it joins the main river, yet they do prefer it to the main river, which has always plenty of water; and the nets, knowing this, always drag it in preference to the main river; and that they are justified in their confidence was proved on this occasion, by their coming back in about an hour—while we were fishing a splendid pool and run which I do not believe had seen a fish since Tuesday—with eight fine fish.

Here, as elsewhere, the cry was, "You should come in the grilse season for sport." I got quite to hate "the grilse season." In some instances the old familiar, "You should have been here last Tuesday," in the shape of "You're too late for the earlier spring fishing," became evident; but "You should come next week," in the shape of laudations of the grilse-fishing, everywhere pervaded the atmosphere. "Man never *is* but always *to be* blest." The grilse are, of course, more abundant than the salmon, and either they dwell longer in the lower reaches of the river, or they take better while they are in them, as is the case in the Ness and Dee.

We did nothing and saw nothing. On our return down stream we found an angler fishing one of the best casts. He had risen a salmon and was sticking to him; but the probability was that long before he left fishing him, the fish was gone onward in his upward course.

The next day was Sunday, and I took a walk up the river some four miles or so, to look at the Orrin, one of the chief tributaries of the Conon. At present the little river was low, not much larger than a good-sized burn, but the wide expanse of gravel and stones swept over and lying bare near its junction with the Conon, showed that when it did come down, it was a considerable stream. Some distance up a fall occurs, which stops the further ascent of the salmon, and here, of course, very many of them find their quietus.

It was a lovely day, that spring Sunday, warm and delicious. I picked out a shady spot behind a dyke, and sheltered by some bushes, whence I could gain an uninterrupted view of the river, which ran turbulently in a fine rattling salmon stream at my feet, an irregular chain of mountains breaking the background up into all kinds of fantastic peaks, backing up the picture. Here I brought out my luncheon and my flask, and, dipping the pannikin into the crystal water below, I restored the body while I invigorated the mind with the bold, healthy, natural scenery before me. Anon the charms of tobacco were added to the symposium, and my placid enjoyment was perfect. All other sound was lost in the rushing of the river and the plash of gurgling water, save now and then the shrill "cheea, cheea," of the peewits, as they fluttered restlessly about overhead, uneasy at the proximity of a human being to their nests; or the occasional plunge of a salmon as, *liber et exultans*, he cut his way through the clear stream on his route to the mountains.

The warm air was instinct with insect-life, newly sprung into existence. The sky was deeply blue and without a cloud; the distant hills looked stilly and impassively on, as though all that passed around them was the mere dropping of atoms into an hour-glass compared with their concerns—the concerns of giants who had gazed on the creation! Aye, and on wondrous scenes long, long before it. *The* creation, as if there had never been a creation before ours! Εν αρχη. When was that αρχη? Did these hills see it? or, when did they commence? I gazed at the hills, and longed to stand upon the highest of them at eventide. Indeed, by half closing my eyes, and stopping my ears to the sound of the waters, I could almost, by an effort of the imagination, fancy myself there.

To be out on the wild moor, on the lone hill-side, far above the habitation of man, with no companion but nature, as night is coming down and closing in the prospect upon all sides, is, to those unaccustomed to these solitudes at such a time, an eerie thing. How intense is the stillness! The silence almost makes itself felt, and seems to fall with a chilling effect upon the faculties, as though it would arrest them; by degrees those which are most required, as hearing, become sharpened to an extraordinary degree, and sounds that in the mid-day, and in the hum of the lower world, would escape the ear, fall on it with peculiar effect, and the languid breath of the scarce moving night wind rustling the pendant larches far below, comes swelling up, soughing softly onwards, as it rises and falls through the withered stalks of tall heather, or over the boulders of primeval moss-clad rock, tossed hither and thither in some former and tremendous convulsion; or bringing with it, mayhap, the hushed roar of some far-distant waterfall, the sound of which falls dreamily on the senses. How, in the midst of such silence, the shrill whistle of the plover and curlew, or the fall of some stone or fragment of rock, worn from its bed by the weather of ages, as it goes trip, tripping, or thundering down the precipice, from crag to crag, bursts with startling suddenness upon the ear, which is now nervously anxious and on the stretch to catch every sound; while things, familiar enough by day, become weird and strange in the stilless of evening! Or to be out, haply, when the wind rages and howls through the mountain passes and corries, while the thunder bursts around, and the lightning scathes and scars the adjacent peaks! Or to be benighted while the softly-falling snow, whirling along in masses hour after hour, heaps itself up in heavy drifts, obliterating all roads, and concealing under its treacherous surface secret and dangerous bogs, rifts, and hollows, which may prove sepulchres; or, while he is searching for the trodden path, tempts the wanderer further and further out upon the endless moor, where he loses himself in floundering through the murky night, and gladly lies down at length, worn out and weary, to sleep the sleep of death in a snow shroud! Or when the heavy mists arise, obscuring the mountains and blotting out the valleys—taking strange, uncouth, and spectral forms, that impress the mind more powerfully far from the deep solitude they appear in! There is a solemnity in such associations calculated to impress the mind strangely. Is it any wonder that the mind of the Highlander, who passes his days from youth to age in scenes and amid sights like these, should be strongly tinctured with vague superstitions? Consider the shepherd who spends many a long dreary night on the hills, wrapped in his plaid, with no companion but his faithful colley, and no roof but the eternal stars, and who is constantly seeing and hearing unwonted phenomena which his rude intellect is incapable of accounting for, exaggerated and distorted as they are by varying mediums of sight and sound, which often take so wide a range as to afford appearances so striking and apparently impossible as almost to warrant a belief in the supernatural. Would it not indeed be strange if some belief in kelpies, bogles, witches, fairies, and ghaists were not a portion of his creed, almost as firmly believed in as his religion?

"Ghaists!" as poor old T. used to say, "Will onyone say there's nae siccan thing as ghaists? whilk is a belief clean against the declaration and manifestation o' the Sacred Buik itsel! Mon," he would continue, "d'ye ken hoo my wife Meg seed a ghaist in the year o' our Lord aughteen hunder an' twenty-nine? Ay, Meg,"—and then he would tell that long tale, with a tremendous preamble, to the effect that Meg was engaged to wash up at the great hoose, and had risen, much against his persuasion—as he had been somewhat alarmed earlier in the night, and did not like to be left alone—about four in the morning; that Meg, firm to her promise, dressed and set out in the dark; that he was beginning to feel very eerie and uncomfortable, when of a sudden "the door bangit open fit to flee af the postel, and in rushed Meg, a' ramfeezled an' tousled, an' scraigin oot 'Steek the door! steek the door!' joost dinged hersel' doon by the chimla lug richt awa' intil a swund. 'An Meg, woman, what's wrang wi' ye? what ails ye? Hae ye seen onything?' I asked. An' oh! she lookit, an' lookit, an' glowered sae eldrich-like, I was faurly skeert oot o' ma saven sanses wi' fear mysel', and I'd a mind to get into the meal airk, an' pit the Bible a top o't for safety, d'ye ken, for deil a ghaist or a bogle o' them a' daur face thot, mind. An', as for Meg, a' she could was to sit chittering an' wringin' her hands, an' scraigin' oot till ye'd thocht the roof would fa', 'Steek the door, steek the door!' An 'Meg, wooman, in the name o' a' that's abune, what hae ye seen?' said I again; an 'Oh! a dunna a dunna,' said she; 'but steek the door, steek the door!' an sic was the affack o' that veesitation upon Meg, my wife, that she never could and never did tell whatn she had seen to this day. And noo does ony mon after thot mean to tell me he disna believe in siccan a thing as a ghaist?" Deep, indeed, are the superstitions of the Highlanders, and firm was the belief formerly that their own race was the most ancient in the world, as "old as their hills," in fact. There is a capital story told of a dispute between a Welshman and a Highlander as to the pre-eminence of their races in point of descent. Taffy lied most vain gloriously to prove their direct descent from Adam, but Sandy knocked him out of time by declaring not only that Adam himself was a Highlander, but he quoted even the very Gaelic which Adam made use of when he first saw Eve, and which words he avowed to be still carefully preserved (somehow) amongst the annals of his family; and in proof of his assertion he rendered his claim in the following verse:

When Eve, all fresh in beauty's charms,
First met fond Adam's view,
The first word that he'l spoke to her
Was "Cai mair tha thu an diugh."

Pronounced as "Cummir ashin du;" which means in English, "How are you to-day?" After this, it is needless to say, that even Taffy collapsed.

The next day being Monday, of course there would be fresh fish in the river, as the river was in fine order for fish to run, so I made a start early to get to the upper pools in good time, Fergusson promising to join me in the middle of the day. There was no mistaking which were the streams, as they were marked enough, and I had spotted them the day before. Early as I started, however, I found two gentlemen there before me, one of whom is a resident, and works the river pretty constantly. They were fishing the best stream—a fine, rapid, rattling stream; having fished the one above it previously, which I did not know at the time. There were but these two streams below the Orrin for some distance down. There is, however, a good cast or two up above; the one opposite to the rhododendron walk at Brahan Castle is a capital one. I fished the upper stream down twice, and twice rose a fish about half way down it; but he came very shy, and, although I plied him with various flies, he would not take, which was not wonderful, for the day was broiling and the river was full of snow-water, as were most of the rivers now; and by the time I had fished the stream down twice—as it was a very long and heavy one to fish, requiring deep wading and long casting to cover it—I was tolerably glad to take a rest and a weed. By this time the anglers had left the lower stream, in which they had done nothing; they also having twice risen a fish in the upper stream, I found, though not the same fish I rose. So we exchanged, and they went on to fish the upper and I the lower stream. The lower stream was a pretty long one, and it was such a tempting-looking one that I fished it over three times with three strange flies. But it was useless; I did not get a touch or an offer of any kind. By this time the day was well on, and as the other gentlemen had fished the upper stream out of the boat, and had pretty well disturbed it, we decided to go down. I tried two or three nice-looking runs down on my way to the lower pools, but without any encouragement at all. At the tail of a pool called the Green Bank I handed the rod to Fergusson for a few casts, being tired with the hard, hot work. He moved a fish, which touched the fly and would not come again, though we charmed him with various tunes. On the lowest stream of all, which required a very long heave across, up came a fine fish at me at mid-stream, making a most brilliant rise; but he did not take, and on looking at my fly I found the gut tied round the bend of the hook, so that I had been towing it through the water tail foremost; the feathers working all the wrong way gave it a strange and wild appearance, which seemed to have some attractions for Master Salmo, for when I reversed it he declined to inspect it further, clearly reading "Dangerous" written up in the *salar* dialect. Not another fish could I rise, so I went home; and as Tuesday was scarce likely to be better than Monday, I arranged for a start south the next morning. Having so done and written my letters, it rained all night of course, and was a dark drizzling day, when I have no doubt I could have killed a fish or two—if they had been in the way, and inclined to rise, a conjunction which is desirable for success in salmon-fishing. I give three standard flies for the Conon, and they are standard flies for any river, being capital general flies. No. 1. Tail small topping, and sprigs of gold pheasant tippet; one turn of bright red brown pig's wool, continue half way up with orange yellow, and the remaining half of the body with black pig's wool; body dressed roughly; silver tinsel and black hackle over the black wool only; wing a short gold pheasant tippet feather, covered with a nice bright peacock wing, with two shortish jungle-cock feathers at the cheeks. No. 2 is similar, save that the upper half of the body is medium light blue instead of black; the black hackle only to be dressed on the shoulder; wing the same, minus the tippet feather. These two flies, with perhaps the slightest modification of the wing, would kill anywhere. No. 3. Tail as before; a turn of black ostrich herl over it, a few sprigs of dark yellow pig's wool above it; copper colour up to the shoulder, and the rest a dirty light purple; body not so rough as the others; silver tinsel, and a black hackle from head to tail; wing peacock wing as before; no jungle. This is a capital plain fly, and I make no doubt would be a clipper for Thames trout.

The river above Brahan for very many miles, save with the exception of one or two small bits, belongs to Sir William Mackenzie, of Coul. Salmon, however, cannot go further up than Loch Luichart, as there is a high fall there which stops them. The fishing was for several years rented by Col. Murray, and it affords excellent sport at times; far better than the lower part, as the pools are finer and the water altogether better and more holding.

The next day found me in Inverness, again *en route* for the Spey. I was bound *imprimis* for Aberlour. There I was to meet my brother-in-law and an old friend Mr. D..; and Sir A. Cumming had also promised to get me a day or two in the lower part of the river at Rothes, which is usually the best water on the river. On the way up, the river, which is crossed by the rail, looked to me decidedly thick, as well as high, which boded no good for the fishing; and when I arrived I found that neither of my friends had done anything that day, though Mr. D. had a nice fish the day before. The river was very full, and was far too high for fishing, save it might be just about the tails of a pool or two. The heavy snow that had fallen so lately, lay thickly on the hills which line the course of the greater portion of the upper part of the Spey; and when a westerly wind and a warm sun come together, it melts the snow wholesale, and down comes the river a good foot. Every night the river rose eight or nine inches or more, and every afternoon it fell again; and it is needless to say that when a river is jumping up and down in this way, if it was full of fish, the chance of sport would be small, though there are a few fish which will always take in any water, and it was with some such hope we fished, for Aberlour is not a water that fishes well when very high; but, on the other hand, it fishes well and longer in low water than perhaps do other parts of the Spey which fish better when high. To show how unfishable the water was, I may say there are a dozen good streams and pools which are fishable on it, and during my stay we could only fish three of them; and if sport be indifferent while such a state of things exists, I do not think there is much to be said about it; the reason is pretty evident. Anyone who expects to have sport when a river is two feet higher than it should be with snow-water, expects that which he is scarcely likely to realise. Not that I think the fish will not rise in snow-water, because I know full well that they will. Doubtless it makes them a little picksome and capricious, but it has not the effect of stopping them altogether; and if the water be not too high, the persevering and skilful angler may always hope to meet his reward, though it may not be large. Superadded to these drawbacks, however, we had a far worse one than easterly winds and cold weather, which I do not think generally prove insurmountable obstructions to salmon-fishing. Indeed, cold weather is so natural in the Highlands in the early part of the year, that if salmon did not rise in it, they would seldom rise at all at that time. We, however, had broiling-hot sun, regular July weather, just as we had been having at intervals for some time, and that I look upon as far worse for fishing than any other wind or weather it is possible to have. On the first morning we found that the river had risen very suddenly nearly a foot. We crossed it, however, to our fishing on the further side. Above the ferry was about the best stream, in the then state of the river, we had, and we had but three. I say the best stream—I should have said what would have been the best stream but for the ferry boat, which was regularly several times daily pushed by a large iron-shod staff or towed by a chain up to the very best of the stream, in order to allow for the drifting in crossing, a proceeding which, of course, utterly spoilt it for hours. Having only three streams fishable, it was exceedingly annoying to have the best one spoilt. We fished such of it, however, as the boat had left untouched, but without seeing a fish. We then went up to a fine pool above; and here, noticing the water (which looked very thick) closely, I observed, apparently, a great quantity of sand held in suspension in the water, and when I took off my waders I found a great quantity of sand deposited in them. Some lock or dam must have burst, we concluded, which accounted for the sudden rush of water and brought down this sand. They were launching a number of rafts of timber up above, we found out subsequently, and that, no doubt, was the reason of the disturbance. It quite spoilt our fishing, however. From this we went down-stream to a pool called Campbell's pool, a pretty cast enough, and in this my friend Mr. D. rose a fish, but he came shy. We fished one or two other streams without result, and went in to lunch. The day was so bright that it was hopeless; and as we had plenty of writing and reading to do, we did not go out till evening; but the river, which had fallen a little in the morning, was rising again, and fishing was all but useless—we did nothing. The next day was just a ditto of the last, the river jumping up and down, but on the whole lower than it had been since my arrival. We went up to some very nice water about a quarter of a mile further up, where there was a succession of fine runs of some two hundred yards or so in length, with a fine rocky bottom and rattling streams. The water was now clear of the sand which pervaded it yesterday. I saw a fine fish show himself in the neck of one of the streams, but the fish was clearly running, and not in a taking spot. The water was a great deal too high, but there was just an eddy here and there, where a remote chance lay of a fish rising, but the chance proved even more remote than it looked, as we rose nothing. I would not wish to fish a prettier piece of water, and if fine deep streams and eddies, with huge rocks at the bottom, constitute favourite lying ground, the salmon had it here. Anon we travelled down to the boat pool, still fishing hook and hook about, as dividing the stream rather. Half-way down a fish came at me with a very brilliant rise, even in the midst of the hot sun, as salmon will at times. He gave me a good deal of play, and finally I got him out; he was about 15lb. but was not in prime condition. There was a great deal of doubt as to what he was. Was he a kelt, or was he not? It was almost as close a thing as I ever saw—his head and shoulders were all right in shape and proportion, and his gills were perfectly clean and bright, but he was a little thin in the flank, and his colour was not good; and so with something of a misgiving I gave him the benefit of the doubt and turned him in again—but to this day I am not certain I did not turn in a clean fish. I described the fish to one of the oldest and most experienced anglers on the river in those parts, and he said that he had once or twice met with such fish, and on one occasion he was just as doubtful as we had been; but the fish had been gaffed, so he took him home; and doubtful and poor as the fish looked, he said that it cut and looked perfectly red and clean, and that he never ate a better fish in his life. I have heard more than once of such cases: still it would never have done for me to have killed a fish which the most distant suspicion could have rested on. So he went his way, and I went mine. The next day the river was up and down as usual. I fished in the morning, but did nothing; and in the afternoon my brother-in-law and myself drove over to the Fiddich, which is about twenty minutes' drive from the inn. The Fiddich is a charming little burn, running between high banks, with hanging woods here and there, which if the angler be not provided with wading-boots—as I was not, unfortunately—entails some pretty tall scrambling. The most of the fish in the Fiddich which I caught, ran small—the usual burn trout, in fact, but there are better fish in it, for I saw them, and caught one or two: a minnow in the sharp runs would, no doubt, produce some big ones. There are here and there a few nice pools, and in the lower part of the stream there are often a few sea-trout to be had, but they cannot go far up the stream, being stopped about three-quarters of a mile from its mouth by a weir. I got about two dozen little trout, and my brother-in-law about a dozen. I should like much to fish the Fiddich about the end of this month (May), and to follow it up into the mountains a few miles. It would prove a delightful scramble, and I am sure the quantity of trout one might take would be considerable, as in some places they rose two or three at a cast, and that part of the stream being nearer to the village and railway-station is more fished. Of course, anyone who expects to take a creel full of half and three-quarter pounders will be disappointed.

On our return we found, of course, that Mr. D., by sticking to the river while we went trouting, had got a fish—in fact, he said he would as we drove home—a niceish fish, too, of 8½lb. It was the fish he had risen in the Campbell's pool, and, of course, he had the laugh of us for going trouting when we might have got salmon. I also found a note from Sir A. Cumming, appointing to meet me at Rothes early the next morning for a couple of days' fishing, which he had a general permission for; and as they had been taking fish pretty regularly on that water, I calculated on some sport. I made all ready for a start, but early the next morning a surly-looking keeper brought me over a note from the gentleman who had the management of the fishing, saying that the proprietors had suddenly come down the evening before, and were going to fish, and that he had sent a note to Sir A. Cumming to let him know of it. It was just the same misfortune as happened to me at the Blackwater. It was particularly unfortunate too, as had I known of it earlier I could have got fishing on one or two capital fisheries up the river without the least difficulty, but my time was too short now for me to get leave and to make use of it. The morning came up dark and cloudy. The river was in a little better order than it had been. My brother-in-law went down to a pool some distance below, where, I believe, he got a kelt.

Mr. D. went up to the upper water, and I went to Campbell's pool. I had fished it half down when a fish took the fly quite out of the stream, and in the dead water just where the cast ended. I did not see him come, in fact every fish that was taken took deep under water. Somehow, if they did come to the top, they generally refused; and the first notice I had of him was the giving him an awful drag as I was drawing out the line for a fresh cast. This, of course, was not at all agreeable to him, and he dashed out into the stream at double quick, where we performed the usual *pas de deux;* and after a time I introduced him to a new partner, in the person of my gillie, who, by hook and by crook, stuck so fast to him that he found it impossible to shake off the acquaintance. He was a nice shapely fish enough of 8lb. As if it had only been waiting for the purpose, as soon as I had landed my fish, the sun burst out as bright and hot as ever, and the day was crippled for fishing. After lunch we did little more. Mr. D., I think, got a kelt.

By the way I omitted to give the dressing of the "Highlander" I find. Two turns of silver-twist and gold-coloured silk for tag, one topping for tail, and black ostrich herl over; gold-coloured silk nearly half-way up the body, if the fly be small—if large, a few turns of silk and then yellow pig's-wool will be better. Above this, olive-green mohair, silver tinsel, and a pea-green hackle from tail to head; jay over it at the shoulder, and black ostrich herl head. Wing, sprigs of tippet, with gold-pheasant tail and mallard, with a little pintail over this. Doubled jungle-cock feathers—*i.e.*, a long and short feather on either side; over all a topping, and blue macaw points—and a very good fly it is when the fish like pea-green hackles.

CHAPTER XXIII.

THE AVON—BALLINDALLOCH—THE LEGEND OF THE COO HAUGH—SPEY FLIES—GRANT TOWN—THE PASS OF KILLIECRANKIE, PERTH—HARRY OF THE WYND—STORMONTFIELD—CARGILL WATER—THE ISLA—PEARL FISHING.

THERE is a very pretty river, a considerable tributary of the Spey, which runs into it about eight or nine miles above Aberlour—the Avon. It belongs to Mr. Macpherson Grant, of Ballindalloch. Leave to fish it is generally confined to gentlemen staying at the Delneshaugh Inn, at Dalnas. It had the reputation of being a very fine trout stream; and there was also a capital chance of a salmon—almost as good as on the Spey. As there are some excellent pools in it, under the convoy of a first-rate performer with the rod—the worthy pedagogue of Aberlour, who was employing one of his holidays in his favourite pursuit, and was going to fish the Spey near Avon-mouth, and who undertook to set us off in the right way—we started for the Delneshaugh Inn, to which we had a very agreeable drive, as our companion pointed out the various objects of interest to be seen along the road. One of the stories he told us was rather amusing; it related to the old mansion-house of Ballindalloch, the original site of which was to the south-east of the present castle, and within fifty yards of the turnpike-road. Here the laird attempted to build his house; but when the walls had arrived to about twelve or fifteen feet high, every night the work that was done the previous day was thrown down and demolished! while persons who watched by it declared that they heard a hoarse sepulchral voice bellow forth "Big upon the coo haugh!"—

("Build upon the cow valley," haugh signifying a low-lying fertile valley). The tale of terror was told to the laird, but the laird was something of a sceptic. In the first place, if the devil had anything to with it, of course he would naturally be a Scotch devil; but then he would be a devil of some attainments, and not a common vulgar yokel like this, whose language savoured more of the bricklayer's labourer than of the well-educated Scotch demon. "Big upon the coo haugh," indeed! He'd "big" the rascals! No doubt it was the masons wanting to prolong the job. He'd catch 'em! Accordingly, accompanied by his butler, the laird went to watch for himself. When, lo! a mighty tempest arose; the walls were hurled over as though it were a card-house; and "Big upon the coo haugh!" was roared forth with such supernatural energy that the laird almost, if not quite, swooned with terror. Furious grew the tempest; big trees and little trees were blown up and whirled through the air like straws! and, entangled in the branches of the trees, the laird and his attendant were blown for a good quarter of a mile clean across the river, and lodged up in the tops of two large trees that stood close together on the other side of the river, and were uninjured! Here they remained till the morning, afraid to move or speak. When the storm was passed, they cautiously descended, fearing to wake the genius of the storm afresh. "Jock," said the laird, who never expected to see his follower again; "Jock, is that you?"—"The deil kens best!" quoth Jock. "It's a pairt o' me, onyhow."—"Dinna blate on, then; an' we'll tak' the adveece o' yon chiel, whilk is tendered in a way that one canna weel withstaun, and wee'll joost "big upon the coo haugh;" which it is needless to say he did; the demon whose abiding place he had previously invaded thereafter leaving him at peace.

Now I have mentioned this little legend, not because there is any particular novelty in the story—save in the laird being blown across the river into the tree tops without damage to life or limb—but because it is a legend so very often told in many parts of the country. I am sure that this story of the pulling down of the work done by day, in the night, until the builders change the site, has come under my notice at least half a dozen times, and that too in places so wide apart that there could not be any suspicion of their having a common origin; one of these places being the Isle of Wight, which is about as far from the north of Scotland as could well be. Whence, then, could have arisen a belief or a superstition so widely indulged in? for I have no doubt that there are scores of places where the same story is told, which I have not come across. The places where the event has been said to occur are generally wildish parts of the country —what could be the foundation for the story? Setting aside the supernatural, could the solution afforded by the scientific gentleman's servant in "Pickwick," in that difficult question about meteors caused by Mr. Winkle's dark lantern, and reputed by the said servant to "Thieves."—Could Thieves offer any solution? I confess myself much puzzled, for the story is too general to be without some foundation.

The inn at Ballindalloch is a comfortable little angling public, where an angler might be in the heart of fine scenery, and enjoy some pretty trouting, with a few sea-trout, and a chance of a grilse or a salmon now and then; and the Avon is a very pretty little river. When I saw it it was in spate, so doubtless many of the pools looked finer than they are wont to. On the other hand, the trouting did not show to such advantage. The day was very hot and bright as usual, and the snow-water was coming down heavily in the river, and snow-water is as bad for sport with the trout as it is for salmon, as it checks the rise of flies and keeps the insects under the stones and out of sight. I had been persuaded by my gillie that a small trout-rod would do to fish the water, but when I got there I was sorry I did not bring a larger weapon, as I could not fish the salmon pools properly; and, after trying two or three, I took off the salmon-fly, partly because I could not work it properly, and partly because the brightness of the day and the great body of snow water in the river gave small hopes of sport, particularly as I could not fish the water properly. The trout also rose very badly, very few rising, and many of those which did refusing. My brother-in-law and myself managed to howk out some dozen or fourteen of them, losing one or two fair ones—my companion lost one which he set at 1lb. Several of the fish were half-pounders, one or two a trifle above; but fish of three-quarters and a pound are not very rare, though they rarely top 1½lb. They are nice game fish, and give good sport. The river runs in many parts over pebbly and sandy pools and streams, here and there by rocks and stones, and when in fair order is, I should think, a very pretty river to fish. The minnow would, no doubt, tell tales in the many sharp streams at the heads of the pools. As I wanted to get on the next morning to Perth, I had my traps sent on by the last train from Aberlour, and caught the train at Ballindalloch (which is about one mile and a half from the inn), and went on to Grantown, where I slept, catching the down train on the Highland line the next day.

The flies for the Spey are strange-looking things—long wool bodies, the lower half yellow, the upper black or yellow, and dark claret or purple; some of altogether dirty olive-yellow. The hackles are large black-and-grey heron hackles, or the long feather—not hackle from the back of a peculiarly-coloured cock. This feather is of a shiny, brown hue. All the hackles are laid on the wrong way of the feather, so that they stand up very awkwardly in appearance, but they play much more in the water. In order to secure the hackle as much as possible, the tinsel (which is often silver and gold, side by side) is laid on the reverse way to the hackle, and over it—a process which is difficult to do neatly, the fibres wanting so much picking out. The wings are brown turkey or peacock, or mallard, or dun turkey. These flies can be varied by varying the materials and colours above-named. The best fly I found to kill, however, was a black-bodied fly, with gold tag, silver tinsel, black hackle, gallina shoulder, pintail wing, with two or even double jungle-cock feathers, and a topping over all. This is an old pattern, and a very general favourite.

Grantown is very properly so named, being in the heart of the Grant country; and every other man's name in the place—to judge by the shops, &c.—is Grant; and how the dickens they manage to indicate this Alexander Grant from that Alexander Grant, or that one from t'other, and t'other one from another one, and another one from some other one, and so on, would puzzle any stranger. I believe the fashion is as follows. You go to the place and *ask* for Sandy Grant. The answer is, "Whilk one; there's twenty Sandy Grants." Well, you want the big one. "Oh! Muckle Sandy Grant. Hey, mon, there's joost twal Muckle Sandy Grants." "Twal?" "Ay, twal." "Stop a bit, it's the red-headed one." "Oh! Muckle Rhu (red) Sandy Grant. Weell, there's sax Muckle Rhu Sandy Grants." You make one more shot at it. "He squints." "E-how, then, it is Muckle Rhu Gley (squinting) Sandy Grant. "Weell, an' there's twa o'm still, and whilk is't ye want?" Finally you explain that the man you want has a long nose. "Oway, it'll be Muckle Rhu Gley Lang-Nebbit Sandy ye'll be wantin. Why did ye na say sae at first. Yon's him." The humorous verses of Sir Alexander Boswell may be remembered in evidence of the multiplicity of Grants:

Came the Grants of Tullochgorum,
Wi' their pipers gaun before 'em;
Proud their mothers are that bore 'em—
Feedle-feedle-fum.

Next the Grants of Rothiemurchus;
Every man his sword and dirk has;
Every man as proud as Turk is—
Feedle-feedle-dum.

I believe this jocular effusion roused the bile of a scion of the clan, who forthwith called Sir Alexander out for poking fun at them. There is a very comfortable hotel at Grantown, which I commend to the notice of travellers.

The next day I betook myself to the train, and was soon bowling along "doon the lang glen" which culminates in the Pass of Killiecrankie. The scenery along this line, as it winds through the narrow glen for many miles, with abrupt mountains on either side, is very fine. Loch, river, stream, and mountain whirl by in rapid succession, until we strike the infant Garry where it commences—a small burn—and we skirt it mile after mile until it becomes a fine salmon-stream. As we progress, the scenery becomes finer and more striking. The precipitous rocks, clothed with fine wood, descend abruptly to the river, and the gorge deepens. It was clearly just the place for a Highland fight, and where a handful of men might hold the pass against an army. Here it was that Bonnie Dundee—or, as he was termed by the Covenanters, the Bloody Claverhouse—fought his last fight and died in the arms of victory, in 1689. Turning his back upon the Convention, who refused to hear him, he rode forth at the head of a small band of fifty followers; and being asked where he was going, he waved his hat and is said to have answered, "Wherever the spirit of Montrose shall direct me." "Brave Dunniwassals"—not "three thousand times three," but about three thousand times one—came to his standard; and having gradually drawn General Mackay, who commanded the army of the Covenant, 7000 strong, into the defile, he ascended the water of Tilt, came round the Hill of Lude, and rushed down upon the foe, broadsword and buckler in hand, and completely swept away the greater part of the opposing force. General Mackay escaped, with a remnant of the right wing, but Dundee received his death-wound as he was bringing up some of his men. A stone still stands near Urrard House which marks the spot where he fell. With all his faults (and they were many), he was a gallant soldier and a skilful leader. There is no need to quote the verses which have immortalised him—they are in every child's mouth. As we pass along, Blair Athol is behind, Dunkeld the terrible—

Oh! what a toun, what a terrible toun;
Oh what a toun is the toun o' Dunkeld!—

is in the rear: terrible now only for the formidable style of its architecture, which abounds in a multiplicity of little extinguishers stuck on to nine houses out of ten, without regard to fitness or use; and we stop at Perth at last, where the welcome repose of the British Hotel, kept by Mr. Pople—who did his best, and very satisfactorily, to make me comfortable—received me. I found the house, being so handy to the railway, very convenient; and others appear to think so too, for in the grouse season it is necessary to send word beforehand if beds are required, or the house is full.

On my arrival at Perth, I found that Mr. Paton the gunmaker —who fills the same useful post in that town as Snowie does at Inverness—had arranged everything for me, had obtained permission beforehand for me to fish upon many of the best waters on the Tay, and had, generally, saved me a good deal of trouble. He also took great pains to show me the various waters, and many other objects of interest about Perth, for which I felt very thankful to him, for his experience at once suggested what was worth my seeing in the fishery line and what was not. Perth was formerly the capital of Scotland, and was fortified by Agricola. It is placed on one of the most picturesque sites in the kingdom. It is said that the Romans were so struck with the beauty of the situation, that when they first saw it from the high ground they exclaimed, "Ecce Tiber! Ecce Campus Martius!" There is a great deal that is interesting to the tourist in Perth—the church where John Knox preached his first sermon against Popery; a very quaint old house which is shown as part of the building in which the celebrated Gowrie conspiracy was sought to be carried out by the seizure and captivity of King James by the Ruthvens (other authorities, however, assert that not a stone of the original building is standing, its site being occupied by the Town Hall); while the neighbourhood of Perth contains a great variety of objects of interest—amongst them are Scone Palace, the ancient palace of the Scottish kings, but now the seat of Lord Mansfield; Kinfauns Castle; the north and south Inches—two beautiful public meadows of great extent, on the banks of the Tay, the former of which is now the race-course, and was, in the reign of Robert the Third the scene of that remarkable combat between two rival clans, which is related by Sir Walter Scott in the "Fair Maid of Perth." The clans engaged were the Mackays and the Macintoshes, and thirty champions a side were chosen to contest for the victory. One of the Macintoshes was missing on the day, and an armourer named Wynde took his place, for half a French gold dollar. Twenty-nine of the Mackays fell in the combat, and the thirtieth, as described by Sir Walter Scott, swam the Tay and escaped, ten of the Macintoshes, with Wynde, remaining masters of the field. I need not say how curiously I scanned the scene of this exploit. More peaceable games are carried on there now, amongst which the national game of golf appears to prevail the most.

The Tay is navigable up to Perth, and the whole of the waters above and below Perth, for many miles up are regularly netted, and large quantities of the finest salmon which comes to the market are captured daily throughout the season; some of the tacksmen paying very large sums in rentals—I heard of one who alone paid something like 8000*l*. a year in rentals.

In order to save time, as soon as I arrived Mr. Paton proposed that I should go at once to Stormontfield. We could thus spend an hour or two there, and see all that was required without breaking up a day for the purpose; and accordingly he drove me up to the ponds, which are some six miles or so from Perth. Here we found our old friend "Peter of the Pools" at home, and delighted to see us. Peter took us all round the works, and gave us every information in his power. The Stormontfield hatching and rearing ponds, which have achieved a worthily-earned world-wide fame, occupy a portion of waste ground on the banks of the Tay, about sixteen feet above the level of the river. From a mill lade which runs along the upper part of the ground, pipes are conducted into an oblong filtering pond. The water is filtered from this into a canal, which runs the whole breadth of the boxes, and from this the boxes are supplied. Sixty new boxes had been added to the number since the last year in order to increase the accommodation. These boxes are six feet long, and there are twenty-four of them in a row. There are sixteen rows, with a narrow pathway between each. They are partially filled with gravel, largish stones being laid upon the top, amongst which the ova lie perdu, the whole occupying, as Peter told me, seventy feet square; but I should think that either he or I must have made some mistake in this, as I fancy the area must be much larger. At the lower end of these boxes is another canal, and into this canal as soon as the young are forward enough to seek their own food, the whole of the fry migrate without any persuasion on the part of their keepers. From this canal a sluice allows them to escape into the first rearing-pond. This pond is 223 feet long by 112 wide, and was meant to contain some 200,000 fry; but, as with only one pond they could not rear more than one lot of fry, they could not hatch every year, accordingly another pond of larger dimensions had afterwards been added to the works, and was ready to receive the fry of the year's hatching. From these ponds a sluice allows the egress of the smolts to the river when they are ready to go. The fish pond was then filled with some 150,000 little parr, in the most lively and active condition. It is astonishing how well these little fellows seem to know feeding time. Take a piece of boiled liver and crumble it up, and throw it into the pond, and, instantly, some fifty or a hundred of the fry, about the size of large minnows, rush to the spot, and in less than half a minute every fragment of it disappears. Gulls are great enemies of Peter's, and he gives them a dose of shot whenever he sees them paying their regards to his domain. The mischief these winged depredators do to the fisheries may be estimated by the fact that in one, which he shot while it was robbing his pond, pretty near a score of parr were found; and when the hundreds of gulls we see hovering over the shallows day after day on salmon rivers in the spring, and the number of smolts each one devours *per diem*, are taken into consideration, the loss to the Tay alone must be far larger than Stormontfield can replace.

During my stay I saw the late Mr. Buist, and had a chat with him upon Stormontfield and fishery matters. I also called upon Mr. Brown, the author of the interesting little work on the "Stormontfield Experiments," I was anxious to meet him, as his experience and knowledge of the statistics of the Tay fishings was very considerable; but, unfortunately, he was confined by severe indisposition, and he was unable to see me. He too, alas! is since dead.

The first morning, in company with our worthy host, Pople—to whose care we confided the provisioning department, without due consideration of which a fishing excursion on Tay or elsewhere is not complete—we started for the Cargill water. They have a strange but a very good plan at Perth of taking fishings. For example, a person in business cannot of course fish every day in the week, and, consequently, he does not, perhaps, care to go to the expense and trouble of taking a fishing to himself, which he may be unable to avail himself of; and the rent too would be larger than he would like to pay; and therefore he rents the fishing for so many days per week as he may wish to fish. Suppose he only wishes to fish one day, he rents a day of one of the proprietors, paying from 10*l.* to 20*l.* for it, according to the day and the repute of the water. Again, on the Tay the opposite proprietors have three days a week each. They do not both fish on either side of the river whenever they please, as they do on Tweed, but take the whole of the river on alternate days, varying them week and week about—this being necessitated from the method of fishing adopted on the Tay, for, as will be seen presently, two boats could not fish simultaneously. This plan of taking the water is a capital one for residents, and brings a little fishing within the reach of moderate means. Most of the waters are rented in this way, though, of course, there are some where the entire fishing is taken by one person. The day was hot, bright, and still, as usual, and the water crystal clear. There was a very small chance of our catching fish in such weather and water.

The Isla, a considerable river, which often shows good sport both with salmon and trout, being a capital trout river higher up, runs in at the top of the Cargill water, and, as we were waiting for the boat to come up, we saw a man at the mouth of the Isla, pearl-fishing. The process was a very singular one. He did not dive down amongst sharks and all sorts of monsters, as do his Çeylon brethren, but he sat in a little square deal box (like a packing-case) about five feet square. A rope was stretched tightly across the river by means of two pegs driven into the banks. On this rope the box was threaded, as it were, by means of a couple of rings or wheels, one on either side of the front of the box. By taking hold of this rope, the fisher could pull himself from one side of the river to the other. The method of procedure is thus: Having fixed his rope, the fisherman commences fishing near one bank of the river. Taking in one hand a huge black tin cylinder, somewhat like an overgrown Wellington boot with a glass sole to it, he holds it by a handle, with the glass just dipping into the water and looking into the other end surveys the bottom of the water, through the tube. The glass (which is but common window-glass) being under water, the broken vibrations which occur on the surface do not affect it, and he is enabled to see the bottom even in twelve or fourteen feet of water, distinctly. Of course, clear water and a still bright, day are desirables. As soon as he discerns a pearl mussel, with a long staff which he holds in his right hand, he prods straight down upon it. The end of the staff is split, and the split is kept open by a wedge. When the mussel is fixed in the split, it is hauled up, detached, and cast into the box, and another prospected for. When the ground below him is cleared of mussels, the fisher pulls himself along the rope for a yard or two, and recommences operations. This goes on until he has worked over to the other bank, when he takes out one peg, shifts it up or down a few yards, crosses, and then shifts the other, and begins collecting again. When he has a sufficient number of mussels, he opens them with his knife, feels round about the beards, where the pearls are mostly found, and removing any pearl that may be there, throws the shell and fish overboard, when the eels—who are expert fishers too in their way—soon finish him. A great number of pearls are found, and some of them of large size, before the fisher finds one of pure water, while one of good shape as well is very rare. The great proportion of the pearls are dark, brown, discoloured substances, of all sorts of shapes—rounded on one side and flat on the other is the most general shape. The man showed me one pearl, about the size of a No. 1 shot, of a most brilliant water, and perfectly round; he asked 25*s.* for it; but such a find is, of course, rare, though sometimes a piece of unusual good luck will turn up, and pearls of great value are discovered. But the large pearls are mostly pear or egg shaped. The older mussels, and those which have a rugged or irregular shell, are the most probable pearl-bearers. The part of the river where he was then fishing produced plenty of pearls, such as they were, but very few of any value, as the bottom was too muddy. The mussels in the Tay and its tributaries, in the Forth and Teith and other rivers in Scotland, in the Donegal and other rivers in Ireland, produce pearls, while those of the Thames, where they abound also, though of a different species, do not. A curious question arises, viz., whether, if the Tay mussels were transplanted to the Thames, they would retain their pearl-bearing qualities; or is there anything in the soil or water which encourages this property in some rivers?

But the boat was waiting for us, so we speedily took our seats and arranged our tackle. *Imprimis*, the boats are large wide praam-shaped craft, better adapted for dropping down stream than rowing up. We three all sat side by side—"Three jolly fishermen all of a row"—with our faces to the stern. Over the stern we each projected a rod, one at each corner of the stern, and one over the middle, and each line had one or two flies attached to it. After a time the middle one was changed to a phantom minnow;

thirty or forty yards of line were then let out. The line was stopped by being lapped round a stone which was laid on the stern-board, and away we went rowing ziz-zag across with the head of the boat up the stream, and dropping a little at every board, so that pretty well the whole of the river was combed with five or six flies, or with three or four flies and a minnow at the same time, and with such a profuse choice it would be hard if a salmon could not suit himself if so inclined. This method of fishing is called hurling on the Tay. But we combed as fine a piece of water as there is in the Tay—full of rough rapids and splendid runs—in vain; not a salmon did we even rise. It was hardly to be wondered at, the day was a roaster. One good trout was hooked and lost on the minnow, and I killed one of 1½lb. upon it subsequently. After lunch, having obtained permission, we fished the next water down. But it would not do, not even a kelt would show, and we were finally obliged to retreat empty-handed. When the fish are rising well I can easily fancy this plan of fishing may be very exciting at times, as it is not a great rarity to have two fish on at once; and such a thing even as three being hooked at the same time, and all landed, has I believe been known, though this is, of course, a very great rarity. One salmon seems to me quite enough to engross the attention of one angler; and what I should do with three rods, each with a salmon on, and each plunging here and there and everywhere, I am sure I do not know. I could manage to hang on to one by each hand, but what in the world should I do with the other? I never tried to hold a rod between my teeth, nor could I play a salmon between my knees. Stay! I have it. I would stick the butt of the rod down my back between the collar of my coat and my spine, and, by keeping a stiff back on him, I have no doubt I could manage to work him. Eureka!

CHAPTER XXIV.

LARGE BULL TROUT—THE STANLEY WATER, MR. BRIGGS'S ADVENTURE ON IT—LUNCARTY WATER—GLENALMOND—BESSY BELL AND MARY GRAY—BLEACH WORKS—THE BERMONEY BOAT—HURLING ON TAY—TAY FLIES.

THE next day was like the last—hot, bright, and unbearable for fishing. In the morning I strolled down to one of the fish-factors to look at the fish. They were not very numerous, but there was one fine salmon of hard upon 30lb., and there was an enormous bull-trout of 32lb. A huge beast he was, and would no doubt, on the slab of a London fishmonger, figure as a splendid Tay salmon; for the general public would never have known but that it was really a salmon, the difference in general appearance not being very striking; only when the fish came to table would it be discovered that he was not as pink as some salmon, and was rather dry and flavourless—which would have been attributed to his being rather large, coarse, and overgrown perhaps, and a mental note would, no doubt, have been taken, not to choose such large salmon in future. After this I walked up to Mr. Paton's, and went all over his establishment, where a variety of breech-loaders and other guns were in progress of making, for Mr. Paton manufactures all his own guns, and having been for years practically engaged in the business, he overlooks and sees to the proper workmanship and finish of all of them.

In the afternoon we drove out to the Stanley water, which is some seven or eight miles from Perth. This water is classical and world-renowned, for it was here that Leech derived his inspiration for the cartoons of old Briggs catching that historical salmon. Here is the "Cat hole" where he hooked his salmon, and there that tremendous run he took him down—and a very nasty run it is! and there, too, is Hell hole, where the redoubtable salmon sulked! and that, as I live, is an exact sketch of the very spot where that wonderful gillie is taking his "sneesh!" and here Mr. Briggs landed the fish clasped in his embrace; and there is the very boat, too, in which he sat beaming upon the river, with the three rods spread out before him! Who could fail to recognise the scene where befel the greatest event in Mr. Briggs's sporting career? It is splendid water that Stanley water—such a succession of rattling, rapid streams and swirls, that I doubt if there be so fine a bit elsewhere on the Tay. It was too early for any chance of moving a fish, so we had walked on up the river to inspect the water. Above the Stanley water comes the Burnmouth water—a fine, long, open pool, for a considerable portion of it, which always holds fish, and that too of the largest. At the top of the Burnmouth water is the Linn of Campsie, where the rocky shores approach each other very closely indeed, and, with the exception of an insignificant side stream, the whole of the Tay here pours in a resistless volume through a narrow neck not much more than twenty yards wide, into a deep, dark, foam-flecked swirling pool below, which resembles a huge basin. A fine view of the Linn is obtained from the high rocks which overhang the north side. Here formerly a monastery stood, and faint traces are still to be seen of its walls. The scenery is very fine, and is alone worth a visit. Having seen all that we cared to see, we scrambled through the woods, over the cliffs, where a slip or a fall in places would drop one into the river, one hundred feet or more below, back to the Stanley water. The boat was ready for us, and embarking with two rods, each with a brace of flies on, and one with a phantom minnow, we commenced the usual see-saw to and fro. A good many fish were rising and showing themselves. They were kelts, old red winter fish, and a few clean fish—but not one would even make an offer at us; and after about a couple of hours assiduous hurling without any result, we gave it up, got back to our trap, and so home, It was clear that, barring the accident of a dark and windy day—which seemed to avoid us as much as possible—fishing in the Tay was hopeless. It was also full late for spring-fishing, and too early for grilse.

The next day I had an invitation from Mr. Marshall, of Luncarty, to fish his water, and to look over his bleach works, Perth being famed for having in its vicinity the first bleach works established in Scotland; and in the morning he very kindly drove in and fetched us, and we had a very pleasant drive to Luncarty. On the way, Mr. Marshall pointed out to me the various objects of interest on the road. About five or six miles from Perth he pointed to the left, towards Glen Almond. "Yonder, out by Lynedoch," he said, "lies the grave of Bessie Bell and Mary Gray." The story of these poor girls is so romantic and interesting, that I make no apology for extracting it as I find it told in "Black's Tourist."

The common tradition is, that Bessie Bell and Mary Gray were the daughters of two country gentlemen in the neighbourhood of Perth, and an intimate friendship subsisted between them. Bessie Bell, daughter of the Laird of Kinnaird, happened to be on a visit to Mary Gray, at her father's house of Lynedoch, when the plague of 1666 broke out. To avoid the infection, the two young ladies built themselves a bower in a very retired and romantic spot called the Burnbraes, about three quarters of a mile westward from Lynedoch House, where they resided for some time, supplied with food, it is said, by a young gentleman of Perth, who was in love with them *both*. The disease was unfortunately communicated to them by their lover, and proved fatal, when, according to custom in cases of plague, they were not buried in the ordinary parochial place of sepulture, but in a sequestered spot called Dronach Haugh, at the foot of a brae of the same name, upon the banks of the river Almond. The late Lord Lynedoch put an iron railing round the grave, and planted some yew trees beside it.

The following pathetic little ballad, which Allan Ramsay supplanted by a much inferior song, has fortunately been recovered by Mr. Kirkpatrick Sharpe:

O Bessie Bell and Mary Gray,
They war twa bonnie lasses,
They biggit a bower on yon burn side,
And theekit it ower wi' rashes.

They theekit it ower wi' rashes green,
They theekit it ower wi' heather;
But the pest cam frae the burrows-town,
And slew them baith thegither.

They thocht to lie in Methven kirk-yard,
Amang their noble kin;
But they maun lie on Lynedoch brae,
To beek forenent the sun.
And Bessie Bell and Mary Gray,
They war twa bonnie lasses;
They biggit a bower on yon burn side,
And theekit it ower wi' rashes.

"Pennant's Tour." "Chambers's Ballads," p. 146.

Poor things! What a melancholy termination to their young lives, and how tenderly and simply is their history given.

A little further on, the site of an old battle-field, between the Danes and the Scots, in the reign of Kenneth III., was pointed out to me. The Scotch were almost routed, and were about to fly, when a peasant, named Hay, and his two sons, who chanced to be ploughing hard by, came to their assistance, armed only with their plough-yokes. Their appearance and courage re-inspired the flying soldiers. They rallied, and, turning upon their foes, succeeded in gaining a complete victory over them. The king was so sensible of his obligation, that he ennobled the Hays and gave them all the territory his falcon could fly over, and the Hays became lords of a very extensive domain there. They bore on their crest, in memory of their victory, a peasant carrying a yoke over his shoulder. Well, indeed, did they earn their fame, and nobly and richly were they rewarded.

The bleach-works were very interesting, and we saw all the improvements made by science in the process of late years, and they are not very numerous, except in the drying process, in which cylinders heated by steam are employed, instead of the old plan of hanging the cloths in a large store with open jalousies, where in cold weather, they used to be frozen hard and stiff. I noticed a considerable smell of chloride in one of the processes;

but this gets a good deal diluted before it reaches the river, and the leats themselves have trout in them; it is probable that no great harm is done to the fishery. Mr. Marshall, besides being very partial to angling, would scarcely, if he could avoid it, poison his own water. In one of the processes, where the cloths were rolled up, an immense number of stampers (similar to ore-crushers) are used to beat the cloth, and the din made by these stampers when they are in work is something almost infernal. I stopped my ears and bolted, being somewhat sensitive in my auricular arrangements. After looking at the works, we went down to the water, where Mr. M.'s boat was in attendance, and we went through the usual process of zig-zagging to and fro over a beautiful piece of water, where, if the weather had been reasonably favourable, we might fairly have expected to get something; but the fish clearly preferred stopping at the bottom and chancing boiling to coming to the top, with the certainty of broiling; so we saw nothing of the salmon, and after a couple of hours' fishing, during which Mr. Paton killed a nice trout or two, we went in to lunch, and after lunch our entertainer drove us back to Perth again.

It was now pretty evident that fishing on the Tay was at an end for a season. I had seen some of the best waters, and determined to take a look at the celebrated Bermoney boat. Accordingly, on the next day, we got into a boat and essayed to row down; but we started too late for the tide, and after meeting the young flood, and finding that it would be decidedly harder work rowing than walking, we left the boat at a quay about a mile or so below Perth, and walked the remainder of the distance. It was a pleasant walk, and the view of Kinfauns Castle is very beautiful. Many nets were at work as we walked on, and about four miles down we came to the place where the celebrated Bermoney boat is worked. The plan is a very simple one. The water to be fished is a creek or fork, and from the shore—some little distance down, across to the outer point of the creek, which is a promontory projecting down stream—a rope has been laid down and fixed by means of a peg at either end. When they want to shoot the net they take up the rope and pull themselves along by its aid, and are thus enabled to make quicker and easier work of it than they would with oars. Now that I have seen the apparatus, I am satisfied that no judges could have declared it to be capable of being brought under the category of "fixed engines," as neither net nor boat is ever supposed to be stationary. It happens that the town have the fishery immediately above this. The creek is a very favourite resting-place for salmon when the tide is rising or at the full, but they will not rest in it when it is low or ebbing fast; consequently, if this creek could not be fished—and it could not well be fished, they say, in any other way—the fish that rest there at high tide, instead of being swept up by the B. B., would be grabbed by the town. *Hinc illæ lacrymæ!* Eleven fish were so taken the day before we were there, and eleven fish would probably fetch 25*s.* apiece, so the point is worth fighting over.

The fishings in the Tay altogether must be very valuable; but I think if they did not net so many of the angling pools so incessantly, they would do better with the angling, *i.e.*, the value of the angling would increase to such an extent that it would cover the little loss there would be by nets. As it is, the spring fishing on the Tay—and I think very much from this cause, combined with the style of rod fishing adopted—is very far from being so productive or valuable as it ought to be. On a mile of the best water on the Tay they had taken the season I was there about a score of fish, and they seemed to think that was a very fair take, as none of the other waters had done anything like it. I confess that I was astounded at its smallness for a river like the Tay, where every cast might and ought to almost swarm with salmon. When we think of the enormous rents that are paid on many rivers for rod fishings, the smallness of the sum realised for the rod fishings on the best part of the Tay is surprising. I subjoin a list furnished to me by persons competent to make it; it is a fair estimate of the value, &c., and I took the statements down as they gave them to me. Starting down stream from the Birnam Hotel water, which is the first water of any note, we come to

	£	Miles.
The Delvin and Murthley waters, belonging to Sir A. Mackenzie and Sir W. Stewart. It lets for about	60	2
Cargill and Ballathie waters: from Isla mouth to Cargill-bridge, and from Cargill-bridge to the Old Oak Tree, belonging to General Richardson Robertson and Lord Willoughby; lets for	96	1½
Stobball and Tay-mouth waters: from the Old Oak Tree to the Linn of Campsie, the best water on Tay, belonging to Lords Mansfield and Willoughby; valued at about	48	2
Burnmouth and part of the Stanley water: from the Linn of Campsie to Hells Hole; Lord Willoughby and the Duke of Athol	48	1¼
Stanley water: from Hells Hole to Thistle Brig; Duke of Athol, Mr. Howard, and Lord Mansfield........	48	1
Binchell and Blackrock water: from Thistle Brig to Luncarty; The Duke of Athol and Lord Mansfield	48	2
Scone and Redgorten water: from Luncarty to Perth; Lord Mansfield and Mr. Maxton Graham	48	4
Total *	£396	13¾

396*l.* for nearly fourteen miles of the finest river in Scotland! one that has, perhaps, if not the finest angling water, yet as fine as any other, and a river, moreover, which gives to the nets more fish than any other river in Scotland. What can be the reason of this? It is not because it is boat fishing, because the Tweed is boat fishing, and many other rivers I could name also; yet, I have known one-sixth the length and less water on the Tweed fetch a great deal more money. It would not be a very wild assertion to say that, instead of nearly 400*l.* a-year, these rod-fishings, if they were what in a river like the Tay they ought to

* This was estimated in 1865. The rentals have been doubled since then, and the sport greatly deteriorated owing to increased netting, but still I let it stand.—F. F.

be, should be worth nearer 4000*l*. Angling pools ought not to be netted, or very sparsely; if they are, the fish are rendered restless, and will not rise, even if they are in the river—and then the question arises, which is the most valuable, net or rod? Indeed, a medium course might be adopted if every proprietor was not so desperately jealous of his up-stream neighbour as to fear to leave anything for him. The fish produced by the rod might be given up, and, if the water was not harried as it is, these should be considerable in number; while the expense of men and tackle, which must be very considerable, would be done away with, as the angler would find all that. Of course, such a plan could not be pursued unless all up-stream proprietors agreed to adopt it. It would not do for a few on the angling water to say we will not net, if those above them did. I am quite sure that if they gave over the netting, in time they would find the angling rents would pay them better than the present system.

As regards the style of angling adopted on the Tay, I cannot say that I like it. It is a very lazy style of fishing. Boat-fishing at the best is a terrible pull-down to the noble sport of salmon-fishing, but when you do not even cast the fly, it becomes, to my fancy, very tame work when sport is slack. Salmon fishing under any circumstances is apt to become wearying when the fish do not rise; but much *solatium* is to be obtained by practising a neat, or a light, or a long cast, and in devising various expedients to tempt the salmon up, and at every likely cast the excitement is kept up by the constantly renewed expectation. But in hurling there is no skill whatever required; indeed, it scarcely needs even patience, for the angler may take the most comfortable and easy chair, or a seat equivalent to it, stick up his legs Yankee-fashion, put a long regalia in his mouth, and plunge into the last new sensation novel; and thus, being rowed gently to and fro, with the wash of the stream and the lap of the oars, may either lose himself in his story or in sleep—to be awakened from some dream of gratified ambition, or just as that lovely and most delicious of heroines has been found out in murdering her fifth husband by slow poison, by her only son, an elegant and popular young minister of the Church of ——, by the shout, "There he is, sir!" and the "birring" of his reel. No, it is not salmon-fishing, to my mind, unless it be for gouty practitioners. Added to this, the practice of sweeping the river with so many flies, of rowing constantly across and across the streams all day long, must, I should think, have a tendency to shy the fish and to keep them down. It may be difficult to fish such a large stream as the Tay satisfactorily by casting, but still I fancy if each party on either side kept to his own half of the river, as they do on Tweed, and fished only that half, that the doubled rods would catch as many fish as they do now. My sport on the Tay was so very moderate, that perhaps I am pronouncing a hasty and inexperienced judgment. It may be so, and it may be that upon further experience I should come to a different conclusion. Still I should like to see the Tweed plan well and fairly tried. I think that the fish, being less disturbed by the boats, would rise more freely, and that this might counterbalance the difficulty there would be in covering the half of the water by casting. If, however, I do err in my judgment, I do not feel very bigoted in my opinion. The Tay is a very large river, and it is just possible that it has already been found ineffective to fish it as I have suggested. If this be so, I must apologise for intruding my ideas.

The Tay flies are strange-looking ones, being usually tied upon long-shanked round-bend hooks; tails, wisps of pigs's wool, claret or yellow, with a topping a bit of mallard or sprigs of a gold pheasant's tippet; bodies, yellow or red for the lower half, and blues of various shades above, or yellow, claret, and blue. Where there is claret in the body a claret hackle from head to tail, with gallina at shoulder, where it is almost blue, with black hackle at shoulder; wings, turkey of various shades; a light dun brown lightly speckled with a lightish point to it, is the feather preferred, the lightish point being considered a great desideratum. Where the fibre is not long enough for the large spring flies, it is usual to tie another pair of wings on half way down the body—broad silver tinsel; dirty browns, clarets, and blues, are all favourites, with longish hackles and dun turkey wings. But the flies are numerous and various, and the angler will always find the best choice at Paton's, or elsewhere, so I need not attempt a long description of a score of flies.

With respect to the Tay and its tributaries I may say a few words before leaving the district. I wrote to Mr. Paton to ask him for information, and his son, Mr. L. Paton, who carries on the business at Perth, while his father is at the London establishment at 108, Mount-street, replied to my question. I cannot do better than give his information in his own words. First, then, anyone may fish the Tay from the right bank for either salmon or trout for about three or four miles above Perth, thence downwards, on both banks. From Perth downwards, it is a sort of disputed point, whether the public may fish by boat or not, as the tide comes up above Perth. Anyhow, the public do fish it, and there is no attempt to prosecute. From Perth upwards the first hotel water is Birnam, and the next Aberfeldy, the Breadalbane Arms, and both waters show fair sport, and at times are really good. On the most of the river, trout fishing from the bank is permitted, except where the river runs through or past private pleasure grounds, such as Scone Park, Stanley Cottage, Stanley House, Stobhall, Taymount, Murthly Grounds, Dunkeld Cottage Grounds, Castle Mongies, and Taymouth Castle. It is capital for trout, from Ballinluig to Aberfeldy, and, I am told, quite free. On the Earn all the fishing is in the hands of proprietors, or shooting tenants. The two best trout streams falling into it are the Devon and the May. The latter is all preserved, the former only partly. The Almond is free, except where it runs through Lord Mansfield's policies at Logiealmond and Lynedoch, but is only a trout river, and the trouts run very small. The Isla is free both for salmon and trout, and a good number of salmon are killed in it in the back end of the season. It is a very sluggish stream and requires wind not a little. Higher up it is a capital trout stream, and is all free. It is, of course, very well fished, principally by Dundee visitors. The Ericht flows into it, not far from Coupar Angus, and is an excellent trout stream, especially about six miles above Blairgowrie, where it is called the Ardle. A fine stretch of the Tummel can be fished by staying at Mr. Fisher's hotel at Pitlochrie, and no charge is made, and good sport is often got in April and May. The Hotel is a most comfortable and well-conducted one, near to the falls of Tummel and the pass of Killiecrankie. The rest is preserved. The Tummel is a capital trout river. The Garry and Tilt are both fully preserved. The Braan is a fine trout stream, no use below the Rumbling Bridge, but above that free. Amulree is the best place to stay at, as you can walk down as far as you like and fish home. Splendid salmon fishing may be got on Loch Tay either at the hotel at Killin or at that at Kenmore the fish run very large, often from 30lb. to 40lb. and over. The charge is £5 a-week for the fishing, and the angler keeps his fish. The phantom is very deadly on Loch Tay, fly being of little use; three, four, and five fish in a day are not at all uncommon. There are other hotels which have the privilege of letting boats on the lake. The fishing commences early in February and holds till May.

A portion of the Dochart which runs into Loch Tay at Killin may be fished by staying at the hotel at Luib, and sometimes good sport is got there. There is railway accommodation to Killin direct *viâ* Stirling.

CHAPTER XXV.

THE TWEED AGAIN—SPROUSTON DUB—MRS. JOHNSTONE'S—A FISH IN THE DUB—SMOLT SLAUGHTER ON TWEED—THE TEVIOT—AE MAIR I' THE DUB—A VERY HOLDING "PRISON"—TWEED FLIES—CLOSING REMARKS.

I HAD promised to meet a friend on the Tweed, at Sprouston, and, as I had somewhat extended the time set apart for the trip, as soon as I could leave Perth, I made for Kelso. On reaching it I found a note from my friend, saying that he could not come; and as the weather and water did not promise very favourably, I was glad to shorten the time of my stay, though after all things turned out a trifle better than I expected. On the evening of my arrival, I walked over to Sprouston to arrange with Kerss, and to see my old acquaintance, Jamie Wright, and to get a few slaughterers from him. "She"—that is, of course, the river, for rivers are always feminine genders in Scotland—"was verra sma'," and verra sma' flies were required to do any good; and, having ordered half-a-dozen double-toothed (double-hooked) tempters for the morrow, I walked up to Mrs. Johstone's to see if any of the gentlemen who belong to the club were at home. I found two; one of them, who was leaving the next morning, had been out trouting, and had picked up a capital dish of trout, in number about forty, and varying in size from three to the pound to 1lb. and over, and beautiful fish those pounders were. Altogether it was as handsome a dish of fish as one need wish to catch. Mr. H., the other gentleman, had taken a salmon about 7lb. Mrs. Johnstone's is, for the benefit of those who do not know it, a most comfortable abiding for the angler. It is a sort of half-club, half-public, somewhat after the fashion of the well-known Tibbie Shiels. Over the mantel-piece in the sitting-room is a card registering the notable fish killed by members of the club within the last few years—and there i'faith is a goodly list, few under 30lb. Against each fish is the date and place of his slaughter, the name of his captor, and the fly that tempted him, as thus: "35lb. Sept. 10, 1863, Capt. ——; Sprouston Dub; the Durham Ranger,"—or 36lb. Oct. 1, 1862, the Rev. ——; the Prison; Jock Scott,"—and so on; and amongst the list is the red-letter fish, a 46-pounder, whose capture was chronicled in *The Field* some years since. Confound the list! it made my mouth water. It was like a bottle of sweets stuck on a high shelf out of reach, to a child.

Early next morning I was about; but the exigencies of posts and letters, and journals—those horrible drawbacks to an angler's enjoyment—kept me dilly-dallying about for an hour or two. What a relief it would be if one could only get where posts and newspapers are not; "Oh, for a lodge in some vast wilderness!" with not even "pony expresses" to worry one periodically.

I got to the river at last, and found Kerss waiting for me. He had to go up and fetch the flies, so I waited for another spell, but at last we go off. I had Sprouston Dub for my water, and the morning, for a wonder, was dark and windy, and there was a very nice curl on the Dub; and I thought, if ever a fish rose on it, it should be now. Out of my six flies I selected one called the "Kate," and began to fish with it, Kerss dropping the boat slowly down the Dub at every cast. I was about half-way down when, "There he was, sir," as a smart boil in the water told that *something* fishy had come up to look. But he did not touch, so after a short rest I pitched him the two-hooked tempter again, and let it sink a little, when he came and took it fairly. And now, what was he? was he a kelt? No! per Baccho! he was not, for there he jumped clean out of the water, and settled all doubts on the question. He was a beautiful clean fish of about 12lb. He gave some very fair sport, and although my hooks were small

—not larger than sea-trout hooks—there were two, and they held on to him like grim Death on a dead nigger, and vain were his efforts to get me into difficulties. I landed, worked him in, and Kerss popped the net under him, and he came out as good, if not a better fish, than any I had killed during my trip, 11½lb., and as "ansum as a picter," as the Thames fisherman would express it. He was duly admired and christened, and consigned to the till until further orders; and we went to work again. Fished the Dub, but gave it a little rest while we lunched. I tried it again with a change of flies, and near the lower end up came a big 'un to the temptations of Jock Scott; and he began playing very vigorously, so much so that I felt pretty confident I was in another clean one; but presently he showed his back above water, and he was of the kelt keltic. Whereupon I "put the pot on," and got him out as soon as I could; which was not easy, for I do think that a kelt is the hardest fish in the head of any I know, and the way in which he manages to bore down and keep his head well down amongst the rocks, and his tail well up—stands on his head, in fact, is remarkable. When we did get him out he was a poor thin brute of some 14lb. or 15lb., and he was so exhausted with the pully-hauling he had partaken of, that he lay a long time at the bottom of the water before he was equal to make a move. He disappeared at last, however, so I conclude he recovered.

After this the wind fell almost to a calm, and it was quite useless trying for salmon, so I put up my trout rod, and worked for trout. I did not catch very many, as the day was not quite all that one could wish; but I caught two or three "punders," as they are called; and what game fish they are. It is astonishing how long and persistently a pound fish will play, you cannot haul him out just as you please. Your tackle is fine and your hooks small; and if you attempt to take your own way too much with him, he will break away to a certainty. I was fishing with a strong, double-handed rod, and not a very small fly, yet was I quite astonished at the time they took to kill.

One thing had taken my attention, and that was the numbers of boys I saw fishing the river at every bend, and I mentioned it to one of the fisherman. "Yes," he said, "and most of them are killing smolts. It is too bad, and ought to be put a stop to." I made inquiry from others, and what I gathered may be seen from the following letter which I sent to the *Scotsman*, in the hope of inducing the conservators to put a stop to such terribly wholesale destruction:

Sir,—Will you allow me to call attention to a most-disastrous and mischievous practice at present very widely followed on the Tweed? I am, as you are perhaps aware, at present engaged in Scotland on a mission for The Field in reporting upon the various rivers that come under my notice, and pointing out any matter which strikes me as requiring attention or amendment. In the course of my journey I have come down to the Tweed; and on the first morning I arrived here, I was struck by the number of men and boys whom I saw passing along the banks of the river between this and Sprouston, and, on remarking on it to the fishermen, they told me that the greater majority of them were engaged in smolt killing. The smolts are very forward on the Tweed—more so than any other river I have been on; and they are this year remarkably fine, and promise well for a good grilse season, if they are not swept away in the manner they are being just now. We made a calculation (and I have purposely put it at the lowest figure) that there would be at least fifty rods about Kelso daily; each of these would, at the lowest compute, get two dozen of smolts. Many could get four or five dozen, or even far more than that. Suppose this work to continue for only a month, instead of all the season, when the parrs are taken instead, something like 40,000 smolts are the tally which the little poachers of Kelso alone rob the river of. Supposing that only one in twenty of these come back a grilse—and it is a fair calculation—there is a loss of 2000 grilse to the river. But consider this practice being carried on in every town and village on the Tweed: and is it not a wonder that any smolts at all get to the sea? So ravenous are those little creatures that the coarsest tackle will take them; and they will devour fly, worm, grub, and almost anything with equal avidity. In fact, a withe stick and a hook will take a dozen or two with very little skill; and so great is the quantity taken by some of the more experienced scamps, that I am assured that last season some of them in Sprouston took more smolts than their families could eat, or than they knew what to do with, and they were actually thrown to the pigs. Now, if only a tithe of this is true, it is scandalous and abominable in the extreme. No river in the kingdom pays so heavily for protection as the Tweed. Year after year we have terrific accounts of the tremendous engagements fought by that active and energetic officer Inspector So-and-so with the poachers of Peebles and Galashiels, that the spawn may be duly deposited in the beds; but what is the use of all this ratepaying and head-breaking if after the spawn has been deposited, and has passed through nearly all its dangers, and having become a perfect fish, needing but a short trip to the sea to bring it back a 4lb. or 5lb. grilse, it is allowed to be captured and killed to any extent with impunity? I constantly see the reports of the scientific gentlemen at the mouth of the river, who are seeking to establish certain points in the history of the salmon, and these reports complain loudly of the vast and rapid decrease yearly of the salmon smolts; and if practices such as I have noted above are allowed, it is not to be wondered at. One raid on the part of one bailiff would effectually stop the practice which is at present depreciating the river; and how it happens that no bailiffs ever do come up and see to this abuse, I cannot understand.

I should have treated upon this in The Field, and not have troubled you, but that the matter is urgent. The smolts are now getting together, and in a week or two enormous destruction will have been done if the mischief be not promptly stopped; and it will be two or three weeks before my chapter on the Tweed can possibly appear in The Field.

Francis Francis.

This letter produced two or three others from other correspondents, shewing that the evil was not confined by any means to the Tweed, but was just as rife in its tributaries; and when one considers the hundreds of miles which there are of these tributaries, upon most of which parr are found, and the hundreds and hundreds of anglers who do not hesitate to bag them to the number of from one or two to ten or twelve dozen daily, it is impossible to calculate the awful destruction dealt to the Tweed from this source alone. When the vast increase of anglers is taken into consideration, this source of destruction is quite enough to account for any falling off, however great, of the salmon fisheries. Formerly anglers were few and far between comparatively speaking, trout were very plentiful, and the same inducements to poach smolts did not exist. The case is much more serious now.

Another point much complained of is the impracticable state of some of the caulds. There are two or three in the river, which the fish cannot, save under very favourable circumstance, surmount. I think the one at Melrose was cited as an example.

The next day was Sunday, and towards the afternoon I walked up the Teviot some four or five miles. The caulds in the Teviot are very bad. I saw a great many huge kelts jumping in the pools, and I could not see very clearly how they wère to get out of them without a very heavy spate. The lower part of the Teviot for about a mile or so is very pretty trout-water; above that mill-dams dyke it up with long dead pools, with short intervals here and there. These pools, however contain some fine trout, and are the salmon-pools also. Of course a strong breeze is needed for sport. It is needless to say that the Teviot, more particularly the lower part, being so handy to Kelso, is tolerably well fished. Late in the season it gives fair salmon fishing after a flood.

On Monday I fished the Dub again, and it was a fine, rough, dark day—a capital day for the Sprouston water. But I tried the virtues of the Kate, Jock Scott, the Black-and-yellow, and the Drake on it, but failed to move a fish. I then went down to the slap in the cauld, at the back of which a contumacious fish resided. He had risen once or twice to flies, but always came shy. I tried him deftly with the charming Kate, and he came and inspected that young person, but did not break the water. I tried him with Jock Scott, and he just looked at it, but it interested him less than the other. At intervals I tried him with some half dozen flies, but they would not do. Then I thought, "Let us try him with a larger fly, the day is dark and rough." Accordingly, I put up a dun-wing, and at the very first cast he came more boldly than he had at all; but he would not buckle to, so I was obliged to leave him to his own sulky and abandoned. devices. He was a most rude, suspicious kind of fish—a fish devoid of that noble confidence and trust in his species and the human race generally which is so refreshing to meet with in the arid deserts of conventionalism and civilisation—none of that chivalrous sentiment about him that prompted the crusades and knight errantry. I could not do more than I did to provoke a combat—nailed my colours to the mast, displayed my shield, I even trailed my coat-a-more,' and I proclaimed my Kate to be the fairest and most captivating young person in all those parts: and this cowardly, sneaking salmon would not try conclusions with me. A low kind of fish—very: I went my ways—quite unworthy of my attention! I had no doubt whatever that he would be caught with a worm in the first water that came down, and a very proper fate too. He was very sour grapes, that fish—very sour!

"We'll have another try at the Dub, Kerss, there's always one more there," I said.

"Ay, indeed," said Kerss dryly; "there's always ae mair i'the Dub and sometimes twa." Accordingly I kept on the dun-wing, and tried it up the Dub, and, as luck would have it, just in the best bit of it up jumped a capital fish, making a most brilliant rise, and fastened. From the first there was little doubt that he was a clean fish; indeed, at this time of the year the betting was 3 to 1 in favour of a clean fish, as kelts were nearly all gone, and the few that were left had all been hauled about, and would not rise well. After a little nasty play, in which the fish fought hard for some foul ground where rocks did congregate, I beat him out of it, and got him within comfortable distance; and although he manifested a decent reluctance to come into the net, he slipped gracefully into it at last, and turned up a fine fish of 12lb. After this exploit we went to lunch, and found that Mr. H. had hooked and lost two fish; one he was sure was a clean one, the other was uncertain. I tried the Dub over again and again, but did no more; and wanting a dish of trout to take home with me, I betook myself to trouting, and got up a respectable basket, but nothing remarkable. I had to leave off rather early, having to catch the evening train, and as I left the Dub I saw Sir R., who was fishing the opposite water, fast in a good fish, which I believe he landed; and just as I was tackling up Mr. H. got hold of a fine fish of 16lb. or 17lb., which had been seen several times playing round the Prison, and had often been tried for but without success. This time, however, he had taken bravely, and an exciting struggle took place. That Prison is a very remarkable cast. It consists of a huge tabular stone, which stands up in the middle of the river, and between the stone and the south shore is a sharp ledge of rock, a narrow gut, and a very nasty bottom ground. Round this stone the fish kept working, never coming near the surface, but playing deeply and dangerously in such ground. Mr. H. landed on the north shore, thinking that he had taken the steel out of him a little; but Salmo had not half done yet, for, making a rush round the upper face of the Prison, he got into the deep narrow gut, taking line out bravely. He was a gallant fish, and played nobly. Mr. H. got into the boat again perforce, and followed him. Deeper and deeper he shot under the dangerous ledge of rocks, the very dungeons of the Prison, when suddenly up flew the rod-point—he had cut him fairly; Salmo triumphant, though sore—the angler sore too, but not triumphant. Packing up my traps I bade adieu to my fishing, and made my way back to Kelso, and thence to the rail.

Sprouston Dub is too well known to need description. It is perhaps the finest and most holding pool for large fish on the Tweed. It is a long pool and is rather dead water out of the stream, as is evidenced by the fact that you may cast up-stream apparently and draw down, and the fish rise quite as well as when you are fishing the reverse way; indeed, the first fish I caught was caught thus. The probability is that when the water is high there are eddies which in places run up-stream. However that may be, the fact is so far noteworthy as being unusual. Kerss is a well-educated, superior man, and I was fortunate in obtaining his assistance in the boat, his experience being great; and, strangely enough for that part of the world, he never touches whisky, and that is no light praise for Tweedside, where whisky is a complaint which a man takes like the measles. He has known the water all his life, and his family has rented it for many years.

I have mentioned two flies specially—Kate and Jock Scott. They are flies which would kill, I feel certain, not only on Tweed but anywhere. The other flies I used are tolerably well known patterns; indeed, Jock Scott is an old, well-tried favourite. The Kate: tag, silver wire and yellow silk; tail, a small topping with short kingfisher at the but; body, darkish red silk and wool; hackle of the same colour at shoulder, with yellow-orange hackle over it, silver wire; wing, mixed fibres of wood duck, gold pheasant tippet, black partridge, green and yellow parrot, blue macaw; topping over all, and two jungle cock points at the cheeks; black head.

Jock Scott: silver wire tag, small topping, with point of Indian crow for the tail; body, orange-yellow silk the lower half, over this is tied three or four toucan points, as in the Popham, over the buts of these a couple of turns of black ostrich harl; the remaining half of body black; silver wire; black hackle at shoulder, with gallina over it; mixed wing of white tip turkey, bustard, black partridge, a few red and green fibres, two short jungle cock, with kingfisher points at the cheeks; black head.

The flies were, as all Wright's flies are, pictures. He certainly does tie an admirable fly, and these little double-hooked fellows were the deftest little beauties imaginable. If I wanted a batch of flies for general fishing, I know no one I would sooner apply to, as he is a practical man, and with the assistance of his apprentices ties the flies he sells, and is not likely to fit you out with a showy stock of rubbish, as is too commonly the case where fine old standard back stocks are kept. He keeps no back stock, simply because he can sell his flies faster than he can make them; and if you want flies you have to wait while they are tied, unless you order them well beforehand. Most of the waters on Tweed are in private hands, taken by the year or on lease; rods may be taken by anglers on the Kerss's water at Sprouston, which are usually let by the month, and there are few more holding waters on the whole of Tweed. Of the trouting, &c., I have already spoken.

Probably a worse spring season has not been known for many years in the north, than the one I have written of. March was remarkable for very low water, and bitter easterly winds. April, on the other hand, turned out very bright and warm, and the falls of snow on the mountains having been very late and very heavy, the rivers were kept up far above good fishing height, by constantly melting snows, which made most of them equally impracticable in another way. When this settled down into something like fishing-water, sport improved somewhat, but the early spring fishing was lost.

THIRD RAMBLE.

CHAPTER XXVI.

HELL GATE—INVERARY—DUGALD DALGETTY—LOCH AWE—PORT SONNACHEN—CLADDOCK—KIT NORTH AND HIS FRIEND.

EARLY in May I made my way to the mouth of the Clyde, to the lovely sea-loch side watering-place called Row, on the Gare-loch, opposite to Greenock and Rosneath, to join my friend Tupman in a fishing trip to Loch Awe, and after a brief preparation, we made tracks by steamer from Greenock *viâ* Loch Long up to Loch Goil-head, where we took coach over the mountains, through a pass most inappropriately and inaptly termed Hell Gate—for if the difficulty of getting through the real one at all approaches that to be met with in this, I fear that Old Hornie would have but a small congregation, and that "Facilis descensus Averni" would have to be re-written. To be sure this would be "ascensus," which rather alters the case, for it is all terrible uphill work. And here, though it is exceeding early to begin story-telling, I did hear one while in Scotland, which bore so upon this point that I can't help telling it; for we must be babbling, my masters. B., a well-known manufacturer and philanthropist in a small way, was commenting to a friend, C., a canny, shrewd old rule-of-thumb contractor, on the good that philanthropy effected, and he concluded thus: "I wonder, Mr. B., whether we shall be permitted to look down upon our good deeds hereafter, and to watch the fructification of the good seed we have sown here." "Ha!" said B. curtly and cannily, "but maybe, Sheriff, that it's *looking up* ye may be." From Hell Gate we descended to Loch Fyne, and so across to Inverary, and thence by trap thirteen miles to Port Sonnachan on Loch Awe. The beauty of those salt-water lochs must be seen to be appreciated, and even I, who have seen most of the finest scenery in Scotland and Ireland, was surprised at it. In the summer thousands of tourists throng the steamboats; but those who want to see these scenes comfortably and without the British tourist should go in May if the weather suits, which is before the tourist season. The coach is a sort of cross between a diligence, an omnibus, and some other unnameable vehicle. It is a mode of conveyance certainly, but the road being awfully hilly, as the Irishman said of the sedan chair without a bottom, "Bedad, av' it wasn't for the look of the thing, I'd as lave walk altogether." As we landed from the ferry boat at the little pier at Inverary Tupman repeated Burns.

> Whatever stranger visits here,
> We pity his sad case,
> Unless to worship he draws near,
> The king of kings—his Grace.

Burns certainly was a terrible Democrat, and it was not likely that Maccallum More would escape his wit if Burns ever chanced to sojourn at Inverary; and though, no doubt, the time is long gone by when it was "a far cry to Loch Awe," * and the Campbells were not the most desirable of neighbours—when a chief of the clan had but to nod his head to cause the fall of any head, or any half-dozen of heads, that were obnoxious to him in Inverary—still the name of Argyll is not likely to be unknown in Inverary for some years to come. Inverary is one of the few

* The origin of this well-known cry, which was afterwards employed in a different signification by the Campbells, arose during a desperate fight between Cawdors and Campbells in Strathnairn in 1499, for the possession of Marian, a ward of the Earl of Argyle, whom Campbell of Inverlivor was conveying to Inverary. In the heat of the battle Inverlivor shouted in Gaelic, "'S fadah glaodh o Lochow 's fadah cobhair a chlam dhoaine." (It's a far cry to Loch Awe, and a distant help to the Campbells.) Walter Scott gives another meaning to it when he puts it into the mouth of one of the Campbells, speaking to Dugald Dalgetty, at Inverary Castle, in the "Legend of Montrose."

places that one comes across in these iconoclastic times, which Time has touched lightly, and with a little stretch of imagination, and a removal of a few of the more modern tenements, one can recognise the market-place, and guess at the spot on which stood the gibbet, laden with its horrible wealth of corpses, and which first opened the eyes of Major Dugald Dalgetty of Drumthwacket that should have been, late Ritt-master to the great Gustavus Adolphus, Lion of the North, &c., &c., to the wasp's nest he had invaded—one can see the cowering Highland women, mourning their slain at the foot of the gibbet, with their heads buried in their plaids—can hear Major Dalgetty conducting his defence before the Marquis of Argyll in the long gallery of the gloomy old castle of the Argylls. The present one is gloomy enough and ugly enough in all conscience, and how the mind of architect could ever conceive such an amazing structure passes comprehension.

"A dead fly," said a clergyman, "maketh the ointment of the apothecary to stink."

"Reverend sir," said Captain Dalgetty, "in respect of the use to be derived, I forgive you the unsavouriness of your comparison; and also remit the gentleman in the red bonnet the disparaging epithet of 'fellow,' which he has discourteously applied to me, who am no way to be distinguished by the same, unless in so far as I have been called fellow soldier by the great Gustavus Adolphus, the Lion of the North," &c., &c.

One can see the frowning Marquis immersed in his schemes of intrigue, and hear the whispering of his followers as they eye the bold free lance with looks of anything but love and kindliness —at least we can see and hear all this "in the mind's eye, Horatio."

Lunch was despatched, and we speedily mounted our trap and bowled away for Loch Awe, thirteen (posting) miles; for some distance we drove along the banks of the Aray, a pretty salmon and sea-trout river running through the lovely grounds of Inverary Castle, and in which, along with its neighbour the Shirrah, his Grace had given me a very kind permission to fish either then or later in the autumn when they would yield capital sport, as they are not often fished, and the fish that do enter them are fairly unsophisticated; but they were dead low now and useless. Port Sonnachan at last, and Host Cameron's comfortable angling inn open to receive us. It stood on the far shore of the lake, and we had to ferry across, and the ferryman demonstrated to us that the M'Gregors were not all gone, but that there was a cateran or two still left. There is a big new hotel on the near side, I believe, but I prefer the humbler hostelry. But here we are on M'Gregor's land, what splendid scenery it is.

> Glen-Orchy's proud mountains,
> Colquhirn and her towers

(see "The M'Gregors' Gathering," for the extent of their territory) are all there. Magnificent mountains; rocky shores, clad with the most varied foliage; little rippling bays and pebbly strands; sparkling waters; here and there a mountain burn pitching over a waterfall. Nature has indeed dealt with a lavish hand, and art has done little to disturb her. Along the northern end of the lake the mighty Ben Cruachan, 3700 feet in height, heaves up his huge back, rugged and storm-furrowed, to the skies, surrounded by his vassal mountains; on the other hand, Ben Lui (Laoidh) hides his sharper peaks in a fleecy nightcap that should portend rain in May, but unfortunately only portends snow in *this* May. All along the foot of the Ben Cruachan, which comes tumbling and sliding down to the lake, we float, drifting before the wind, casting right and left in the inky waters, now ruffled by a March wind. "There he was, sir!" cries Donald. Again we cover the timid quarry, and this time the dropper comes dribbling over him in the way that is so irresistable to a loch trout, and he comes at it again in a style not to be mistaken. A smart chuck of the rod sticks the steel in him, and the line cuts through the water. The rod bends as if I were fast in a 3lb. fish at least, but I know better; it is a good pound fish, and that is all, but he fights as hard and as heavily as many a stream trout of more than double his size will. Bang! bang! bang! out of water he jumps like a harlequin from a trap, as I said, an honest pounder. "Ready with the net, Donald? That's it; and, as he is No. 1, we'll wet him." And the brown and golden captive with his big black spots gets a knock on the head and is pitched into the creel, while we perform the mystic ceremony of Glenlivat at his obsequies.

See yonder wee burnie between the rocks, that runs its little porter-coloured flood down into the crystal lake from last night's rain. There is surely a good trout or two there. "Cannily, Donald, cannily, for—(singing)—

> I've put up the woodcock and yellow,
> I've put up the red and the teal;
> 'Tis the bonniest flee that a troot can see,
> If it's tied upon trusty steel.

"Cannily, now, cannily"—

> Just in the dubious point where with the pool
> Is mixed the trembling stream, or where it boils
> Around the shore, or from the hollowed bank
> Reverted, plays in undulating flow.
> There throw, nice judging, the delusive fly:
> And as you lead it round in artful curve,
> With eye attentive, mark the springing game.

And there he springs sure enough. Thomson must have had this spot in his mind when he wrote these lines. But land the fish, Donald, a pretty ¾lb. and his brother is behind that small stone, no doubt, Donald. "Ay, mony a gude throot I seen oot o' that." I send an invitation to any of the inhabitants of the fortress in question. It is at once accepted by a fine lusty trout, who, like a hearty good fellow, takes my invite as freely as I offer it, and not only comes home with me to dine, but even stands the dinner, or part of it. Onward we go, but the trout have become insensible to our seductions for the rest of the drift, and, as we turn again to renew it, Donald advises a change of flies. Accordingly off come the claret and the green, and on go the favourite red and teal, that kills on every loch, and the woodcock and yellow. This latter fly resembles a good-sized cowdung very much, and has been the best fly by far on Loch Awe lately. The flies, too, are a size smaller, as the wind is a trifle less and the sun is bright.

"There goes the first fly I've seen on the water this morning!" as a small member of the *Phryganidæ* flutters past, and the flop of a good trout follows it. Then several flies come out, and four or five good trout commence, as it is termed here, "rising to themselves." I duly cover them, and picked up three of them in succession; then occurs an interregnum, and I get another and another; and then another long interregnum, and so to lunch on a romantic island, about which there is a legend of course, as there is about most of the islands of any extent in the loch.

Meantime the wind falls, and we cross to the other side where it strikes better; and, yonder, too, is Claddich, formerly an inn where much good company assembled. Kit North and his friends held "high jinks" here many a time and oft, and here, no doubt, was laid the foundation of the amusing "Noctes," the scene of which was placed in the arbour at Buchanan Lodge, in which North, the Shepherd, Tickler, and the English Opium Eater, were engaged. The solemn gravity with which North and the Shepherd lie against each other in relating their angling exploits is too good to be forgotten. Fisherman's weight is a proverb, unfortunately; and fishermen's numbers, when they count by dozens, are not always strictly accurate to "a dizen or twa," we fear. Listen to this:

"*Shepherd.*—What creelfu's you maun hae killed!

"*North.*—A hundred and thirty in one day in Loch Awe, James, as I hope to be saved—not one of them under——

"*Shepherd.*—A dizzen pun', and twa-thirds o' them aboon't, a'thegither a ton. If you are gaun to draw the lang bow, e'en pu' the string to your lug; never fear the yew crackin'."

"*North.*—My poor dear old friend, M'Neil of Hayfield, on the other side of the lake, opposite Claddich—God rest his soul, it is in Heaven—held up his hands in wonder as, under a shady tree, I laid the 130 yellow shiners at his feet. Major Mackay—

A lambkin in peace and a lion in war—

acknowledged me as a formidable rival now in angling as in leaping of yore; and poor Stevenson, now no more, wreathed round my forehead a diadem of heatherbells. and called me king of the anglers!

"*Shepherd.*—Poo! That was nae day's fishin' ava, man, in comparison to ane o' mine on St. Mary's Loch, to say naething about the countless sma' anes—twa hunder about half a pun', ae hunder about a haill pun', fifty about twa pun', five-and-twenty about four pun', and the lave rinnin' frae half a stane up to a stane and a half, except about half a dozen aboon a' wecht, that put Geordie Gudefallow and Huntley Gordon to their mettle to carry them pechin' to Mount Benger on a haun-barrow.

"*North.*—Well done, Ulysses.

"*Shepherd.*—Anither day, in the Megget, I caucht a cartfu'. As it gaed doun the road, the kintra folk thocht it war a cartfu' o' herrins, for they were a' preceesely o' ae size to an unce; an' though we left twa dizzen at this house, and four dizzen at that house, and a gross at Henderland, on countin' them at hame in the kitchen, Leezy made them out forty dizzen, and Girzy forty-twa aught. Sae, a dispute ha'in arisen, and o' coorse a bet, we took the census ower again; an' may these be the last words I sall ever speak gin they didna turn out to be forty-five!"

On this, North caps him with a tale of a 90lb. salmon, killed in three hours in the Awe, when—

"*Tickler.*—Mr. De Quincey, now that these two old fools have got upon angling——

"*Shepherd.*—Twa auld fules! you great, starin', Saracen-headed Longshanks! If it werena for bringin' in Mr. North intill trouble, by ha'in a dead man fun' within his premises, deil take me gin I wadna fractur' your skull wi' ane o' the cut crystals."

On this Mr. North turns out the gas, and they adjourn to supper.

After this, all other fishermen's tales must wax feeble and colourless. What would one have given to have been present at one of these evenings at Claddich, when wit, poetry, learning, humour, and the most sparkling conviviality went to make up such evenings as we shall never see or hear of again! No other sport but angling could produce such a concatenation; and well may we be proud of our craft, brother anglers.

But time progresses, and we must return to our fishing. A little further on we pick up Tupman, who has been sketching Ben Cruachan all day, and who will work at the sketch desperately all to-morrow and wash it all out next day, and call that giving "it an atmosphere." On we progress, now drifting, now rowing slowly, picking up an odd trout here and there; but it is far from a good fishing day—a hot sun, not too much wind, and that very cold from the N.E.—a bad fishing day indeed; and so we reach home and dinner, my basket being eleven trout that weighed 8½lb. T. did not add to the total anything but the sketch. Two other gentlemen had come in, one with thirteen and the other with nine fish, that averaged a trifle under half-a-pound each, my lot being rather above the average.

The next day, Tuesday, I tried the opposite side of the lake, but a number of boats were out, some from Dalmally; thus it happened that, as we started late, we could hardly get into a bay without finding a boat there, and it is not etiquette to cut into the same bay, to say nothing of its being very little use unless you cut into the front of the other boat, which none but a cad of the first water would do. This put us about a good deal, and we crossed to the other side again, but the wind there was too mighty, and the trout would not move; got lazy, sought out sheltered nooks, and gave my mind more to smoking and mooning than fishing. Lunch, too! yes, by Jove, lunch would be a distraction, and we'd catch some perch and cook 'em, and that would be a distraction too. Here is an island handy, and two to one there are perch in the bay round behind the trees. Go on land and turn over some stones, and collect half-a-dozen worms. Then a spare hook is hunted up, a bit of lead stuck on the line, and a cork from a soda-water bottle improvised into a float, and now we are all ready. Seeking a sheltered cove, where the water is about ten or twelve feet deep, in goes the worm, and hardly is it to the bottom when plump goes the cork under water, and away it streams for the middle of the lake. A chuck of the rod brings on a grand pulling-hauling match, and a fine yellow-sided, black-barred perch of a pound soon makes his appearance on the surface. He is followed by his brother of three-quarters, and then two of a half, and two more of three-quarters, and we have enough; and hey for the island! We build a fire of peats or dried sticks, and broil our perch delightfully; a hard boiled egg, a bit of biscuit and cheese, a big pull at the flask, and lunch is over, and the wind having fallen so that there is little hope of fishing, we will lie back and muse among the heaps of stones which form part of some old ruined stronghold, where every kind of villany was practised centuries ago; and if these old stones could tell their story, if each old broken window had a tongue, we fear they would malign the good old times sadly. Meantime the smoke of our huge *pipe en bois* curls slowly upwards among the quivering leaves into the tender green, freckled sky above, and we become sensible that Donald is maundering a legend of the island to us. For there is hardly an island of any size which has not its legend, and most of them had strongholds on them as well. On this island, if you please, we had the gardens of Paradise, and goulden apples guarded by a fiery dragon or a big flying sarpent with a terrymengous tail—I couldn't quite make out which, except that he had a forked tongue and spat venom. And Sir Fraoch, who loved the Princess Miggoo, went to the island to get the Princess some aiples she wanted, and when he got there the sarpent opposed him, and wound round him, and spat venom at him, which scorched pieces out of him, and broke his sword between his teeth, and was scrunching him to death, when Sir F. whipped out his skene-dhu and ripped up the dragon's wame, and so touched his feelings that, giving a loud shriek that shook Ben Cruachan, he plunged into the lake, in a torment of foam, and was never seen more; and then Sir F. went into the garden, which stood joost ower yonder, and plucked as many apples as he pleased. But if, as Mark Twain says, the tail of the sarpent wasn't over them all, the breath of the sarpent was, and had poisoned the apples; so that when he and the Princess ate of them—how they managed to bite golden apples I do not know—but they both died in strong convulsions, and were buried under the two big rocks up yonder. But the pipe is out, so is the legend; and once more we betake us to the lake. We did but little, however, and came home with only eight moderate fish, and found Tupman—who did not finish painting till two, and had then gone down to Crow's Island and back—calmly and loftily jubilant, as if he could do it whenever he liked, with nineteen fish, weighing 11½lb.—the best dish I saw at all, and all taken in about two hours. T. was superb over it, expansive, genial, condescending.

CHAPTER XXVII.

A PLEASANT LUNATIC—AN UNPLEASANT FEROX—ARD-HONEL—ONE GOOD DAY—ECCE ITERUM FEROX—BOCK AGIN—GENERAL FISHING ON LOCH AWE.

THE next day was bitterly cold, with a heavy breeze from the S.E.; we went down to Crow's Island. There were one or two boats in the best bays on the north shore, so we did very little good; got only thirteen fish between us, but they were a fair average size. The only other gentleman in the inn, Mr. D., got into a taking bay, and picked them up rapidly, getting twenty-two; but they were very small, and not what is known as Loch Awe trout. This day Tupman met with an odd adventure. He is a most fervent fisher when sport is good, but soon gets disgusted when it fails, and, being disappointed on this occasion, he landed some five miles down the lake and walked home. On his way he passed a cottage, from which a respectable-looking old fellow of sixty or seventy or thereaway, looked out, and, seeing T., hurried back, obtained a thick stick, and, glowering at him furiously, hastened on before him to a little wood that he had to pass through. T. had been reading reviews of "Eugene Aram," sport had been bad, and, worse than all, we had left the whiskey at home. The afternoon was gloomy, so was T., and he muttered to himself,

> "A mighty wind had swept the leaves,
> And lo the corse was bare.

I'll paint that—capital subject—'Eugene Aram finding the corpse of Harold.' No it wasn't Harold—it was what's-his-name,

Never mind! Wonder what that old fellow went in and got that stick for? Pity I left my fishing rod with the spike in it behind; I would have spoke him fair if he offered violence. As it is—hem!—I wonder which way I had better go." Just then a decent-looking woman came out of the cottage, and, seeing T. advancing, threw down her besom and hastened out to the wood, reappearing in a few minutes, leading the unhappy old lunatic (as he proved to be) out by his collar. He looked at Tupman from time to time while he was led unwillingly home, as if he would have liked to try whether his skull was timber-proof or no. After this T. hastened home and liquored up as speedily and effectively as he conveniently could; and when we arrived, hours after, chilled to the bone and fagged out, he was chirruping if you please, and, like Hotspur's dainty lord, was

> Neat, trimly dressed,
> Fresh as a bridegroom, and his chin new reap'd
> Looked like a stubble land at harvest home.
> He was perfumed like a milliner.

and he offered us invidious suggestions touching our making an elaborate toilet for dinner, which were received with the scorn such preposterous propositions merited, and we took a sherry and bitter instead, and then two, and felt better for it.

The next day was the worst of the whole. The wind was all over the loch, east, west, north, south, coming in flaws with a dead calm behind. Now it would blow for half an hour steadily, and a fish would look up; then it flew round to the opposite direction, and there was very little of it. I don't know anything more annoying than this sort of weather, which just keeps you on the point of expectation without any fulfilment; you can't catch fish, and you can't quite leave it alone. How often have I been humbugged by just such conditions! The cautious Tupman was wise for once, and sketched nearly all day, letting Donald fish for his own amusement, which suited him down to the ground. Cameron went out with me himself, but even his well-known skill failed to alter the luck. We trolled a little at last, as the fly became manifestly useless; I had tried the artificial minnow going and coming on previous occasions, but did nothing. On this day I determined to try the natural bait, and got a couple of small trout from the burn; for, let what will be said of it, the natural bait will beat the artificial, particularly with big fish. Unfortunately, my bait was two sizes too large for the hook that I had out, and the bait was not properly armed; for just as we passed down above Crow's Island, well out on the lake, a tremendous bang at the rod announced a visit from Mr. Ferox, and I had on a big fish for half a minute—alas, only for half a minute. I had jumped up and was preparing for the struggle, had seen all clear and ship-shape, and was on the point of telling Cameron how to manage the boat, when—horror, agony, and everything else expressive of catastrophe!—the rod top straitened, and the bait came away before I had even got a run from the fish. On looking at the bait I could discern very little trace of his teeth, a pretty sure sign of a big one, but he had opened one of the hooks. Of course I collapsed—that is to say, I became all slack and limp after being smartly wound up for mortal combat; for I had particularly wished to catch a ferox of Loch Awe, and it is excessively and specially aggravating to lose that which you have long intensely desired just at the moment of victory; but there's many a slip twixt hook and lip, and none know it so well as your old fisherman. What the size of this fish was I cannot say, but he struck heavily, and took a bait fully five inches long—he might have been 5lb., or 10lb., or even 15lb. I determined for a bigger set of tackle on the morrow. The fish was gone—that was a great fact. It was no use crying over spilt milk—that was another.

> The last links are broken which bound me to thee,
> And the last words are spoken which rendered thee free,

and they didn't rhyme with Shem or Japhet.

I settled the bait again, and, with an "artificial" towing

alongside on another rod, I went solemnly on my way down the lake. "*If* I'd only done this! *If* I hadn't done that! If—if if—the fish had only done the other! What a pestilent word is your if! "Much virtue in an if," is there? I'm not at all convinced of that. I'm in the humour to argue the point. For that matter I often am. In this case I should perhaps have said something improper, "if" it had only been proper to do so; but, as I am noted as a great regarder of propriety—few more so—I only smiled and beamed, and sang something sweetly and softly from Dr. Watts or Mrs. Hemans, and improved the (unfortunately) shining hour by sundry sentimental and beneficial cogitations.

I append the verse I sung on the occasion:—

> How doth the gentle ang-u-ler improve each shining* hour,
> By gathering troutlings all the day whene'er he has the power;
> How busily he throws his line, how neatly spreads his fly—

I was at a loss for a rhyme here when T. broke in—

> How thirstily he takes his drink whenever he is dry.

"Pass that flask here, Cameron. Here's health to men and death to trouts."

T. and myself only mustered ten fish between us at the quay, and they were not tritons. Our friend Mr. D. had, however, picked up a ferox of 2½lb. on the Phantom, and I took stock of him. He had all the outward distinguishing features of the fish—large mouth, powerful jaw, very long incurved teeth, almost hooked in fact (one of the strongest distinctions in the ferox) purple bloom on the back, and one more which I never heard of before—I do not know if it is peculiar to Loch Awe—viz., ten or eleven large red spots on the after and lower part of the body, *and only there,* for the red spots never advance beyond the ventral fins, or above the dorsal line. Beyond them the spots are all black, but upon all the Loch Awe feroxes this curious fact is, I am told, observable; and the men say that there is always one more spot on one side than on the other; usually

* This should be cloudy, I think, or shady.

they are said to run ten and eleven. This may be a point too far to carry the theory, but I saw that the position of the spots was as I have described; indeed, it is rare to see more than an odd spot or two on a fish of that size that can be called red at all, and the appearance of such a cluster on either side of the fish's flank is of itself somewhat striking.

Keener than ever after this, I routed out a good set of Thames trout tackle, went to bed, and dreamt of a single combat with a sort of mermaid ferox at the bottom of the lake, where I conducted my affairs without the slightest inconvenience from change of element, although I was not conscious of the possession of gills, and without even the intervention of macintoshes; and I was just at that stage in the conflict when I was vociferating "Have you a red spot on your left tail?" "No." "Then it is—it is my long-lost mermaid"—when a knock at the door, and "hot water, sir," dispelled the illusion, and I once more woke to the consciousness that the weather was very cold and the wind was N.E. And cold enough it was, and there was reason for it, for Cruachan, Ben Vreck, and Ben Lui were all heavily capped with snow, and the wind blew to us straight off them; the most expensive and cuttingest Sheffield razors were nothing to it. Nevertheless, the water was dark and well curled, and we determined to make a start of it and to try it. Cameron decided to go with us, and he and Donald would do the boat well; so we made straight shirt-tails down the lake, as they say on the other side of the water, with plaids and great coats, two or three apiece, sou'-westers, comforters, a muckle whisky flask, and all the necessary paraphernalia for comfort during the ethereal mildness of a severe May. We decided to go down a good distance, even to Ard-honnel, Ard-chonnel, or Innis-chonel, as it is or has been variously called. This venerable castle is some eight miles down the lake. It was, according to old chronicles, in existence in thirteen hundred and something, and how much before that *I* cannot depone, and no one else can. There is a legend about it of course—and, like all these legends, to make a grim pun, it is full of *awe*—wherein sons shoot their mothers, and mothers prophesy the picking out of their sons' eyes by eagles, and there is the usual burning, robbing, and ravishing peculiar to the good old times, when any chief hanged whom he liked on his own doom's tree. However, the roof that sheltered these old iniquities no longer exists; but the strong walls that contained them still stand, and probably will do so when the iniquities and the weaker walls of the present day have passed away for ever. Farewell to thee, fair Innis-chonel! I had a good day's fishing under thy walls, so my memories of thee are pleasant, and apart from the unholy old legends that float about thee.

Tupman and I did well on that last day, for the breeze held truly, and, cold though it was, the fish rose fairly all day, and we basketed between us fifty trout, forty of which weighed 20lb., bearing out the half-pound average. On the way back, passing above Crow's Island, as nearly as possible in the same spot as I had run the ferox on the day before, I got another heavy pull; but the hooks did not get hold at all, and when I came to look I found that he had seized the bait very carefully and judiciously by the head part, where there were no hooks. For unfortunately, although I got a larger set of hooks, I could only procure a still larger bait, and nearly half the bait was unarmed, and thus Mr. Ferox had again escaped me by skin of his teeth. Lucky ferox! Long may you commemorate your escape! Well indeed may he

> Stand a tip-*tail* when this day is named,
> And rouse him at the name of Francis,
> Then will he strip his teeth and show his scars,
> And say These wounds I had on Francis' day.
> Old trout forget; yet all shall be forgot,
> But he'll remember with advantages
> What feats he did that day.

And a pretty duffer he'll make me figure in the annals of Troutcatchiana, kept at the bottom in one of the crystal caverns of Loch Awe by some hoary-headed old Lord Chancellor Ferox! Well, well! one must bear one's burthens, and one ought to do it meekly; but, as Mr. Chuckster said on a notable occasion, "my worst enemies, sir, never accused me of meekness." When we got home, to show the extreme uncertainty and variableness of lock fishing, our friend D. had only six moderate trout. T. and I had as nearly as possible taken equal numbers. If there was any difference, he was one or two ahead of me; yet ordinarily I should say that I was much the better fisherman of the two.

The next day we left, and returned to the Clyde. I know no pleasanter spot to spend a fortnight in, wind and weather permitting, than Loch Awe. If the rambler be a keen fisher, there he may indulge to his heart's content either in fly fishing or trolling. In the first he will, judging by the list of takes of past years shown in the book kept at the inn, pick up from one dozen to two and a half dozens of good trout to his own rod, which will average half a pound. Now, when I say this I mean honest *weighed* weight. If I were speaking loosely by ordinary fisherman's estimate, I should certainly say they averaged three-quarters, and that several of the fish would run over a pound; but Cameron won't let you guess weights, he scales the fish to an ounce, and as it is they run nearly a pound, which is all the difference. But these Loch Awe fish are among the gamest I ever handled, and for their size are tough antagonists; they jump out of water, and scurry hither and thither, with an agility that keeps the angler in pleasant excitement, and a pound fish is a strong fighter who will take ten minutes to kill. They are capital eating, cut red and firm, and mighty good for breakfast. Now and then you will take a sea trout or two—I got hold of two one day, but the largest was only some three-quarters of a pound.

For fly fishing, May and early June are the best season. Trolling certainly is not as hopeless a case as it is on some lochs I could mention, only one never sticks at it when the fish are rising; and, as that is the time when they would also be running it is mostly pursued at the most unfavourable and unlikely times, and is therefore not so successful as it might be. But, though the ferox is not nearly as plentiful as formerly in Loch Awe, there are still a good few in the lake, and a bottle of preserved dace would, I am sure, answer well here. The practice now is to use artificial baits—the Angel, the Phantom, &c.; and, excellent as the Phantom is, and it is universally used in all this part of Scotland, still it cannot equal the natural bait, which many fish, I am sure, might be killed with. The ferox do not as a rule run large—under 6lb. I should say—but every now and then a thumper makes his appearance; one of 17lb. was taken a day or two after I left, as I heard. Ferox are generally indifferent eating, but the 2½lb. fish mentioned above was by no means a bad fish. We had him boiled for dinner, and the head and tail alone were left when we had done with it. I stole the jaw, however, to bring it home for comparison, and then, like a fisherman (I was going to say something else), I forgot to compare it. There are a few salmon in the lake, as well as sea trout; but the throws are not well known, or the fish are capricious, and the lake is very large, so that it is more often an accident than not when one is hooked. If the angler likes to go in for pike and perch, unfortunately in some bays there are plenty. The perch often run large, but I never happened to get hold of a pike, though I trolled a good deal at times, which rather surprised me. Still, I must believe that there are plenty; for if they once got into the lake, they couldn't fail to increase. Formerly they were kept down a good deal by set nets; but no one seems to have any interest in doing so now, and the lake, which had greatly improved under this regimen, is now, I am told, going back again under its abandonment. Surely the innkeepers might do something, if the proprietors are supine. Mr. Malcolm, who is a very large proprietor on the lake side, and is also a sportsman, if he only gave the word to his keepers, might do much good. He is building a large hotel at Sonnachan, and, in the interest of the coming customers, he might at least help to keep the pike down.

There are several good small lakes near Loch Awe (Loch Avick is the largest), it gives nice trout of three to the pound, and plenty of them bright merry yellow fins, but they wanted much walking, and I was lame and could not reach them; they form a very agreeable change, however, to those who *can* walk. The flies that killed best were the yellow and woodcock (a large cowdung, in fact), the red and teal (a soldier palmer with teal wing), and the green and teal—green and crewel body, silver thread, black hackle, and teal wing. There are several stations, but the best for sport, from all I can learn, is Port Sonnachan. Ford was spoken of to me as an excellent station, where the fish ran large, and sea trout were plenty; but it is at the far end of the lake, is more difficult to get at, and the choice of ground is small, as you must go and return over the same ground every day. At Sonnachan you can go either way, and can fish nearly the whole of the best part of the lake, which you certainly could not from Ford. It is a good plan to fish to Ford one day and back the next. Cameron also has the right of a day a week at Taynuilt, which is on the Awe, about eight miles off, and sometimes gives first-rate salmon fishing; but to get the first of the casts one must be early afoot.

Cameron's is not a swell hotel—such hotels are my abomination—but a comfortable, snug little angler's inn. Cameron himself is a most skilful brother of the angle, and a right good judge of weather and wind. His wife is an excellent cook, having presided at a large club in that position. The living is good, the wines and spirits far beyond the average in quality, and the charges certainly moderate. If the traveller be an artist or lover of the picturesque, he will be enchanted with Loch Awe's beautiful and grand scenery. It is simply a paradise for the overworked citizen who wants laziness and perfect rest; indeed, Paradise it is held to be by some of the natives, for there is a story of a picturesque-hunter meeting a native, who pointed out various fine views and strange sights, and who finally asked, "Wad ye see Awdam's grave?" "Adam who?" was the reply.

"Joost Awdam's—oor common feyther—Awdam 'n Eve's. It's joost aboon yonder brae. There's some says it's at Tobermory, but a says it's joost here." I am reminded that Adam wasn't buried in Paradise ; but never mind, if the story is not altogether true it is *ben trovato*—a new Ben for those parts.

CHAPTER XXVIII.

LOCH LEVEN—THE BALBRIGGAN BROTHERS—ARCHY MACQUOID—HIGH JINKS—FATHER FAIRLICHT.

WHO has not heard of Loch Leven? of Loch Leven trout?—at Groves's, in Bond-street, at Heaven knows how much a pound, and not to be had there now, or anywhere else except by accident, at anything a pound. Formerly nets were used on the loch, and the trout were sold; and by the time they were sold in London, when at all scarce, 5*s.* a pound, or even far more for fine fish, was not, I believe, at all an unusual charge. The last dodge about Glasgow is to sell sea trout, worth about 10*d.* a pound, for Loch Leven fish at 2*s.*; but the net is now only used to slay the pike and perch, which unfortunately are too plentiful, and the lake is kept solely for angling purposes. The wisdom of this course has been gradually developed; for whereas not very many years ago a hundred or two of pounds a year would have represented the takings of the proprietor, now thousands more accurately record it. The tariff is 2*s.* 6*d.* an hour, and there are few days in the season when there are not from ten to fifteen or twenty boats out on the loch. The great strength of the loch rests on its approachableness, and the system of competition adopted by the numerous Scottish angling clubs at Glasgow, Edinburgh, Stirling, Dundee, and many other towns, from which the loch can be reached in an hour or two by rail. These clubs engage usually from six or seven to ten or a dozen boats. So much by way of introduction.

The place was Harris's Hotel, in the small town of Kinross, and we sat down to dinner, nineteen keen water-whippers. It was the period of the annual competition at Loch Leven, and the Balbriggan Brithers, of which I have the honour to be a member though a non-effective, had come out to do friendly battle among themselves, and to see who was best man and who was the luckiest. Provost Doublegang had presented a silver salver, 14in. across, to be fished for, the capturer of the greatest weight of Loch Leven trout in one day to be the winner, and for days and weeks before surreptitious visits had been paid to Archy Macquoid's, the Balbriggan tackle-maker, in search of the raal "hechum pechum" (a very favourite fly on most of the Scotch lakes in the South), and mysterious consultations were held daily in his little back room. It was surmised that the Sheriff (that's our friend Dingwall, and the keenest fly-fisher of our club) had made a sly visit to Embro' to consult Mistress Hogg as to the precise dressing of that excellent lure, and had come back with some momentous secret that was to land the salver for him in his dining-room at any odds. Then how he would ask three or four of those whose baskets came nearest to his in weight to dinner afterwards, and call our attention to the salver when something was being handed to us on it, as "a sma' trifle, ye ken, Mr. Wilkins—joost a token o' respec' like frae a few friens for teachin' them hoo to thraw a flee on Loch Leven," and the sly twinkle of the eye, and the hearty "haw, haw," afterwards, with which he would accompany this little bit of mild chaff, we could well foresee. The Sheriff certainly had been to Edinburgh, ostensibly on business, and if he could go there a fortnight before the competition and not call just to ask "Hoo his auld frien' Mistress Hogg fan hersel' aboot then," he was no our Sheriff, but some impostor. "Joost a chaungling," as Father Fairlicht, the oldest member of our club put it, "who had fa'en asleep, disguised, wi' a muckle whusky flask beside him in the middle o' ane o' the fairy rungs by Miggat, an' after twal' hoors o' haird sleepin' had waukened up and fan himsel' quite anither man, d'ye ken." The true fiery brown never caused more trouble to poor Martin Kelly than. did the directions of "the brithers" as to their flies to Archy Macquoid. This is the sort of thing that occurs two or three days before the contest.

Enter Girzy Macquoid, ætat. 11.

Girzy.—"Here's Mr. Mockintire's Jean, to ken why ye haena sent up thae aipple greens?"

Archy, himsel'—"An' hoo am I to sen' up thae aipple greens, when Maister Mockintire his sel' disna ken ava whatna shed o' green *es* an aipple green."

Girzy.—"Weel, what'll I say till Jean?"

Archy.—"Say till her! Why, say that her maister's a dubitable auld deevil, that disna ken his ain min' twa chappins o' the clock thegither. I've sen' up three lots o' thae aipple greens, an' they're a' wrang. See, noo, gi'e her that lot; it's joost the first yane I sent. It was a' wrang then; like enow it'll be a' richt the noo," adds Archy, pawkily; and Mr. Mockintire's Jean bammocks off rejoicing.

Girzy.—"Here's Meestr Macklehoose comin' oop the street wi' his hat aff and the rain drops patterin' aff his bald pow like peas from an ashet. My certies but he's a grand sicht the noo."

Archy.—"Lord safe us, dinna say't, and they red an' teals no even in haun yet! The mon'll gang wud, daft and clean distractit. For he's bet half a dizen o' sharry wine he'll beat the Shirra. See, now, I'll gang oot at the back yet, so's ye mayna tell a lee, an' ye'll say am oot, and ye dinna ken when I'll be bock—maybe no till the morrow, sae he needna think to wait," and so on.

But here we are, with the secrets of angling safely locked up in our pocket books, our books locked up in our creels; the cunning casts, made up in several varieties, ready to come forth and deal death and destruction on the morrow. Dinner, with much fun and merriment—for Father Fairlicht, the chief humourist of our party, is specially great to-day—is happily over, and we proceed to draw for boats. There are nine boats allotted to us, with a list of their names, and nine tickets, each with one of these names on, are placed in one hat; and eighteen, with the names of the competitors on, in another.

"Mr. Fairlicht and Mr. Crotchet," cries the secretary, after perusing two tickets drawn from one hat. "The Wullie Waught," he continues, as another ticket from the other hat is handed to him. "That's your boat, gentlemen."

"Weel, weel," says Father Fairlicht, while the secretary is noting this down in his list. "Noo, Mr. Crotchet, we'll hae nane o' your legerdemain; for I'm no' pairtial to findin' my sandwiches chainged into panetils and my whuskey into Apsom salts." Mr. Crotchet is a dab at conjuring tricks, and has already conjured the soup ladle off the table and into the Sheriff's pocket, whence it had been extracted, amid roars of laughter and much discomfiture to the Sheriff. In this fashion the list is made out, until each boat has its two allotted piscators.

"What's come till the whusky?" mutters the Sheriff, with a serious change of countenance, "It's naething at a' but sugar and het watter," and he makes various wry faces, to the great amusement of the company, for the incorrigible Crotchet has contrived to substitute a bottle of plain water for the whisky, for the Sheriff to compound his toddy with.

"Noo, Sheriff," says Fairlicht, "I'll be a bet against you, and I daursay Crotchet will be one against your partner, Macklehoose." A bet is merely a bottle of wine. That is how we pay for our wine at our dinners, and we allow no other kind of bet; and we generally have a bet or two all round."

"Done wi' you, Faither. Book that bet, Mr. Secretary," says the Sheriff, and the bet is booked accordingly. A few more bets are then made, but most of them have been made before, and the secretary then reads them over to see if he has them all booked right. Mr. A. bets Mr. B., Mr. C. bets Mr. D., and so on; and then all the business being duly competed, we call on the Sheriff to promote the conviviality with a song; and after the usual objections, the Sheriff, who is a jovial soul, skewers a fly on the ceiling with his right eye, keeps the other one carefully on his tumbler, to see that Crotchet does not beguile it in any way, hooks his thumb in his waistcoat hole, and sings Burns's "Lassie wi' the lint-white locks" very well, and reaps a loud round of applause. One or two other songs are given in the usual way, and then Father Fairlicht is called on, who gives us an original song of his own, which runs in this wise:—

THE ANGLER'S SONG.

Air—"Duncan Davidson."

Nae royal road has yet been found
The trout or salmon tae beguile,
A peasant boy may beat the king,
Wi' a' his tinsel an' his style;
A wee pook out the auld coo's tail
Has aften prov'd o' mair avail
Than a' the flees we e'er could wale
Wi' a' our skill and patient toil.

When trout were dull and unco dour,
Tae passin' boats we raised a shout,
Our faces were baith long an' sour,
We felt a little put about;
Our arms were sair an' like tae crack,
An' pains were fleein' down our back,
We thocht that we had lost the knack
Tae throw the flee an' whip them oot.

We threw them here, we threw them there,
Wee flees an' big we vainly try,
We threw them wi' the greatest care,
An' heaved a sentimental sigh;
But ne'er a trout would gie a peep,
The schule had skailed, an' aff they sweep,
An' in their lairs are sound asleep,
Or slyly keek wi' cautious eye.

A gude three-pounder fell tae me,
But how it cam' I ne'er could learn,
Jist chance-like, wi' a trailin' flee,
While haflins sleepin' in the stern;

The whirrin' pirn skreigh'd loud and lang,
Up tae my feet I quickly sprang,
I lik'd the singer an' the sang,
  I kent the lad had ta'en the earn.

Sometimes they rise at every throw,
  When in a merry mood to dine,
Their gleamin' sides wi' silver show
  The splendours o' the starry mine;
The muckle trout are on the feed,
They seize the floating flees wi' greed,
We play, or pu' them in wi' speed,
  To throw again the waving line.

A trusty frien' wi' feelin's kind,
  An' siller a' our wants tae meet,
A well-gaun pipe, an easy min',
  Are tae an Angler joy complete.
We toast wi' glee the eager wish,
"Here's health tae men an' death tae fish,"
And hope tae see a splendid dish
  O' trout lie shinin' at our feet.

It's gude tae see the auld folk douse,
  An' wisdom drappin' frae their lips,
Or sometimes jist a little crouse,
  The outcome o' their wee bit nips;
They've had their day, an' tales can tell,
Which micht be measured by the ell,
O' a' the won'ers that befel
  The "Angler" in their Hielan trips.

We maun obey kind Nature's laws,
  Altho' the road we canna see,
An' in our journey mak' a pause
  At our firesides tae rest a wee;
Our weel-lo'ed waunds we lay aside,
Then frae the scene we quietly glide,
For ever here we daurna bide,
  Whate'er our station or degree.

It is needless to say that this literally brings the house down, and the Father's health is drunk with many tokens of respect and goodwill, and the kindly old man, with the head of a sage and the fun and frolic of a boy, and now and then a flash of keen trenchant wit worthy of a first-class humourist, rises, with a smile on his lip and a wee something in his eye that adds additional brightness to it, and in a few well chosen words thanks us all with an earnestness which we can see comes from his heart, and then, winding up with a joke at the Sheriff's expense, which is so original, applicable, and funny, that it sets the table in a roar, sits down under cover of the smoke; and so the symposium progresses; and when the sma' hours came on, and a select knot of half-a-dozen eager old flailers got together over the toddy to exchange notes, it was hard to think of bed. What lochs and streams, what flies and rods, what deep fishing lore, was then unfolded! Among that half-dozen there was not a stream or lake of note in Scotland that had not been fished, and we wandered at will, north, east, south, west, and found nothing barren. Heigho!

> Gather ye rosebuds while ye may,
> Old Time will still be flying!

and bed-room candlesticks will reproach us, while Harris, good fellow, looks on complacently and as satisfied as though time were really "made for slaves" and beds for sluggards. "Let's have t' other glass. Was that one or two that struck last?" But no matter; Mrs. Caudle is happily at home in the bosom of her family, and we shall not be reminded that our clothes smell of filthy tobacco, and that there is a dreadful odour of spirits any where; so "Put out the light, and then put out the"—Snaw-aw-craw—waw-w-w.

Morning beams bright and joyous. One enthusiastic angler who couldn't sleep has been tying flies in the next room since five in the morning or thereaway—confound him! as I sleep next to it; others are punctual to the minute; and, haw-yaw, it's half-past seven, and breakfast will be ready at eight sharp. A Scotch breakfast, my friends, is just, to use the words of the poet,

> A thing of beauty and a joy for ever.

The last spoonful of raspberry jam, the last taste of marmalade has disappeared, luncheon baskets are packed. The omnibus is waiting to convey us and our impedimenta to the little pier. The pier is reached; Mr. Marshall, the tacksman, is there to allot to each the boats, and the names of the boats are called; two men coming forward as each is named, they having, like ourselves, balloted for the boats the night before. Rods were soon ready, and each taking his place—one angler in the bow and the other in the stern; I being an odd man, and not competing, had a boat to myself—and away the whole fleet of boats started for the far end of the lake, the wind suiting to drift from that direction. As the far end of the lake is a good four miles from the pier, and the boats are very large, roomy, and heavy, it is a smart bit of collar work against the wind; so leaving the men to toil over it to the best of their ability, and allowing the flies to trail astern at the end of a long line in the hope of attracting a "happening fish," we put up our legs and light the morning pipe. How grand to the real smoker is the first morning pipe! He has just answered a bothering letter or two, and noted that Bostocks have gone down seven-sixteenths, and is troubled as to whether they will recover or make a further decline, and doubtful whether he ought to have sneaked away from business last night on the plea of going to visit his ailing maternal aunt, or whether he ought not to have sold Bostocks to-day, and then the keeper on the "bit shootin'" that he shares with three old cronies "awa'" up Nevis side, too, has written to say that "disease is very bad, and though we are not as bad as our neighbours, yet the birds are still dying," thus leaving it to be concluded that there are hopes even yet that we may not be behind the worst of our neighbours—a dispatch similar to the above literally came to a friend lately—but the cool, ruffling breeze soon carries off the vapours, and, as the first rung or two of tobacco smoke circles away into the clear air, our cares go with them, and we see over again the unfortunate Queen and her brutal ——. But stay! No. On second considerations, we won't. Let her misfortunes and her errors rest in peace, so far as we are concerned. The scenery of the lake is not very picturesque. The Castle Island, perhaps, is the most striking thing about it. That we will not trouble at present, for we have left it astern while lighting our pipe. As we approach the far shore the boats spread out and diverge like the spokes of a wheel, covering a wide space of the lake. Overboard go the anchors, that we may not drift too quickly, and broadside to the wind we commence our drift.

I do not know anything so pleasant to the angler as fishing a new water, and particularly if it be one of a great reputation. With what eagerness one gets up one's tackle and makes the first few casts! how one longs for the first fish! It was my first visit to Loch Leven. After some twenty or thirty casts a sudden sharp splash announced a rise, and the bending rod-top told of a fixture. Spang, spang, came a small bar of freshly-chased silver out of the water, and in two minutes after my first Loch Leven fish lay gasping on the bottom of the boat. They are wonderfully like sea trout. Had I taken the fish just fresh from the sea at Ballinahinch or on the Tay, I should have basketed it as a sea trout without another look or another word. We drifted on far out into the loch, but did no more. Another drift produced us a rise and a refusal. a third one fish again, a fourth nothing, and then the wind sank and things looked gloomy. Suddenly a cloud arose, and came rapidly down in a heavy squall of wind and rain, and the lake was soon gloomy enough for anything. The wind shifting to the west, anon the sun began to peep out, and we rowed towards another bay known as the Green Island to my men, though not generally. As we went along I had a rise and a refusal; then another, also a refusal; then a third, hooked and got off; and then trout began rising all over the lake. The blue and yellow dun (known as the hare lug) was out quite thickly, and the fish fully appreciated its gastronomic merits. Presently a heavy splash and a drag told of something larger than common, and away raced a good fish, taking out line and playing boldly at first for a minute or two; but he soon adopted more cautious, sluggish, and dangerous tactics, boring down to the bottom towards the weed, and smacking the line with his tail—which I felt most of the big fish do subsequently many times, and it is a nerve-disturbing operation. A steady strain, however, soon brought him to the top, and a fine trout of 2¼lb. made his appearance. He was just a wee bit thin about the flank, and might have been a little better later on, but he was by no means a bad fish. Then I got rise after rise, and refusal after refusal. One fish I just hooked and lost, but I should think that I rose ten fish for one that fastened; and so it was all the while that the fish were well upon the rise. I am sure I rose thirty or forty fish that refused the fly entirely. The same thing happened to all the anglers; indeed, it generally does happen more or less on Loch Leven. Anon I determined to change the temptation, and to see whether a new move would answer, and I took off all the Loch Leven flies and put on Loch Awe favourites; after which I missed far less fish, though the fish did not come up nearly as fast. Still I got two more good fish, one of 2lb., another 2lb. nearly; they were not in as good fettle as the first, however, the last being very kelty. Altogether I got eight fish, that scaled 9lb. 12oz. The best two baskets of the day were fourteen and thirteen; the third the same as mine, 9lb. 12oz.. but with nearly double the number of fish. Had the fish taken only moderately well, I should have had a prodigious take. My experience, too, I found was that of all the other boats; every one had risen heaps of fish that refused in the most aggravating way to fasten. I have very little doubt in my own mind, from this and the next day's experience, that this is, as it is stated to be, owing very much to the prevalence of minnow trolling, which now is practised here to far too great an extent. Wherever fish rise really well to the fly, as they do in Loch Leven, minnow never should be allowed, as sooner or later it seriously injures the fly fishing. The effect of it soon becomes most palpable; many of the fishers who had been out on the day that we came down complained that the ground around them was trailed over by five or six boats, one after the other, with two or three minnows out; and we all know that fish will not rise, or rise very shyly indeed, when they have had minnows over them often at any recent date. If it is not practicable to prohibit the minnow altogether, it should be greatly reduced; it catches the largest and the worst fish, which should not be caught at all, and I am quite satisfied that if clubs frequently have as bad sport as they too often have now, the lessees will find it affect their profits seriously. It is not fair, either, on the clubs which use only fly and no minnow; indeed, it is particularly hard on them, because they are the main support of the loch.

The second day on the lake was almost as bad as it could be; the wind had been blowing a gale all night, but was more moderate in the morning. At first, to glance at the lake, one would have thought the weather perfect. There was a fine fresh S.W. breeze, that looked like slaughtering trout to a large extent, but the old hands shook their wise heads, and said it was just the worst wind on the lake for sport. The result proved them correct, for before half the day was over it grew squally, and black "crows' feathers," in which no fish ever rises as a rule, swept over the water incessantly. It was a hopeless task; I kept on trying—big flies, little flies and moderate flies—but it was all of no use. I got only three fish, that weighed something over 4lb., while the best bag of the day was but 7½lb. It is a curious fact here that the best wind that can blow is an east wind—with that sport is pretty certain; and the worst is a S.W. wind.

Loch Leven is a large loch, some eleven or twelve miles round, shaped rather like an ill-grown pear, with the Castle Island in the middle, and owing to the moderate and very uniform depth there is a great extent of fishing ground, and of course a great extent of feeding or food producing ground. That the food of the lake and that alone makes the fish what they are I do not at all believe. There is an abundance of small shellfish, which, from the casual glance I had of them, I take to belong either to *Bythinia* or *Hydrobia*, species common enough in large areas of water; but I cannot be certain, as I did one of those stupid things that one does sometimes. I had plenty of them on the first day; but thinking that, as they were so abundant, I need not trouble to carry them home that day, I put it off till the next. The next day I was getting up some weed which abounds in the lake, a very pretty mossy-looking plant—the *Chara flexilis* according to botanists—and could find no shellfish on it; and on desiring the men to row to where I could get some, they told me I should be sure to find plenty in the fish, as never a fish was killed without finding his stomach full. Satisfied with this, I went home, opened my fish, and did not find one. I subsequently wrote to Mr. Marshall to ask him to send me a boxful, but these though promised never came to hand at all. Another lesson—never to put anything off, and never to trust to chance or anyone else if you can help it. The abundance of this particular kind of food no doubt gives very pink flesh to the trout; this we find in all lochs where these small shellfish are plentiful. I have seen the same thing in Loch Conn in Ireland, and in other lochs, where the fish are by no means well-shaped, fat fish, and certainly anything but silvery like the Loch Leven fish. But still the flesh is a bright pink, and of good flavour, though they have dark green olive skins, and are not very bright in colour. I am inclined to think there is something, from all I can see, in what Mr. C. F. Walsh advanced some time ago, viz., that these fish come of a race of imprisoned sea trout. We know, from the Tasmanian experience, that sea trout will and do breed without ever having been to the sea; and, that fact clearly established, considerable light is thrown upon many dark places, and the main difficulty in the theory of their being descended from sea trout, but slightly modified by long residence in a lake and by a descent from fish naturalised to lake existence, vanishes. The big fish that I saw were in the end of May as like sea-trout kelts a good deal out of condition as any I ever saw, and I certainly never saw any other lake trout but these silvery fellows in such a condition at that time of the year. The shape, colour, appearance, everything in the outward indications that one could judge by, are infinitely more like those of a migratory trout than those of the brown trout; and a Loch Leven trout of a pound, as I have already said, would be bagged by 999 anglers out of a thousand as a sea trout without question if caught in a river. One curious fact, however, is noticeable, that the adipose fin is very slightly red-tinged at the tip, which is not the case with the salmon or salmon trout, but is the case, though to a much greater extent, with the bull trout and common trout. Then, on the other hand, it has not that white stripe along the anterior edge of the anal fin which one finds in the brown trout, but not in the bull trout. Structural differences are so hard to determine, and they seem in different varieties of different species so often to run into one another, and to vary so much according to the clean or unclean state of the fish, that no formula I have ever seen yet has been laid down that will enable one to pronounce safely and positively on species. I puzzled over the gill-cover formation at one time, and had fish of all kinds from all parts of the country sent me, and I finally came to the conclusion that it was utterly unreliable. I then tried fin rays, and that, I became equally satisfied, was quite untrustworthy too—individuals of admittedly the same species constantly differing in the numbers of their fin rays. Vertebræ, again, became equally unsound; and finally I came to the conclusion that the less positive we are upon any point of species among the *Salmonidæ* the better, for even the most learned know but very little about it. I took down the number of fin rays that I found in the Loch Leven fish, and they run as follows: Dorsal 12, pectoral 14, ventral 9, anal 10, caudal 19. *Salmo fario* (the common trout), as laid down by Yarrell, agrees in this formula, except that it has eleven rays, or one more, in the anal fin; *Salmo trutta*, on the other hand, agrees in all but the pectoral, where it has one less; and I have found quite as great differences between two specimens of admitted brown trout taken from different streams. Certain of the fish found in Loch Lomond are said to belong to the same species, and a new species has been set up, named *Salmo Levenensis*, in order to cover difficulties and dovetail facts, by reason possibly of imperfect knowledge of the habits of fish. The fish of Loch Ard, too, and elsewhere, are also said to belong to the same species. When I come to treat of Loch Lomond I shall be obliged to recur to this again.

One more fact I must chronicle. As I have already mentioned, the fish feed largely on the shellfish; but on investigating the stomachs of those I killed on the second day I found that they had been feeding on beetles—some of them wee black beetles, some larger, and perhaps half an inch long. Anglers of Loch Leven should bear this in mind.

Loch Leven flies are like most of the ordinary Scotch lake flies. The white tip with red body known as the Hechum-pechum is held a great medicine by some. I did very little with it, but killed most of my fish with Loch Awe flies and the light and dark hare lug. Flies can be bought at the office on the pier.

CHAPTER XXIX.

LOCH LOMOND—ITS TOURISTS—LUSS—THE MACGREGORS—SIR JAMES COLQUHOUN—FISHING AT LUSS—ROWARDENNAN—INVERSNAID—THE HEAD OF THE LOCH.

HAVE you ever been up Loch Lomond? Has anyone in Scotland never been up Loch Lomond? Has anyone anywhere else never been up Loch Lomond? Don't be alarmed; I am not going to conjugate the compound verb, "To go up Loch Lomond." To persons who have not been up Loch Lomond, I say, go there; to those who have been, I may add, go again. If you want to go pleasantly, choose some day in June, before the strong flood of tourists has set in, and don't choose either Saturday or St. Monday—and the same may be said, perhaps even more forcibly, of the Clyde steamers—unless you wish to study the habits of the Glasgow rough, who shines even among roughs, and who is pre-eminent in roughness. A few odd tourists are rather good fun, and if you like to make yourself a little busy among them, or if you don't get out of the way of them, you may derive some amusement from the study of them. Let us take a glance at them. First there is the eating tourist. No sooner has he, or she, or it, or both, or all three, slid off the pier at Balloch into the boat than a suitable station is chosen for the prosecution of the important avocations of the day. A big basket is opened and the business of the day commences, and until exhausted nature cries "Hold, enough," and a strong internal sense of suffocation comes on, jaw-bones are kept moving. No sooner is the home supply exhausted, and a fair half-hour allowed for it to settle, than the lady or gentleman begins once more to feel quite faint from prolonged abstinence, and the eating-saloon is sought out and the pangs of unassuaged hunger are temporarily mollified by a heaped-up plate of half-raw beef and ham. Their principal amusement is feeding the gulls with the fragments which they cannot find room for themselves, and they take profound interest in seeing these edible waifs gobbled down and wrangled over. It reminds them of the time when they were children, and wrangled over the last morsel of apple-pie themselves, and they feel quite melancholy and regretful if any chance bit remains unappropriated. As for the scenery, they care nothing about it. They come on Loch Lomond because it gives them an appetite, and there is no pitching and tossing, as there sometimes is on the Clyde boats, which rather has a contrary effect. The last we see of them is opening a large paper of "sandwiches," which they have procured somewhere, probably of the steward, as the train leaves Balloch for Glasgow late in the evening. May their "bosoms' lords sit lightly on their throne," if, as in probability, nightmare should rule over that portion of their anatomy twixt night and morning. Then there is the sentimental young lady tourist, who sometimes may be in a position to drop the "young," who sits and gapes at Ben Lomond with an abstracted wrapt attention that becomes very comic; a book is in her hand, but it droops by her side in "The Inexpressibly Gushing Sensation which pervades the Circumambient Empyrean." Her thoughts, like the late Sir Edward Lytton's, being expressible only in capitals. She eats not, neither does she drink, save of inspiration, though, no doubt, she will ply a decent knife and fork at the *table-d'hôte* at Inversnaid by-and-by, when nobody notices her, and if Ben Lomond were Ben M'Intyre, who serves in Mr. Grocer's shop in Sauchiehall Street, she couldn't be more devoted to it. Then there is the drinking tourist, who goes into a steamboat because it is a public-house all the way. Though he usually brings a soda-water bottle, full of whisky, in either of his coat pockets, in case the steamboat should run short, a constant recurrence to those faithful companions makes a beast of him in due time, and a nuisance to all around, until, happily, a few more applications send him off, snoring like a hog, under the lee of some convenient trunk or bulkhead—Unfortunate beast! Then there are the spooney-couple tourists, who ought to be put down by Act of Parliament or municipal regulations. They are either on their honeymoon trip, or ought to be. They pretend to try and get out of sight—as if anyone could get out of sight in a Loch Lomond steamboat; the slightest possible isolation, obstruction, or concealment suffices for them; and the amount of semi-surreptitious hugging and kissing that goes on under the half-shelter of a cloak or an umbrella is calculated very much to disturb the equanimity of those who are not spooney. Then there is the sketching tourist, amateur and artist; Tupman usually takes to him, and they get up a polysyllabic talk about art, which, I am happy to say, I do not understand in the least. And next, the travelling tourist (chiefly Yankee), who, if you enter into conversation with him, will soon acquire an accurate knowledge of you and all your affairs, down to the maker of your hat and the price of your pantaloons; the practical joking tourist—a pest to all his friends and acquaintances, and not always safe even upon strangers; the tourist who is always fidgetting about his carpet-bag and his umbrella; and the tourist who is always in such a hurry, and so on, and so on—the full description of whom would require more time and space than can be given to them. But here is Luss, a pretty little Highland village, belonging to Sir James Colquhoun, charmingly situated on the shore of the lake; and the steamer stops at the little pier to take up and set down passengers. Rossdhu, the splendid seat of Sir James Colquhoun,* is here. At the entrance of the Glen stand the ruins of Banachra Castle. All these spots are immortalised by Sir Walter in that splendid song of "Roderick Vich Alpin."

* Poor Sir James! His tragic end within a month or two of the publication of these notices will be in the memory of everybody.

Proudly our pibroch has thrilled in Glen Fruin,
And Bannochar's groans to our slogan replied;
Glen Luss and Rossdhu they are smoking in ruin,
And the best of Loch Lomond lie dead by her side.

It is impossible, in spite of all the halo of romance which Sir Walter and others have cast over them, to regard the Macgregors as anything but highly objectionable neighbours; and viewing their doings by such lights as are afforded by even their friends, one can but sympathise with the desire of their neighbours to be rid of them. Highland cowstealing may have been a much more gallant thing than highway robbery; but still, if we go into them closely, the difference is not very much, save in the name—and "What's in a name?" A cow stealer by any other name will not smell any more sweetly; and whether one's throat be cut by a Macgregor or a Bill Sykes it comes to pretty much the same thing, as far as we are concerned, though, perhaps in one case we might get a decent burial, while in the other we should be left to the crows and foxes, or, romantically putting it, "eagles."

The Fruin, one of the best white trout streams on the lake, runs in here when there is any water at all. The Fruin yields fine sport, the fish often running up to a very large size, even to 7lb. or 8lb., or more. Season tickets can be taken to fish this stream, and many neighbours avail themselves of the privilege. The stream gets a good deal fished, of course, and when the water is fine the fish are proportionately shy. Still a ramble up Glen Fruin is well worth the trouble, if only for the ever changing and lovely scenery it discloses.

There are four anglers in our party to-day. Shall we shoulder our rods and baskets and go on shore, and try among the delightful maze of islands which makes this part of the lake so lovely? The question must be determined by the state of the lake, and whether there has been a flush of water down the Leven lately on a Sunday—for, alas, the naughty irreligious Scotch fish will travel on the Sabbath, though their proprietors won't. We should see few enough of them if they wouldn't, and it is only on a wet Sunday that they have a chance of getting up, the Leven being blocked at all other times by the nets and the filth that comes from the factories at Levenbank. The stock of sea fish that thus gets up is small, and Loch Lomond is a very large area, so that, unless fresh fish have come in within two or three weeks, the stock of fish in this part of the lake will be low, as it is not very good fishing for the lake fish. At the best, half-a-dozen sea trout, some of them running up to 3lb. or 4lb. weight, with a stray grilse or even a salmon now and then, a few lake trout, and perhaps a big pike or two, may reward the angler, and this is pretty much the character of the water from Luss up to Rowardennan. Thence upwards the sea fish are less plentiful, but the lake trout increase until, from Tarbet upwards, past Inversnaid to the head of the lake, the trout fishing on any really fair day becomes very good, and a score of nice fish, running from half a pound to 1½lb., with an occasional big one of 3lb. or 4lb., may be entrapped by the use of the fly and minnow.

There was a small head of fish just before our visit, so we resolved to take our chance, and after suitable refreshment at the little inn at the top of the village, we got us into a couple of boats and started. It was a very bad day for fishing. The wind was strong enough, too strong indeed, but it was in a bad airt, and the sun was as bright as it could be, the water being low and clear to a degree. I hooked four or five sea fish on the minnow, one of near 2lb., but whether I bungled them, or they took badly, or the wind was in the way, or anything else was the matter, I don't know, but I somehow lost them all to a fish, some almost as soon as they struck, and others when half way up to the net. No doubt there are few anglers who have not experienced this sort of day; a day when everything goes wrong, do what you will; a disgusting day; a humiliating sort of day; a day you don't care to remember. I think four or five small brown trout, the largest somewhere about ½lb. to ¾lb., and very ugly beasts too, was our lot, and our friends were no better. And yet the day before two friends of mine did well up the lake towards Rowardennan, taking the one seventeen trout, one of them 4½lb., and the other sixteen and a pike of 14lb.; but they were mostly taken by the minnow, and many of them were sea trout. This is an unusually good take for that water.

The scenery at Luss, among the islands, is most charming, one never seems to know where you are going, or how you are coming out, or going to get back again—rocky, woody, of all sorts, sizes, and shapes, with cold grey stone, or warm birch; there they seem to be by dozens, a perfect archipelago or maze of islands, and all lovely in turn, what a place for picnics!

Failing in doing much at Luss, we took the late boat on to Inversnaid, where we arrived at 7.30; and here Mr. Blair's hospitable hotel received us with a good *table d'hôte* tea, at which various nationalities presided—Swedes, Danes, and Americans, appearing to have a weakness for Loch Lomond. The next morning I took a boat with a friend; I fished fly, he trolled a minnow. A fine S.W. breeze came on as we got about a mile up the loch, just under Rob Roy's Cave, a natural hole in the rocks, apparently caused by their tumbling together, and of no great extent. The fish rose well at the fly; the minnow was less successful than it usually is, taking only some half-dozen fish, and those all of the smallest, all the best fish and far the largest number coming to the fly. We worked up to the head of the loch, where we lunched, and then worked back again to the hotel, which we reached comfortably by tea time, when we found we had twenty-one trout weighing 16½lb., and two small perch, which took the minnow. A good many fish were hooked and lost, perhaps half as many more. The best fish was 1½lb. I saw quite as fine a dish taken two days afterwards round the head of the loch by one of the keepers while I was fishing Loch Arklet. The next day I again tried the head of the loch, but took the opposite side of the lake, in which are some very fine bays. Indeed, I should think the far side the best, but the fishermen say no. The result was very small; I got only five fish, losing eight others that were slightly hooked, but the reason was that it was a dead calm, and the water all day was like a sheet of glass, when lake fishing is all but hopeless. I did get a languid pull now and then at the minnow when a slight air gently ruffled the surface for a minute or two; but fishing was hopeless, and the fly a perfect superfluity. But for the fact that we had a good stock of fine live minnows, we should hardly have got a single run. It is a great comfort to Loch Lomond fishers that they can always get a good store of live minnows at Inversnaid. Some years ago the proprietor of Loch Arklet, in order to increase the food of the lake, stocked it—and the Arklet burn, which runs out close to the hotel at Inversnaid and makes a fine waterfall some thirty feet high there—with minnows, and they have increased in both to a surprising degree, so that there is no difficulty in obtaining any number of minnows desired. There are one or two charming islands with ruined castles on them hereabouts which were the strongholds of turbulent chiefs in days gone by, and the scenery here is lovely. I know nothing more pleasant than a cigar after a good day in front of the Inversnaid Hotel, just within hearing of the waterfall, with the glorious lake and magnificent mountains before one.

The next few days I fished over Loch Arklet, Loch Katrine, and Loch Chon, and as I had to return to Glasgow on some business, I did not then fish Loch Lomond again, but came back a few days after to have another turn at Loch Lomond and at Loch Katrine. The first day after my return I took Loch Lomond. Unfortunately the day turned out very wet. For an hour the fish came on well, and I took seven or eight trout, one of which weighed 4lb., the others about 1lb. and ¾lb. each, and half a dozen perch. A friend who was out in another boat over the same ground doing about the same, save as regards the large fish, his largest being about 1lb. The largest fish gave me a tough job, for he was over large for the net, and when being lifted into the boat jumped clean out of the net and fell at least

4ft. into the water. "Phansy my feelinks," as Jeames de la Pluche was wont to say when Thackeray portrayed him, on seeing by far the best fish I had had hold of at all, and which looked to me 5lb. and over, taking a rocketer out of my net into the air, kersquash into the water. What hook that ever stuck in a minnow could be expected to hold? and my triangles were exceedingly small, and I of course bade farewell to my fish, not in the least expecting him to hang on after such usage. But somehow one of the little toothed gum ticklers did contrive to keep its place, and after another scurry off and more careful manœuvring I once more got him under and into the net; but the boatman was clearly not used to landing big fish in small nets, for once more the fish bolted. I fear that had I spoken outwardly what I thought inwardly, the Highland bluid of my henchman would have boiled some, and that I should have been told, like the angler on the Tweed, that I "might fesh by mysel;" so I wheeled the fish round again, and this time we did manage to bundle him into the boat somehow; and a fairly handsome fish this big fellow was—a wee bit thin in the flank, where out-of-condition fish always do show it, but not bad coloured. A very well-mended kelt he looked to me, and I should have put him down as a sea trout. He had all the appearance of it, and ate very miserably being of a dirty white colour, and poor and watery in consistence as to his flesh; but I was assured by those who are supposed to know Loch Lomond well that it was just one of the lake trout. I cannot understand it, however. The contrast in the edible condition of the flesh as compared with other lake fish made it the more unaccountable. There are two distinct kinds of trout, it is said, in the lake; one the ordinary brown and yellow fish which no one can mistake for a moment, and the other a bright silvery fish that looks all over a sea trout, that has the grey fins of the salmon trout, and that even adopts the lively jumping tactics of that fish. They are scarcely as silvery as a fresh-run sea trout, being a trifle rusty and tarnished, but in all other respects I can see no difference.

They certainly look to me exactly like sea trout that have not gone down to the sea in their regular turn, but just stay in the lake and recover condition there, and thus in time take upon them some few of the characteristics of the lake trout. As I have before said, we know that, from the Australian experiment, it is not an absolute necessity for salmon trout to go to the sea to enable them to recover the condition necessary for spawning. I have long thought that this was just a question of condition and food. No doubt change of water and food does, like change of air and diet with us, improve condition much more quickly; but, of course, a big fish like a salmon wants so much food to recover him, that we can easily understand he could not find it sufficiently plentiful in a river. We know that in some cases salmon kelts do mend partially, though we do not know how far, or whether any ever do recover sufficiently to breed. Sea trout, however, could of course recover nearly as early as common trout, and no doubt in many instances do so. I have frequently, in many lakes and streams, found undoubted sea trout, and that, too, in fairish condition, and at a time when the sea trout had not begun to run. These fish were, I have no doubt, mended kelts, and, to all appearance, fairly mended too; but of course they lacked the lustre and brilliancy of fresh clean fish new from the sea; and this is about the difference in appearance, so far as I can see, as regards these Loch Lomond fish. It is quite possible, also, that they may be the children of fish that have not gone to the sea, and thus still more have weakened the migratory instinct, or there may be something hybrid in the breed. However it be, they are wonderfully different from the ordinary brown trout of the loch, and I have serious doubts of the brown trout theory, and even more of the *Salmo Levenensis;* and, in a review of the facts, I am strongly inclined to think, with Mr. Walsh, that *Salmo trutta* Levenensis*ed* would be nearer the mark.

But we are leaving the lake. The big fish was, of course, put in the place of honour, and he looked very imposing in it. And so we float on, the pleasant south-west wind just tossing the water into ruffling wavelets that plash crisply against the boat, now and then lifting her to and fro with a soothing motion, and fish after fish essays to capture, to his cost, the feathered bauble at the end of our line, which carries such a sting in its tail, and, like pleasant vices often indulged in, proves at length so difficult to shake off that they vanquish their victim in the long run, and haul him away to the shades when he least expects it. But it is luncheon time, and here, in this rocky cavern—where desperate men may really have taken refuge for all we know—in the cool shades, gazing at the tender light and green foliage that traces the air without, will we take our luncheon, and smoke our mid-day pipe in silent peace and contentment, and sing with Izaak Walton to the music of worthy Doctor Sellé,

> Oh, the gallant fisher's life,
> It is the best of any;
> 'Tis full of pleasure, void of strife,
> And 'tis beloved of many.
> Other joys are but toys,
> Only this lawful is;
> For our skill breeds no ill,
> But content and pleasure.
> Oh, the gallant fisher's life, &c.

Alack and alas, why does not somebody write such songs now-a-days? Why are we deluged with horrid music-hall jingles, as vulgar in matter as in tune, and as devoid of wit as the wretched jokes that convulsed the Court during the eternal Tichborne trial? As for our ballads—heaven save the mark! What read you there, my lord? Why, as Hamlet answered, "Words, words, words," nothing but words; no sense, no feeling, no sentiment, no imagination; nothing but jingle, jingle, jingle. Well, "You that jingle may" for me, I'll none of it. But the day is over. Evening comes on, and, after a comfortable tea-dinner at Inversnaid, we smoke our last pipe with Blair, the proprietor of the capital hotel we are located in, and listen to the hushed fall of Arklet burn, as it pitches over into the dark foam-flecked pool below, and gaze dreamily at the shadows as they deepen on Benvoirlich and Benvean, and wonder when that patch of snow will vanish far up Benreoch, for it is now late in June, and still it shows no signs of going; and watch the fleecy clouds that float from mountain to mountain across the lake, now "like a camel," anon "backed like a weasel," and presently "very like a whale;" and so evening comes down upon the lake, and as the air gets damp and chilly, we will retire and counteract the vapours with a toddy.

I forgot to say that on this occasion I found the water quite thickly studded in places with the cases of the May fly or green drake; and the next day I saw a good many on the water—there must have been quite a decent rise of them the day before; bnt the trout did not seem to notice them—perhaps they were hardly thick enough. I believe, too, they come out strongly on Loch Awe, and there at times the trout do notice them; and on a smaller lake, Loch Kulliper,* near the Crinan Canal, a heavy rise of Mayfly comes up, I am told, and the trout, which are particularly fine, take well then, though somewhat shy at other times; and a few Mayfly show on most of the southern lakes.

There are two very nice burns at Inversnaid—one on either shore of the lake—which give capital sport after a shower of rain; but they are private, and leave has to be obtained; and on one of them, I believe, there is little difficulty in this respect. At the head of the lake too, and in the mouth of the Falloch which feeds it, there is (unfortunately) capital pike fishing; and 80lb. or 90lb. of big fish may sometimes be taken by an expert. A friend of mine, who is a fair trout fisher, but no great adept at the Thames style, picked up 74lb. or thereabouts two days running last year; and as nearly all the salmon have to pass up the Falloch to spawn, as it is the largest feeder of the lake, and the greater portion of the smolts have to come

* This is phonetic, I believe, Keillbar being the correct spelling.

down and run the gauntlet of these brutes, I am quite sure that the fisheries at the Leven mouth must be seriously affected by the numbers of pike here; and if anyone would go and stay at the Ardlui Hotel, which is close at hand, and seriously attack the pike for a week in October, they would get capital sport, and do no end of good; and, though they might get small trout from the burns, I would advise a good stock of dace and gudgeons to be bottled beforehand—a good silvery dace would be a very attractive bait. I intended to take some up, but neglected it, and was sorry for it all the while I was there. The burn trout are not bright enough to show well.

I did not meet with the far-famed powan of Loch Lomond. It is not so often taken now as formerly, and keeps lower down the lake towards Luss. Now and then one or two are found in the maw of some big pike. The powan is one of the various species of corregoni found in the British Islands, of which we know for certainty of four—the vendace of Loch Maben, the gwyniad of Wales and Cumberland, the powan of Loch Lomond, and the pollan of Lough Neagh and other Irish lakes. The two which approach nearest to each other of these are the powan and pollan. But there is a remarkable structural difference in the formation of the mouth and the bones of the mouth figured in Yarrell, which enables the line to be distinctly drawn. They are mostly (except in the case of the vendace, which serves, like the whitebait, to hold together gorgeous feasts) only held in moderate repute for the table, and should be eaten when freshly caught. They afford no sport to the angler, rarely taking fly or bait, though tho pollan, having a rather larger mouth than the powan, is a trifle the best fish in this respect. They will make good feeding for the great lake trout, which I hear that the late Sir James Colquhoun introduced into the lake, where they no doubt will thrive abundantly.

CHAPTER XXX.

A MYSTERIOUS STRANGER—LOCH AIR AN DALLANAIGH—A GREAT EXPEDITION—THE MYSTERIOUS STRANGER ABSORBS AND LIES, AND IS LEFT LYING.

DREAMILY I sit at the door of my hotel, gazing at the lofty mountains that surround Loch Lomond. Tupman smokes beside me, enraptured by the most peculiar effect of cloud scenery that I ever saw. It is the time of dusk—there is a darkish cloud over the sky upon the far shore, the edges of which are fleecy white. through which the setting sun shines in a very peculiar way. The back of this cloud seems to act as a sort of looking-glass reflector, and throws a light upon the mountain-side which, late in the day as it is, shows every rock and hollow far more clearly than we could possibly see them at the brightest mid-day. Indeed, if a man or a sheep had been on the mountain-side, I fully believe we could have seen them, which, I am quite sure, we never could do at mid-day. Such a curious illumination I never saw before: it was as if a strong lime-light had been hidden behind the cloud, and the full force of it thrown on the mountain. It lasted for some fifteen or twenty minutes, and gradually died out. Tupman was in ecstasies, and the power of hard words and art roots he brought to bear on it quite left me floundering like a stranded porpoise. I opened my mouth to reply now and then, but I found nothing to say to him—not a word of more than five syllables. I thought of "poluphloisboio thalasses," but it was not appropriate, and I could not at the moment make it so, I sung softly a line or two of that funny old glee, "Aldiborontifoscofornio, Chrononhotonthologos," which produced opprobrious epithets upon my want of art-knowledge, and I was stigmatised as an ignorant behemoth, but it broke the neck of the scientific eulogium, and I gazed in silence and in peace.

Somebody spoke—a mysterious stranger sat on the seat beside us, smoking a large meerschaum. How did he come there I did not see him come—Tupman did not see him come. Nobody saw him come. He didn't come. He appeared. You remember if you ever saw him, Herr Staudigl, in "Der Freyschütz," and *his* "Zamiel appear"—and that individual in a very uncomfortable dress of red ochre appears. This individual appeared in a somewhat similar way, only without the invocation and without the red ochre, unless his whiskers were ochre—they *were* red. I remember that I was fascinated by his whiskers; Tupman confessed to being taken with his forehead, which was narrow, pointed, and æsthetic. Æsthetic—but that was Tupman all over; of course I couldn't say it wasn't, for I didn't exactly know what æsthetic was. By the way, does Tupman himself know? *Mem.*, The next time he says a thing is æsthetic I will say it isn't, and let him show how it is. I expect he'll flounder, and then I'll give him another touch of "Aldiboronti," &c. But what was this mysterious stranger? He wasn't a keeper. He wasn't a pedlar. He wasn't a bagman. He wasn't any kind of tourist that we were familiar with. He wasn't quite a gentleman; but he was an indescribable mixture of many things. He spoke fair English, or fair Scotch, as it suited him, and seemed quite at home in the country, and, in spite of everything against him, his whiskers inspired confidence. Tupman wouldn't have the whiskers, but never mind. He was one of the finest smokers I ever met; as a drinker I never saw any one equal him, except myself; and I think twenty years ago I could have run a dead heat with him. As a *raconteur* he was inimitable and inexhaustible—by Jingo, sir, he even beat me—he had so much natural wit, such amazing power of ready invention, and such indomitable cheek. It was the cheek that did it; that's what it was. Now there is my particular weakness, I haven't a particle of cheek in my composition. Oh, if I only had! What have I not lost in the last thirty years or so for the want of it? *Audace et audace et encore audace.* That is the secret of success, no doubt of it. He could sing a good song, and had the queerest collection of good songs I ever came across. He talked of fishing, and he talked very well of fishing, interspersing his conversation with stories and anecdotes of men and things often of a very surprising character; indeed, we sometimes almost doubted the truth of them, but there was a clearness and circumstantiality of detail —a minute delineation—about them that set scepticism aside, and, as it were, almost compelled credence. He talked of a small lake in a lonely valley, away on the skirts of Ben Lomond, not known to anglers, and rather difficult to find. Loch Air an Dallanaich he called it, and I made him spell it, as these Gaelic names come out all over the shop, as it were, in point of spelling. In this lake the trout were as long as "that"— indicating with his hands something that might have been fourteen, eighteen, or twenty-four inches, and he told a tale of a tremendous single combat that he had with a monster one he tackled once, which got away, of course, and was still in the lake; and he so inflamed our curiosity that we besought him to conduct us to the mysterious lake, which at length he promised to do on the morrow. We were to take plenty of provision for a long day, and a very sufficient—indeed an unusually large—stock of whisky. This he said (with a grin, which I understood afterwards) was indispensable if we wished to find the lake. Tupman has a sort of flask, a big flat thing that holds rather more than three pints, which slings at his back, and has a lock on it which has provoked the anathema maranatha of many gillies; and if we each took our largest flasks full besides, and a caulker upon starting, we might survive the day. Of course there was no house, or even a sheiling, within miles, and so we went to bed to dream of enormous trout in mysterious and unknown lochs.

The next morning early, each laden with rod, basket, lunch, and flask, we started. It was but "six or seven miles, *or so*, across the hills," and we were very merry in anticipation of grand sport to come, as the wind was S.E., just the right wind for the loch. So our unknown friend said, and we stepped away bravely. An hour or two's stiff walking found us breasting a very steep hillside, and after surmounting it, the unknown called a halt, and we took our first refreshment by a little rivulet. "Is it much farther?" asked Tupman. "Only just among those hills," was the reply. Tupman's face visibly lengthened. There was an undesirable bit or two of climbing to be done, a sort of thing which T. objected to when it came too often; but re-invigorated *pro tem.*, we went on. Another hour found us among the hills in question. Up we went, and down we went, and still no loch in sight, but to all our questions when we should see it, "Just presently" was the reply. It was actually getting towards noon, and still no lake was in sight; and we began to think that the lake was a myth, when our companion proposed that we should anchor under the shade of some rocks and lunch, where a little dripping spring made a basin of sweet cool water, and the gentle breeze pleasantly fanned our heated brows, and we sunk into three mossy, ferny seats without a murmur of dissension. Leisurely we despatched our lunch with good appetites, then we qualified our whisky with the spring, and fell into a lazy smoke and chat. It was a lovely scene below us—broken, rocky, feathery mountain ground close to us, and wooded slopes below, with green, peaceful glens in the hollow.

"See yonder white house among the trees?" asked our acquaintance, indicating a house far below, which stood out prominently.

"I met our friends W. G. and Bob L. there a few years ago. They were on a walkin' tour, and thought they were unknown; but *I* spotted them, bless you! although, of course, I wouldn't pretend to know them, for fear of scaring them off, for people often like to be *incog.* in the Highlands. Then we had a most delightful evening. Glorious, glorious."

"And you found them very pleasant fellows?" I asked.

"Pleasant is not the word, my friend—not the word at all. If you'd only heard G. sing "John Brown's Daughter," and seen the way he danced the break-down to it, I give you my word you'd have been convulsed. Beat the Happy Land dance into sky blue fits."

"Indeed; really."

"Truly, oh truly! As for Bob, the conjuring tricks that he did were wonderful. The pea and thimble was nothing to him. The three card trick he was such a dab at that he actually won one and ninepence halfpenny off me at it, and what's more, I paid him, though I was never very famous for ready cash, and actually he kept it. Now, you'll hardly believe that! Then he got to doing tricks with a match box and three matches of different lengths, and in the course of that I had the honour to suggest a reference which afterwards became famous. He was manipulating three matches very cleverly, and he showed me the trick. 'The audience,' says he, 'would of course stake their pile upon this match, but this is *the* match after all.' 'And so you see you sell 'em,' said I. 'You see you sell 'em,' he replied, repeating the words once or twice. 'You see you sell 'em,' he continued reflectively—'sell 'em.' 'What is it? Ah! I have it—*luce lucellum*—*ex luce*—exactly.' And that was the first of it. Odd, wasn't it?"

"Very singular," I replied. Tupman nudged me, and pulled down his left under eyelid when our friend was not looking. After this we wandered away to the revolutionary state of things now in progress, and so, easily to the old French revolution, and by chance to Canning.

"What, George?" said our friend, who got through his whisky with amazing rapidity, and was growing loquacious. "George—hic—hic—I remember him when I was a boy—quite a young one, I'll allow." Our friend did not look above fifty at the outside, but his was an uncertain phiz which might have existed longer, and it was just possible.

"Remember him! I should think so. It was only just over there—yonder," pointing to a hill some three or four miles away —"that he first composed "The Needy Knife-Grinder," and I had the honour of helping him." Tupman and I glanced furtively at one another. "I remember, I was going up the hill a-fishing, with my rod over my shoulder, and coming round a rock, in a little natural amphitheatre—show you the place by-and-by—I happened on a fellow walking to and fro, repeating verses aloud to himself, and I heard him recite—

Rough is the way,
Thy wheel is out of order,
Cold blows the wind;
Thy hat has got a hole in——

And he paused and repeated the line, as if looking out for another, when, remarking that he had torn the seat of his trousers in sitting on a jagged rock, I called out to him, "And so have your breeches!" He clapped his hand behind, proved it was true, and then slapped his hand on his thigh. "The very thing," said he:—

So have thy breeches!—
Cold blows the wind;
Thy hat has got a hole in,
So have thy breeches."

"Thanks, good youth! thanks, most apt and excellent stranger!" and we instantly cottoned and collogued, and had a long chat, in which I gave him some new ideas, I flatter myself. "Didn't know George from Adam then, and not until afterwards, when I met with the poem in the anti-Jacobin, and recognised my own handiwork, and made a few inquiries." Then he told us a story of how he captured and held a live stag in position for Landseer while he painted it, and how he suggested the lions in Trafalgar-square, and even put Paxton up to the Crystal Palace, and suggested the Income Tax and the Police to Peel, with many other remarkable coincidences.

"I say, Frank," said Tupman, while our friend went to mix another glass at the spring, "this chap's lying, I think."

"*Do* you think so?" I replied in a doubtful undertone. "Well, it is just possible; but he's a very original liar if he is."

"And now for a song," said our friend, and we sang all round —singly and then collectively and in chorus, and the three-pint flask began to evince signs of weakness. I proposed to go, as I thought we should get no fishing, but this our friend wouldn't hear of. He was getting on a bit, and said that "This was much better fun than fishin'—blow the fishin'! We'd just sit where we were, and make out the day, and go fishin' t'-morrer!" After another hour, I thought it desirable to move, as it was some distance back, but this again our companion wouldn't hear of. It was all right—he was "our guide, philoshopher, and friend," and there was plenty of time after finishing "t'other flask." I noticed that he experienced a difficulty in the word philosopher, and thought that something must give way soon, and I ventured to mention that if we were to reach Loch Air an Dallanaich to-night we really ought to be moving. Whereupon, with a look of pretenatural sagacity, our friend said "Needn be in sh deush of a 'urry, th' loch 'il come to ush fash 'nuff and no mishtake." His meaning was not apparent then, though I puzzled my head for some time to account for it, but at last I thought of the man who sat down in the square (which was turning round and round to his vision), under the profound belief that he had only to wait there till his own house came round in due turn so as to save all walking. No doubt our friend was under a similar delusion, but he seemed to care little for anything except the whisky flask, and ten minutes afterwards, our guide, philosopher, and friend, in the middle of a deep swig at the flask, collapsed suddenly, and fell back in the ferns, overcome by the heat of the afternoon, and soon began to snore like a nine farrow sow. Here was a pretty state of things. We shook him, but beyond a grunt could get nothing out of him. Tupman, in a rage, threw a pannikin of cold spring water over his face and shirt-front, but that too had no effect whatever. What was to be done? Were we to wait till he had slept off his attack? That would take four or five hours, and perhaps six or seven, by which time it would be dark night. Where were we? Did even our guide, philosopher, and friend know? This we doubted, for one or two little incidents, which before were hardly noticed, led us to think that he did not, and that he had utterly lost the way to the lake he was looking for before lunch. At any rate, we would just ascend that pinnacle of rock to see where we were; but before we went we stuck the two lower joints of our friend's rod in the ground, with his handkerchief tied to it, to find our way back to him by, and then we set out. We got to the peak, but quite lost sight of the handkerchief in doing so. We thought we could easily find our way back to him, and we could make out the way of getting down the mountain quite plainly, so we set out to return, and make one more effort to rouse up our guide; but, betrayed by the numerous sheep tracks among the rocks, we soon lost our own way, and wandered about for a good half-hour; of course, we shouted, but our companion would not have heard it had he been three yards away instead of probably three times three hundred, and so we wandered on for another hour disconsolate. At length it became evident that something *must* be done if we didn't want to spend the night on the mountains. It was useless looking any longer for our guide. He was a blind guide, a drunken philosopher, a false friend, and must take his chance. A night out would not perhaps be a very great discomfort. If it was, it was his own fault, and we could not help it. So we set to work seriously to get out of our difficulty, and, as luck would have it, five minutes after we saw a smoke, and in ten minutes more stood before a shepherd's bothy. It was a snug little hut enough, composed of turfs and heather. The architecture was of no great consequence. There was a peat fire at the back, and with a hole in the roof for the smoke—a dog barked, and a man stood before it. We explained to him our position; he had a little English, and understood us. But when we mentioned Loch Air an Dallanaich he smole a smile, and when we told him all our adventures, and how we had left our friend, it expanded into a broad grin, and he called to a companion, who came to the door of the hut and saluted us very respectfully, but without any servility. Him his friend addressed rapidly in a torrent of Gaelic, and when he came to Loch Air an Dallanaich his friend was as much on the grin as he was, and they chuckled to one another till I began to lose patience, but our new acquaintance said he had no doubt our friend had found the loch he went in search of, for Loch Air an Dallanaich, rendered into English, was simply "Loch blind drunk;" and after a moment of vexation I grinned too, while Tupman roared, as he delights in a sell. In the end we left our friend to the shepherds, who promised to relieve him, as the dogs would find him easy enough; and after administering to them the last of the whisky and a chunk of negro-head, which is almost the most grateful offering you can make a Highland shepherd, our acquaintance took us round a spur in the hills, and in half an hour pointed out to us Loch Arklet dimpling in the evening sun at our feet. It was easy to find our way down to it, and the high road ran alongside of it; so, thanking our conductor, we made the best of our way home, having, so far as we were concerned, sought Loch Air an Dallanaich in vain. We found out afterwards that our friend was a sort of peripatetic reporter for one or two newspapers, but Loch Air an, &c., was his stumbling-block. He was a very clever fellow, and capable of even brilliant things in the general utility line, but for his weakness which reduced him to the condition of a literary pedlar.

While at Loch Lomond I made the acquaintance of Andrew Clerk, the well-known tackle maker in New York, probably the first in the United States; a Scotchman originally, he had migrated to New York, and made a very good thing of his talent. For health's sake he was wandering among the old familiar scenes of his youth, sketching; and he was no mean artist, and handled his brush as well as his rod. We had many very pleasant confabs about sport in Canada and the States, and he gave me a good deal of information. It was very pleasant to meet a person from the other side of the Atlantic whose knowledge and experience was so extensive on the precise topics which are most interesting to me.

CHAPTER XXXI.

LOCH ARKLET—POACHING AND PIKE—LOCH KATRINE—TRYING THE PATERNOSTER—THE WATERWORKS EXTENSION OF THE LOCH—HOW I WENT UP BEN AN AND BENVENUE—LOCH CHON AND ITS PIKE, &C.

LOCH ARKLET is pleasantly situated about three or four miles from Inversnaid, by the side of the road on which the coach travels between Inversnaid and Stronaclachar, which is the place of embarkation for tourists going down Loch Katrine and through the Trossachs. At one end of Glen Arklet stands an old fort (Inversnaid Fort), which was erected in 1713 to keep the M'Gregors in proper order; who, if I remember right, returned the compliment some time after by sacking it. The remains of the old ruined walls may still be seen. It has an interest in the fact that at one time it was commanded by General Wolfe, who must have learnt here some of that experience in dealing with rocks and mountains which he afterwards carried to Quebec. On the further shore of Loch Arklet a tumble-down gable and a wall or two is pointed out to tourists as Rob Roy's house. I heard a tourist on the coach remark to another, as he regarded it somewhat scornously, that "it wasn't up to much." Loch Arklet is in private hands, being held by the lessee of the shootings of Glen Arklet, through which runs the Arklet burn already mentioned, and this, of course, also goes with the shootings. It is a very romantic burn, pitching down many falls, making deep, unseen lynns in its dark ravine, and these lynns, I understand, hold some very nice mahogany-coloured trout of from ½lb. to ¾lb., though they are scarcely as handsome as the Loch Arklet fish. I fished Lock Arklet by permission, but this lake, which had once one of the best names for giving sport of any lake in Scotland, is sadly fallen off. Two causes contribute to it; the pike have terribly increased for one, for we took, while fishing, quite as many pike as trout on our minnow tackles, most of them only wee fish of a year or so old, which augurs ill for the future, as they are just the fellows to clear off the fry wholesale. I hear of pike of 8lb. having been taken from it; and in a small lake like Arklet, there is no chance for the trout to get away from their enemies, they are brought so close together. There, too, I heard that not only Loch Arklet, but many other lakes hereabouts, had been skinned last winter and the winter previous by poachers, who swept out the small burns at spawning time, often getting two and three hogshead of trout in a night. No lakes can stand this double depletion for more than a year or two, and, unless it is put a stop to rigidly, they will shortly not be worth the angler's notice at all. I fished round the lake three times in a fine breeze (albeit it was northerly, which is not a good wind for fishing at this part in June). I changed casts several times, and I never got the symptom of a rise—not one. We then trolled round and round, taking only seven trout in the end, and as many pike. They were beautiful fish, however, of ¾lb. average, and on the table unequalled, though hardly as game in the water as the Loch Lomond fish. No doubt under the new proprietor's management the poaching of the burns will be stopped, and, as it is not difficult considerably to reduce the pike by employing set nets and trimmers, the fishing may possibly be greatly improved in the future. The lake can easily be re-stocked from the burn below to any extent, and such a charming lake as it is, so capable of giving fine trout, it would be a thousand pities if every chance was not given to it. It is rather a shy lake to the fly I understand. From the peculiar formation of the valley I have little doubt that at one time Loch Arklet extended over a far larger space than it does now, but natural causes no doubt have contributed greatly to reduce it. Indeed, more than once it has been proposed to drain it altogether, which might very easily be done by laying a pipe through to Loch Katrine, which is close at hand and at a much lower level while the water which it gives would be welcome for the Glasgow supply drawn from Loch Katrine.

On the next day I tried Loch Katrine ; from the little I saw of it, I have a high opinion of this loch. With a good breeze and a fairly favourable day, from two to three dozen of fish may be taken on it—beautiful golden trout up to 1lb.—and now and then of course a larger one. As the day was very hot, close, and windless, I was in no hurry to start on my fishing, but waited till the steamer came into Inversnaid at eleven, drove over to Loch Katrine by the coach to Stronachlachar, and there took a boat, and fished round the loch head; but there was not a breath of wind, and the fish would not look either at fly or troll, so I set my wits to work, and determined, as the lake thereabouts was not very deep or foul, and the bays rather flat and level, that I would try to paternoster it. Accordingly I rigged up a gut line, with a bullet at the bottom and two hooks, one two feet off the bottom, and the other five feet (the top hook took all the fish); then putting on a couple of live minnows, I directed the boatmen to pull a stroke or two between every cast, and casting towards the shore, drew the line in towards the boat. So we worked along through one or two bays, catching two or three very pretty fish indeed, when a little breeze sprang up, and we went to the fly for an hour or two, and then a tremendous squall with heavy rain drove us ashore and soaked us; after which we returned to Stronachlachar, with only half a dozen ¾lb. fish, and one about 1lb. But from what the boatman told me, which was confirmed afterwards by friends who have stayed there, there are few better lakes in Scotland—wind and weather permitting—than Loch Katrine, and there is

> Ample space and verge enough
> The characters of death to trace

on many a right stump of a trout.

The operations undertaken for the supplying of Glasgow with water from Loch Katrine have considerably extended the area of the loch; for in order to mitigate the severity of the work of tunnelling, &c., they raised the level of the lake considerably by means of a dam at the lower end, so as to get a sufficient slope and fall also. This of course has caused the flooding of a low-lying meadow here and there; and along the shores where the slope was gradual the waters have run some distance inland, and one constantly in shallow bays comes upon a low row of black jagged stumps of trees standing just above water, and here and there just under; and very nasty-looking obstacles they are, and you have to be careful with your spinning-tackle in such places, or grief comes upon you. The trees have been partially submerged and killed by this rise of the lake, and only their stumps are left of them. No doubt the trout profited *pro tem.* by the new feeding ground opened to them. In one instance an ancient graveyard was submerged, and I was told that the Laird whom it belonged to wanted very heavy compensation of the Glasgow folks for disturbing the bones of his ancestors. Unfortunately, neither the Glasgow folks nor the Court which he appealed to took a sentimental view of his rights in respect to his ancestor's bones, and the *solatium* which they gave to his pious grief was unsatisfactory.

As I have said, I subsequently returned and fished Loch Katrine again with a friend, but on this occasion it was bitterly cold—as cold as it is in March; and the usual genial north wind, which attended so many of our efforts during this tour, blew half a gale. Now Loch Katrine lies at a very high level—higher indeed than most of the large lakes in this district—and the result is that a cold wind is extra cold here. It is also owing to the natural coldness of the water, rather a late lake, fishing best in July, as the insects are not fully ripe till then, and the trout, of course, are not active in pursuit of them. The altitude at which the lake stands, and the nature of the surrounding hills particularly, render it liable to heavy squalls of wind, which frequently drive the angler ashore, to walk some five or six rough miles home again. On my second visit with a friend the day was dark, gloomy, and cold—most unfavourable; the result was only six moderate trout and three beastly pike, ugly, slimy kelts, with a foul smell and malignant aspect; for pike, alas! have invaded this lovely loch among the others, and they must do no end of mischief. One feels inclined to wish that the man who introduced pike into the Highlands at all had been hanged, drawn, quartered, and hung up to feed fishes. I saw several Mayfly out on the lake—it was on the 14th of June; but it was quite evident that the trout were away in the deep water out of the cold for shelter, and were not on the shores at all, for not a Mayfly was taken or even looked at. Had the fish been on the casts, if they had not risen to the fly, at least they would have come to the minnow; and what makes me more sure that the fish had retired into the deep water was that two or three of our fish were caught and hooked when we were crossing the lake in quite deep water, in places where it was perhaps fifty or sixty feet deep. I have often done this in crossing lakes, but seldom when it was a really good fishing day on the shores. It may be just possible, of course, that on really good fishing days one does not waste time by crossing the water more than one can help. Loch Katrine is rather an uncertain loch; but there is a large range of good fishing ground, which extends from end to end, though I think the head is the best ground, and holds the best fish, and Stronachlachar Hotel is the best spot to fish it from. This, of course can be reached by the steamboat from the Trossachs end of the lake, or by the coach from Inversnaid. Get the lake in a nice S. or S.W. breeze in July, and two, three, or four dozen of beautiful fish of $\frac{1}{2}$lb. and $\frac{3}{4}$lb. up to 1lb. will reward you.

I cannot forbear here from relating one adventure which I had on my first visit to Loch Katrine.

It is nearly twenty years since I first saw Loch Katrine and the Trossachs, and even then I did not fish Loch Katrine, for, if I remember me aright, there was a savage M'Gregor who set folks at defiance in the fishing way there. I fished that lovely Loch Achray, however, but the sport was only middling—the trout few, and not large—and in default of sport I set myself to climb mountains, at that time a very favourite occupation of mine. I never could come near a mountain but what I must get to the top of it, and as the sport was poor on the lake and the wind nothing to speak of, I set off to walk up Ben An. I do not suppose that in the world there is a lovelier bit of scenery than that eastern end of Loch Katrine, and Scott certainly did not waste his encomiums. Every moment disclosed fresh beauty as I steadily plodded through the birch, and made up the long gradual slope that precedes the real climbing, where

> On the north, through middle air,
> Ben An heaves high his forehead bare.

And that forehead is as stiff a 1200 feet as one need wish for. Nevertheless, I breasted it vigorously, for in those days I felt rather like young Malcolm (having had about six weeks' scrambling in the Highlands, and, as if

> Right up Ben Lomond I could press,
> And not a sob my toil confess,

which, allowing for poetical license, was pretty much my own state, and in due time I clambered up the last bit of peak, and stood on the top. The top of Ben An is a wonderfully small space—a mere extended platform. The peak goes up like a needle. There is a slight elevation at one end, with a narrow ridge, if I remember aright, not more than fifty yards or so long, and a slight expansion at the other. Standing on the elevation, one looks right sheer down a tremendous precipice almost into the lake. It is a prodigious sight, and most extraordinary sensation to stand up there and gaze steadily down. As for the view, it is magnificent. Beneath my feet,

> One burnished sheet of living gold,
> Loch Katrine beneath me rolled,

promontory, creek, bay, one beyond the other, melting into delicious indistinct harmony in the far distance, purple islands between, and on the opposite shore,

> High on the south huge Benvenue,
> Down on the lake in masses threw
> Crags, knolls, and mounds confusedly hurled,
> The fragments of an earlier world.

But all this is a bore, and perhaps superfluous, as almost everybody has seen it. "But, hallo, what is the meaning of this? This is too bad. If Benvenue is not higher than Ben An!"—Now the cause of this reflection and remark was thus:—Being of an aspiring, Excelsior-like nature, when I do go up a mountain I do not like anything to be above me in the neighbourhood but the sky. I like to go up the highest mountain, if there is one higher than another. From below, Ben An, from its peculiar sharp peak, looked the highest, and lumpy old Benvenue did not look so high by a great deal; but when I got to the top of Ben An, and looked across the lake, it was impossible not to see that the lumps were above the peak, and that Benvenue was the tallest. I was disgusted, and I went down again, thinking small things of Ben An. I had been decoyed up on false pretences. It was a humbug, a swindle, and so I went back to my fishing, sorely discomfited, and flailed away for an hour or two without success, looking at Benvenue from time to time.

"Where is the Goblin's Cave," I asked, "That's it, sir; that deep rift three parts up the side of the mountain," responded the boatman, pointing out the hole. "And that is the Coir nan tonskin,"—the cavern or den of the goblin, who is or was a sort of a brownie, and a cross between a man and goat, as it was said—evidently a descendant of the Satyrs—and just above it that mass of birch must mark the Beal a-nam-ho, or Pass of the Wild Cattle. It was very interesting, very; but I was getting hungry. So I concluded to return to my hotel—the Trossachs. Here a roast duck and a pint of port put me on good terms with myself, and rather friendly with all mankind. I sat outside the window and smoked my largest regalia. One glass of toddy promoted reflection. "And I hadn't been up the highest mountain after all." Confound that Benvenue. There was the Goblin's Cave, too. I'd never seen a goblin. Suppose one took one's whisky up there, and lighted a fire in the den or cavern, and waited till dark—would one see a goblin? They were called jolly satyrs, I remember; why shouldn't they be so still? It was not half a bad idea. It was a weird sort of thing to do, and rather recommended itself to me. It was something to say I'd done afterwards. Another glass of toddy decided me: I wouldn't be beat. I filled my flask, put a large box of matches and a biscuit in my pocket, pulled my hat down, and, without saying a word to anyone, off I started. I had four miles to go to reach the foot of the mountain; so, as it was well on in the afternoon, I went off at a good fast trot, which took me along the bank of the stream to the foot of the mountain in half an hour, or a trifle more, and I began to ascend just below the Goblin's Cave. The first five or six hundred feet or so was a species of huge stone quarry, and every step up that I took a mass of big rubble and large stones went rolling away behind me. It was very nasty, not to say dangerous work; but I worked on steadily, and reached sounder ground anon, but it was horribly rough still. I plodded on for an hour and more upwards, almost without a moment's pause, foot and hand helping each other. I often wonder now, when a steep flight of stairs makes me puff a bit, how I did it; but I lived in a hilly country then, and shot daily over some very abrupt ground, and practice, no doubt, helped me. However, knowing that the dusk was coming on, and the descent would be dangerous, I lost no time, and kept on —up and up and up—and now I began to think that I ought to be somewhere about the neighbourhood of the Coir, but I could not find it, and I still kept on ascending. At length I became sensible that I was getting toward the top, and supposed I had passed it (the cave), which I had—but I wasn't near the top yet; for as fast as I got to the top of one huge bulge of a slope,

I found there was another beyond, and so I went on and on for another hour or so—now stumbling over rock, now up to my knees in a moss. At length I made one more struggle up another bulge of rock, and there was nothing before me but space—illimitable space. I had reached the top at last, just as the sun was bowing his adieu. Knowing that there was no time to lose, I rested five minutes to get my wind, and ease the pulses that were beating all through me like sledge hammers with the tremendous toil, took a refresher, turned round again, and commenced to descend. Then I found that a furious wind was blowing right in my face. The evening was coming on; and, alone on the mountain side, thousands of feet above my fellows, with plenty of danger to season the feat, I began to think that I had done a remarkably stupid thing, and that if I got home alive I should be very fortunate, and have to thank Providence for an escape I did not deserve. Onwards I stumbled, downwards and downwards, and as the light was fast fading I knew that I could not spare a minute; but I would not be rash. I have a peculiar faculty of locality, and an object once seen rivets itself on my memory, and I knew that I had but to keep on going down, and to avoid slips and precipices. Still, with all I could do, the way was horribly dangerous. Once or twice, when going down very steep bits, the wind was so furious that it nailed me back against the rocks, and if I had wanted to fall forwards I could not very easily have managed it. That helped me a little. Where I was going I did not know, but I still went on downwards. I expect that I must have run half a dozen narrow chances of being dashed to pieces. Once I did slip, and I thought that all was over with me, but I was brought up with a tremendous shake by my feet coming in contact with a ledge of rock, which I found by feeling to be about a foot or eighteen inches in width. I estimate that I fell about a dozen or fifteen feet, and then I stood considerably frightened, with my back against the rock. Which way to move I did not know. Fortunately a huge rock on my right sheltered me a little from the wind; a large tuft of dry grass and moss grew beside me out of a rift, and a sudden idea occurred to me. I pulled out my box of matches, struck a dozen of them at once, and thrust them into the tuft of dry stuff, and a bright blaze sprung up for a minute, by the aid of which I saw that the ledge ran round the big rock. I could see nothing immediately below but the scarped rock. The light was speedily blown out by the wind, but I had seen all I wanted; and keeping my back to the rock, I stepped past the smouldering embers, and shouldered my way carefully round into a dried-up watercourse. Down this I scrambled with bruises and broken shins galore, until at last by good luck I hit upon the stone quarry I had started from. It was no child's play going down this loose stuff, for big stones rumbled down before and behind me; but fortunately I avoided all serious mischief, and at last found myself once more on firm ground at the foot of the mountain. I paused for a few minutes, refreshed myself with a pull at the flask and a dozen whiffs at the pipe, and then set off at a run for home. The path, which was rather broken, ran beside the stream between Katrine and Achray. Once or twice I stumbled, and found myself with a splash almost up to my waist in the stream, but this was rather refreshing than otherwise, so I did not much mind it; and, scrambling out, I once more ran on, and finally reached the hotel a very pretty scarecrow, torn and dishevelled, bathed in perspiration, wet to the skin, just at twelve o'clock, having been better than seven hours away.

"Good gracious, sir, where have you been?" said mine host; "we were quite uneasy about you."

"Up Benvenue," I replied.

"What to the top?" I nodded, and drank a deep draught.

"At this time of night, and since you dined here?" I nodded again, and took another draught.

"Good heavens, sir, you don't mean it? Why, you must have run all the way."

"I did," I replied; "there and back."

"And without a guide, too? Why, I wouldn't send a gentleman up in the day-time without a guide. It's the maddest thing I ever heard of, and how you escaped alive I can't imagine."

"Well, I had a narrow squeak or two, and that's a fact; but now if there's any cold meat, I'd like to recruit a little. Then send me a soda and whisky and a bed-room candle." There were about a dozen tourists in the coffee-room, who looked at me and whispered from time to time. Evidently they regarded me as an unusual specimen of their genus. Having walked and run about fourteen miles, and gone up two mountains in the day, I slept well, and thanked Providence that for my folly my bones were not left to the foxes and crows in some lonely corrie in Benvenue. This was my first acquaintance with Loch Katrine.

Loch Chon is a charming lake to look at; the scenery is very beautiful. It lies in a valley which runs almost from Loch Arklet right through to Aberfoyle, and the Pass of Aberfoyle is second only, if it is second, in point of beauty to the Trossachs. Loch Chon is rather secluded, and is one of a chain of lakes, big and little, that are made by the burn that runs through the valley. There is no inn near Loch Chon; probably the inn at the Clachan of Aberfoyle, the Bailie Nichol Jarvie, is the nearest, and that is some five miles or so from the lower end. The lake itself is some two or three miles long; and, as the road along it is about one of the worst in Scotland—and that is saying a good deal—it is desirable to have the boat (for there is but one on the lake, and that belongs to Mr. Blair, of Aberfoyle) as near as it can be to the point whence you start. We, coming from Inversnaid, had to drive the whole length of the lake, the boat being at the lower end, and then to send the trap back to the farmhouse at the head of the lake to put up, all of which caused loss of time and trouble; but as the fishing and boat belong to Mr. Blair, of Aberfoyle, application must be made to him; of course he keeps the boat at his own end of the lake, and Aberfoyle, no doubt, would be the best place to fish it from.

Loch Chon once had a name second only to Loch Arklet in giving capital sport; but in those days the burns were carefully protected by a gentleman who held it, and the pike steadily netted. This has fallen into desuetude, and much that is true of Arklet is true of Chon. It swarms with pike, and the burns get poached in the winter, so the trout are not plentiful. It is, too, rather a sulky loch, and the fish rise capriciously to the fly; but it used at times to show fine sport to the minnow. Now, however, the pike monopolise by far the larger share of the sport; if a London pike-fisher wants sport, just let him go to Loch Chon in October, and I warrant him a full basket on every likely day, and some big fish; for at the lower end, among the reeds and lily pads, there are pike of 20lb. weight and over, I hear. No one ever thinks of going there on purpose to fish pike, so the real jack-fisher would have untried ground all to himself. There would be no difficulty about bait I expect, as any number of small trout could be had out of the burns, though a jar of preserved bait would be indispensable as a stand-by; and further I would recommend a long rope and a stone or anchor to prevent drifting. With this I commend Loch Chon to the notice of my London friends, some of whom I doubt not will visit it some fine autumn, to the pleasure of themselves and the great profit of the lake; and if they only take out 200 or 300 pike, it will be some relief. The pike we took on our minnows averaged 3lb. or 4lb. each. Up to three o'clock, though there was a good breeze on from the usual quarter, viz., north, we had not a trout nor a rise, though we got several pike on the minnow. I then got a rise from a good fish, who repeated it, but did not take hold. Soon after we got one on the minnow, then I got one on the fly—the only one we caught on the fly all day—and the day resulted in five trout and seven or eight pike, the trout being none over three-quarters of a pound. A northerly wind, however, is supposed to be a very bad wind, and this perhaps was one reason for our want of sport; but pike and poaching must tell their tale, and when you catch double the number of pike that you do of trout, the prospect begins to my mind to look blue—indigo hue, in fact—particularly when the pike have spread themselves all over the lake, and are not confined to any particular bay or favourable ground, as is usual in most lakes, but take your minnow all over the best trout ground. It is imperative, if some of these lakes are not to be destroyed, that something vigorous should be done. That good large lakes can be destroyed by pike, there is no doubt. If the proprietors were determined to carry on war against the pike, it is not very difficult to do so; but to check the poaching, unless they are owners of the land also, or can interest those persons seriously in putting a stop to it, is, I fear, not so easy, and nothing can be done without a close time for trout in Scotland being established by law. The ruin of many of the lakes in the Highlands, which is proceeding, would be a great misfortune to Scotland; for the anglers largely contribute to keep open the inns in the wilder and more out-of-the-way districts for many months in the year. Allow the fishing to be extinguished, and the profit to be had from tourists and travellers alone will not in many instances suffice to keep these inns open, the season being so short. The result will be the abandonment of such inns and the closing of those parts of the country to the fertilising influence of strangers' money, which now helps to bring comfort into many a wild, out-of-the-way strath and glen. Surely these are considerations of sufficient weight to procure a fence time for trout. I do not pretend to enter on the sentimental view of the case, but I have a notion that the trout is at least as valuable a creature as the tomtit, or the black-headed gull. I should like to see the tourist handed in a dish of tomtits or black-heads, instead of a smoking ashet of brown, crisp, red-fleshed "throots," just fresh from the crystal lake, and to hear his exposition of the case after he had discussed his supper.

My experience of Loch Chon was not a favourable one, the day was utterly bad and no doubt far better sport could be got on a more suitable occasion.

CHAPTER XXXII.

BUCHLYVIE — BAILIE NICHOL JARVIE AND THE CLACHAN OF ABERFOYLE—LOCH ARD—CAUSES OF ITS DECADENCE — ROB ROY—WALTER SCOTT'S GENIUS.

LOCH ARD had so bad a name that I had been advised not to trouble it. A friend, however, told me that good baskets had been taken lately, so I determined to look it up, and accordingly prosecuted a rather tedious railway journey to Buchlyvie—not an interesting place according to the old song—

> Baron of Buchlyvie,
> May the foul fiend drive ye,
> And a' to pieces rive ye,
> For building sic a town,
> Where there's neither horse meat, nor man's meat, nor chair
> to sit down.

Hence we drive about six miles across a somewhat monotonous, uninteresting, dreary moor. As we leave it to the peewits and crows, we see not the winding Forth nor the peeps of pleasant nooks not far removed from the high road. The afternoon is warm, the jog-trot of the veritable rocking-horse who drags our cart has gradually somehow soothed down our musings, and our pipe is out, when the appearance ahead of three persons on horseback suddenly attracts our attention. They are mounting the rustic bridge which crosses the Forth close to Aberfoyle. Their riding coats are heavy and square cut, rather peculiar, and perhaps a bit old-fashioned at the first glance—a new kind of Ulster, I suppose—with large hoods to them. And—no—yes—they are actually riding in their long wading boots, turned down for convenience no doubt—brother fishermen evidently; and now they ride down into the Clachan of Aberfoyle, and stop at the door of the inn to which we also are slowly, very slowly, approaching. They dismount, and after a minute's pause, to remove a peeled willow wand which rests across the door, they enter. In a few minutes, we in turn approach the door, and as we do so, we hear through the open door a harsh, loud voice call out, "We are three to three. If ye be pretty men, draw!" Then there was a noise as though all the crockery was being smashed up by fireirons, followed by a tremendous smell of burning, as if all the sheeps' heads in the clachan were being singed at the same time. Then the noise ceases, and we peep inside the room, and, lo! it is our old friend Bailie Nicol Jarvie himself, with the red-hot poker in his hand, and Master Frank Osbaldiston and Galbraith sheathing their swords after the tuilzie, and Iveragh displaying a big hole in his plaid that "ye might put a kail pot through," singed by the Bailie's poker—odd we did not recognise them at first, wasn't it?—and so the scene vanishes, and nothing is left of it but the poker—the immortal poker—so long the outward and visible sign of the Bailie Nicol Jarvie Hotel at the Clachan of Aberfoyle, and we shake ourselves up into wakefulness, and dismount to the welcome of our friend Blair, who has taken the inn, and determined to rescue it from the depths of dirt and discomfort into which it had unfortunately of late years subsided. Formerly the fishing in Loch Ard was good, and the hotel was fairly comfortable. Both, however, were neglected together, and both alike got out of order. Loch Ard suffered from a severe visitation of tapeworm, which attacked the trout to such an extent that, after a day's fishing, it was nothing very unusual for the angler to find a tapeworm or two in the bottom of his fishing creel. Many trout in other lochs have been visited by this scourge, but not to the extent found in Loch Ard. I also discovered tapeworm largely in minnows sent from Loch Katrine, about one minnow in five or six being troubled with it, and those usually the finest. These specimens were sent to Dr. Spencer Cobbold, a great authority on such matters, and he declared them to be of the species termed *Lizella digramma.* All freshwater fish are more or less liable to *entozoa,* and tapeworm is not at all unknown in trout; but this appears to have been a most unusual outbreak. The causes are, no doubt, as recondite as the attack of tapeworm upon grouse, and therefore I can offer no satisfactory suggestion upon them, particularly as it is a subject which I am but little acquainted with; and whether there is any connexion between the attacks or no I have no notion. Some of the old Highland keepers say that the embryos of the tapeworm that attacked the grouse have been washed off the moors in rainy weather into the burns, and so carried down into the lakes; but I believe that the parasite attending on one animal does not, as a rule, transfer its attentions to another, though there may, of course, be exceptions to the rule, as in the case, for example, of *Trichinæ.* However, there is no doubt that, from this and other causes—chiefly the poaching of the burns during the spawning season, Loch Ard has suffered a good deal, and is not so productive as heretofore, the run of trout being smaller—in fact, belonging to a different and younger generation. When the late Mr. Dick lived upon the lake and farmed the fishing, he looked pretty sharply after the burns, and saw that they were protected. Since his death there has been no protection at all. The burns have been fearfully and shamefully poached in the spawning season, and all the best fish of the lake captured—and lakes may stand some poaching, or some pike (which latter abound in Loch Ard), or some tapeworm; but they cannot stand all three, and Loch Ard yielded under it—and so, for a season or two, it got into disrepute, and was but little visited by the Glasgow anglers. This temporary abstinence has contributed, in a sort, to neutralise some of the want of protection, and it is now a little better than it was.

Loch Ard and Aberfoyle present good illustrations of Walter Scott's descriptive genius. Anyone who has read "Rob Roy" carefully cannot fail to identify every spot described in it. Here is the

Bailie Nicol Jarvie Inn already noted. Further on we can easily recognise the place where Helen M'Gregor met the soldiers in search of her husband, and shot the sergeant. Up at that scaur above is the identical thornbush from which Bailie Nicol Jarvie hung suspended by the skirt of his coat—one could almost swear to it; and yonder is the high cliff above the lake off which Morris the gauger was hurled. Here it all is, graphic and living to this day, and we can trace the action just as we can trace the action of the "Lady of the Lake" through the scenery of the Trossachs. Scott never left anything to chance; he never evolved scenes out of his head or his memory, but set himself laboriously to stereotype them irom nature. It is told of him that once when out for a walk with a friend, his friend returned to him after a slight divergence, and found him seated in a little dell, paper and pencil in hand, jotting down the names of every shrub, tree, and wee floweret, moss and lichen, every circumstance of light and shade, &c.; that he might make use of the picture in some future work; and this peculiarity of habit in all his descriptions it is that keeps his novels and poems ever fresh and ever green. Contrast with this studied accuracy of detail the practice of another great writer, Bulwer. I have never forgotten a scene in "Pelham." Pelham is on his canvass for Parliament. He enters one house; they are eating blackberry pudding. In another he finds the garden flaming with *crocuses* and *sunflowers.* Such a botanical blunder never could have happened in any work of Scott's; and thus it is that, even though handicapped with forty or fifty years extra, the works of Scott will exist when those of Bulwer are forgotten. Leech in his sporting pictures had just the same careful habit of sketching bits and compounding pictures from the actual life, as I had reason to know personally; and the reason we have no Leech now, and are not likely to have, proceeds, I fancy, from the absence of that care in more modern caricaturists. They trust too much to imagination and too little to nature.

But this is not fishing, and my admiration of Walter Scott, and the marvellous accuracy of his descriptions of scenery, which we cannot fail to recognise throughout all this district, has led me astray. On the largest island in Loch Ard stands a small house, built formerly by the Stirling Club for refuge in coarse weather; it has a large fireplace and an oven, with a table and forms, and really is a great boon in wet weather, as I found it on one occasion. There stood the stronghold of some ancient chief in days gone by, and the peaceful fishing house no doubt is constructed out of the stones of the old fortress. Round about this island and the adjoining bay is some of the best ground in the lake.

There are two lakes at Loch Ard, the lower and the upper lake. The lower is much the smallest of the two, but holds some fine trout and plenty of pike. The first day I tried the lake I did very well, considering the day, which was dark and gloomy, with a fitful breeze that only made a decent ripple now and then; but Loch Ard fishes with less wind than any loch I know of. Give the slightest disturbance of the surface, and you may hope for fish; and even when it is quite calm you may still in a dark shady corner pick up a trout or two—indeed, it must be a very bad day that sees you come in clean from Loch Ard. I put out a minnow and rowed along the south shore, casting as I went; a bang at the minnow soon told of the presence of a fish, and a bright, silvery, handsome fish of half a pound, very like the Loch Leven trout, but certainly not identical with them, came dancing in. Then one came to the fly, and another and another. The minnow did not pay, and was soon taken in; indeed, I only took three fish with it all day, as minnows abound in Loch Ard. I believe, however, that it does best in the evening, as I heard of a good basket being taken with it then. I fished hard, being desirous of seeing what the lake could do, and I worked the lake pretty evenly and carefully, wasting but little time over luncheon and such distractions. But the cuckoos have ceased calling on each other across the lake. The last twitter of mavis and merle is over for the night, and little beyond the faint plash of rippling wavelets and the hum of insects is heard.

The landing place is at hand: a couple of strokes urge us into it, and the cart is waiting for us. So we tackle up our rods, &c., count up the fish, remove our belongings to the cart, and bid adieu to Loch Ard, our take amounting to twenty-five pretty fish, of which three scale a pound each, six three-quarters of a pound each, and the rest vary from three and four to the pound up to half a pound. The other two boats out did badly; one got eight, and the other only six. The next day was almost a dead calm, being hot and bright, and the lake very low; but by letting out a long line and trailing my flies I picked up a few trout. This is a capital plan when the trout rise falsely at the fly, they will often at such times take the trailed fly freely, the reason being that it is a foot or eighteen inches under water, and they have not as good a chance of detecting the cheat as they have on the surface. In this way I frequently got two on the cast at once. Now and then a slight breeze sprung up, and then we deluded a trout or two; but the minnow was of no use at all. I tried it by myself in the evening and got a pike of four or five pounds; but that was all. We mooned about a good deal, and spent some time in the hut. This place is a great resort for pic-nics with the Stirling and Glasgow folk, and the quiet fisherman, as the summer evening steals over him, often hears the silvery voices of "fair ladyes" joining in "Row, brothers, row," or the dear old "Keel row"—those simple and pleasant melodies that somehow spontaneously burst forth rippling over the waters from the sweet throats of the pic-nicking lasses. *Ay de mi.* Time was when this sort of thing was a special and rich delight to me; but half a century of years dulls the edge of pic-nicking enjoyments, and I prefer a quiet smoke after lunch, with a good instalment towards a satisfactory bag of trout when the day shall be over. After this we loiter about and drift hither and thither over shallows and deeps, mocking the cuckoos and watching the wee divers, but with an eye to business too, till we find the shades of evening drooping down. My boatman and I did not set our horses together well, or I might have killed many more fish than

I did. He was a capital man, no doubt, for a lad or a muff, as he knew the lake thoroughly and had certain set ideas as to his functions; but he was as obstinate as many mules, and as bent on having his way and not letting you have yours as any boatman I ever met and endured through two days' fishing. I got only thirteen fish, averaging about the same as the preceding day. The other boats got, one a dozen, and the other six, but the one with a dozen was away at six in the morning, and so had four hours' start of us.

On the third day I had intended to drive up and fish Loch Chon again, as I was assured that our former day on it was a very unfavourable one, that it was doubtless owing to the north-east wind, which the lake never fished well on, and that several people had had decent sport on it, &c.; so I resolved to give it another try. But when I got up in the morning and found a good breeze from the north-east, I did not think, with my past experience, that I would have another turn at it; so I resolved to stay on Loch Ard, merely changing my boatman—and I think I got the best fellow for boatman of all the lot; he is a tailor and lives near the lake. He knew his work; could row stoutly, and did not spare his labours; did not hurry you over your ground; did as you told him; was not bad company; wanted very little to drink, and took the weather as he found it without shirking or shrinking—all of which are in my eyes cardinal virtues in a boatman. Unfortunately, however, though we had a good breeze during a part of the day, we had a pelting rain throughout the rest, so that we got wet through, and had to take refuge in the Stirling Club's pavilion, and light a fire there till we had dried ourselves; worse than all, the water had broken, and was covered with a thick beastly scum that parted in greasy waves and slimy wreaths when the oar was dipped in it, and resembled tar refuse on the water more than anything else. What this comes from I cannot pretend to say. We have something like it on the Thames at some seasons of the year, though hardly so thick as this was, and it is said to come from some change in the weeds at the bottom. Loch Ard is at the bottom in all the bays, as far as I could see, just like a grass field, the weeds being short and thick, like the side of a down. No doubt this scum comes from them in some way; however that may be, I felt quite sure that it was fatal to fishing as soon as ever I saw it, and so it was, for I only got ten fish all day, and those of the weeëst. Perhaps the ten might, with a penny piece or two, weigh 3lb. I do not know what the others did, but I fear not much, for I left the lake and took my cart away for Inversnaid from the top of the lake, as I had to be at Luss for a competition of the West of Scotland Club the next day; I had, too, to leave early to catch the other cart from Inversnaid, which I had told to meet me at Loch Chon head, and thus I bade adieu to Loch Ard.

Oh, that drive from Aberfoyle to Loch Chon head; what a delicious bit of scenery it is! To my thinking, it almost equals the Trossachs. Lake upon lake, pool, brawling burn and waterfall, mountain and fell, rocks, ferns, heather, fitful cloud and waving wood—it is just fairyland, and like a pantomime or a drop scene at a theatre, only real, and one can fancy that

> Here in cool grot and mossy cell
> The rural fays and fairies dwell.

One seems to want to lie down in the heather with a cigar and gaze on it all day without moving; to "listen to the waterfall," and to skylark and mavis, curlew and grouse cock, and drink in all sorts of heavenly and earthly sounds and scenes in exquisite and healthy laziness, in perfect *abandon* to the bliss of complete rest of mind and body; to re-instil into one's faculties some of that essence of nature which is gradually worn away in the daily friction of the world. Oh, ye toilers and moilers among men—oh, ye paterfamiliases, whose wearying struggle it is to keep up with the world and the insane requirements of society, who race with bankruptcy and paralysis and get beaten on the post—don't take your families to the seaside, don't be cheated by hags and devoured by bugs, and humbugged by conventionality into the belief that you have enjoyed yourself when you know you have been miserable and devoured of ennui; but if women *will* go there, *send* 'em, and come here yourselves for a season. So shall you have rest for your souls, and fortify yourselves with powers of endurance against the shocks of business and the agonies of Mrs. Grundy in the future. The walk from Aberfoyle, say to Stronachlachar on Loch Katrine, which is about ten miles, is simply delicious.

As regards the improvement of the fishing on Loch Ard, two things are required—the destruction of the pike and the protection of the burns at breeding time. Perfect protection cannot be had without a regular, legally qualified close season from November to March; though, if the lessee of the lakes has the goodwill of the proprietor and the landowners, he may do a good deal to stop the slaughter. But a close time for trout in the Highlands must be had before long, or many of the lakes will be extinguished as fisheries; this will extinguish the inns, which, as a matter of course, will extinguish the tourists, and great loss to the districts will be the result. The destruction of the pike in Loch Ard would be comparatively an easy task, for I never saw a lake which could so easily be dealt with by nets. At the head of each little bay is a fringe of rushes and reeds from 20 to 40 or 50 feet or so deep, and in these the pike spawn and bask during the warm weather to a very considerable extent. A Thames powsing net run round the outside of these weeds would take every pike in them. A Thames powsing net is a single-walled trammel about 40 yards long, with a 3in. mesh for the lint and a 10in. walling. It is fixed at either end by a couple of ripecks (iron-shod poles) thrust into the ground, the ends of the net being lashed on to the poles. The first pole being fixed at one end of the rushes, the net is run out as quietly as possible all round the rushes until it is all out, the other pole is then stuck in, and the net thus makes an upright wall round the rushes on the lake side. Then go into the rushes and beat them with the oars and plunge them with poles all over, and every pike in the rushes will bolt out into the net and be caught. This should be repeated at intervals of two or three days, until the supply of pike becomes exhausted, when the rushes may be left at rest for a season. Just before spawning time in April would be a capital time for the work. The double-walled trammel, which is used as a set net for pike, being anchored out at right angles to the shore and left all night, would answer equally well for this work; but forty yards would hardly be long enough for these rush beds—sixty would be better, or two nets might be joined together. It would be hard, however, to explain to a Highland boatman how to do these things; and therefore I strongly advise the Glasgow Club, who are moving to preserve these lakes, to hire a regular old Thames netsman to come up and bring a couple of nets with him, wlth ripeck irons (poles he can get there in any number) and all the tackle complete, and let him show them for a week how to punish the pike on Loch Ard. They would have a man or two there from other lakes to help him, and thus the method would easily be learnt and disseminated, and 10*l.* or 15*l.* would be the outside of the cost, and a deadly blow would be dealt at the increase of pike in the Highland lakes.*

I may say here that I got safely to the competition at Luss, next day, but, owing to unfavourable weather, it was a poor affair, hardly worth chronicling.

Before closing with the freshwater fishing I may state that the flies used in all the lakes are very similar. The bodies are mostly rough wool bodies, red, red and yellow, black and red, orange, yellow, and green, with silver or gold thread; hackles black or red, and wings of teal, drake, or woodcock. It is always desirable to have two sizes at least, one for rough and high, and a smaller for low and calm water, and the best advice I can

* I am happy to say that these representations have not been futile. The West of Scotland Angling Club, with whom I am in correspondence, have, during the past season, put watchers on some of the burns, and have ordered pike nets for Loch Ard and Loch Chon, and they deserve great credit for their public spirit and sportsmanlike determination.

give to help to make a basket is to keep on fishing. Never allow yourself beat, persevere. If one fly doesn't do, try another. If casting does not do, trail. Somehow determine on getting fish, and don't yield to the pleasant advice dealt out by the poet, who says:—

To my way of thinking,
There's nothing like drinking
While the fishes are blinking
And winking at me.

It is jolly, it is seductive, but delusive. Stick to your fishing while you are about it, and if you must drink, wait till you get home in the evening.

There are a few other lakes in this neighbourhood which may be summed up shortly. Loch Achray I have mentioned already. It is a small but very pretty lake, and may be fished from the Trossachs Hotel, which it is close to. It is not a free rising lake at all, but there are good trout in it, and very large pike unfortunately. Some four miles to the south is Loch Dronkie, but that, I think, is in private hands, though anglers from the banks are not interrupted. It is very similar to the rest. I fished it once only many years since, but sport was bad, the day being bright and still, and while there I picked up the lead belonging to an otter, which was, perhaps, an additional reason for bad sport. The trout run almost equal to those of Loch Chon, and the sport is somewhat similar. Loch Vennachar is a fine lake and fishes better in spring. Indeed, Vennachar and Ard are the two earliest lakes hereaway; it often gives a salmon or two to the lucky fisherman. It is much affected by the Stirling anglers. Callander is the best station for it, as it is also for Loch Lubnaig. This, too, is a large loch, but the trout are not so large as in the other lakes, though very plentiful; I never fished it, but for a change it might suit the wandering piscator. The Loch of Menteith has a few good trout, but not many, being full of pike and perch, of which any quantity can be taken. I have said nothing as to rivers, as I fished none;

but the upper Clyde with its tributaries might well engross the angler for a summer ramble. Starting from the Elvanfoot Station on the Caledonian line as the topmost on the Clyde, five or six tributary burns first form the river, the most considerable of these being the Deer and Powtrail waters; between this and Abington three other burns fall in; and between this and Lamington, other three, one Duneaton water, a considerable one, and next come Garff water, a capital stream, and Culter water, which flows in at Symington, which is a capital station to fish the middle district of the Clyde from, accommodation being obtainable at most of the above stations, which are also stations on the Caledonian Railway. From Symington, where there is a good inn, the fishing is good past Thankerton, till we come to Carstairs Junction; just above this the Medwin falls in, and to this there are many fine burns—indeed, curiously enough by means of a cut for a sawmill, a portion of the Clyde water is diverted from the Medwin Burn into the Tarth water, and so down the Tweed, so closely do the sources of these two important rivers run into one another; Dippool and Mouse waters run into the Clyde near Lanark, and are the last worth notice. They are excellent streams, and yield remarkably fine trout in places. The upper Clyde, too, is well stocked with fine grayling, which often exceed the trout in size. Salmon fishing may be had in the Awe by going to the inn at Taynuilt and taking a day ticket, 5*s.*, and sometimes it is not to be despised if the water and weather are suitable. It is a fine river to fish, and coming from so large a lake is seldom very low. Orchy and some of its tributaries, with one or two lakes, can be fished either at Dalmally for the lower water, or for the upper parts Inveroran, and in the autumn the Orchy gives very fine salmon fishing, and all these places can easily be got at from Glasgow. Lucky Glasgow! though any one going to Dalmally from the south would take the rail to Tyndrum, and thence coach to Dalmally. Taynuilt lies further on, and may be got at best from Oban. The Teith, another very nice river, gives good sport at times both with salmon and sea-trout, as well as brown trout, a good stretch of it is rented by the proprietor of the Dreadnought Hotel at Callander. So that the angler has a choice of lakes and rivers at Callander. The Teith is celebrated for its pearl mussels, which are, or were, at one time very abundant.

CHAPTER XXXIII.

The Clyde compared with the Thames.—The Sea Lochs.—Sea Fishing at Row.

The case of the Clyde has often been cited as a reason why salmon should be able to get up the Thames. The two cases present no parallel, except in so far as that both rivers are more or less polluted; but here all similarity ends. In the one instance we have the pollution of a population of between 300,000 and 400,000, and in the other of one of 3,000,000 or 4,000,000. In the one instance there are numerous towns and villages above to add to the filth, and in the other nothing of any account. In the one the area and length of river into which the pollutions are poured is probably about a mile, and in the other about eight miles. Eight or, ten miles below Glasgow the water, as I saw it, is pure enough for any salmon to live in; while twelve or thirteen miles down, where the Leven runs in from Loch Lomond, salmon and sea trout are taken habitually. There is nothing of this kind on the Thames. Then again, the Clyde at Glasgow and for a long way below is very narrow—hardly as wide as the Thames is above Abingdon; and when a heavy spate comes down it, the river at Glasgow rises ten, fifteen, and even twenty feet, I have been told. Is it not quite evident that when this happens the body of filth must be overpowered and swept out by the tremendous force of the clean water coming down in flood; and that while this high water lasts, the river flowing by Glasgow must be comparatively pure; and if it only lasts from twenty-four to forty-eight hours, that is long enough for a salmon to run clean past Glasgow, or for smolts perhaps to be carried down? If the Thames had a flood down it 20ft. deep now and then, we might hope to see salmon up it. No doubt in ordinary water at Midsummer the Clyde stinks as badly and looks as foul as the Thames, and thus it is that people are led away in their comparison of the two. Besides all this, there are the two facts that salmon do pass Glasgow, and are constantly seen above it, at least, I believe so; whereas they do not pass London, and are never seen above it, and the parallel therefore does not hold good.

Glasgow is especially fortunate in having so much good free trout fishing within easy reach. Most of the lakes I have noted are no further off than a mere trip to one of the stations on the Thames would take one; and with this difference, that when you get a good day's sport your fish are worth a great deal more than the hire of the boat comes to, which can seldom be said on the Thames. The average cost of boat and man is about 5*s.* or 6*s.*, about half what it costs you for punt and bait on the Thames. But Glasgow also has a variety of lovely seaside villages, within a very short steamboat run, all about the mouth of the Clyde, on the shores of those noble salt-water lochs which run into the land for miles and miles, and form almost arms of the sea; there may be had splendid and safe yachting almost all the year round, and to persons at all troubled by sea sickness it must be a great comfort to be able to carry this out in comparatively calm water. As for the sea fishing, there is no place round the coasts of the British Islands, nor, so far as I know, anywhere else, where such a variety of delightful sport can be had. A little 5 or 6 ton yacht, fitted with fishing apparatus, a trawl, a seine, and a trammel net, with a spillet and lines various, would enable one to provide oneself and friends with fish for eight months out of the year, and leave a good deal to dispose of besides.

I cannot imagine anything more delightful than a summer spent in exploring these lochs and discovering the various kinds of fishing and the best localities for them. Whiffing for lythe, saithe, mackerel, sea trout, and other fish may go on from early spring to late autumn. In the spring sea trout take the minnow well, and I have known 30lb. weight of beautiful fish from 1lb. to 4lb. each taken by one fisherman along the shore by Helensburg. Almost every kind of salt water fish is caught in abundance in the inlets about the mouth of the Clyde. In one day I took whiting, codling, flounders, wrasse, saithe, gurnet, and father lashers. I got Angus, the pier-keeper at Row, to procure for me a good pot of rag worms, which are very fine thereabouts. By the way, Angus and I became friendly: he is an institution of Row. The Queen, I think, mentioned him in her book, and Her Majesty never mentions anything unworthy of mention, nor commends anything unworthy of commendation; apart from all ordinary respect and loyalty I have a great respect for her judgment as a woman, and Angus was worthy of notice—a fine old fellow, sturdy, honest, independent, and thoroughly Scotch. A very good specimen of the old class of Highlander is Angus. With my rods and pot of rag worms I pushed off in a little boat of Angus's about half a mile from the shore, picked out a spot not too much in the run of the tide, and with a couple of trolling rods, each fitted with a light lead or pair of chopsticks, and a couple of stout gut hooks, I had for two or three hours till the tide turned my hands pretty full hauling in fish, frequently two at a time. Some of the codling went up to two pounds weight, and were capital eating; and frequently while reeling in one lot, the point of the other rod was going hard, and had to be left to itself, so that I could not get them in fast enough. Had there been another hand at the other rod I should have largely increased my take; as it was, I got abont four score of fish various as above noted. As I went more particularly for flounders, they formed the major part of the fish, and capital eating they were too; but a row of another half mile would have taken me specially into the whiting ground, where large takes are made. I had two or three turns at this fun, and enjoyed it greatly, the boat being quietly at anchor, with scarcely a motion; and to many persons fond of the sport but with weak stomachs, the advantage of this is incalculable. I only wish I had had time and opportunity to explore the Gareloch with my rods and chopsticks; but I could not do everything.

Having heard a good deal of the splendid sport to be had with the lythe and saithe in the mouth of Loch Goil, just above where it opens into Loch Long, I was anxious to get a day there, and I found two friends willing to join me—one of whom had often been there before, and knew how to arrange, and what boatman to get. He talked of so many stone of fish that he took on this and that occasion, his largest not being over 10lb., but a good many of 8lb., and so on; and when fish are reckoned by the stone, and by 8 and 10-pounders, it sets all my piscatorial mania a-going, and I long to be at them with an eagerness that obstacles cannot daunt. My friend, however, was not very sanguine of our making a large bag in the daytime, most of his sport having been had at night. The saithe particularly did not feed well by day, and were shy; lythe we might get a few of, and perhaps a sea trout or so. I, however, had made up my mind that they would bite just to oblige me, and was anxious to go and try my luck at least; so we went We had a lovely drive from Roseneath to a little village on Loch Long, opposite Ardentinny, where two sturdy boatmen where waiting for us. Unfortunately, our old friend the north wind attended on us as usual, and came rollicking down the loch to meet us as though it were whistling "Slap bang, here we are again; here we are again; here we are again;" and, as a very little wind is best for the sport, it did not add to our probabilities. My friends used a tackle made of three stout hooks, tied on gimp in the fashion of the Stewart worm tackle. On this they hung a big rag worm, as large round as my little finger, and then plunging their rods up to the middle joint in the water, waited the result as we rowed away. I had on one of those corkscrew spinning sand eels, and in order to give it a flavour I had cut a strip from the side of a small saithe I picked up, and wound it round the screw, and tied it head and tail. It was a noble bait, and spun like a top. We had not long started, and I was just paying out a long line when forty or fifty yards astern up rolled a brace of porpoises; a minute after I had a most tremendous bang at the rod. "I'm in him! I'm in him! a porpoise! a porpoise! by Jove." Porpoises feed on sand eels, remember, and it was not impossible, only if it had been a porpoise he would have smashed everything to powder; but whatever it was, in the very commencement of his first run, off he went—the hold gave. What an unlucky chap I am, as a poor dear old friend, now no more, would have said, and often did say upon such occasions when he was inclined to chaff, as he usually was. "Just like my luck, eh, old fellow?" and so it was. The fish was gone, and what he was we didn't know, but the *cognoscenti* opined that he was a big sea trout, and, probably, much the most valuable fish we should hook that day.

After this we took up our lines, having gone over the best ground thereabouts, and rowed away for Loch Goil, a good stiff three or four miles row, with a strong wind ahead and a heavy boat. When we entered Loch Goil we went over the likely places—some shallow rocky ground about 200yds. long, rowing across and across, but we got nothing. The fish were not feeding. So as we were sharp set after our drive and row, we fed instead, going ashore to do so. Just as we had done lunch I saw one or two gulls hurry towards the spot we had left, and pounce down in the water. "The fish are feeding; I saw one or two break the water; and there's another, and another," said my friend, as the splash of a large fish or two was seen half a mile off, and we put to sea again. As we approached the spot, every now and then a big fish or two would come up to the surface with a rush, driving the small fry—herring soil—up to the surface, when the gulls would swoop down and pick up their share of them. Up and down the ground we went, through and through the shoal. My friend got a small lythe of 1½lb. weight, and I hooked a good fish of 3lb. or 4lb.; which served me as the former one did; but we could not get on with the saithe. Every now and then three or four big fish broke water, and at one time there were fifty or sixty big fish, many of them 10lb. and 12lb. weight, dashing up the foam in all directions, all round the boat, often within ten or a dozen yards or so of it, for several minutes. It was a splendid sight, and made us very eager, but never a pull could we get from them. My friend, alas! was only too true a prophet. If we liked to stop all night, and the tide suited, we might catch wales and whales. I was sorely tempted. I had a good mind to stop, but I'd a better one not to; so, after trailing along the shore through a spot called the "lythe hole," famous for monsters of this species, we returned to our trap with four small lythe and two or three codlings; a lamentable end to my "great expectations." I have no doubt, however, that from all I heard a night's fishing would produce something considerable from what I saw of the fish *to be taken*; and all the fishermen quite concurred in what I had been told.

These lochs are the great breeding ground for all kinds of fish, and from the presence of the herring soil no doubt the herrings also deposit their spawn in them. The heads of the lochs are mostly fed by small rivers, which are hardly large enough for salmon, but they are fine white trout streams. There are also many smaller ones that fall in in other parts, and nets are frequently drawn round the mouths of these at night after a fall of rain, and frequently with profitable results to the net. Rowing softly along these lochs on a still night, with moon or stars only lighting the scene, the dark shadows of the cliffs and mountains thrown down on them from the rocks above, the phosphoric sparkles as some big fish breaks the surface in pursuit of his prey —the long trail of brilliants left behind in the boat's water— the solemn quietude and silence of the night, are striking circumstances under which to enjoy one's sport; and if the fish are well on the feed, and one's musings are broken every now and then by a tremendous rugg and plunge of an 8lb. or 10lb. fish I can quite understand how agreeable "a nicht wi' saithe" is, and how pleasant the reminiscence.

I was very much surprised at the scarcity of oysters in these lochs, most of which present to all appearance the finest oyster ground in the world. I know of no place where oysters would be likely to reach such fine quality as in Lochs Fyne, Long, Goil, and the Gareloch. As regards Loch Fyne, it struck me that the water was charged with minute matters, such as Diatoms, &c., upon which oysters feed. I had not an opportunity of examining and testing the particles, but such was the appearance of the water as I stood on the pier at Inverary. Clear almost as crystal as the water was, you could see every small object, no matter how minute, that was held in suspension, and it seemed as if the water was charged with them, and heavily too. It has been laid down as a principle by shrewd ostreaculturists, that where there are no signs of oysters ever having existed—considering how oyster spat must have been wafted all round the coast over and over again—the probability is that the place is not very suitable for oysters. This test, however, will not apply to these grounds, because oysters are constently found, though not in such large numbers as to make dredging for them a paying pursuit. I know that oysters are found in the Gareloch, and there are few places that I know of so suitable to all appearance for oyster cultivation as the coast all down by Helensburgh and Row. It reminds me strongly of the coasts at the Ile de Rhé, where the *parc* system of cultivation was first tried with such signal success. Considering how valuable oysters are, and what a profit is realised out of a well-stocked, well-managed fishery, I wonder that no one in Glasgow has ever thought of utilising these flats and these fine salt water lochs. Judiciously dealt with, I feel certain that handsome revenues might be drawn from them. I have now concluded my notice of the fishing in this part of Scotland, merely adding that there are few spots that I am acquainted with better worth a visit from the wandering angler. Taking

Lochs Vennachar and Ard as the earliest lochs, he might in succession fish Loch Awe, Loch Lomond, Loch Chon, and Loch Katrine, and spend a pleasant season, as I did, before the tourists swarm too much, for finding your inn choke full, with considerable difficulty in obtaining refreshment, and the certainty of having to share the inside of the stage-coach for the night with two or three others instead of having a downy couch to rest your wearied limbs on, is anything but delightful, and the noise and snobbery of the whole thing is a very bad sauce to take with the picturesque.

FOURTH RAMBLE.

CHAPTER XXXV.

The Start for Thurso—A Gale—The Cruive Pool and the First Fish—Strathmore—The Linn of Skinnet—A Brace of Fish Bagged.

It is a good many years ago since I went to Thurso; yet every incident that then occurred is as vividly impressed on my memory as if it were only last season. I purpose, with the aid of my notes, to recall them. In those days the railway went no further north than Aberdeen, and one took ship from Aberdeen to the sweet-smelling Burgh of Wick, where the staple is herrings, the talk is ever and always of herrings, and the smell is also of herrings. The train deposited us in the cold grey Granite City about three o'clock in the afternoon; five o'clock saw us on the quay, embarking on board the old paddle-wheel which plied to Orkney and back. It was a calm afternoon in March when we steamed away from the mouths of the Dee and Don; and when well on our journey a sumptuous Scotch tea, with haddies and other delights, prepared one for all hazards. My family have all been sailors for generations, and some of them have played a creditable part in the history of their country's wars; but I do not call myself a good sailor, though I am not what others would call a bad one, having been much acquainted with and used to the sea. My father, though an old captain in the navy, to the last day of his life could never go to sea without being sea-sick: and I believe he shared that peculiarity with the great Nelson himself. Having a very little of the family failing, I laid down a basis of action, and, after taking a stiff caulker of Glenlivat and fortifying myself with a comfortable smoke, prepared to leave the deck and turn in, particularly as I saw a low-lying bank of clouds in the north-east, which looked to me threatening. I pointed them out to the steersman, who did not share my opinion.

I'm a capital sleeper, aboard or ashore, and can get to sleep anywhere, and in five minutes I was in the Land of Nod. I had wandered in that paradise about three hours, perhaps, when a crash and a tinkle awoke me. It was the face of my watch, which I had hung up to a hook in my berth with too long a purchase. "Hullo! what the dickens! why, it's blowing a gale of wind, and a stiff one too!" The long easy swing and regular beat of the engines was exchanged for a most violent pitching, tossing, and thumping, while the wind howled and whistled like twenty thousand theatrical gods during a long stage wait. I don't like being below in coarse weather, so in five minutes I was out, dressed, and on deck. It was a splendid sight, being as near a downright furious storm as need be without being quite that. The waves were big enough for anything, and as black as ink, with a ridge of curling white angry foam on the top. It was a real ugly night, and the steersman allowed that I had been quite justified in my expectations. It was about one o'clock, and we were opening Wick Harbour; but in such a gale we could not enter it, and, as we could not do anything else till we attracted their attention on shore, we lay-to for about four hours, which was worse than before. At length, having succeeded in our object, we worked round the head in front of us into Sinclair's Bay, where we were in shelter, and, a boat having been sent in a cart across country from Wick to meet us, we all landed, and walked into Wick. Here a wash and a breakfast refreshed one, in spite of the herrings, and a dogcart sent in by Dunbar from Thurso took up me and my belongings.

Away we bowled for Thurso, eighteen miles, over a very dreary, dull road, with a not too conversible driver. About half-way we passed a nice sheet of water, Loch Watten, which holds good trout, up to 2lb. I was told. In due time Dunbar's Hotel, at Thurso, received me; but when I crossed the Thurso, my anticipations of sport went down into the heels of my boots, and I felt quite limp and faint. There was what they called a river—that is to say, a lot of stones of all sizes, with a small puddle here and there; but there was not as much water running out of it altogether as would fill a respectable water-butt. Here was a bright look-out! To think I had come some 900 miles or so for this! I got some lunch, however, and by the time I had done Dunbar came in, and I imparted to him my mistrust; at which he laughed. and said, "It did not matter a bawbee. The Thurso fished better and better the lower she got, if there was only wind, and she'd fish well for a month yet without a drop of rain. The gentlemen up at Strathmore were getting their two, three, and four fish a day each; and if I'd come out with him in the evening I should see him kill a good fish, and perhaps two, not two miles up the stream."

A little reassured at this, I lighted up the calumet of consolation, and, taking a flask of distilled comfort in my pocket, I sallied out up the river with Dunbar, who over his shoulder wielded what Homer would have described as "no small part of the mast of a vessel," but which he called a rod; it would have made perhaps rather a tasty hop-pole. We passed a likelyish pool or two, which were of no use then, and at length reached a long deep, still, sullen-looking pool, some forty or fifty yards or so wide; this was called the Cruive Pool, though cruives there were none. It was the scene formerly of a most prodigious take of salmon—I forget how many they got out at one haul, but it was something awful—twelve hundred and odd I think. Dunbar put up a fly—such a fly! The Thurso flies, as exhibited by the natives, were no beauties in those days—I have a lot of them by me now, and I look at them now and then, when I've been inspecting a lot of really nice flies, just for distraction; but the fish approved of them, and that was enough. There was a nice breeze on, and as the fly lighted for the third time on the water a short chopping rise betokened a sea trout, of which there are generally a few, though of no great size, on the lower pools. Then a big boil said "salmon" to us, but whether clean or foul we could not tell, as he would not come again; and then, after carefully combing the pool all over, we went up to the next, which I think was called the Kelt Pool, and commenced afresh. In a few minutes there was a dull ruffle of the water, and the reel was screeching a music compared with which "A te o cara" by Mario in his best days would have been uninteresting. Again and again the fish bolted up and across the pool; but Dunbar—who has, or rather had then, a very heavy hand on the fish, with tackle of the severest—soon rolled Master Silversides over and over. He had a little jointed gaff at his side, liking always to gaff his own fish—a practice I strongly object to, as being always the cause of loss of time, and often of loss of fish. After three or four false chops and misses, he got the gaff into the fish, and hauled him out, a nice new brilliant fish of 11½lb. His health was duly quaffed, and a libation made to him, and once more the long line fell straight as an arrow across the water; for D. was a fine fisherman without doubt, and many approve of heavy play, and think it always the right thing. Five minutes, ten minutes, passed, when suddenly a spanking fish of some 14lb. or 15lb. made a most dashing rise, and was fast; he travelled about at a great rate, but at the second run he contrived to get quit of the steel, and bade us *au revoir*. "Wait till I catch ye up on the Linn, ye beggar!" said Dunbar, wrathfully. A change of flies then took place, as the hackle was cut; after which, though we tried for half an hour, only one faint rise rewarded us, and so we walked home lightly enough.

"It's easy walking now," said Dunbar, "but I've seen in the winter time when this two miles would tax a strong man to get to the town. I recollect once, when Mr. Thistlethwaite was up here, he started out up to Amester. It looked threatening, and we advised him not to go; but he was a wilful man, and would to Cupar. It came on a heavy storm of wind and snow, straight in his face, and he tried to come back; but not getting home so soon as we expected, we got alarmed, and sent out a party to look for him, and found him under a hedge about three-quarters of a mile from the town, nearly done for, and if we had not sent to look for him he'd have been a dead man ere morning. Ye've no idea, unless ye've tried it, of the force of a Highland snow storm."

The next day I started in the trap for Strathmore, which at that time was the lodge where the whole of the gentlemen were. I was put down at Halkirk, a little half-way village, while the trap went on to the lodge with my impediments. At Halkirk I found my gillie waiting to conduct me on to the water which was that day my beat. The last comer always went to the bottom of the water, and took the lowest beat, which included Amester, the Cruive Pool, &c.*; but, as the next beat was not thought much of, and was a long distance from Strathmore, it was not in use to-day, and was at my service. It comprised a longish dull pool, called then the Linn of Skinnet, close to which now Brawl Castle stands, with sundry other smaller and uninteresting pools up towards Halkirk. There were six beats on the river; the Linn, far the best water on the river, was at the top. The other beats down to Halkirk were supposed at that time of year to be rather indifferent. One in particular, called the Rocks, was of no use till May, though there was a pool on it, called the Sauce pool, of which more anon. We had a four-mile walk down to our water. A trap was to pick us up in the evening at Halkirk and take us to Strathmore. I tried down some of the pools above Skinnet, but they were too low. In one—I think the Red Brae—I got a rise, and after a little perseverance hooked and landed a kelt, and then another. Arrived at Skinnet, I changed my fly, and put up one of a couple of dozen I had bought of Blacker, poor "Ephemera's"

* The names of most of the pools have been changed since then.

protégé. Very prettily tied flies they were too; but so they ought to have been, for he charged enough for them, having the ball at his toe then. I remember that the fly was dressed thickly with three different coloured hackles—red, blue, and yellow, I think; for it was a new one to the river, and, as it proved a rattling taker, it took itself off out of my box the next evening without leave.

I had not long displayed the glories of my tricolour to the salmon of Skinnet, when in mid-water there was a fine no-mistake-at-all-about-it rise — a regular head-and-tailer, which says to the salmon fisher in the plainest terms, "I'm come for that fly, and I mean to have it." I chucked him under the chin for old acquaintance, and got him to come home with me, though at first he did not seem a bit inclined to cultivate any closer acquaintance; for he bolted up stream, down stream, and across to the other side with great determination, and for some ten minutes I was alternately winding-up and letting out vigorously. He wasn't a striking fish, however—few of the Thurso fish are, for the river is very dead and still, as regards the best pools—but he made as fair a fight as it was in him to make, and when his time was come surrendered without any vulgar fuss, like a gentleman, and his life-blood stained the heather." No, there I'm wrong—there is not much heather just there to stain; it is mostly grass, for much of the banks of Thurso have a very meadow-riferous and lawn-like aspect. My prize scaled 12½lb., and was a very thick, handsome, sturdy fish, and while I took stock of him I made my lunch, after which a pipe and so forth, and then at it again.

Whilst at lunch I had seen another fish rise on the other side of the river, and further down; so, as there was a ford just above, my gillie played the pious Æneas to my Anchises and pickabacked me over, and I made to the spot. It was just off a sort of point that inclosed a little bay. I had marked the fish well, and at the third cast a boil and an obstruction told me that my friend was in attendance. I gave him a drag, and he made the reel screech once for about 40yds.; but after that he never took out a yard of line, but kept roaming round and round the little bay just noted, in and out, backwards and forwards. It became tedious, so I laid the butt well into him, brought him speedily within reach, and my man, who was not bad with the gaff, whipped him out before he had quite made up his mind to come. He was the brother of the other fish, and scaled the same weight to an ounce or two. I rose two more fish, and marked them down for future use, as they would not be persuaded, and then walked down to Amester, where I lost a fish from a slight hold; and after another half-hour, as we had above four miles across the moor to walk, and the trap had to pick up other anglers on the way home, we tackled up, handled the fish, and made tracks homewards. One other gentleman only was down the river that day, Col. P.—he had one fish only, a ten-pounder, while the occupants of the Linn—for the beat was shared that day—had four; the rest had none. At Strathmore I was introduced to the other five piscators who were my future comrades. We all dined, smoked, toddied, and chatted fishing together for the rest of the evening till bedtime; and I thought that, if only the commissariat were pretty good, I could manage to make out my month well enough at Strathmore.

CHAPTER XXXV.

My Snuggery at Strathmore—The Linn of Skinnet again—A Good day—My Yankee—Sir C. Blois and the Sauce Pool—An Awkward Predicament.

Strathmore was a very jolly abiding place; the victualling was pretty good and the liquors very fair—the company most companionable. The sport continued brisk, and got better as time went on, so that we were all in a good humour, and bent on enjoying ourselves. But all the bedrooms were full at the lodge; so, as the last comer, I had to take up with one of the keeper's houses, where there was a large and comfortable room, and as I had the place to myself I rather enjoyed it, for I went to bed when and how I liked, or not at all if I didn't like. I built up the peats, made a roaring fire, and wrote letters; had a last glass of grog—perhaps two—with many last pipes; and I sometimes even made night hideous and set the dogs howling by practising the cornopean, which I was then learning. I hope no one cursed me for my untimeous notes—I think I should have cursed myself had I been anybody else; but if they did I didn't mind it, and, like Dick Swiveller, who took to the flute at night as a consolation, I at least thoroughly enjoyed myself. But to my narrative. At breakfast next morning we all met together—six good men and true—the late Sir F. Sykes, the late Sir C. Blois, Col. P., Mr. W., Mr. D., and myself. What a jolly, pleasant party we were! what yarns we had when round the fire of an evening! How every capture of the day was discussed! I never heard an angry or a cross word the whole time I was there, and that is something to say, for I *have* heard brother anglers quarrel like Kilkenny cats, and use much worse language; but then our beats were so marked out that we couldn't conflict or collide in our fishing. We did not allow cards, and we never talked either religion or politics or philosophy, and eschewed all the ologies. After breakfast, those who had to go to the more distant beats mounted the trap, their sandwich cases and pocket pistols loaded, and were dropped at their respective stations one by one, where their men awaited them with their rods, and were collected again at night. Those who were close home went leisurely and comfortably down to the river; the last fish killed on the Linn, which was close to the house, being always sent in every day for dinner, and the result was that the fish was often almost wagging his tail when he was popped into the pot, and that was salmon in perfection; it would break like a carrot.

The second day my beat was the Linn of Skinnet by right, so I went to it and soon began to kill fish, taking a 14-pounder within half an hour of my advent. Then I did the honours to a 15-pounder. These were the two fish I marked the day before. I lost no time, for I was as keen as a first-class Sheffield razor, and ere long I was fast in another, that played brilliantly for a Skinnet fish; but he too was landed, and scaled 10lb. After that I moved down a little, and the tricolour being waved over a likely cast brought another victim to the guillotine, and another 15lb. one soon graced the grass. Hurrah! This was something like a day; four fish before lunch! Well done, Thurso! The fish then took a rest, and finding they were off, I laid my four prizes out before me and feasted my eyes on their beauty, while I feasted my whame on something else. While I was feeding my gillie took my rod and went down to a sort of dyke or ridge of rocks that run out into or just above Amester pool, and took a cast on his own account. Presently I saw him fast in a fish. "Bravo!" said I to myself, "that'll make up the score to five; though I would have preferred killing the fish myself perhaps." My attendant drew the fish ashore, not having a gaff, and tailed it out, and, after dislodging the hook, to my great surprise pushed it back into the water again. I asked him when he came back why he turned it in again, and he replied that it was "joost a late bagget (female fish big in spawn), ye ken," which I thought strange enough, of course, as one does not often see a female fish heavy in spawn in March though it happens occasionally. After lunch I fell again to fishing at once, and in about half an hour I was fast in another rattling fish. Up and down rushed the fish, and at length made straight towards me. Now under my feet was a shelving bank, with a thin fringe of tall reeds. Seeing that the fish's intent was to bolt into these reeds, I shouted to my attendant to go down the bank and splash the water with the gaff to keep the fish off, as I had no power over him; and he could easily have done so without wetting a foot, having long thigh boots on. But the more I shouted, the less that calm and seemingly imperturable individual regarded. I could not comprehend it. He looked on as if he really wished the fish to take to the reeds, which he immediately did, and hanging me up got clear. I repeated "How doth the little busy bee" and "Twinkle, twinkle, little star," in the sweetest voice; but my calm friend just replied, "Hey, mon, ye canna kill every fish ye heuk." "Confound you!" I roared, "but I could have killed that one if you'd done as I ordered you." To this the individual deigned no reply. I was so angry that I had to smoke two pipes to compose myself; but when this essence of coolness and cheek proceeded to take up the rod and walk off to try his own hand again, I talked to him kindly and affectionately, and he put it down as if there were an insect of "the flea specie," as poor old Jemmy Hall used to call it, somewhere about his ear, and lighted *his* pipe. This fellow had left Thurso for a tour in the States a year or two before, in order to see what he could make out of the rivers there; and, as he made nothing, he came back again much worse than he went, and was called the Yankee sometimes, but more often "that somethinged Yankee." I need hardly say that he did not exactly suit my requirements, and the next day I gave him him his mittimus. I did no more that day, but got home duly, and my four fish raised a sensation rather, and "Skinnets" went up in the market. After dinner I told my news and lamented my lost fish; and Mr. W., after a strong word about that Yankee," said,

"How many fish had ye?"

"Four."

"And they average 15lb. apiece, or 60lb in the gross."

"Just so."

"And ye'd four miles to walk across the moor, and bad walking." I was forced to admit this.

"Ah! if he'd been the first fish, you'd have killed him fast enough, and the bagget too, which was as much a bagget as I am; but that confounded Yankee thought 60lb. quite enough to carry four miles, and that's the whole of it."

Mr. W. had hit it, I felt sure, but this only made me more raw, for, rather than lose the fish and the chance of a good score, I'd have carried them home myself; and, as I said, I presented my friend with a highly ornate and embroidered "sack" the very next morning. As it turned out, I should, with six fish, have headed the week; for the Linn men of the day only did five, and those *up* to 12lb. The next day I took Halkirk, and some water above and below—one decent pool called the Rae Beg I think, but of this I am not sure. Halkirk was one of the prettiest pools in the river, being rocky and streamy, but it rarely gave a fish, being everlastingly disturbed by ducks and other economic poultry, and also by the brats of children who persisted in pelting real or imaginary ducks, or swimming impromptu boats, &c., or doing some other violently disturbing nuisance all day long; and many a sly whip was taken at the pool, too, when there was no one handy or likely to be. Nevertheless, I wasn't half-way down it when a lively thirteen-pounder came to my beck, and, after visiting all his friends in all parts of the pool to say farewell, he allowed himself to be converted into merchandise, and five minutes after I was dancing a jig with his sister. My step did not suit her, I suppose; so she dissolved the connection and returned to her chaperone, or perhaps her big stone. I tried up and down, but it was of no avail; and until late in the afternoon, when I returned to Halkirk, I did no more; then, however, I coaxed a nice 12lb. fish to hook on, and had just landed him comfortably when I saw the trap coming, and so home.

By this time my friends began to look on me with curiosity; for while four, not to say six, fish out of Skinnet in a day was something to coax, two out of Halkirk was more. The next day I tried the Rocks. The Rocks was certainly the prettiest beat on the Thurso to look at, the pools being rocky and rattling, but somehow they seldom held fish until the weather got somewhat warmer. Up to April the fish seemed to like the warmer and muddier or peaty bottoms of the deep still linns. Of course there was a pool or two in which a fish might lie—one called the Sauce Pool, which lay some three or four miles from Strathmore, being one of them; but, as a rule, at this time of the year, the beat was regarded as little better than a probable blank. *Apropos* of this Sauce Pool—so called because of certain scum or froth which was caused by the slight fall at the entrance, and the broken foamy water it produced—some days after my visit to it, when I barely gave it a careless skim over, Sir Charles Blois had the beat. Sir Charles was an old Namsen fisher, having been one of the earliest of the British anglers who penetrated up to the stupendous Fiskum Foss, pretty well known to a good many British anglers since then. He showed me on his gaff handle one day a notch which he had cut to measure the length of a big fish, that weighed either 52lb. or 54lb. (I forget which), that he had killed in the big pool below the foss. He was in the boat by himself. He hooked the fish, rowed and managed the boat, and played his fish, landed, and gaffed him all by himself; and when the size of the fish is considered, that is a feat for anyone to be proud of. Sir Charles further told me that he hooked four other fish on the same morning, or as large or larger than the one he caught, and all of which he lost, chiefly for the want of a boatman; but he had a strong taste for fishing by himself, and could not bear to be looked at while fishing. On the afternoon when he had "the Rocks" he thought he would walk down and have a look at the Sauce Pool. Accordingly he put his rod over his shoulder and stalked off across the moor by himself. When he reached the pool it was in fine order, and he had barely made his third cast when a rattling fourteen-pounder came at him and gave him five or six minutes of smart play; but Sir Charles soon shortened him home and gaffed him, much pleased with his luck at getting a fish out of the Sauce Pool. He thought, however, that he would try another cast, just on the off chance, and he did so, when he was speedily rewarded with another rise, and soon a fine twelve-pounder was dancing on the grass beside his comrade. Then he sat down and gave the pool a rest for a time, congratulating himself upon the unusual feat he had performed. Still, having a grain or two of faith left, he went at it again, when a bigger head and shoulders than he had seen yet put up and gulped in his fly, and in some ten or twelve minutes Sir Charles had the great satisfaction of depositing a magnificent eighteen-pounder by the side of his friends. "Who can tell but what there might even be another?" thought Sir Charles, and faith there was another—a fifteen-pounder—and he came up nobly, fastened well, and was speedily laid by the rest. By this time the evening was coming on, for four fine salmon are not caught in the waving of a salmon rod; and then it suddenly occurred to Sir Charles that it was just possible that he might have a difficulty in getting them home. He was not a very powerful man, and, beyond that, had an objection to carrying his own fish; and there they lay in all their brilliant panoply, close on sixty pound of salmon, to be carried across the moor some three or four miles. What should he do? If only a shepherd were in sight! but no, none appeared. He thought of hiding them, and leaving them and sending for them; but it would be dark before anyone could get to them, and if they were left all night it was a hundred to one but some vermin would find them out. What was to be done? He almost wished them back in the pool again, only the triumph of howking four fish out of the Sauce Pool was, as he knew well, *the* triumph of the season. At length two children appeared far off. Sir Charles telegraphed and shouted. The children, amazed at his antics, were rather inclined to run away at first; but at length he got them to approach near enough to understand his wishes, and so the splendid catch was conveyed home, to the wonder and admiration of all beholders, as it is the fashion to say.

The next day Sir F. Sykes had the same beat, and in the afternoon he too thought he would comb the Sauce Pool, in case there were any "leavings"; so, asking me to go with him for a walk, he took his big spliced greenheart—a novelty in those days—from Forrest of Kelso, and off we walked. Arrived at the pool, he asked me to pick him out a fly, as I was a lucky man. I did so—an old Namsen fly with a warm taking body, which I have always fancied, and which I have described in my Book on Angling as the Namsen, and after a few casts Sir F. got fast in a smart fourteen pound fish, which I gaffed for him; and but a few minutes after he hooked, played, and lost another, I think by being too severe with him. Sir F. was a very tall powerful man, and used a tremendous rod—indeed, I think his rod was a twenty-one footer, and I could not wield it. He could kill a fish very quickly if he was well hooked, and could put out a very long line against the wind; but if fish were only lightly hooked they were apt to get off, when lighter play would have landed them. However, it showed me that there were for certain six good fish in this small pool waiting for me two days before if I had only fished it properly; and it served me right that I didn't get them, or most of them as I might have done.

On the day Sir Charles killed his fish I had the Linn. The Linn *par excellence* was the finest beat on the river, and was always an object of desire and calculation, for it was crammed with fish. It was a long, deep, still pool, rather canally, but, as far as I can remember now, perhaps a mile or a mile and a half long, and all good fishing water. Above it was a long stretch of thin trout water, which ran up to Loch Beg; and the Linn was the favourite lying place with all the fish, (and their name was legion,) which did not care to run the thin water for the lake. So much desired was the Linn that anglers would split their days with a friend when they had a bad beat—that is, Sir. F. and Mr. D. would fish it together when it was Sir F.'s day, and again when it was Mr. D.'s day; so that they got two days a week each instead of one on it, though of course they did not get the sport that they would fishing it alone. The angler whose day it was on the Linn always was up and taking a peep at the weather by daybreak, and rarely wasted any time after breakfast when it looked favourable, as the fishing commenced not one hundred yards from the lodge. My first day on the Linn was a bad one; there was no wind, and I only took three fish, and those not remarkable ones—four, five, and even six or seven fish being not at all unusual; three were thought poorish, two bad, and one duffing in the extreme. Three times while I was there were ten or more fish taken on it by one rod.

CHAPTER XXXVI.

THE MOORS ABOUT STRATHMORE—STALKING THE WILD GOOSE—A WONDERFUL EEL—LOCH BEG—DISAPPOINTED OF A SPATE.

THE moors about Strathmore were plentifully stocked with game, and as one walked across them many an old grouse cock would go "conking" away as a warning to his mate to lie close and keep dark. There was also a great deal of other stuff in the shape of ducks, geese, snipes, and plovers, and all sorts of wildfowl rare and common, about; indeed, Dunbar, who was no mean taxidermist and naturalist, had made a fine collection of rare birds. All these latter things we were at liberty to shoot if we chose, and now and then we massacred a few plovers, &c., for a pie—though it was a great shame, as it was the breeding season—and we used to eat their eggs for breakfast. But the geese, of which there was a large flock about the place, were a great nuisance to the little farmer below, who had a large patch of barley just beyond the river. The beasts had a strong taste for barley, a perfect contempt for strong Scotch expletives, and any amount of respect for a gun, which they took care to keep at a very wary distance from. They were the most cunning critters I ever came across. Talk of geese saving Rome by their wide-awakedness! That was only once, and after all only by a fluke—a gobble or two caused probably by accidental indigestion from eating too much of the maccaroni of the period. These beggars saved themselves half-a-dozen times a day, and by the most astonishing devices. How hard I tried to get a shot at them, and always failed! I had a rifle with me, which I knew how to use, and I declare that I took as much trouble to try and stalk them as some would to get within range of a stag of ten, an old bull moose, a 14-foot tusker, or a mangy "man-eater," but always in vain. One day in particular I drove them off the barley, and they went away for a small shallow loch about two miles off; so I took a wide range of about ten miles or so, more or less, to get the wind of them, and to get under the shelter of a bank which rose up on the south shore of the loch, and would afford safe hiding. The moors were much intersected by deepish but narrow gullies or drains, and one could often travel some distance up them; and, after a very cautious but tedious scramble of several miles in from four to eight inches of bog water, I approached the bank behind which the geese were. Cautiously, cautiously, I crept on up to the bank—not a whisper, not a creak, not the wag of a hair. On I swarmed up, up the bank, like a wild Indian after scalps, pushing myself along by a sort of Archimedean screw on my stomach, which, ahem! was—alas! that it ever should come to be so with us—less in my way, not to put too fine a point on it, in those days than it is now in prosecuting such enterprises; indeed, I am doubtful if that mode of progression now wouldn't be something more than inconvenient. On I squirmed then, however, crunching beetles and squelching snails, dismembering daddy longlegs, mangling my shirt front while on—which, I am free to confess, is not the best way of mangling it—and filling my vest pockets with various botanical and entomological curiosities. At length, by remarkable acrobatic skill and incredible athletic exertion, and much dampness in various prominent and inconvenient places, I reached the brow of that bank. I peeped very cautiously between two tufts of heather, and there—

Oh, frabjous day! calloo callay!

I would have "chortled in my joy," if I had known how, and it would'nt have alarmed the geese. There were about fifty of 'em squattling about the shore of the loch, and only some sixty yards away.

Alas! unconscious of their doom,
The little goslings play,

As what's-his-name might have said. The unerring rifle was gradually pushed to the gap in the heather. It creeps over the brow like an iron snake in the grass. There are two gander-pots—grandpapa geese standing with their heads erect and looking on like two prime ministers, or a brace of beadles, or a pair of Alexander Selkirks as Dickens puts it, at the gambols and guzzlings of their belongings, with that air of stolid stupidity so remarkable in a bird who is so often stuffed with *sage* notions. This attitude is broken now and then by a short sharp waggle of the tail, which means nothing in particular that ever I could discover—and I have asked many a goose why he did that, and he never could tell me yet. I have surmised, maugre more precise information, however, that the goose had occasion to wag his tail, and did it because he preferred it to leaving it still. These two old sinners, who were digesting their feloniously acquired barley in complacency, were exactly in a line, and, in default of having that wonderful eel by me which I once read of, and the veracious history of which I append below, I could string them with one bullet. I am lowering my eye to the "imminent deadly breech." I know I shan't miss 'em, for I am good up to 200 yards, and I feel now like Hawkeye taking a good shot at that Indian in the tree on the other side of the river. "I'll make you smell sage and onions, my shavers; only wait a minute; there'll be goose for dinner to-morrow," I whispered. My forefinger steels to the trigger; an electric thrill shoots through it; the moment of combustion has arrived—it is here; when "ca waw!" two of about the largest sized shrieks that were ever uttered by the throat of that ridiculous and intrusive skunk, the *Larus ridibundus*, were yelled just over my head. "Here he is; I've got him." "Ca waw!" screeched the wretch again; but once was enough. The geese were on the further side of the loch in the twinkling of a goose tail, on their way back to the barley; I was the only one of the flock left, and "was left" like Hon. Miss Ullin's papa on the banks of Loch Goil, "lamenting." I sent a futile bullet after them to quicken their way, and then pitched the other barrel up at the black-headed cuss above. This, however, wasn't in his contract; it was clearly extra work, and the pay didn't suit; so with a half-frightened farewell shriek, he turned and sailed off. I quickened *his* way too, for just as he turned I let him have it, and I was only an inch or two behind him, for I cut a feather out of his tail which made him wabble some, and he really did make tracks as if he meant it.

I didn't go gandering again after this, it was not satisfactory, but contented myself by taking long pot shots into the brown of them 200 yards or more off, whenever I saw a knot of them together in the barley-field; but I never perforated one by accident, though they didn't like it, for I cut dirt considerably close to them once or twice, and at last it was quite a caution to see how they bolted as soon as my grey cap and the gleam of my rifle topped the dyke. Yes, it is my opinion that if the Romans had only been half as clever as the geese, and had had a reasonable allowance of black heads among 'em, they would have preserved their Capitol, not once, but for everlasting; and those little hills they made so much fuss about would have been eternally crowned with temples like the National Gallery; and then, only think—why, they might have imported from the barbarian the Duke of York's column, the Northumberland lion, the statue from Leicester-square, and a few other of our national art treasures, with instruction to themselves and advantage to us. We could even have spared them some Scotch padrones and a sprinkling of bagpipes.

This is the veracious history of the wonderful eel that I spoke of; it reveals facts in natural history hitherto unknown, and quite worthy the attention of the most eminent physiologists of the day. As for the shot with the revolver, it was a pretty good one on the whole, but nothing to make a brag of, and I fancy from the tone of the article that it was thought to be something remarkable, which is a mistake:

The way they catch geese (states the *Buffalo Republican*) on the Western waters is sufficiently wonderful without at all taxing the incredulity of anyone. They are very fond of a small and very active eel, armed with sharp head and teeth, whose habits insist upon its swimming very near the surface of the water. It is very seldom the geese can get hold of this choice morsel, and when they do, they have a grand jollification over it. This eel the hunters use as bait for their geese-ships. A short time since two hunters went out to catch wild geese. One hunter laid down in his canoe with a trout line attached to his wrist, and on the other end, in the water, was tied the nimble, sharp-headed eel before spoken of. The canoe floated slowly through the marshes, and came gradually among a large flock of geese, and the eel swimming along close to the surface. One venerable *bon vivant* of a goose gobbled up the eel, like a flash; also, the eel had made its way through the body of the epicure, and lo! the goose was "on strong." Another goose, afflicted with a luxurious palate, swallowed the eel, but without any particular satisfaction, as the eel, hardly noticing an obstruction, travelled through the "goose-grease" with scarcely an effort. And so this identical eel travelled and travelled until seventeen geese were on the string, and our scientific friend, thinking he had been fortunate enough, commenced hauling them into the boat. But, wonder of wonders, the seventeen geese rose upon their wings as one goose, and before our friend of the canoe could make a will or say a prayer, he was lifted bodily from the canoe, through the combined efforts of the seventeen geese attached to his wrist, and ere he was aware of it was thirty feet above the water. A friend of his on the shore saw the difficulty, and, his revolver fortunately being loaded, shot off the string and rescued his friend. So, instead of wild goose, our hunter got cold duck; and, although he fishes no more for wild geese with eels, he is prepared to affirm, asseverate, or swear to the truth of the foregoing.

Not liking my beat next day, I thought I would take a turn at Loch Beg. Loch Beg was a capital beat from about the middle of April, but before that it seldom fished well; and it was then turned into a beat, if another beat was needed. It was a small rocky loch, with small bays and inlets, about enough for one rod when the fish were taking well. I had a notion that I would spin it, and was rigging out my tackle, which, among other things, comprised a large sized, heavyish Archimedean minnow, which had the call then—the Phantom, which now everywhere prevails, not having been invented. Mr. W., a very dry sort of chip, took up the minnow, and gravely inspected it between his finger and thumb.

"Are you going to show this to the fish of Loch Beg?"

"Such is my intention," I replied.

"Vera ingenious—remairkably so; I shouldn't wonder if you left it there."

And faith he was right, for when I got to the lake it was blowing half a gale of wind, which was pretty nearly the normal state of the wind there; it never blew less than a third of a gale, or say a quarter, except when I had the Linn, and then it usually either stopped in Orkney or went off into Sutherland on a visit for the day, the consequence being that I would get two or three fish where almost everyone else got five and six. However there was plenty of wind on Loch Beg, and much more than plenty; the market was overstocked. There was a boat on the lake, and we put off. My gillie was not a Gulston nor a Knollys with the timber. Now and then he caught a double crab, when he immediately dove on his back into the bow of the boat, to the delight of the fishes and Father Æolus, and my gentle irritation. Why he didn't fracture the base of his skull now and then I couldn't make out; I never saw a man try harder. However, we went gyrating about here and there and everywhere in the most erratic and playful manner. If I saw a salmon rise, instead of the fly or minnow we put the boat over him in a jiffey, which didn't answer the same purpose.

Then we went ashore, and rigged up an anchor or killick by the aid of a rope, chain, and a big stone. This answered well for fully two minutes and a half, and I began to think that my friend W. was a jolly old bird of ill omen, all croak and no fulfilment, when she slipped her stone and drove bang on to a lee shore, while my gillie described what Sheridan in "The Critic" calls "two revolving suns and two revolving moons" with his oar blades, and then dittoed it with his heels again. I had just made a long cast down wind, to my own great admiration, and of course couldn't get the line in; the boat gave a brisk jump from a lumping wave which sent me into a sort of hip bath at the bottom; and, as she stranded broadside on the big stones, we jumped out knee-deep and hauled her ashore to save her planks and get out our traps, all wet through. There was the rod with the whole 75 yards of line out; but that was all—there was nothing at the end. The mermaids of Loch Beg had captured my minnow tackle, cut it off, and hung it up in their tackle shop below. I saw Mr. W. on the further shore, chuckling—if ever there was a chuckle in him, which I confess I doubt, for he was a grave senior—at the attempt I had made to spin Loch Beg. There were two or three good fish rising steadily, from time to time, in the loch, and both he and I tried them with a fly, but eventuated nothing—not even a boil. Loch Beg was as yet clearly no go—a beggarly Beg. That evening it began to rain. Now, those of my readers who are salmon fishers know well what an interesting and even delightful phenomenon a downfall of rain may be; one gets wet through on a salmon river with an equanimity one never displays anywhere else. The river was low; we wanted, or thought we did, fresh fish up; would it rain long enough? It looked very black outside. But Dunbar shook his head, and read the paper. We were snug round the fire, and a faint spit and hiss on the turfs now and then told us it *was* raining—even if the rush and pelt of the storm without had not announced the fact pretty clearly.

"By Jove, how it is pelting down outside," said one.

"Give us a water as sure as death, if it will only last; and they're catching lots of fish in the bay, I hear," quoth another.

But Dunbar shook his head and smoked silently. "If it will rain till about ten or twelve to-morrow, say, it will do, and it really does look as if it had set in; only hark how it is coming down. It's my day on the Linn on Tuesday, and by then, I should say, there will be heaps of fresh fish. I say, D., shall we share our days next week?"

"I'm agreeable."

"Very good, then, we *must* come upon them." But that perverse Dunbar still shook his head. "The wund was no in the right airt." The oracle had spoken, as oracles mostly do, in the most aggravating manner possible. About half-past eleven I retired across to my quarters. It was raining delightfully, and was as black as a wolf's throat. I hugged myself, for it was my day on the Linn on Friday, and I wasn't going to share with any one; so I revelled in the idea of a regular slaughtering, and went to sleep and dreamt that I had killed eight fish in the Lynn, seven having been the top limit as yet. About six in the morning a knock came at the door.

"Het water, sir."

"Oh, eh! Archy, come in. What sort of a morning is it? Raining like mad, isn't it, eh? and how's the river?

"Na, sir, na, it no just but an ordinar morning. The wun's gane doon too, an' the rain ceased or one o'clock. It'll be no great day for the fushin', I'm thenkin'. The river'll be thick an risen an inch or twee."

"An inch or twee!" and I expected to see a great porter-coloured flood, of three feet or more, rolling onwards from far Ben More to the sea. Well, well, to be sure—of course if it ceased at one there was no more to be said, so I got up and went to breakfast.

"The river's just where she was three days ago. But there's plenty of fish in the river, she'll fish well if we've only wind for a fortnight, and I'll back that we kill six hundred fish in the season," said Dunbar; and he knew pretty well what he was talking about.

CHAPTER XXXVII.

Durley Castle—A Legend—The Pot of Gold and the Devil's Pool—Loch More—A Sporting Fish—Trouting and its Pleasures—A Practical Joke—A real Big Day on the Linn.

There was one place which had a great charm for me, and where I mooned away one or two Sunday afternoons in April, when the weather was fine and warm, the lark singing, and that was at Durley Castle. Durley Castle was an old ruined tower, situated in a sheltered dell about the middle of the Rocks. In the middle of a large flat-bottomed irregular basin, as it were, of some acres in extent, a rocky mound rose upon which stood the ruins of a solid square tower, built in the rudest way, with large flat stones; round the base of the tower, on two sides, flowed the Thurso, making here a deep dark pool, for romantic and legendary purposes pronounced unfathomable. The tower at present was little above the adjoining plateau, though when at its full height, no doubt the upper stories rose well above the plain. Here, reclining against the rocky bank, courting the sunshine, with the song of the lark, the hum of early bees, and the gurgle of the water as it flowed rippling into the pool, I smoked and read and mused alternately; a boy whom I had for a gillie told me fragments of a maundering legend about Durley. The deep dark pool, overshadowed by the Castle, was called, "The Devil's Pool," and there was a pot of gold at the bottom, only no one could find the bottom, and the devil of course took care of the pot of gold. A fair maid, daughter of the chief who held Durley Castle, whose name I have forgotten, indeed, I am not certain I ever heard it, loved a young man in her own clan, whose only fault was that he was below the lady in position and means. Meantime, a famous sea rover, who chanced to put into Thurso bay, saw her and loved her, and made various offers to her father of the most precious gifts in his possession to induce him to give her to him in marriage; but the chief was fond of his daughter, and did not want to part with her, but was at length induced to promise her by the present of a wonderful casket, which, open when he would, always was full of gold; spend how he might, he had but to close the lid, and when he opened it, lo! it was full again. This, of course, was obtained from a Norway sorceress, who sold winds and wealth, and blights, and all sorts of things, and bought souls and other trifles of that kind, and no doubt the price paid for this inexhaustible casket was something diabolically beneficial. However, the maiden was pledged by her father to the rover, and as she did not approve of him, she wandered about in a miserable kind of way until she came upon a palmer grey, who was of course a saint in disguise, who shammed weary and faint and hungry, because if he really was a saint he couldn't well be either, at least such is my notion of saints, but I may be wrong. She of course compassionated, and he, as in duty bound, did the like by her, when he drew from her her tale of distress, and she took him home and fed and tended him; and even the chief paid deference to his venerable appearance. And when the next morning came the chief took from his casket a piece of gold, and laid it on the saint's palm (he being a palmer) to help him on his way, whereupon the gold piece curled and smoked and frizzled, and turned into a withered leaf—to the amazement and conviction of the chief—and the saint became suddenly beautiful and saintly, and, seizing the casket, he hurled it out of the window into the deep, black, unfathomable pool below, and a pair of huge brawny hairy arms, with talons like a tiger's, came out of the water and caught it as it fell, and it disappeared beneath the pool amidst a bellow of supernatural laughter, and there the pot of gold has lain at the bottom of the pool ever since, and will lay (I don't like

like to say "lie," being suggestive) until some one can hook it up, but as the depth is so profound, no one is likely to. Whereupon I gaged the profundity with my running line and a stone tied to it, and, alas for romance and imagination, nowhere did I find the pool more than about eighteen feet deep, but the peat coloured water and the over-shadowing castle and rocks make it look very black, gloomy, and profound. "What became of all the rest?" Well, upon my word I never inquired, for I didn't care much about them, and being practically-minded, I forgot all about it in sounding the depth of the pool, and having ascertained that, of course the legend was, if one might say so, "busted."

I didn't care to go "down"; it was a long, dull drive there and back, and I thought I would go up and look at Loch More, the largest loch on the river. For there were many small tributary lochs, and one fair-sized one, Loch Calder, which fed it from small burns, scattered about, but salmon only went into the two that were on the river itself—viz., Loch Beg, already mentioned, and Loch More, which lay some way above Loch Beg—the stream between them being sharp and shallow, like that just below Loch Beg. Loch More was known to be full of fish, but it was too soon for it, and no boat had yet been taken up on it. A day or two previously, Sir F. Sykes had walked up to the point where the upper and spawning stream flows in, and at that point had hooked a good fish, which went straight out to sea (made for the middle of the lake), and could not be stopped. It ran out all his line—nearly 100 yards if I remember aright—and broke him. I therefore picked out my longest line, 120 yards, to try conclusions with any fish I could meet, and away I started for Loch More. It is rather an open, exposed loch, and somewhat uninteresting in form. However, we made our way to the feeding stream, which was here little more than a good-sized burn, stealing into the lake over a bar of brilliant sand and gravel. There was of course a deepish hole just outside the point of entry, and a broken eddy or two showed the moving of the water. The breeze was moderate. I fished the mouth carefully, and after a few casts a big boil showed on the surface, but the fly remained untouched. I gave him a rest and tried him again; "no go." I then sat down, picked out a smaller fly of the same colour, and waited for a cloud. It was not long coming, and I again pitched the fly slantindicularly down stream into the loch, and, giving it a minute's pause, began fishing it home a foot under the surface. Just as I was working up to the bar a slight boil, a heavy tug, and a bending rod told me that the ball had commenced. I never in my life saw such a fish as this; he was perfectly mad, and flew along the surface like a steamboat, leaping and plunging in the most extraordinary way. I don't believe he was ever four feet under water the whole time of his voyage out. Straight for the middle of the lake he steered, taking out line with wonderful rapidity and steadiness, and it became clear to me that he was going to play the same tactics as the fish that broke Sir F. I have often told the story of this fish before—indeed, I have related it in my Book on Angling, the play was in my estimation so brilliant. The fish continued these pranks until he had out fully 100 yards of line, and even at that great distance, and with that length and weight of line in the water, he continued to jump and spring clean out of the water twice or three times, looking, so far off, no bigger than a good-sized sea-trout; and one could hardly believe that there was any connection between us—it seemed impossible. However, slight as the string was, and far afield as he had roamed, it was destined to work his downfall. I looked down at the rapidly decreasing bulk of the reel, or rather of the line on it, and began to give it out very gingerly; then I got the rod up, and got a pull on him, and he evidently found the pace too good to last; but he made another bolt, and got out half a dozen more yards, though I made it hot and hard work for him by sinking the line as deep as I could. Then I got another pull on him, and he submitted to be led back a few yards, when another short bolt showed that he was not beaten. I never met a more determined or desperate fish for his size.

And so we went on, I winning back ten or a dozen yards now and then, and he bolting and taking back seven or eight of them. Slowly but surely, however, the bulk on the reel was growing. He had long done skylarking, and now fought deep and stubbornly; but his circles grew smaller and closer, and at length I got him under the rod again. He caught sight of me, made one frantic rush for fifteen or twenty yards, and then threw up the sponge and came in on his side, and my attendant tailed him out on the shelving sand. He was a pretty fish of 12½lb., and one of the most gallant fish I ever killed. I'd go all the way to Thurso to-morrow for such another fight. There were no more fish to be had that day; so I went home proud of my victory, for no one else had killed a fish, owing to the rain.

The trout in the Thurso were not very good specimens, but small, black, and tadpoly as a rule; but there were some better ones up near to Loch Beg, and as they wanted some for breakfast at the lodge, I walked off up there with my trout rod one afternoon, determined to bring back a mess. They rose at almost anything, of course, and there were plenty of them, and often two at a time came home on the line. There was nothing up to half a pound, three or four to the pound being the best of them. Such as there were, however, I whipped them out merrily, and wading up the stream, casting left and right, my basket soon began to assume a decent weight and proportions. Arrived at Loch Beg, I passed round, and once more struck the stream between the lakes; and here the fish were a trifle larger and brighter-coloured, and my basket got heavier and heavier. So engrossed was I with the sport, which is one I am partial to, that I did not observe evening coming on apace; at length, however, I became aware of the fact, and, having four or five miles across the moor to walk in wading boots, I hastily reeled up and turned my face homewards, congratulating myself on the capital basket of fish I had. It couldn't go less than 20lb., as I judged—the soldier palmer, black gnat, and grouse hackle being the best executioners, as they will be nine times in ten on

Highland streams. On I trudged, on and on, and the sun got low, and the walking was not good; for, though the moor was level enough to the eye, it was full of those nasty little blind gullies which one couldn't see, but perpetually plumped down into some two feet deep, and this took it out of one rather when often repeated, because one had to get out again. And then there were constant tumps (hard lumps of peat crowned with heather or bents), which I kept kicking violently against; and everything combined to knock one's wind out. And then I became at last aware that 20lb. of fish at my back did not lighten the walking, particularly when at every slight mishap the beastly basket would slip round under my chin, and have to be shoved back into place again. "Never mind, I'll be even with those trouts at breakfast to-morrow," I grumbled. It was only about four or five miles to the house, exclusive of temporary aberrations which so constantly occur when there are no foot-paths and nothing to guide one—and these generally make the distance half as far again; and then it *was* across the moor, and that was equal to a very long extra on the high road in point of labour. Truly the real distance itself was nothing; but somehow, as Angelina found it when looking for Edwin,

Wilds immeasurably spread,
Seem lengthening as I go.

Angelina hadn't to carry a fishing basket with 20lb. of trout in it; and that horrid creel kept bumping the wind out of me too, till I began at last to get out of conceit with the idea of trout for breakfast, and to think that one might even put up with salmon steaks if one hadn't this inf——. There's another! Whop, rumble, roll, bang! and I scrambled out of the forty-ninth gully, stumbled over the hundred and fifty-sixth tump, and saw the slit of that beastly creel just under my nose for the nineteenth time. Right again, and once more out, on and then squash into a bog next. Creel round again. That makes twenty. Bless the creel! 20lb. of fish twenty times under one's nose. Why it's 200lb. at least. All right once more, and on we go to

Joppa. Hallo! What's that wet on my side, and what a smell of whisky there is! Why, if I haven't smashed my flask in that last burster. I was just thinking that a gentle drain would perhaps improve things; and the tobacco being in the same pocket is wet through, too, of course. All right my brick! as Mr. Swiveller said to Destiny; on we go again, and let's see who'll get tired first. Whop, squash; in again, creel once more round my neck and right under my nose, saying like the clown in the pantomine, "Here we are again!" "Now I've had almost enough of this," said I, driven to bay at last; "and if those chaps want trout for breakfast, they may go and catch them themselves." So I took hold of the creel, opened the lid, and turned it upside down, and left the trout, with a sort of savage satisfaction, to the foxes and wild cats and stoats, who no doubt, as Lord Russell says, were "obleeged" to me. After that the road soon got better, and I reached home just as dinner was over. So hurrah for trout fishing!

In the evening, while we were in the middle of our smoke and talk, there were sudden screams and alarming yells in the kitchen, with a villanous smell of saltpetre. What was it? On inquiring we heard that "Sandie's neb (nose) was just blawed clean aff his face, and his pipe blawed joost clean down his throat. He was just smoking quietly by the fireside, when the whole thing blew up." There was an appreciative grin on the face one of our friends at this. The fact was, the lad was employed about the house, or as a gillie or odd man at times, and he had a bad habit of snapping up unconsidered trifles; he wasn't exactly dishonest, for you might have trusted him with gold, but he looked upon tobacco, cigars, and such things, if left about, a lawful flotsam and jetsam, and several times a cigar left on the mantelshelf overnight was missed by its former owner in the morning. One of our friends thereupon unrolled the outer lea of a big cigar by the assistance of the steam from the kettle, cut a hole in the body and inserted a little plug full of powder, and then neatly replaced the leaf and dried the cigar in the sun.

All being prepared, he left it on the mantelshelf as usual, and missed it as usual. Sandy got his nose well scorched as a result, and I fancy it *was* a lesson, for no more deadly insult could be offered to Sandy after this than to ask him if he'd "have a cigar."

Another trick played by my friend D. on his gillie is worth recording here. D. had a goodish muckle whisky flask; yet somehow, no matter how full it was, it never would hold out the day. He supposed that his gillie must help himself pretty freely to it, as gillies often will, just to drink luck to the fishing. But when and how was it done? He hardly ever lost sight of him long enough for him to be able to get out the flask and take a good drink. Still the whisky did go somehow, and he resolved to find out where. Accordingly he made the strongest possible solution of Epsom salts, of which a table-spoonful would be a stiff dose, and filled the flask with it, keeping a surreptitious one in his own pocket for his own use. The morning was a good one for fishing, and Mr. D. had not been at the river half an hour when he stuck fast in a strong fish. The fish was running well, and D.'s attention was fully occupied with him, when there came from behind him the most extraordinary sound, compounded of coughing, spitting, gurgling, and retching. D.'s eye twinkled; he took a half-glance over his shoulder. There was his friend, flask in hand, hacking away at a great pace, and gasping as if dissolution were imminent, but he couldn't get rid of what he had swallowed, which was a good part of a wine-glass full, as speed had to be made on these occasions, and he had therefore disposed of a good stiff dose at a couple of comprehensive gulps, which sorely exercised him for the rest of the day. D. took no notice, and never referred to it, but looked on with perfect complacency at his follower's pale face as every twinge of the whame sent a thrill through him, as if it were all right and all in the day's work. He told him in the most kind and fatherly way that he thought he sat up and smoked too much of a night, and that it made him quite pale, and lost him much of his good looks, and so on; all the while the salts of Epsom were playing at corkscrews and nutcrackers in the most recondite portions of his interior, and it was all he could do to suppress his qualms and groans when D. was giving him such good advice. But the bare sight of D.'s flask was a powerful fetish and a strong taboo for the future. It was the accursed thing to be put away, and not to be meddled with on any consideration.

Three weeks had passed, and my turn came round again for the Linn. It was a wonderfully favourable day, with a fine strong brisk breeze, and the water apparently in perfect order. I had not been at the water long before I killed my first fish, a nice fish of 10lb., and in the next hour I had added three more to the score, 12lb., 12½lb., and 13lb. each, and it became clear that I was in for a big day. Sir F. Sykes came down to chat and look on, and just as he came I had a good rise, up in the neck of the pool, where there was a little stream; and the fish, which was a heavy one, made one good rush down stream, and then began grubbing about the bottom like a barbel. He never quite sulked, but he kept poking about like a dog looking for a bone in a dust heap. Do all I could—stone him, pole him, splash the water—I could not induce him to work. Now and then he would sail slowly over to the other side, and then as slowly back again; but work he wouldn't, and tire himself he wouldn't either. I tried a long line, I tried a short one, but it was all of no use; and what was the more aggravating, good fish were rolling and tumbling about on all sides of me. I would have laid hard hold of the line and tried conclusions with him; but we had seen the fish at first, and both Sir F. and I agreed that, judging from his length, he was a 20-pounder, and "the fish of the season." And I did not want to lose the best fish of the year so far; so for two weary mortal hours did that confounded fish meander about, as if the rod above him were nothing at all. At length, when I was a deal more tired apparently than he was, I got him over under our bank, and by a great strain raised him a foot or two. Sir F. laid down on the bank and buried the gaff handle deep in the water, and as I led the fish by he contrived to stick the gaff in him, and hauled him out kicking. He was a long lean red fish, and weighed 18½lb. only. When he came into the river at Christmas possibly he scaled 3lb. or 4lb. more. He *was* the biggest fish so far; but a few days after Mr. D. caught a 22-pounder close to the house, and I think I lost that same fish a week before in a jiggering match, as I hooked a heavy fish there, which jiggered himself off the hook. But I had lost most valuable time, and if I had got rid of him early might have killed half a dozen other good fish. Sir Charles Blois came down just as he was landed, and wondered why I didn't do this, that, and the other; but as Sir F. said the fish was well handled, and nothing more could be done, I was satisfied. Three minutes after, I had a spanking rise from a good fish in nearly the same place. This one was no sluggard, but worked like a Trojan, and in about five or six minutes I deposited a handsome fish of 16½lb. by the now growing heap. Barely time for a sandwich, a drink of whisky, and a light to my pipe, when I was fast in another, and this too was a good one, apparently the brother of the last; but somehow as he was making his run the handle of the reel got caught in the cuff of my macintosh, the top of the rod rushed down to the water, and the stout salmon gut snapped like packthread. I soon put up another fly, *turned up my cuffs*, and at it again, and for the rest of the afternoon I was kept pretty merrily at work, for I killed four more fish, when they went off, and I went in to get five minutes' rest and a wash before dinner. My take was ten fish, weighing 135lb. For weight it was not beaten that season. Sir F. took ten in the Linn a few days after, but they were smaller fish, and weighed but a little over 100lb.; and a Mr. D—z, a new comer, a few days after his arrival, took eleven fish—they too only scaled about 110lb.; and but for that sluggish fish I might have done far more. My back and loins, however, the next day told me that I had done quite enough, for it was a strong breeze all day, and hard work casting against it; and so hard did it blow at times that it was difficult to say whether it was the wind blowing against the rod or the fish pulling that one was fighting most.

CHAPTER XXXVIII.

A RUN WITH A BULL (NOT A BULL TROUT)—A GREAT TAKE IN LOCH MORE—TROUT FLIES AND SALMON—SHOOTING BLUE ROCKS FROM THEIR NATIVE TRAPS—THURSO FLIES.

A DAY or two after this I had an adventure with a bull. I went down to fish the Rae Beg water; but the pools were shallow and the fish sulky. I only got one fish, almost 6½lb., the smallest fish I caught or saw while at Thurso. I had with me for an attendant a laddie about 13 or 14, a smart little chap enough, but he was only a boy. As we were plodding along I saw coming down the bank of the river a black Highland bull, and on the other side of the river was another like him. The one on the far side was on his own ground, and had a herd of cows with him in the distance. The one on our side was astray by himself. As the moor was very open, and there was no shelter anywhere, I did not quite like it, for they were working themselves up into a tremendous rage, tearing the turf and bellowing loudly.

"Is that bull dangerous, think you, laddie?" I asked.

"Weel, the laddie that has charge o'm keeps gey an' far awa from 'm, so I think he may be!"

"What are we to do, then? We must not stop here, for if we do, one or the other or both the beasts will be after us."

As they came down the bank seeking a ford and roaring defiance, I did not like to hurry away, and I thought that the correct thing to do would be to walk majestically back the course I had just come. I confess that the old theory about the majesty of the human eye occurred to me; but I felt that if it should not prove immediately effective the result would not be satisfactory, and there would probably be too little majesty and too much funk in mine to awe the savage beast effectively. I doubt if the human eye is as majestic as it used to be. Then I remembered how the black man in "Sandford and Merton" deftly seized hold of the bull's tail and thrashed him into a good humour; but that veracious history did not tell us what the bull would have done if the black man had missed his tip—that is, his tail; and I did not think it would suit me to furnish the corollary. Besides, I always hated corollaries, even at school, as they were something more to do after the problems ought to have been over—corollaries are a swindle to the schoolboy. No, clearly a gentle and majestic walk back the way we had come, so as not to lower the Scotch laddie's opinion of English dignity and valour, was the right thing. Just then the laddie shouted out, "He's coomin'! he's coomin'!" and bolted like a wild goose. I looked back—a hasty glance over my shoulder—and there, horror of horrors, came the bull thundering down the bank about eighty or a hundred yards away, straight for us, having just caught sight of us. An open moor before us, no shelter whatever but a river—which we might have taken to, only there was a bull on the other side too, and likewise cows, which count for something in a scrimmage. I really am ashamed to admit it, but I—I bolted too. As I bolted I glanced back; the bull was gaining. It might have been a very pretty race to a looker-on—equal to the boat race, in fact; but the bull here was Cambridge, it was all 3 to 1 on him, and the horns of a bull are much worse than the horns of any other dilemma I know of. Fortunately, just then we came to a place where peat had been cut, and there was a bank four or five feet deep. "Bob down, hide!" I called to the boy, who was close to me; and I jumped down and crouched under the bank. To the bull it would look as if the earth had suddenly swallowed us up, and as if

> Each warrior vanish'd where he stood,
> In broom or bracken, heath, or wood.

It was a risky thing to do, and a valiant thing, for the bull might have advanced to see what had become of us, when he would have had us in a trap. But there was nothing else to do, so we did this; and fortunately just then, as the bull was gazing in amaze—at least, I conclude he was—a bellow from the other beast attracted him; back he went to have it out, and, finding a ford just there, he crossed, and then there was a battle. O for the pen of Homer, translated by our own William—or rather our late own William—to describe it! They charged one another, like little earthquakes or iron-clad express trains; now one was knocked head over heels two or three times over, and now the other. Oh, if they would only kill one another! At length the cows on the other side came to the assistance of their champion, and they gave our bull almost as sound a dressing among them as a bull could desire. I do not know if this is what is meant by being "cowed," but it had that effect certainly. Meantime, we took the opportunity to walk off to the farm, Mr. Henderson's, about a mile off, to whom I gave my fish. I told him of the bull, and asked if it was his. "No," he said, "no; it'll no be our chiel, for he's awa noo—and ours is a quiet chiel too." By way of showing how quiet he was, he related various instances of his playfulness—how he had killed a woman, tossed two children, &c.; finally, he went to the river with us to see, and found it was his very own chiel, quiet enough now, for he had had a tremendous thrashing, enough to have satisfied even an Irish bull, though that is an irrepressible beast too.

We had had enough fishing and returned home, and then we found that everybody had had a big take but myself; two or three of the fishers had been on Loch More, on which two boats had been put the day before, and one on Loch Beg. The others divided the Linn, and so forth; and the result was that the six rods had killed forty-two fish, from 22lb. down to 9lb. or 10lb., and they were all laid out in the cellar. It was a splendid sight to see such a beautiful lot of fish all taken by the rod in one day. But the Thurso is certainly a wonderful river for fish when all goes well, though there are prettier rivers to fish.

After this I moved down to Thurso; for my month was up, and I wanted to have a day at the rock pigeons, of which there are swarms on the coast. I killed another fish or two, for the lower pools were still at my service when no one else was on them; and one day I went up to the Cruive Pool with my single-handed trout rod. for there were some very nice trout in the tideway, and a few merry little sea trout. While I was standing looking at the pool above the cruive, I saw several fish rising in it, and, more from idleness than anything else, I pitched my little trout fly over the nearest, when, to my huge surprise, he rose and took it. I struck him, and away he went, but I had only about 20yds. of line on my reel, and what to do I knew not; however, the fish relieved me of any trouble, for the hold gave. I then covered another fish I saw rising, and he also took; and he, too, after a short turn, went off. The hook was too small, and I had no larger with me. I then tried another fish, but with exactly the same result; and I rose and hooked five fish in succession, but the fly would not hold, and they all got off. The last fish I allowed to take the fly down with him, giving as much line as I could before I struck him, and then I hit him as hard as I dared, and I did begin to think at last that I was going to kill him, for I ran up and down merrily with him for a quarter of an hour; but at last the fly came away as in the rest, and I then ran off home as hard as I could run, and fetched my salmon rod, but when I came back they were quite off, and not a fin could I stir.

It was a lovely morning when Dunbar and I sailed away round the coast in pursuit of rock pigeons. The green wavelets lapped against the bow of the boat as the pleasant breeze bore us along. On the one side the broad Northern ocean, with the high land of Orkney in the distance; on the other the gigantic frowning rocks, six or eight hundred feet in height, which guard the iron-bound, or more appropriately rock-bound, coast. Sea-birds by thousands—gulls, razor-bills, cormorants, and many other species—swam, flew, dived, and screamed on all sides of us. Here a big rock stood out, black on one side with cormorants, and white on the other with gulls, who religiously kept their own territories, it being death to infringe the other. To and fro flitted the restless pigeons, and over all, in widening circles, sailed and chattered or screamed a graceful peregrine. But here is a huge cavern—a big rift in the rocks. We paddled very gently in, fending off the rocks. As we reached the mouth we all set up a sudden shout, the boatmen banging on the thwarts with trenails to frighten the birds. Out rush a score of big blue rocks right in our faces, and begin circling up to get out of the gap. I secured a brace right and left, a feat which considerably raised my reputation for holding straight with Dunbar, as one doesn't often bowl over a brace of real blue rocks in their native wilds right and left. Dunbar also did execution and, having picked up our slain, we backed out and sought another cave. This continued with varied success till mid-day, and then we landed in one of the coves, and scrambled upon the cliffs, had our lunch, mooned about, saw a high cliff, the highest of all, from which a coastguard officer precipitated himself into the sea many years ago through jealousy. His wife was very handsome, and he found that she was carrying on an intrigue with another man, or thought she was, and, in a fit of rage and despair, he mounted and made straight for the highest cliff, intending to ride over it; but when the horse came to the verge he stopped his gallop in a sudden fright, and it was supposed shot the poor wretch headlong over the cliff, for he came back to his stable alone, and the footmarks of the horse were tracked to the cliff edge in the short turf; the body was never again seen. By and by the pigeons began to return from the corn fields to their homes in the rocks. There was a very strong wind blowing off shore, and if anyone wants to see what pace a pigeon can travel, he should see these wild "rocks" travelling down wind under these circumstances. We lay down under a bank, and looking up could see the pigeons come over the brow almost a mile off, and we had barely time to settle ourselves and get our guns ready when they were over us and away like a flash of lightning. Talk of partridge or grouse driving, or a rocketing pheasant! it is a child's play to it. If you didn't hold a couple of yards ahead you had no chance; and often when the distance that I pitched my gun in front seemed almost preposterous to me, it was quite wonderful how they came in for the thick of it. And it was also surprising the amount of shot they carried away. We left the boat below to pick up the slain, but our bag was, after all, very meagre for the lot of shooting we did. I think it only amounted to nineteen pigeons, for, of course, we lost several; but the amount of powder and shot we discharged I should not like to say.

This was the last bit of sport I had at Thurso. I had greatly enjoyed myself there, and was sorry to leave. We had been the pleasantest little social knot of brothers of the angle conceivable. Sport was good; everybody was satisfied, no one disappointed, and there were therefore no heart-burnings and no jealousies, and no trying to cut each other out, as I have seen at other places. Indeed, the system of beats in rotation did not admit of this; and, added to this, the charge then was very moderate compared with that at the present day, so much has salmon fishing grown in popularity of late years. The flies have changed so on the Thurso that it is not of much use to name those I killed with then; but I may say that a Britannia with a green hackle (I first introduced this fly to the river) I found very killing, and also a good large Butcher. The water is deep, and large flies are required in early spring. On the whole, I think I killed rather more than a fish and a half a day during my month, which is pretty good; but I had great luck with them, only losing six or seven fish, exclusive of those on the trout rod, in the whole time. Good as my fishing was, it has since then been very far surpassed. The deeds of this season, 1874, probably will long remain on record as unsurpassed in fishing in the British Islands, the salmon slaughtered during a few weeks having been something altogether prodigious and unparalleled.

CHAPTER XXXIX.

THE RIVERS ON THE NORTH, NORTH-WEST, AND WESTERN COASTS, WITH SOME NOTICE OF THE INLAND LOCHS, AND THE RIVERS OF THE SOLWAY FIRTH.

SOME information, scanty, but enough to guide the angler, I venture to append of the rivers and lakes to the north and west coast, much of it being from residents or actual visitors of the localities. Coming round to the west of Thurso, there is the Forss, a small water which yields fair sport with the grilse and sea trout at times, but it is held usually by the shooting tenant. The Halladale is a somewhat larger water, and holds about a dozen good pools near the mouth. The best sport, however, is had with grilse and sea trout. Mr. Dunbar, the lessee of the Thurso, also rents and sublets the Halladale. The Naver is a largish river; indeed it is a river of size and consequence. It is let with the shootings, and, save by permission, cannot be fished. It is a fine salmon river, running out of a large loch—Loch Naver,—close to Aultnaharra Inn. The Naver is a very early river, the fish entering it in December, and rising fairly to the middle of August, the only desideratum being water and weather, and a convenient place to live in, as the river is long and inns wide apart, the Naver being rarely without fish. Loch Naver fishes well for both salmon and grilse, and there are plenty of tributary burns and lochs which give good sport with the trout. I made some flies for it for a friend who rented shootings on it, and had the privilege of fishing it two or three years since; they were of the Black and teal pattern, and did good execution, I believe. Bettyhill would be the best station for the lower water; Aultnaharra for the upper. To fish the river at all thoroughly, however, requires a good many long drives as the inns are quite at the top and mouth of the river, and are more than thirty miles apart. The Borgie, Hope, and Grudie or Dionard, are three small rivers let with the shootings, or held by the Duke of Sutherland himself. Loch Hope, perhaps, gives the best chance of sport, as it is a fine sheet of water. When they are not let, the Duke's agent at Tongue often gives leave, and there are some inns convenient to the rivers. Passing round Cape Wrath we come to Rhiconich Inn, by staying at which a little salmon fishing may be had on the Inchard and Loch Garbet-beg, and any quantity of trouting in the neighbouring lochs. And next we come to one of the best fishing waters for its size in Sutherland, viz. the Laxford and Loch Stack, which abound in salmon and sea trout. The Laxford is by no means a large or heavy river, and Loch Stack is quite a small sheet of water compared with many of its neighbours, and the stream is a short one, but the crowds of sea trout and salmon that constantly swarm up it are prodigious. The public have not much interest in it, however, as the fishery, with the deer forest and adjacent shootings are let to the Duke of Westminster, and the neighbourhood is rather out of the way, Lairg being the nearest railway-station.

The Inver is a nice river, and often gives good sport; it is the outlet of Loch Assynt. Loch Assynt fishes fairly in sea-trout, salmon, and grilse, and is noted for its *Salmo ferox.* Fishing can be had on Assynt by stopping at the inn at Inch-na-damff. Lairg is the nearest railway-station, and is thirty-three miles distant. There is a mail-car, however. The Inver is reserved, as is its neighbour the Kirkaig. Both these rivers formerly were in the hands of Mr. Mackenzie, the innkeeper at Loch Inver, who let them out by ticket only; these also, I fear, are among the has-beens, and have been for some years out of the public market. Very fine sea-trout are taken in the Kirkaig, and there are grand brown trout in the Inver. Between Inch-na-damff and Altnalough Inn, and in the neighbourhood, are many beautiful lakes, some of which give fair sport, notably Loch Mulach-Corrie, celebrated for its fine gillaroo trout, Loch Boarlan, Loch Urigall, Loch Meaddie, and Loch Awe or Ah, as it is sometimes called. In these are variety and wealth of sport enough for any moderately satisfied angler. The Kirkaig is the last of the Sutherland streams, and divides Sutherland from Ross. There are few streams of moment on the western shores of the Ross.

The Broom, which runs into Loch Broom, is a niceish stream, and gives plenty of salmon, grilse, and sea trout. The best season for it is in August, but it is rented with the shootings, and is not open to the public. The two Gruinards run into Loch Gruinard, each run out of good lakes; on the lesser one only can fishing be had by ticket on application to Mr. Mackenzie, of Dundonnell. The railway only brings one within about fifty miles at Auchnasheen, but there is coach and mail car for nearly the whole of the rest of the distance. Indeed, this railway which runs from Dingwall right across Scotland to Strome Ferry, on Loch Carron, forms not only the communication with all these western shores of Ross and Inverness, but forms the high road to Skye and Lewis, or The Lews, as it is the fashion to call the Hebrides. There are not many rivers in Skye that can be called salmon rivers. The Snizort is the chief, and that is nothing remarkable. There are plenty of smaller streams holding sea trout, but they are mostly let with the shootings, and are not open to the public. There are plenty of lochs, some of which give good sport with sea and yellow trout. Loch Coruisk, celebrated for its magnificent and wild scenery, gives fair sport, and is open to the public; and visitors to the Broadford Hotel occasionally get a day on Loch Kilchrist, which holds a few salmon. There are a good many small rivers and some fair lakes in the Lews which show good sport with sea trout, and also with salmon, but the best are all let with the shootings, and leave has to be obtained.

To return to the mainland, the best river in Ross-shire on the west coast by far is the Ewe, which runs into the sea at

Poolewe, and drains Loch Maree. The Ewe is a very short river from the sea to the loch, so short that the great wonder is why the fish rest in it at all, but do not run through at once to the loch ; or why in so short a transit they rise so well as they do at the fly, both of which circumstances are unusual. The Ewe was first made famous by Sir Humphrey Davy, and it was at Poolewe that Halietus Poietes, Ornither and Physicus, fished and talked that remarkably stilted Dry-as-dust which our progenitors delighted in. I have no doubt I am extremely heterodox in my opinions, but for all that I cannot say I like it, and, viewed by the light of subsequent knowledge, even the science which should be the backbone of it is a trifle deficient. The Ewe, however, for all that, is well worthy of his or anyone's commendation, for it has been no uncommon thing, short as the limits are, for an angler to reckon up a score of deaths in a day upon this charming bit of fishing ground. Of course the river is in private hands, but fishing in Loch Maree is permitted, and I believe that Kinlochewe inn at the head of the loch is the best point to fish it from. The trout fishing is unusually good, and the fish run of good size. Loch Maree is a very large loch, and the salmon and sea trout do not take very well on it, or it may be that the best casts are not well known; it holds some charr also. A strong wind which drives the water out of the loch is very bad for the river fishing, as, although it increases the flow of water, the fish will not move in it, even though the river should be full of them. The head waters of the lake run into and intermingle with the head waters of the Conon and its tributaries, which debouch in the Cromarty Firth on the Eastern coast. South of this there are two or three small streams that run into Loch Torridon, two of which run out of very nice lakes, Loch Doule and Loch Damph ; they hold grilse and sea trout in the autumn ; but they are mostly let with the shootings or in private hands ; and the Applecross, a nice little river, of which the same must be said. Next comes the Carron, a really good river, along which the railway runs. It passes through a capital loch, Loch

Dougall, but it is closed to the public. The Shiel is a fair summer river, and holds salmon and sea trout, and can be fished by anglers stopping at Shiel Hotel and taking a ticket, which is 5*s.* a day. It can be reached either by the rail to Strome Ferry, or by steamer from Glasgow to Glenelg. Continuing south there is little worth notice till we come to Loch Morar, a fine loch some fifteen miles in length, within two or three miles of Arisaig. The hotel keeper there has the privilege of fishing, and, besides a few salmon and sea trout, it holds plenty of good brown trout, some of them of large size. The route is by steamer from Glasgow. South of this is Loch Eilt and the river Aylort, which give fine sport. Formerly the fishing was let by the day, but now it goes with the shootings.

Loch Shiel, the next fishing to the South, is a splendid loch near twenty miles in length, it contains salmon, sea trout, and large brown trout, and shows excellent sport; being in a very out of the way district, however, it is little known. I wrote to a gentleman who was fishing it for information, and from his letter in reply I extract the following:—"There is one inn on the loch at Shielfoot, and another at Salen two miles from it, *but they have no fishing attached.* There is no other accommodation for strangers except Ardsheilach, Mr. Ralston's, who has salmon and trout fishing on the loch for three rods, and at present he is full. The proprietors on Loch Shiel are Lord Howard, Sir Thomas Riddell, and Lord Morton, and Messrs. Dalgleish and McDonald of Glenaladale. The best time for fishing is June, July, and August. The salmon nets are put down in May and taken off on the 26th of August. The brown trout average from ½lb. to 1½lb.; the white trout from 1lb. to 4lb. or 5lb., and an occasional ferox makes his appearance. The salmon are of fair average size, are very well shaped and rise to the fly, but the deadliest bait is the angel minnow, with perhaps the blue phantom next; flies, claret and brown bodies with dark mallard or turkey wings; and white trout take almost anything, but prefer blue palmers with yellow head, or *vice versâ.* Steam communication between Oban and Salen daily in the season. The fishing is best done from a boat, as the banks are often boggy; boats can be hired, when the trolling is excellent. The white trout and brown trout fishing is very good, and the salmon fishing fair. The best fishing no doubt is in the three or four mile stretch of river between the lake and the sea. That, however, belongs entirely to Lord Howard and Mr. Dalgleish. The inns are fair Highland inns."

Turning inland from Loch Shiel we come on Loch Arkaig, which contains fine brown trout and an occasional salmon, it can be fished, being open to the public, but is hardly worth going far out of the way for. There is a coach from Kingussie to Spean Bridge, or it can be reached *viâ* Caledonian Canal. Loch Lochy, one of the Caledonian Canal lochs, lies adjacent. The trout fishing is very fair here, and they run of good size. It was formerly a good salmon loch, and an occasional one may be taken now, it is open to the public, but it is badly off for inn accommodation, Invergarry Inn being the best place to stop at, and that is four or five miles from the loch. The Garry is a magnificent salmon river, of a rapid and tumultuous character, it fishes very early in spring, and yields very large fish, and fetches a very high rent. The Lochy belongs entirely to Lord Abinger, and is a capital salmon river, and very productive. A story of John Bright taking a header after a salmon that was running away with his line, the end of which had not been properly fastened to his reel, went the round of the papers some years since, it was on the Lochy that the celebrated Democrat was said to have performed this unusual feat. The Spean, which is a fine salmon river, with plenty of white and brown trout in it, is also let to private parties, it runs out of Loch Laggan, a fine loch seven miles long, which is a fair trout loch, though the trout do not run large, but there are plenty of very respectable feroxes which do. Loch Laggan Hotel may be reached from Kingussie by coach; the innkeeper has boats on it. Loch Treig, in the same district, is a pure sheet of water, but difficult to get at, and not open to the public, it is nine miles long, and gives very good trout fishing.

Further to the east lies Loch Ericht, a very fine loch for fishing; the trout run of excellent size, and there are plenty of feroxes or feroces, as it may suit the critical to pronounce it; Dalwhinnie, which is close to the Highland Railway, is the station for it.

Loch Rannoch, to the south of Loch Ericht, is another splendid trout loch, the sport it yields being similar to that enjoyed at Ericht. Kinloch-Rannoch is the station for it; the hotel is fairly comfortable, and has four or five boats on the loch, but the proprietors do not agree very well about the fishing. East of this again is Loch Tummel, which holds very fine trout, which take minnow better than fly, and often run up to two, three, and four pounds, but there is no inn on the lake, and the angler would have to drive from Pitlochrie, or from Tummel Bridge; Pitlochrie is the best route for the last two lakes.

I was desirous also of knowing something of the rivers that run into the Solway, many of which are very fine rivers, though they are horribly cut up by the nets; I wrote to two or three friends who live there, and there is very little fishing that can be said to be open to the public. The Esk is perhaps the most favourable of them all, it runs up to the head waters of the Tweed and Clyde, and separates England from Scotland for some distance. Tickets are issued for the Esk and Liddle, the full price for the season being 3*l.* 3*s.*, but short time tickets, for the week or even day, can be had of Mr. McGeorge, the secretary of the association, at Langholm. The Cross Keys, near Cannobie, is almost the key of the position, and is within a mile and a half of the Cannobie Railway Station. The best fishing for sea trout and herlings begins in June. The salmon fishing begins at the end of August, when the nets are off, and continues to the 1st of November, though an occasional salmon and grilse may be got much earlier, only they do not take so well. Six miles from the Cross Keys, another good hotel may be found, at Langholm, and there are farm houses on the river, where one could get quiet lodgings. The Annan, with the exception of some two miles near-the mouth, is strictly preserved, though the proprietors do give leave if they know anything at all of the persons applying. There is fine salmon and capital trout fishing on the Annan, while there are also abundance of big chub, locally Skelleys. The Nith, another fine river, is strictly preserved. The Dee, a very fine river, is mostly closed, but there is a portion of it below the Cruives, at Tongueland, where there is a comfortable hotel, on which tickets can be had, the price of which for the season is 6*l.* 6*s.*, or 7*s.* per day. The tickets are issued by Messrs. Martin and Gillone, the lessees; the best season is from June to October, as then the grilse begin to come in, and the angler is allowed two fish a day if he can catch them, the rest being given up. The Cree and its tributary the Minnick are both in the better parts closed to the public, the lower waters being much netted though the upper are protected by an association. They are excellent spring rivers, the fish being small but plentiful. The Bladenoch is not so good as a river; it is later, and the fish are much shyer; leave also has to be obtained here. The Luce is a later river, but the fish run heavy in it. The Luce gets dreadfully netted, but as the fishing has lately been taken by an excellent sportsman, Mr. Dodd, it may be greatly improved. The Stinchar, too, is a fine river and would be a very fine river if it were not so closely fished. Excellent sport, however, is got on it at times, but it is, like the rest, in private hands. There are other rivers and lakes in most of which there is fair, and often good trout fishing in this district, and this there is little difficulty in getting—in many places it is open.

I have now only to thank the angler who has waded thus far, and to bid him farewell for the present.

INDEX

OF

THE RIVERS AND LAKES DESCRIBED OR NOTICED IN THIS WORK.

LIST OF BOOKS

PUBLISHED BY

HORACE COX, AT 346, STRAND, LONDON, W.C.

BY LAKE and RIVER: an Angler's Rambles in the North of England and Scotland. By FRANCIS FRANCIS, Author of "A Book on Angling," &c. &c. Post 8vo, price 8s. 6d.

THE BARB and the BRIDLE: a Handbook of Equitation for Ladies, and Manual of Instruction in the Science of Riding, from the preparatory suppling exercises on foot to the form in which a lady should ride to hounds. Republished from "THE QUEEN" Newspaper. By "VIEILLE MOUSTACHE." Post 8vo., price 5s.

THE QUEEN LACE BOOK: a Historical and Descriptive Account of the Hand-made Antique Laces of all Countries. By L. W. Part I. Mediæval Lacework and Point Lace. With thirty illustrations of lace specimens, and seven diagrams of lace stitches. Price 5s., 4to., printed on toned paper, with plates.

FACTS and USEFUL HINTS relating to FISHING and SHOOTING; being a Collection of Information and Recipes of all descriptions of the greatest utility to the general Sportsman, to which is added a series of Recipes on the Management of Dogs in Health and Disease. Vol. I. of "THE FIELD" LIBRARY. Third Edition. Large post 8vo., price *7s. 6d.* cloth; post free, *7s. 10d.*

THE COUNTRY HOUSE; a Collection of Useful Information and Recipes, adapted to the country gentleman and his household, and of the greatest utility to the housekeeper generally. Illustrated. Vol. II. of "THE FIELD" LIBRARY. Second Edition, enlarged and revised. Large post 8vo., price 5s. cloth; post free, *5s. 4d.*

THE FARM: being Part I. of the Second Edition of "The Farm, Garden, Stable, and Aviary." Valuable to country gentlemen, farmers, &c. Vol. III. of "THE FIELD" LIBRARY. Large post 8vo., price *5s.* cloth; post free, *5s. 4d.*

THE GARDEN: being Part II. of the Second Edition of "The Farm, Garden, Stable, and Aviary." Vol. III. of "THE FIELD" LIBRARY. Large post 8vo., price *5s.* cloth; post free, *5s. 4d.*

THE STABLE: being Part III. of the Second Edition of the FARM, GARDEN, STABLE, and AVIARY. Large post 8vo., price *5s.*; post free, *5s. 3d.*

A YEAR OF LIBERTY; or, Salmon Angling in Ireland. Vol. IV. of "THE FIELD" LIBRARY. Price *5s.* cloth; post free, *5s. 5d.*

POPULAR ILLUSTRATIONS of the LOWER FORMS OF LIFE. Illustrated. Vol. V. of "THE FIELD" LIBRARY. By C. R. BREE, M.D., F.L.S., F.Z.S. Large post 8vo., price *5s.* cloth; post free, *5s. 3d.*

EXPERIENCES of a GAME PRESERVER. Vol. VI. of "THE FIELD" LIBRARY. By "DEADFALL." Large post 8vo., price 5s. cloth; post free, 5s. 3d.

PRACTICAL FALCONRY; to which is added, HOW I BECAME A FALCONER. Vol. VII. of "THE FIELD" LIBRARY. By GAGE EARLE FREEMAN, M.A. ("Peregrine," of "THE FIELD"). Price 5s. cloth; post free, 5s. 3d.

SKETCHES of LIFE, SCENERY, and SPORT in NORWAY. Vol. VIII. of "THE FIELD" LIBRARY. By the Rev. M. R. BARNARD, B.A. The work is admirably adapted for use as a Sporting Tourist's Handbook, while it is of absorbing interest to the general reader. Price 6s. 6d.; post free, 6s. 10d.

DOGS OF THE BRITISH ISLANDS. Edited by "STONEHENGE." Second Edition, greatly enlarged (including new Parts on "Kennel Management of Dogs" and "Judging at Dog Shows and Field Trials." 4to., gilt edges, printed on toned paper, price 10s. 6d.; by post, 11s. 4½d.

DOGS USED WITH THE GUN, containing Setters (with four Illustrations) Pointers (with Illustration), Retrievers (with two Illustrations), Field Spaniels (with two Illustrations), Deerhounds (with Illustration).

COMPANIONABLE DOGS, containing Terriers (with four Illustrations), Bull Terrier and Bull Dog (with two Illustrations), Mastiffs (with three Illustrations), Sheep and Drovers' Dogs (with Illustration).

HOUNDS and TOY DOGS, containing Greyhound (with Illustration), Blood hound (with Illustration), Foxhound (with two Illustrations), Harriers (with Illustration), Beagles (with Illustration), Fox Terrier (with Illustration), Truffle Dog (with Illustration), King Charles and Blenheim Spaniels (with Illustration), Maltese Dog (with Illustration), Pug Dog and Italian Greyhound (with Illustration), Chinese Crested Dog (with Illustration).

On the MANAGEMENT of LARGE and PET DOGS, and TREATMENT of DISTEMPER, MANGE, and WORMS.

JUDGING at DOG SHOWS and FIELD TRIALS.

N.B.—The new parts on "Kennel Management of Dogs" and "Judging at Dog Shows and Field Trials," may be had together, price 1s. 6d.; post free, 1s. 8d.

SHIFTS and EXPEDIENTS of CAMP LIFE, TRAVEL, and EXPLORATION. By W. B. LORD, Royal Artillery, and T. BAINES, F.R.G.S. The work is written expressly for the use of Military and Naval Officers, Missionaries, Travellers, and any who may be obliged to "rough it" in Foreign and Savage Countries; and it is believed that the "Shifts and Expedients" here gathered together will be found of the greatest service to all such. The work contains about 900 pages, and nearly 400 Illustrations. Price 45s., cloth gilt; or in 17 Parts, 2s. 6d. each.

THE ARTS of ROWING and TRAINING. Demy 8vo., cloth gilt, price 4s.; post free, 4s. 2d.

THE SILKWORM BOOK; or, SILKWORMS ANCIENT and MODERN, their FOOD and MODE of MANAGEMENT. By W. B. LORD, R.A. Illustrated. In demy 8vo., price 2s. 6d., cloth gilt; post free, 2s. 8d.

THE COURSING CALENDAR AND REVIEW. Edited by "STONEHENGE." Published half-yearly. Fcap. 8vo.; price 10s. 6d. cloth; post free, 10s. 9d.

ROUND THE TABLE; or, Notes on Cookery and Plain Recipes, with a Selection of Bills of Fare. By "The G. C." Post 8vo., pp. 300, price 6s.; free by post, 6s. 5d.

THE IDSTONE PAPERS. A Series of Articles and Desultory Observations on Sport and Things in general, written originally for "THE FIELD" Newspaper. By "IDSTONE." Large post 8vo., price 7*s.* 6*d.*; post free, 7*s.* 11*d.* [*Second edition in press.*

THE DIAMOND DIGGINGS OF SOUTH AFRICA: a Personal and Practical Account. By CHARLES A. PAYTON, "SARCELLE," of "THE FIELD." With a Brief Notice of THE NEW GOLD FIELDS. With Map large post 8vo., price 6*s.*; post free, 6*s.* 5*d.*

THE FIELD DUPLICATE JUDGING BOOK facilitates the work of the Judges at Poultry and other Shows, by a very simple method of entering and preserving a duplicate judging list. Price 6*d.*; or 2*s.* 6*d.* the half dozen.

THE WISE, THE WITTY, AND THE BEAUTIFUL: A collection of good things in prose and verse, adapted for penny readings, railway travellers, and all who wish to pass an hour pleasantly. In small 8vo., cloth gilt, price 1*s.*; post free, 1*s.* 3*d.*

ALL ENGLAND CROQUET CLUB.—Regulations for the MANAGEMENT of PRIZE MEETINGS. Price 6*d.*; post free, 7*d.*

THE BOOK of DINNER SERVIETTES (Second Edition), which contains a new Introduction on the Decoration of Dinner Tables, and General Directions for folding the Serviettes, of which there are Twenty-one different kinds given, with Ninety-two Woodcuts illustrative of the various Folds required, and the Serviettes complete. In demy 4to., on toned paper, and in fancy cover, price 2*s.*; by post, 2*s.* 2*d.*

THE ART of SKATING; containing many Figures never previously described, with Illustrations, Diagrams, and Plain Directions for the Acquirement of the most Difficult and Elegant Movements. By GEORGE ANDERSON ("CYCLOS"), for many years President of the Glasgow Skating Club. Second Edition. In post 8vo., limp cloth gilt, price 2*s.* 6*d.*; post free, 2*s.* 8*d.*

THE RAIL and the ROD; or, The Tourist-Angler's Guide to Waters and Quarters. In Parts, paper wrapper, price 1*s.* each; in cloth, 1*s.* 6*d*; post free, 2*d.* extra.

No. 1. GREAT EASTERN RAILWAY. | No. 3. SOUTH-WESTERN RAILWAY.
No. 2. GREAT WESTERN RAILWAY. | No. 4. SOUTH-EASTERN RAILWAY.
No. 5 and No. 6. GREAT EASTERN, LONDON AND NORTH-WESTERN, MIDLAND, and GREAT NORTHERN RAILWAYS.

May be had in two vols. cloth, 4*s.* each.

PHEASANTS for COVERTS and AVIARIES: their Natural History and Practical Management. By W. B. TEGETMEIER, F.Z.S. Illustrated with numerous full-page Engravings drawn from life by T. W. Wood. Royal 4to., bevelled boards, gilt edges, price 12*s.*

RAMBLES AFTER SPORT; or, Travels and Adventures in the Americas and at Home. By "OLIVER NORTH." Large post 8vo., price 6*s.*; post free, 6*s.* 4*d.*

A TREATISE on HARNESS, SADDLES, and BRIDLES: their History and Manufacture, from the earliest times down to the present period. By A. DAVIS. In large post 8vo., price 2*s.* cloth; by post, 2*s.* 2*d.*

FOOTBALL OUR WINTER GAME. By C. W. ALCOCK, Hon. Sec. of Football Association. CONTENTS: On Ancient Ball Games; their Relation to Football.—The Football of the Past; its Origin and Early Stages.—The Football of the Present; its Styles and Differences.—Some Eccentric Games at Football.—Practical Football, and How to Play it.—A Few Hints on Football Properties.—The Various Styles of Football, with Rules and Notes thereon. Price 2s. 6d.

REPORTS on SALMON LADDERS, with Original Drawings, Plans, and Sections. By FRANCIS FRANCIS. In post 4to., price 2*s.* 6*d.*; by post, 2*s.* 7*d.*

THE ANGLER'S DIARY, wherein the Angler can register his take of Fish throughout the year. An extensive List of Fishing Stations throughout the World is added. Post 8vo., price 1*s.* 6*d.*; by post, 1*s.* 8*d.*

THE SHOOTER'S DIARY contains Forms for Register-ing Game killed during the Year, either by a Single Gun or by a Party, or off the whole Estate. A List of Shooting Stations throughout the World is also given. Post 4to., price 1*s.* 6*d.*; post free, 2*d.* extra.

THE RURAL ALMANAC and SPORTSMAN'S ILLUSTRATED CALENDAR. Its contents comprise Information of the greatest utility and interest to the Sportsman and Country Gentleman. Illustrated. Published annually. Price 1*s.*; by post, 1*s.* 2*d.*

"WHETSTONES FOR WITS:" or Double Acrostics. By VARIOUS HANDS. Edited by "CRACK." Price 5*s.*; by post, 5*s.* 4*d.*

"You have not the book of riddles about you, have you?"—*Merry Wives.*

OUR COMMON INSECTS: First Steps to Entomology. By Mrs. E. W. COX. Price 2*s.* 6*d.*; by post, 2*s.* 8*d.*

UNASKED ADVICE; a Series of Articles on Horses and Hunting, reprinted from "THE FIELD." Post 8vo., with 11 engravings, printed on toned paper. Price 7*s.* 6*d.*

FIGURE SKATING: being the Theory and Practice of the Art as developed in England, with a glance at its Origin and History. By H. C. VANDERVELL and T. MAXWELL WITHAM, Members of the London Skating Club. Price 6*s.*, by post 6*s.* 4*d.*

THE INTERNAL PARASITES of our DOMESTICATED ANIMALS; a Manual of the Entozoa of the Ox, Sheep, Dog, Horse, Pig, and Cat. By T. SPENCER COBBOLD, M.D., F.R.S., F.L.S. Illustrated with numerous woodcuts. Post 8vo., price 5*s.*, by post 5*s.* 3*d.*

THE GROUSE DISEASE: a Statement of Facts tending to prove the Parasitic Origin of the Epidemic. By T. SPENCER COBBOLD, M.D., F.R.S., F.L.S. With Two Illustrations. Price 1*s.*, by post 1*s.* 1*d.*

Shortly will be published.

THE KENNEL CALENDAR and STUD BOOK, from 1859 to 1873. Including: The Birmingham, Crystal Palace, Leeds, Manchester (Belle-vue and Free Trade Hall), Dublin, Glasgow, Edinburgh, Islington, Ashburnham, Hull, Nottingham, and other Dog Shows, Reports of Field Trials, with Lists of Prizes Awarded, and Pedigrees of Dogs, Names of Exhibitors, Judges, &c., &c.

www.ingramcontent.com/pod-product-compliance
Lightning Source LLC
Chambersburg PA
CBHW032302280326
41932CB00009B/660
* 9 7 8 3 3 3 7 2 3 3 2 9 7 *